GW00787250

COGNITIVE SOCIAL PSYCHOLOGY
A Guidebook to Theory and Research

COGNITIVE SOCIAL PSYCHOLOGY
A Guidebook to Theory and Research

J. Richard Eiser
Professor of Psychology
University of Exeter

McGRAW-HILL Book Company (UK) Limited

London · New York · St Louis · San Francisco · Auckland
Bogotá · Guatemala · Hamburg · Johannesburg · Lisbon · Madrid
Mexico · Montreal · New Delhi · Panama · Paris · San Juan
São Paulo · Singapore · Sydney · Tokyo · Toronto

Published by
McGRAW-HILL Book Company (UK) Limited
MAIDENHEAD · BERKSHIRE · ENGLAND

British Library Cataloguing in Publication Data

Eiser, John Richard
    Cognitive social psychology.
    1. Social psychology   2. Cognition
    I. Title
    301.11   HM291   79-41027

    ISBN 0-07-084104-7
    ISBN 0-07-084103-9 Pbk

12345   WCS   81079

PRINTED AND BOUND IN GREAT BRITAIN

To Chris and David

CONTENTS

PREFACE

In this book I describe a discipline which is wide in its scope, but modest in its claims. Social psychology is the scientific study of human social behaviour, and as such is potentially relevant to an immense variety of phenomena. Yet it is not the only discipline which seeks to study such phenomena, nor does it claim to have discovered the only factors of importance. The understanding of such phenomena which social psychology, or indeed any other social science, can provide is of necessity only partial, and to expect otherwise is to be heading for disappointment.

In fact, many of the criticisms of social psychology are based on such false expectations—for instance, that it is not enough for social psychology to study groups and individuals within a given social, historical, economic, and political context: it is up to social psychology also to provide an analysis of that context. This kind of argument does even less justice to the other social sciences than it does to social psychology. Are sociology, history, economics, and politics mere subsidiary subjects to be picked up in one's spare time, as preliminaries to becoming a social psychologist? Of course, they are not. An acknowledgement of the interdependence and complementarity of the different social sciences does not require us to be jacks of all trades, but masters of none.

There is a difference, though, between refraining from attempting a complete analysis of social context, and ignoring that context completely. Although social psychology *does* aim to say something about human social behaviour which transcends the particularities of context, it cannot succeed if it pretends that such particularities do not exist. There is often a danger of regarding the concerns and preconceptions of a single culture as universal.

Much may be learnt in this regard from cross-cultural research, although this is a field which I have made no attempt to cover. Culture, however, is not simply a factor which influences social psychological phenomena; it is also, at least in part, a product of social psychological processes. Research on such processes may therefore contribute to our understanding of culture and context, even if it is not cross-cultural.

In one small respect, however, this book does try to be cross-cultural. In terms of sheer weight of publications, social psychology is predominantly a North American discipline. Predominantly, but not totally. Many of the major theoretical contributions to American social psychology have been made by people who received their training outside America, and a critical concern with theory remains a hallmark of the best of European social psychological research. I am not attempting self-consciously to put forward a 'European approach' to social psychology, which is in any way antagonistic to an 'American approach'. Nor would I blame anyone for concentrating their reading where most of the best research is still to be found: in the American literature. However, there is good research going on in European social psychology, particularly in areas such as attitudes, categorization, and intergroup behaviour, which have been rather quiet recently on the other side of the Atlantic, and much of this has not been accorded international attention commensurate with its quality. I have not deliberately identified studies or theories as European or American, but I have attempted to give fair, and I hope not disproportionate, coverage to the former as well as to the latter. Even if the traditions are different in some respects, I have attempted an integration rather than an accentuation of such differences.

One deliberate bias in this book should be mentioned. It attempts to describe the cognitive processes underlying human social interaction, but makes no attempt to cover all the different kinds of phenomena which social psychologists have studied. Non-verbal communication is not covered at all. Neither is language, except in so far as linguistic factors are important in the fields of attitudes and judgement. There are other areas also which have been omitted to leave room for others. Chapter 9 (on 'Group Processes'), for example, does not deal with work on leadership, but gives more space to more recent work on intergroup behaviour. I have attempted to describe theories and methods which I believe to be applicable to a large number of issues, but I have not attempted to describe or enumerate all such separate applications. If anyone fails to find their favourite topic adequately covered, I apologize. However, I hope the selection will not seem too arbitrary, or out of step with prevalent concerns. Social psychological research only really makes sense in terms of its relevance to theory, yet many researchers seem reluctant to acknowledge the theoretical basis of their work. Although many studies are designed to test the predictions of superficially conflicting models, they have contributed, sometimes almost in spite of themselves, to the development of a more general theoretical perspective. This perspective is strongly 'cognitive', in that it implies that the business of social psychology is to understand how individuals and groups process information and make decisions in a social context. It is with this perspective that this book is explicitly concerned. The intended level of the book is intermediate. That is to say, I am assuming that readers already have some rudimentary background in general or social psychology, and some commitment to the subject. At the same time, it is not a specialized monograph, so I have avoided, as far as possible, explications of complex mathematical models and statistical methods. Except in a few special cases, I have also kept descriptions of experimental procedures to brief outlines. The book is therefore aimed at bridging the gap between more basic introductory texts and the research literature, as published in journals. I have called it a 'guidebook', as its function is to help you plan your own route through the wide territory that is social psychology. No guidebook, however, can be an adequate substitute for a journey, or for the fun of finding things out for oneself.

Let me acknowledge my deep gratitude to all those who have given me guidance and help in my own journey through social psychology, and in the writing of this book—to Henri Tajfel, who first persuaded me to become a social psychologist, and who has not let me regret my choice; to all my other friends and colleagues, for all they have taught me; to Jean Howard and Diane Hallett, for secretarial assistance; and most of all to Chris, my wife, for everything.

I also gratefully acknowledge permission from the following publishers to reproduce copyrighted material:

Academic Press, Inc., for the passages quoted in Chapter 9 from H. Tajfel, *Differentiation Between Social Groups: Studies in the Social Psychology of Intergroup Relations*, pages 51–76, 1978.

American Psychological Association for Figure 3.8, reproduced from J. R. Eiser and B. E. Osmon, 'Judgmental perspective and the value connotations of response scale labels', *Journal of Personality and Social Psychology*, vol. 36, 494, 1978.

Basil Blackwell, Ltd for the passage quoted in Chapter 8 from D. Mixon, 'Instead of deception', *Journal for the Theory of Social Behaviour*, vol. 2, pages 168–169, 1972.

John Wiley and Sons, Ltd for the passage quoted in Chapter 4 from R. Cohen, 'An investigation of the diagnostic processing of contradictory information', *European Journal of Social Psychology*, vol. 1, pages 476–477, 1971; and for the passages quoted in Chapter 9 from H. Tajfel, C. Flament, M. G. Billig, and R. P. Bundy, 'Social categorization and intergroup behaviour', *European Journal of Social Psychology*, vol. 1, page 174, 1971; and from J. C. Turner, 'Social comparison and social identity: Some prospects for intergroup behaviour', *European Journal of Social Psychology*, vol. 5, pages 19–20, 1975.

Yale University Press for Figure 2.4, reproduced from M. J. Rosenberg *et al.*, *Attitude Organization and Change*, page 3, 1960.

J.R.E.

PART
ONE

INTRODUCTION

SOCIAL PSYCHOLOGY: A COGNITIVE APPROACH

THE TOPICS OF SOCIAL PSYCHOLOGY

Often the closer something is to everyday experience, the more difficult it can be to convince people of the need for its scientific study. The study of the extraordinary has always had a glamour not usually accorded to the study of the ordinary. What happens at the other end of a telescope or microscope, that is the stuff of science. What happens in front of our naked eyes, that is just common knowledge. This is not just a problem for the social and behavioural sciences, although it is now our turn to deal with it: the physical and biological sciences have suffered acutely from this difficulty in the past, and no doubt continue to do so. Yet, if we look at the history of these sciences, we can see that the most revolutionary advances were made when scientists sought directly to explain the obvious. Concepts such as gravity, evolution, infectious disease, were all attempts to account for experiences which were very familiar to scientists and non-scientists alike. These concepts are now themselves so familiar that it is difficult to imagine how the world could have been perceived in any other way, yet already science has moved further on, through questioning once again the basis of what has now become 'obvious'.

Human social behaviour is about as familiar an object of study as one could possibly imagine. We perceive it and participate in it constantly. Even without the help of social psychologists, we feel we know a very great deal about it, and often with very good reason. We are taught about right and wrong, about human nature, about what is done and what is not done, and the lessons we learn bear more than a fortuitous correspondence to our experience. So where does social psychology fit in? Ideally, what social psychology can do is try to answer questions like, *why* people feel and act towards one another in the ways they do, why they hold particular attitudes, why they explain each other's behaviour in particular ways, and why they accept particular roles and rules of conduct. But once again the problem of 'obviousness' reappears. If one looks at the traditional topic areas of social psychology, it seems almost as though social psychologists are welcomed only as troubleshooters, called in to help out when things go wrong, to answer questions to which conventional wisdom has no obvious answer. As social psychologists, we are asked why people are racially prejudiced, attack one another, act destructively and self-destructively, are easily led and persuaded, fail to help one another, and get 'carried away' in a crowd. In short, we are asked to explain apparently *irrational* behaviour.

In many respects, this is fair enough. Interactions between human beings have their uglier aspects, and if these can be understood, then possibly some contribution can be made to the prevention or alleviation of human misery. Indeed, one could argue more strongly that researchers have a real responsibility to try and make such a contribution. But there is still a danger. To be asked 'Why do people behave irrationally?' is to be asked a leading question. It assumes that the behaviour in question *is* irrational, not only in comparison to some logical ideal (for, as we shall see, most social behaviour would have to be called irrational from this standpoint), but in the sense of requiring a different kind of explanation from non-problematic 'sensible' behaviour. In addition, it assumes that, whatever explanations social psychologists come up with, these will *not* be applicable to contexts where conventional wisdom seems confirmed.

If these assumptions are accepted, then the ordinary and everyday—the territory of conventional wisdom—are protected from scrutiny. Yet neither evidence nor logic requires that they be accepted, and hence social psychology has no obligation to submit to the restrictions which they imply. Rather, one could argue that it is these very assumptions, and others which form the basis of so-called common knowledge, that social psychology must challenge and examine, if it is to make any real contribution, either practical or conceptual. The topics of social psychology, then, are not merely different categories of social acts, but also and more vitally the common everyday assumptions which underly such acts and give them meaning.

THEORY AND DATA

Before one starts any investigation, one should have in mind some question that one wants to answer. This sounds so obvious as not to be worth stating, but sadly it seems.often to be ignored in many research endeavours. The motto 'If it moves, measure it' characterizes an unfortunately large proportion of what has passed for research in social psychology and related disciplines. In the short term, following this motto allows one to seem and feel busy, but in the longer term, it is a recipe for disappointment. But having said that, it is not always easy to decide on a question. It takes a little thought. It takes a little theory.

To collect data about how human beings interact with one another is so easy that it is almost impossible. It is easy because human social interactions are going on almost all the time, almost anywhere one cares to look. The streets, so to speak, are paved with gold. The complexity of information potentially available can be quite overwhelming. To get anywhere, one must select and categorize, one must act on hunches, one must decide where the analysis should start and when it should end, in short, one must theorize. As Coombs (1964, pages 5-6) has put it: 'All knowledge is the result of theory— we buy information with assumptions—" facts " are inferences, and so also are data and measurement and scales . . . there is no necessary interpretation of any behavioral example as some particular kind of data.'

In this book I shall be describing a great number of studies where researchers have deliberately set out to test hypotheses derived explicitly from some theory or other. But this is neither the only, nor arguably the most important, aspect of the role of theory in the acquisition of knowledge. Researchers from different theoretical factions may disagree about whose predictions are most accurate, but may still agree about what the measurements they obtain are measurements *of*. Such agreement is by no means universal, but it is often much more widespread than is agreement over the predictive accuracy of any single model. For example, there have been numerous theories of attitude change, but little questioning of the assumption that attitude change can be measured in terms of changes in individuals' responses on an attitude scale. Yet it is precisely here, in the attribution of meaning to particular scores and measurements, that the fundamental theoretical assumptions are made. Without any such assumptions, we cannot even make a start; but neither can we make real progress unless we recognize such assumptions for what they are.

EXPERIMENTATION AND OBSERVATION

Just as the questions which researchers ask depend on their theoretical assumptions, so do the methods which they use. Thus, many of the controversies which present themselves as disagreements over methods are in fact disagreements at the level of theory. One of the most heated of these controversies has been over the value of laboratory experimentation in social psychology. On the one side, there are those who argue that the purpose of research is to determine the effects of independent variables on dependent variables, and that the most efficient way to do this is to perform an experiment in a laboratory where the independent variables can be controlled and manipulated, and the dependent variables can be accurately recorded and measured. On the other side, there are those who argue that laboratory experiments involve situations which bear no relation to any ' real life ' social interactions, and impose artificial restrictions on unrepresentative samples of subjects: to find out what 'really' happens, observations of naturally occurring behaviour are the answer.

There is considerable merit in both these positions, and the fairest conclusion one can reach is the unsurprising one that both experimental and observational studies have a great deal to contribute. Nonetheless, it is important to understand the basis of the disagreement. What is the experimentalist trying to do? In spite of accusations and occasional protestations to the contrary, he usually *is* trying to answer questions about 'real-life' social interaction. He chooses aspects of 'real-life' behaviour and attempts to reproduce them within a laboratory setting. He also chooses situational variables which he suspects might influence such behaviour, and creates experimental analogues for these. Of course, the end-product is artificial, but does such artificiality matter, if what one is trying to do is to discover lawful relationships between independent and dependent variables which are generalizable across contexts and often even across cultures? Of course, the subject sample (usually students) is not demographically representative of the general population, but does such unrepresentativeness matter if one is looking for relationships which are generalizable across different kinds of individuals? Such generalizability, however, is more often assumed as an act of faith than put directly to an empirical test.

Generalizability can be just as much of a problem for the observational approach. The data yielded by an observational study are directly relevant to the 'real-life' situation in question, and are less likely to be distorted by the subjects knowing that they are being observed. This is fine if all one is interested in is just the one particular situation in question, but once the researcher attempts to extrapolate to other 'similar' situations, the conceptual difficulties reappear. How does one decide if two 'real-life' situations are in fact similar? Just as in the experimental approach, one needs to make *theoretical* assumptions about which variables are relevant, and which are the relevant dimensions of similarity. At this point, the experimentalist would claim that he is in a better position than the observationalist to make such decisions of relevance, since the experiment allows him to look at the effects of a number of variables independently, and assess their relative effectiveness and the degree to which they interact, i.e., depend upon one another. Without intervening to control the different variables in turn, the observationalist has less basis to judge which are most important.

Where possible, a happy compromise can be the 'field experiment'. In studies of this kind, subjects do not know that their behaviour is being observed, and instead have to react to what they believe is a naturally occurring event. The problem of extrapolating from the laboratory to the outside world therefore does not arise. At the same time, the experimenter can stage the 'naturally occurring event' so that aspects of it are different for different groups of subjects, and so control and manipulate independent variables at least as effectively as in a laboratory. The main limitations of this method are that it is more difficult to obtain base-line measures of subjects' attitudes and behaviour before any manipulation takes place, and that the number of responses one can hope to obtain from any single subject is usually quite restricted. These limitations, however, are not necessarily insuperable, granted a certain amount of ingenuity, and from another point of view, might be positive advantages. The relative value of a field-experiment approach depends to a large extent on how much it matters, in a specific context, that subjects should be unaware that they are participating in a piece of research.

The important issue, however, is not so much how researchers obtain their data, but how they interpret them. Whether one looks at observational, experimental, or field-experimental studies, what researchers attempt to do is usually to treat the observed behaviour of their subjects as an exemplar of a more general class of behaviour, and to treat features of the specific situations as exemplars of more general classes of situational influences. In a large number of cases, they have then attempted to infer causal relationships between these classes of situational variables and the class of behaviour. Thus, researchers will try to say something about the relationships between, for instance, 'attitude similarity' and 'interpersonal attraction', between 'threat' and 'cooperation', between 'ambiguity' and 'helping', or between 'status' and 'discrimination'. Such terms are the building blocks of much social psychological theory, but how good a foundation do they provide? This is an empirical question, which needs to be answered separately for each specific construct. In an experimental approach, it will depend on how well the relevant variables are 'operationalized'; in other words, how well the variables which the experimenter has chosen to manipulate and measure represent the more general classes of situational influences and the more general classes of behaviour with which his theory is concerned. In an observational approach, it will depend on how well the specific situation and behaviour observed can be classified into the established theoretical categories. The problem is really the same for both approaches: it is merely tackled from opposite sides.

Theoretical advances come when data of any kind force us to rethink such situational and behavioural classifications, and to challenge prior assumptions about their interrelationships, so that our theoretical terms and constructs come to be refined, differentiated, or replaced. Observational studies provide such a challenge by showing what happens 'out there'. Experiments do so by demonstrating relationships which are more subtle and interdependent than our initial preconceptions would have enabled us to envisage.

ASSUMPTIONS OF A COGNITIVE APPROACH

Assumptions of a theoretical nature are therefore implicit in the choice and definition of a research question, in the method of investigation and in the interpretation of data. Inevitably, I have also made assumptions in the selection and treatment of the theories and the research to be described in this book. I hope that these assumptions will seem to be generally supported by the evidence, and not just dogmatic assertions, but that is for you to judge. For the moment, let me just try to put into words what these assumptions are.

The first assumption is that *the individual is an active processor of information*. In other words, the effect of a stimulus depends on how it is categorized and interpreted by the perceiver. Next, it is assumed that *the interpretation of a stimulus depends both on attributes of the stimulus and on the perceiver's prior expectations and standards of comparison*. Stimuli, in other words, are not reacted to in isolation, but in the context of their relation to previous learning and experience. Since stimuli are not reacted to in isolation, but in terms of their relation to other stimuli, this implies the additional assumption that *the individual tries to organize his experience: such organization typically involves selection and simplification*. The extent of such selection and simplification is likely to vary both between individuals and between situations. If each new stimulus had to be reacted to in isolation, and without regard to previous experience, effective and purposive behaviour would be impossible. Hence, *the function of such organization is to provide a guide for action and a basis for prediction*.

The above assumptions apply both to social and to non-social information processing and behaviour. The specific implications for social psychology can be summarized by saying that *social behaviour is the product of decisions*. The way in which a person reacts to any social stimulus or situation depends on how he interprets and categorizes the information contained in that stimulus or situation, on his prior expectations and standards of comparison against which that stimulus or situation is judged, on what he feels is expected of him, and on the consequences he expects to occur as a result of his action. Since a large part of the information which he has to process will be provided by the attributes and behaviour of other people, a person's judgements of others and explanations of others' behaviour will be crucial for such decisions.

COGNITION AND CONSCIOUSNESS

Of the numerous questions which could be asked of this approach, let me at this stage deal with two. The first is, if social behaviour is the product of decisions, are the individuals concerned necessarily able to verbalize how they came to their decisions? The answer that I should give is no, not necessarily, but it is probably worth asking them anyway. The problem here is largely semantic. When we talk of 'coming to a decision', we often tend to think of something that takes a fair amount of time, and may be quite conscious and deliberate. Many social decisions *are* of this kind, and for these it is certainly appropriate to ask people for their reasons, so long as it is remembered that the answers may be deliberately, or unwittingly, biased so as to seem more 'logical' or 'socially desirable', and that assessments of the relative importance of different factors are not necessarily accurate. However, we can also talk of computers making decisions, without any implication of deliberateness or consciousness. This would be analogous to those many instances of social behaviour when people respond spontaneously and 'without thinking'. Usually this will be when the situation is familiar, and/or practised rules of conduct are seen as appropriate. 'Without thinking' here usually means 'without thinking about the longer term consequences'. In these cases one cannot expect too much from asking people for their reasons, as they may find it difficult to distance themselves sufficiently from their behaviour. Still, one may be able to learn a great deal from other kinds of verbal reports, such as their impressions of other participants in the interaction. Nonetheless, I should still regard these instances of social behaviour as the products of decisions, in that they still depend on the organization and *interpretation* of information.

More basic objections to the use of self-reports of decision processes have been raised by Nisbett and Wilson (1977). They take the view that higher order cognitive processes are typically inaccessible to introspection, arguing that individuals may sometimes be unaware of the existence of a stimulus that has an important influence on their response, be unaware of their response, and be unaware of the relationship between the stimulus and the response. According to Nisbett and Wilson, when people are asked to report on their own cognitive processes, they base their answers on implicit causal theories rather than on introspection, and any validity in their explanations is purely incidental: 'Subjective reports about higher mental processes are sometimes correct, but even the instances of correct report are not due to direct introspective awareness. Instead, they are due to the incidentally correct employment of *a priori* causal theories' (page 233).

Smith and Miller (1978) have objected to this conclusion, arguing that it is stated in an unfalsifiable form, and is an over-interpretation of much of the evidence which Nisbett and Wilson cite. For instance, one can hardly blame the individual subject for being unaware of a discriminative stimulus which controls his response, if the experimenter's awareness of the importance of the discriminative stimulus depends on his having conducted an experiment in which the value of that stimulus was different for different subjects, but constant for any single subject. On the other hand, Nisbett and Wilson seem correct in pointing out that individuals do not *typically* monitor their own decision processes in a way that allows for easy and accurate verbalization. To claim that individuals are in principle incapable of accurate introspection (so that any apparent accuracy would be due to chance) would indeed be unfalsifiable, but it is still an empirically demonstrable fact that individuals often find it difficult to report on their own decision processes, particularly from memory. Moreover, the spontaneity of behaviour, which is not normally consciously self-monitored, may actually be impeded by manipulations which increase individuals' levels of self-directed attention or 'objective self-awareness' (see Chapter 6). Verbal self-reports, however, may still be very informative if viewed as 'accounts' rather than as literal truth. They may tell one a great deal about the individual's normative expectations, and the reasons or rationalizations which he uses to justify his behaviour. If *believed* to be true, even the most self-deceptive account may have an important influence on the individual's aims and aspirations.

RATIONALITY, HEURISTICS, AND BIASES

The second main question which is often asked of a cognitive approach is, whether it implies that social decisions and behaviour are necessarily rational. Once again the problem is partly semantic, in that 'rational' typically carries a positive value judgement which seems inapplicable to many of the kinds of social behaviour in which social psychologists have traditionally been interested. Aronson (1972, page 9) has proposed as his 'first law' that 'people who do crazy things are not necessarily crazy', and I feel that this encapsulates much of what is implied by a cognitive approach. The behavioural *product* of a person's decisions may be anywhere from exemplary to execrable, but the way to make sense of the behaviour is still to understand the *process* whereby he arrived at his decision, his expectations, interpretation of information, and so on. There is nonetheless one sense in which a cognitive approach does *not* require social decisions to be rational. This is when one uses the word 'rational' to refer to cognitive operations which are correct and consistent from a logical or mathematical point of view.

Tversky and Kahneman (1974) have described a number of 'heuristics' or biases which influence the ways in which individuals process information. These may be thought of as strategies which are used to cope with complex information, but which can lead to marked errors in some situations. In particular, probabilistic judgements and inferences deviate considerably from statistical principles. The three heuristics considered are representativeness, availability, and anchoring.

The first of these refers to the tendency to judge the probability that a stimulus belongs to a particular class on the basis of how representative or 'typical' of that class it appears to be, with little regard for the base-rate probability of a stimulus belonging to the class. For example, imagine that one found some wild mushrooms, and wanted to decide if they were edible or poisonous. The representativeness heuristic implies that one should base one's decision on how similar the wild mushrooms appear to be to other mushrooms which one knows to be edible, that is, ordinary cultivated mushrooms, as compared with toadstools which one knows to be poisonous. The weakness of this kind of judgement is that it fails to take account of the probability of any wild fungus, chosen at random, being edible rather than poisonous, with the result that a great number of unfamiliar but edible fungi will be avoided. In this example, of course, the costs of eating a poisonous mushroom outweigh those of avoiding an edible one, and most people would be unaware of the statistical probability of a fungus being edible. The same kind of bias, however, can be demonstrated experimentally when subjects are given incentives for accuracy and are told about the base-rate probabilities. A slightly different example of the representativeness bias is the so-called ' gambler's fallacy '. If one knows that a sequence of events is randomly generated, one expects it to *look* random, even if it is very short. So, with spins of a coin, sequence of Heads (H) and Tails (T) such as HHTHTTHT is judged to be more probable than HHHHTHHH.

The availability heuristic refers to the tendency for an event to be judged more probable to the extent that it is more easily pictured or recalled. A headline such as ' Child taken to hospital after eating wild mushrooms ' might increase the ' availability' of information that wild mushrooms can be poisonous. An important practical instance of this is when people have to make comparisons between different kinds of risks. Risks from more easily pictured accidents, such as explosions, may contribute more to the judgement that an industrial process is dangerous, even though they may happen extremely rarely, than continuous and cumulative hazards, such as contaminated atmosphere, which have less immediate dramatic effects. Similarly, certain kinds of risks of mechanical failure may be underestimated, if it is difficult to imagine a particular component going wrong (see Slovic, Fischhoff, and Lichtenstein, 1976).

Finally, the anchoring bias refers to people's failure to revise their estimates adequately when new information is presented. This may happen when they make an initial estimate which they then adjust to give the final answer. However, even with the same information presented, a higher initial estimate will tend to lead to a higher final answer than a lower initial estimate.

All these biases appear to operate in the processing of social information also. Categorization on the basis of similarity is an important aspect of stereotyping, the salience and distinctiveness of information influences people's causal attributions or explanations of events, and primacy effects are observable in a variety of situations which involve the comparison or integration of information presented sequentially over time. There are also many other ways in which individuals simplify the information with which they have to deal, such as the bias towards cognitive consistency, which are less direct translations of the three heuristics which Tversky and Kahneman identify. However, I am not setting out self-consciously to translate the theoretical concepts of social psychology into those of general cognitive psychology, or vice versa. Both social and general cognitive psychology have developed their own somewhat different terminologies in order to describe somewhat different phenomena, and one should not confuse overlap with equivalence. What is more important is the common orientation to the explanation of human behaviour which starts from a consideration of how individuals, singly or in groups, seek, process and interpret information, and choose between alternative courses of action.

Even in the simple situations used by experimental psychologists, individuals do not process information perfectly in accordance with logical or statistical principles, so it seems implausible that they will act more 'logically' in the more complex situations studied by social psychologists. The presence of heuristics and biases, however, does not negate a cognitive approach, since the departures from perfect rationality which they describe are *systematic*. Hence social decision-making can still be regarded as governed by rules, even if these rules reflect individuals' limited capacities for dealing with information, and even if they have to be determined empirically. Indeed, if things were otherwise, there would be no need for an empirical social psychology.

PLAN OF THE BOOK

I have arranged the chapters of this book into two main sections. The first, entitled, *People as Perceivers*, deals primarily with how individuals interpret and organize social information, and with the implicit causal theories in terms of which they seek to explain their own and others' behaviour. The second, entitled, *People as Participants*, deals to a greater extent with how individuals act out their decisions in interpersonal and group situations. This division largely reflects the balance of contemporary research in social psychology which (particularly since the advent of attribution theory, which is described in Chapter 4) is as much concerned with 'social perception' as it is with 'social behaviour'.

My purpose, though, is not to set these two traditions up as opposing factions, but rather to stress their mutual interdependence. Theories of social perception, with their emphasis on individual cognitive processes, are in danger of losing their social context if no attempt is made to apply them to situations where different individuals interact with one another. At the same time, theories of social behaviour may be in danger of losing their psychological foundations if no attempt is made to incorporate an understanding of the decisions implied by social actions.

Finally, in the last chapter, I shall consider how much has been achieved by the theories and research described, and shall tentatively suggest some priorities for the future.

SUMMARY

* Social psychology is primarily the study of ordinary, everyday human social behaviour, and not simply of behaviour categorized as deviant or irrational.
* Research must be guided by theory. Scores and measurements are only interpretable as psychologically relevant data in terms of implicit or expli- cit theoretical assumptions.
* Both experimental and observational methods have their merits and limita- tions. The validity of data obtained by either method depends on the

validity of the theoretical constructs invoked by the researcher to relate classes of situational variables to classes of behaviour.

* A cognitive approach emphasizes constructs concerned with how individuals process information and make decisions in social situations.
* When acting spontaneously, individuals will not necessarily be able to monitor their own decision processes, or be able to recall them accurately. Their accounts of the reasons for their own behaviour, however, may still have psychological relevance.
* A cognitive approach does not assume that social decision making is perfectly rational. Evidence from general cognitive psychology shows that human information processing may be shaped by a reliance on various simplifying heuristics, which can lead to marked departures from formal logical and statistical principles. Comparable systematic biases in social decision making are among the most important topics for study in social psychology.

PART
TWO

PEOPLE AS PERCEIVERS

CHAPTER TWO

ATTITUDE MEASUREMENT, ATTITUDE ORGANIZATION, AND THE PREDICTION OF BEHAVIOUR

THE LOGICAL STATUS OF ATTITUDES

The study of attitudes is both the most natural and the most dangerous point from which to start a book on social psychology. The term 'attitude' is probably used more frequently than any other in social psychology. There are few theories in which the concept is not explicitly or implicitly introduced, and few experiments in which attitudes are not involved somewhere among the dependent or independent variables. Yet the vagueness and ambiguity of the way in which the concept of attitude is conventionally used makes it, to parody Allport's famous statement of forty years ago, probably the most indistinctive and dispensable concept in contemporary social psychology. My purpose in this chapter, however, will not be to dispense with the concept, but to try and determine some of the reasons for this confusion.

At a general level, we all have a rough idea what attitudes are. To say that someone has an attitude towards some object, issue, or person is a shorthand way of saying that he has certain feelings of like or dislike, approval or disapproval, attraction or repulsion, trust or distrust, and so on. We also assume that such feelings will be reflected in the kind of statements the person makes, the way he behaves towards the attitude object, and his reactions to expressions of opinion by other people. Attitudes, in other words, have something to do with feelings on the one hand and behaviour on the other.

So far things are simple enough. The problem comes when one attempts to specify this relationship between feelings and behaviour, and to formulate a definition of attitude which deals both with feelings and behaviour separately and with the relationship between them. For this reason, the various definitions of attitude offered by social psychologists, while they appear uncontentious at a superficial level, frequently involve assumptions, not only about the nature of attitudes, but also about the nature of learning, socialization, information processing, decision-making, memory, and so on. Such assumptions are often treated as self-evident, rather than put to empirical test. As Kiesler, Collins and Miller (1969, page 4) have said 'all too often, social psychologists have tried to make their definition of attitude both a definition and a theory of the concept'.

What has often happened is that social psychologists have attempted to make sense of the relationship between a person's feelings and the behaviour which expresses his feelings in terms of distinctions borrowed from elsewhere in psychology. Thus the distinction between feelings and expressive behaviour has implicitly been treated as one between stimulus and response, or between learned predisposition and specific actions, or between subjective and objective data. In my view, these 'definitions' miss the point. They merely relabel the concept of attitude, without in any way illuminating its logical function.

The main preoccupation of these attempts at definition has been causal inference. The causal status of attitudes generally is unclear. There are times when one wants to say that a person's attitude is a *response* to attributes of the attitude object, and other times when one wants to say that a person behaves in a particular way *because* of his attitude. Also, attitudes, in the sense of a person's feelings, are not things which can be directly observed in the way that a person's verbal and nonverbal behaviour can be observed. Nonetheless, one of the most commonly held preconceptions about attitudes is that we *infer* a person's feelings from his overt behaviour—what he says and does.

This position is in many ways a compromise between two extreme opposing viewpoints. On the one hand, behaviourists would argue that statements about attitudes are no more nor less than statements about behaviour. On the other hand, phenomenologists might argue that statements about attitudes need have no implications for actual behaviour. The compromise, however, is an unhappy one. If statements about a person's attitudes are inferences from behaviour how can one tell if such inferences are valid? How could one observe any statistical association between overt behaviour and inner experiences which by definition are unobservable?

It is a common mistake to assume that because a given statement presupposes that people have inner experiences, it must *refer* to those inner experiences. Consider, for example, a statement like 'That rose is red'. This presupposes the possibility of people having certain sensations associated with the rose which would have been different if the rose was, say, white. Nonetheless, it is a description of the rose, not a description of sensations. If one person says that the rose is red, and another person says of the same rose that it is white, only one of them can be right. The redness or whiteness of the rose is a *fact*. If people disagree about it, that is a problem for them and their opticians, not a problem for the rose.

Things are only slightly different if we consider a statement like 'That rose is beautiful'. This is still a description of the rose, not of the person's impressions. People *may* be more likely to disagree about the beauty of the rose than about its redness, but any disagreement is still a disagreement about the attributes of the rose. Whether aesthetic criteria are absolute or conventional, shared or disputed, communication about them is only possible by reference to what is publicly observable. This statement is similar in structure to many attitude statements—in fact, it *is* an attitude statement—but this does not make it a *description* of the speaker's attitude. It describes the rose, but *expresses* the speaker's attitude. This is what attitude statements do: they describe attitude objects, and express attitudes. Attitude statements, and similar expressive acts, do more than provide a basis for inference. If we understand their meaning and appreciate their context, they *tell us* the person's attitude. Sometimes we may misunderstand a person's expressive behaviour, and sometimes it may be deliberately calculated to deceive, but the same holds true of any other communicative act that one could imagine. A person can lie about his name as easily as about his attitude, but we still feel that we can do more than *infer* his name if he tells us what it is.

In attempting to define attitudes in a way which accounts for the relationship between feelings and inner experiences on the one hand and observable verbal and non-verbal behaviour on the other, many social psychologists seem to have made two crucial assumptions. The first is that attitudes are distinct entities with an independent existence. The second is that their relationship to observable behaviour is causal. I regard both these assumptions as fallacious. The relation of attitudes to expressive behaviour seems to me to be essentially a logical one, analogous to the relation between meaning and utterance. We need to assume that words have meaning to understand verbal behaviour, but we do not need to regard the meaning of a word as something which has an independent existence, nor as a distinct entity which causes the verbal behaviour. Just as words have meaning, people have attitudes, and the concept of attitude is no less important for understanding human social behaviour than is the concept of meaning for understanding language. A person's attitude is the meaning of his expressive behaviour.

ATTITUDE MEASUREMENT

The question of how we measure people's attitudes is one of the basic methodological problems of social psychology. It is also the most appropriate focus for any debate concerning the precision and reliability of social psychological methods. One frequently hears social psychology being talked of as a 'young' science that cannot yet be fairly judged against the exacting standards of methodological sophistication set by the physical sciences. One could not expect chemists or physicists to make precise predictions if they were limited to the equipment of their medieval predecessors, so why, the argument goes, should one expect social psychology to achieve its breakthrough within the first century of its conception?

Relative to most other areas of the behavioural sciences, however, attitude measurement is *not* a new field. Many of the basic techniques in use today are nearly fifty years old or more. Also, with regard to the question of 'sophistication', it could be argued that, in terms of the mathematical and statistical treatment of the data that are obtained, much of what goes on in attitude measurement is just as sophisticated as is typical in the physical sciences. The crucial difference seems to lie in the quality of data obtained, prior to any analysis.

Traditionally, attitude measurement has chosen to base itself upon the dictum that 'everything which exists, exists in some degree'. Attitudes, therefore, are things which may be (if not directly, then indirectly) observed and described in terms of some metric, just as one may observe and describe a person's height or weight. If the measurements one derives do not always turn out to be as reliable as one might wish, then one needs to recalibrate one's observations, or improve one's observational techniques—one does not need to question the validity of the kind of measurement one is attempting.

From the earliest days attitude scaling theorists have acknowledged that their measurements can never completely define a person's attitude.

It will be conceded at the outset that an attitude is a complex affair which cannot be wholly described by any single numerical index. For the problem of measurement this statement is analogous to the observation that an ordinary table is a complex affair which cannot be wholly described by any single numerical index. So is a man such a complexity which cannot be wholly represented by a single index. Nevertheless, we do not hesitate to say that we measure the table. The context usually implies what it is about the table that we propose to measure. We say without hesitation that we measure a man when we take some anthropometric measurements of him. The context may well imply without explicit declaration what aspect of the man we are measuring, his cephalic index, his height or weight or what not. Just in the same sense we shall say here that we are measuring attitudes. We shall state or imply by the context the aspect of people's attitudes that we are measuring. The point is that it is just as legitimate to say that we are measuring attitudes as it is to say that we are measuring tables or men. (Thurstone, 1928, page 530.)

A lack of precision might therefore arise, according to this view, if the 'aspect' of a person's attitude which one was measuring was not the most relevant aspect for one's purposes (as, for example, if one attempted to predict voting behaviour from people's perceptions of the likeability of particular candidates, without regard for their perceived ability).

There would seem, therefore, to be quite a number of ready-made excuses available to account for why attitude measurement appears less reliable than physical measurement, without needing to question the assumption that attitude measurement and physical measurement involve essentially equivalent operations. It is this assumption, however, which is fundamentally in error. Even if one accepts the dictum that 'everything which exists, exists in some degree', attitudes are not 'things' which exist in anything like the same sense that a table or a man exists. If we attempt to measure a person's attitude, what we are doing is attempting to *measure the meaning* of his expressive behaviour. It is possible to measure attitudes only to the same extent, and in the same sense, as it is possible to measure meaning.

The idea of measuring meaning, however, is on the face of it extremely strange, and not at all like measuring tables. We do not typically *measure* the meaning of a statement, we *understand* it. 'Meaning' is not the kind of concept that immediately suggests itself to us as possessed of attributes that can be quantified in terms of some scale or continuum, like height or weight. Moreover, if an attitude is a kind of meaning, and not a kind of 'thing', we have no grounds for supposing it to be any more simple or singular than the complex and multiple acts whereby it is expressed. The use of any single numerical index, or set of indices, can only be a simplification, as Thurstone was well aware. When we use such an index to represent a person's attitude, however, we are *not* giving a simplified description of something inside the person's head, but are offering a summary of our own understanding of his expressive behaviour. How simple or complex we choose to make this summary, and which aspects of his behaviour we choose to emphasize, are functional questions relating to the purpose for which this summary will be used: they are not part of the definition of attitude. This summary takes on the appearance of measurement when its function is to compare the attitudes of different people with each other.

The single most important function which scales of attitude measurement seek to achieve is to compare people in terms of their *positive or negative evaluation* of a given attitude object. Depending on the context and the nature of the attitude object (be it a physical object, a person, a policy, an idea, a task, or whatever), this evaluation might be expressed verbally by terms such as want, like, respect, admire, support, agree with, approve of, enjoy, and so on. Such expressions form the basis of a summary statement to the effect that a person has a (more or less) *favourable or unfavourable* attitude towards the attitude object, or that a person's attitude falls at such-and-such a point on the 'favourable-unfavourable continuum'. Attitude scales are essentially techniques whereby researchers attempt to provide themselves with the kind of data which allows them to summarize people's attitudes in this way. I shall now briefly describe a selection of these techniques.

THURSTONE'S METHOD OF EQUAL-APPEARING INTERVALS

The basic aim of this method is to locate a person's attitude along a continuum ranging from extremely unfavourable to extremely favourable towards a specific object or issue. This is achieved by presenting the person with a series of short statements or 'items' expressing attitudes of varying degrees of favourability and noting the statements with which he agrees. For instance, a person who agrees, on average, with statements expressing a moderately favourable attitude will then be said to be moderately favourable towards the issue. The critical stage of this method is the initial selection of the statements, and the calculation of a measure to represent the degree of favourability expressed by each statement. This measure is termed the 'scale value' of the statement.

To calculate these scale values, and to select the final series of statements, an initial sample of often 100 or more statements is prescribed to a group of 'judges', whose task it is to say, not whether they personally agree with the statements, but how favourable or unfavourable is the attitude expressed by each statement. Originally this was achieved by printing each item on a separate slip of paper, and asking judges to sort the slips into 11 different piles, but a more convenient modification is to print the items in a questionnaire with an 11-point rating scale beneath each item, looking like this:

Extremely   Extremely
unfavourable   1   2   3   4   5   6   7   8   9   10   11   favourable

The judges, therefore, have essentially to ask themselves the question, for each item, 'If someone made this statement, how unfavourable or favourable would his attitude be?' The median, or alternatively, the mean of the different ratings assigned to any given item by the different judges is then taken as the scale value of that item. On the basis of these scale values, and of other features of judges' ratings, notably the degree of variability in judges' ratings of an item (high variability being assumed to reflect 'ambiguity'), the researcher then selects the items to be included in the final questionnaire. When this questionnaire is administered to the respondents, who have to indicate their agreement or disagreement with each item, the average of the scale values of those items with which a person says he agrees is taken as a measure of the location of his attitude along the same 11-point scale from extremely unfavourable to extremely favourable.

The name of this technique reflects the assumption that the measure of attitude derived has the property of an equal interval scale, that is to say, that the difference in attitude between someone at, say, point 2 on the scale and someone at point 6 is the same as that between someone at point 5 and someone at point 9, or that both these differences are twice the difference between, say, someone at point 8 and someone at point 10. Equal differences on the scale, in other words, are assumed to represent equal differences in attitude, in just the same way as equal differences in temperature are represented by equal differences in either fahrenheit or centigrade scales.

Another assumption made by Thurstone and Chave (1929) when they originally proposed this technique was that the scale values derived from the judges' ratings should not be influenced by the judges' own attitude towards the issue. In other words, judges should rate the items similarly, regardless of whether they were themselves favourable or unfavourable towards the issue. As we shall see in the next chapter, this assumption has not proved to be correct. Because of this, one cannot regard a scale value as an *absolute* measure of where a given item falls on the attitude continuum: all it tells us is how that item has been judged *relative* to the other items in the series.

LIKERT'S METHOD OF SUMMATED RATINGS

Likert (1932) put forward his method as a simplified alternative to Thurstone's, which could by-pass the tedious and questionable step of using independent judges to determine the scale values of the items. He regarded Thurstone's procedure of sorting statements into eleven piles as one which made unnecessary demands on the sophistication of subjects, and, therefore suggested that scales could be constructed so as to contain simply two classes of items—those which could be easily classified as favourable, and those which could be classified as unfavourable. Items which were neither clearly favourable nor clearly unfavourable would not be included. To make up for the information possibly lost by this simplified construction technique, Likert adopted a technique of scoring the scale which takes account, in a way which Thurstone's does not, of each respondent's *level* of agreement or disagreement with each item. Each respondent is typically required to rate his agreement with each item in terms of a five-point scale, such as, Strongly Agree, Agree, Undecided, Disagree, Strongly Disagree. For all favourable items, these ratings are then converted to numerical form, with Strongly Agree scored as 5, and Strongly Disagree as 1. For all unfavourable items, the scoring is reversed, so that Strongly Agree is scored as 1 and Strongly Disagree as 5. The ratings are then summated over the total sample of items, to give a score directly related to the favourability of the respondent's attitudes. As with Thurstone's method, scales constructed and scored in this way are assumed to have the properties of equal-interval scales, but they are not assumed to embody any absolute neutral point, and therefore are intended only for *relative* comparisons between the attitudes of different respondents, or of the same respondents under different conditions.

Empirical comparisons of the two techniques have generally vindicated Likert's approach (Seiler and Hough, 1970). The Likert method of scoring is consistently more reliable (Likert, 1932; Edwards and Kenney, 1946), even when applied to items selected according to Thurstone's, rather than Likert's, criteria. In addition, a scale of 20 or 25 items constructed and scored by Likert's method will tend to yield a reliability of 0.90 or more. Thurstone's scales typically need to contain about twice as many items to achieve the same degree of reliability.

UNOBTRUSIVE MEASURES

Although not attitude 'scales' in the normal sense, a number of quantitative indices can be obtained of people's evaluative reactions to some object, issue, or event, which do not depend upon the cooperation of respondents in completing a questionnaire and do not require that subjects know that they are being tested. Such measures may be particularly useful in situations where the willing cooperation of subjects is difficult to obtain, where subjects may be especially motivated to bias their responses in a 'socially desirable' direction, and where the act of answering the questionnaire may have a 'reactive' effect on the very attitude which the questionnaire attempts to measure. Dillehay and Jernigan (1970) have demonstrated that biased questionnaires not only can yield biased responses, but can even change subjects' subsequent attitudes. The use of a pre-test in attitude change research (while it may allow subjects to be used as their own controls, and hence may be more economical in terms of the number of subjects required for a given experiment) is similarly open to the criticism that it may alert subjects to the fact that their attitudes are being tested before the attempt to influence their attitudes is made (Campbell and Stanley, 1963). For such reasons, the potential usefulness of non-verbal, unobtrusive, indices of attitude deserves more systematic investigation than it has typically received.

Where black and white students will choose to sit in college classrooms, for example, has been used as an unobtrusive measure of interracial attitudes (Campbell, Kruskal, and Wallace, 1966). This is not to say that seating behaviour is a 'purer' measure of attitude than could be obtained from anonymously completed questionnaires—this study showed as strong an overall tendency for students to sit near to members of their own sex as to sit near to members of their own race—but it is a measure that is affected by *different* biases from those that might influence verbal self-report methods. Physical traces of people's behaviour can also provide useful data. Chicago's Museum of Science and Industry contains an exhibit in which live chicks can be seen hatching. The popularity of this exhibit is indicated by the fact that the vinyl tiles on the surrounding floor area needed replacement about every six weeks, whereas those in other areas of the museum lasted for years without replacement (Webb, Campbell, Schwartz, and Sechrest, 1966).

As Webb *et al* are careful to point out, both unobtrusive measures and interview or questionnaire methods have their weaknesses. Verbal self-report methods can elicit biased or insincere responses, but can allow the individual to communicate his attitude directly to the researcher. Unobtrusive measures are, ideally, unaffected by individuals' intentions to communicate a particular kind of attitude to the researcher, but the researcher's interpretation of such measures depends critically upon the assumptions he can make about the specific situation in which the data are collected. These assumptions may be difficult to test without altering the situation and hence, conceivably, the attitudes or behaviour under investigation. The weaknesses of the two approaches, however, are *different*. The ideal research strategy, therefore, would seem to be to use data obtained by one kind of method to supplement, rather than replace, data obtained by another kind of method.

SCALOGRAM ANALYSIS AND CUMULATIVE SCALES

Attitude measurement, in the methods so far described, is essentially an attempt to describe people's evaluations of an object or issue in terms of a unidimensional scale or continuum. This is explicit in both the Thurstone and Likert scales, and implicit also in unobtrusive measures, such as the use of seating position as an index of sociometric preference (Campbell *et al.*, 1966). Scalogram analysis, as proposed by Guttman (1944), is not in itself a method of attitude measurement, but a technique of evaluating any measurement device to see if this assumption of unidimensionality is, in fact, valid. It is not exclusively concerned with attitude measurement, but 'is a formal analysis, and hence applies to any universe of qualitative data of any science, obtained by any manner of observation' (Guttman, 1944, page 142).

Scales which conform to the Guttman criterion for unidimensionality are referred to as 'Guttman scales', or 'cumulative scales'. The basic criterion is that, if one individual obtains a higher total score than another person on a given scale, he should also obtain at least as high a score as that other person on each component of the scale. Imagine, for example, that we were interested in devising a test of 'crossword-solving ability'. We could start by finding three crosswords of different levels of difficulty, say one from, *The Times*, one from, the *Daily Telegraph*, and one from, the *Daily Mirror*. We might then give these crosswords to four different people, and see how many clues they could solve if allowed 10 minutes with each of the crosswords. The data we might obtain could look something like this:

Table 2.1 Number of clues solved in hypothetical study of crossword-solving ability. Data compatible with an assumption of unidimensionality

Subject	Times	Crossword: Telegraph	Mirror
1	10	15	25
2	7	12	16
3	1	4	10
4	0	1	3

As can be seen, all three crosswords yield the same rank order of subjects in terms of their performance. For these subjects, therefore, the three crosswords could be regarded as a unidimensional scale of ability. This would not be the case, however, if we obtained data like this:

Table 2.2 Number of clues solved in hypothetical study of crossword-solving ability. Data incompatible with an assumption of unidimensionality

Subject	Times	Crossword: Telegraph	Mirror
1	10	15	25
2	16	7	12
3	1	10	4
4	3	0	1

Since the different crosswords produced different orderings of the subjects in terms of their performance, we should conclude that there were factors which influenced the subjects' performance which were partly specific to each of the crosswords, or alternatively, that the different subjects were influenced by different features of the various crosswords. In other words, the measure of ability derived would not be truly unidimensional.

One of the earliest and best-known examples of a cumulative attitude scale (though not constructed strictly in accordance with scalogram analysis, which it antedates by nearly twenty years) is the Bogardus 'Social Distance' scale (Bogardus, 1925). The respondent is shown a long list of names of different ethnic or national groups, and asked to indicate: 'According to my first feeling reactions I would willingly admit members of each race (as a class and not the best I have known, nor the worst members) to one or more of the classifications under which I have placed a cross'. The seven classifications used are:

1. To close kinship by marriage
2. To my club as personal chums
3. To my street as neighbours
4. To my employment in my occupation
5. To citizenship in my country
6. As visitors only to my country
7. Would exclude from my country

The assumption of this measure is that someone who was prepared to admit, say a Norwegian, to close kinship by marriage, would also be prepared to tolerate the more 'distant' relationships specified by categories 2, 3, 4, and

5. (The inclusion of the word 'only' in category 6 seems to destroy the continuity between 5 and 6). However, someone whom Bogardus' subjects would not tolerate living in the same street, say a Dane, would not be tolerated either in the same club or family. Scalogram analysis is essentially a technique for testing if assumptions of this kind are empirically valid.

To conform to Guttman's criteria, scales typically have to be narrowed down to cover a very restricted, specific range of content, so that the statements are all 'to a large extent, rephrasings of the same thing' (Festinger, 1947, page 159). If one does not wish to lose the information contained in responses to more heterogeneous sets of items, Guttman's suggestion is that one should construct separate scales to measure the separate aspects of the attitude in question.

The unidimensionality of an attitude continuum, therefore, cannot simply be assumed, particularly when the issue is defined in a fairly broad or nonspecific way. As we shall see later in this chapter, the specificity with which one chooses to measure attitudes is crucial to any debate concerning the relationship between attitudes and behaviour. At the same time, it must be remembered that much of the traditional function of attitude scales has been to provide the researcher with easily obtained *summaries* of how favourably or unfavourably a person views a given general issue. Such summaries typically do not make (or, from another viewpoint, typically violate) the assumptions of true unidimensional cumulative scales.

MULTIDIMENSIONAL SCALING

An awareness that unidimensional measures may ignore or disguise important information has led a number of researchers to develop statistical techniques to provide more complex, but also hopefully more complete, descriptions of attitudes. Closely related to factor analysis, these techniques enable the researcher to draw a 'psychological map' in which objects or people perceived as similar to each other are located close together, and dissimilar objects or people are located far apart. Just as one can construct a geographical map from a knowledge of the physical distances between towns and landmarks, so one can construct a psychological map from a knowledge of the 'psychological distances' (perceived similarities and differences) between different objects or people.

As proposed by Torgerson (1958), multidimensional scaling analysis takes as its input direct estimates of the distances between the items being measured. Applied to attitudes, this can either take the form of responses to questions such as 'How similar or dissimilar are these two statements, countries, politicians, etc.?' or such distances can be inferred on the assumption that psychologically similar items elicit similar responses (i.e., two items, both of which a person accepted, would be treated as more similar to each other than two items, one of which he accepted and one of which he rejected). An alternative form of analysis has also been developed, requiring only information concerning the rank order of the distances between each pair of items (Shepard, 1962a, 1962b; Kruskal, 1964).

There are two basic purposes for which these techniques tend to be used. The first is to map the structures of sets of 'concepts' or stimuli, as perceived by a single person or group. These stimuli could, for example, be the statements in a standard Thurstone or Likert scale. If one was concerned, for instance, about whether 'Attitudes towards the Church', as measured by Thurstone's original scale, truly represented a unidimensional continuum, one could obtain estimates or rank orderings of the similarities between the items in the scale and submit these to multidimensional scaling analysis. If the original assumption of unidimensionality was correct, the 'map' revealed by the analysis would consist of a single straight line. If the locations of the different items on this line closely reflected their original scale values, this would provide yet further validation of Thurstone's scale. On the other hand, if more than one dimension was required for an adequate representation of the distances between the items, this would suggest that the scale was more heterogeneous in content than was originally supposed. In a marketing research context, a number of different brands of an article may be compared to find the 'psychological dimensions' underlying consumer preferences.

The second purpose of multidimensional scaling analysis is to map the similarities and dissimilarities between different *persons* or groups in terms of their reactions to a specific object, or scores on a particular attribute.

The basic assumption of multidimensional scaling techniques, whether applied to concepts or persons, is that the nature of the 'space' in terms of which the psychological distances are calculated is constant over all comparisons, i.e., that each element (concept or person) being compared retains a constant position in that space, and that all comparisons must reflect the positions of the elements on all the dimensions of that space. Thus it would be invalid to conduct a multidimensional scaling analysis of attitudes which involved presenting pairs of attitude statements, if a given statement was interpreted as carrying a different meaning, or even as expressing a different degree of favourability towards some issue, in the context of one comparison rather than another. Also, it would be invalid to conduct this kind of analysis on a person's ratings of the similarities between different makes of cars if he were to compare two cars solely on the basis of horsepower, even though they differed in price, but compared another two solely on the basis of price, even though they differed in horsepower.

The validity of these assumptions becomes especially questionable when one attempts to map the conceptual structures of different groups of people by pooling their responses and submitting the *mean* distance scores for each comparison to analysis. Tucker and Messick (1963) and, from a different perspective, Coombs (1964), have developed techniques for jointly representing individual differences and perceived distances between concepts, but these still need to assume that, within individuals, the structure of the conceptual space is invariant over comparisons. Where the conceptual structures of different individuals are mapped separately, a comparison can still be made both in terms of the complexity of the individuals' cognitive maps (e.g., Harvey, Hunt, and Schroder, 1961), and in terms of the dimensions from which these maps are constructed. This reflects the fact that such maps are maps of judged similarities and differences, and that different individuals may select both different numbers, and different kinds, of attributes on which to base their judgements.

Although depending heavily on the researcher's subjective notions concerning what constitutes a 'meaningful' interpretation of a given map, such comparisons can sometimes be extremely evocative in the richness of detail which they provide. A good example, though based upon results of factor analysis rather than multidimensional scaling analysis, is reported by Osgood and Luria (1954) who compared the cognitive maps (or in their terms the 'semantic space') of a multiple personality in each of her different 'personalities'. However, factor-analytic and multidimensional scaling techniques alike carry an important qualification: *Dimensional structures are interpretations which apply only to the specific data obtained and the specific items presented for comparison.* Their validity decreases the more items are added to, or removed from, the original sample. Nonetheless, it is not uncommon for researchers to present subjects with a haphazard selection of items, submit the data obtained to multidimensional scaling or factor analysis, and assume that the dimensions revealed reflect the subjects' basic value systems generalizable at least to other items, and by implication to other issues as well. Eysenck (1971), for instance, felt entitled to delineate the 'structure of social attitudes', and to infer the presence of differences between social classes on a variety of attitudinal issues, on the basis of a factor analysis of a mere 28-item questionnaire. Without any criteria for determining the representativeness of any sample of items, and with the possibility that the items presented may not deal with issues of equal salience to the different subject groups, conclusions of this kind must at best be regarded as speculative (Eiser and Roiser, 1972).

As with any other form of measurement, one cannot hope to get something for nothing. Multidimensional scaling analysis provides the researcher with a powerful technique for reducing complex data to a simpler and more readily interpretable form. The cost of the technique is the assumption that attitudinal structures can be mapped in a manner directly analogous to Euclidian physical space. For the analogy to hold, no item or person can simultaneously occupy more than one position, and neither the structure of the space, nor the positions of any items within that space, can be seriously affected by the act of measurement.

It is arguable that such assumptions are not really very different in kind from those made by other conventional techniques of attitude measurement, so one might as well pursue these assumptions for all the information they are worth. Alternatively, it could be said that the cruder and simpler techniques are less likely to deceive the researcher or his readers with a false semblance of precision. What is certain is that *all* techniques of attitude measurement involve *some* kind of assumption about the nature of attitudes. Measurement depends upon theory for its interpretation. No single method of scaling or statistical analysis can therefore be expected to serve as a panacea for problems generated by the limitations of theory.

ATTITUDE ORGANIZATION

I stated earlier that, while the statements through which a person expresses his attitude may presuppose inner feelings and experience, this inner experience is not the *reference* of such statements. We distinguish attitude statements from other kinds of descriptive statements primarily because they imply a value judgement of some kind, not because they describe different kinds of phenomena. This point is of fundamental importance for our conception of attitudes, since it suggests a picture of the individual actively perceiving, interpreting, and evaluating his external world. It is only because attitudes have an *external* reference that we can describe attitudes as consistent or inconsistent, stable or changeable, normative or deviant, and related or unrelated to nonverbal behaviour.

This picture of the individual as an active perceiver and interpreter of events is fundamental to one of the central concepts of social psychology, the notion of *cognitive consistency*. The basic idea is that people are predisposed to organize their attitudes and beliefs into internally consistent structures. Although defined in slightly different ways by later writers, the essential features of this idea are best introduced by considering Heider's (1946, 1958) theory of cognitive balance.

BALANCE THEORY

Balance theory is an attempt to describe part of what Heider refers to as the 'subjective environment' of an individual 'perceiver'. This 'subjective environment', analogous to Lewin's (1936) concept of a 'life space', consists of certain *entities*, and certain *relations* between these entities, *as perceived by the individual*. The classical example consists of three entities, p, o and x, where p is the individual 'perceiver', o is another person, and x is an impersonal object or issue. (If this third entity is another person, it is conventional to use the symbol q rather than x.) Each of the three relations between each pair of entities can consist of *positive or negative* 'sentiment' (e.g., likes, dislikes; approves of, disapproves of). (Heider also distinguished between positive and negative 'unit' relations, e.g., has some sort of bond or relationship with, has no sort of bond or relationship with, but in view of the conceptual and empirical ambiguities surrounding the status of a negative unit relation

(Jordan, 1953; Cartwright and Harary, 1956) this aspect of the theory has been largely ignored in more recent research.) With two possible relations between each pair of entities, there are eight possible *triads* that can be constructed, as shown in Figure 2.1.

Heider defines as 'balanced' triads containing either three positive relations, or one positive and two negative relations. These four triads represent those situations in which either p perceives agreement with someone he likes, or disagreement with someone he dislikes. The remaining four triads, containing either three negative or one negative and two positive relations, are defined as 'imbalanced' (although the triad with three negative relations was initially considered by Heider to be 'ambiguous'). These all represent situations in which p perceives agreement with someone he dislikes, or disagreement with someone he likes.

Balanced triads   Imbalanced triads

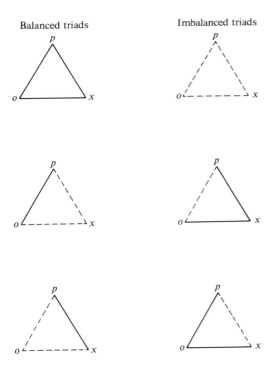

Figure 2.1 Balanced and imbalanced triads as defined by Heider (1946). Positive relations are represented by continuous lines, negative relations by broken lines.

Heider defines balance as 'a harmonious state, one in which the entities comprising the situations and the feelings about them fit together without stress' (1958, page 180); in other words, it is a kind of *Gestalt*. This definition implies a number of predictions that have been taken up by later research. First, balanced structures are more *stable*, in the sense that an individual will be motivated to change an imbalanced structure into a balanced one, but not vice versa. Second, if an imbalanced structure cannot be changed into a balanced one, it will produce 'tension'; hence, balanced states are *preferred* to imbalanced ones. Third, if a person is required to predict the third relation in a triad from a knowledge of the other two (e.g., 'A likes B and A approves of X. Does A think B approves or disapproves of X?'), he is more likely to *predict* a state of balance than imbalance (e.g., 'A thinks B approves of X'). Finally, since balanced states are more predictable than imbalanced ones, they are *simpler* to learn or recognize.

There is a quite literal sense in which balanced states are simpler than imbalanced ones, as can be seen if one applies attitude scaling notions to the theory of balance (Jaspars, 1965). In terms of the approach taken by Coombs (1950, 1964), one can conceptualize judgements of preference and evaluation as depending upon (1) the perceived positions of the judged items in terms of one or more underlying attribute or dimension, and (2) the perceived distances of these items from the individual's own *ideal point* on the dimensions. Positively evaluated items should be close to this ideal point, and negatively evaluated items should be further away. Thus if P represents an individual's ideal point on a given dimension or attribute, and o and x represent the positions of two evaluated items, the schema in Figure 2.2 would represent a situation in which o was preferred to x. Coombs would term a schema a 'J-scale'.

If we wished to extend this approach so as to represent, in terms of the same schema, not only the individual's evaluations of o and x, but also his perception of o's evaluation of x, we could do so by treating a short distance between o and x as representing a positive relation (o is seen as liking x), and a long distance as representing a negative relation. Figure 2.2 would therefore also imply that o disliked x. Applying this to the distinction between balanced and imbalanced triads, one can see in Figure 2.3 that all four balanced triads can be represented by unidimensional schemata. The triad with three negative relations can also be represented unidimensionally, but only in the special case where the individual's ideal point is at the neutral point of the dimension, and o and x are at opposite extremes (e.g., a political 'moderate' might hate both communists and fascists, and also assume that communists and fascists

Figure 2.2 Example of a J-scale.

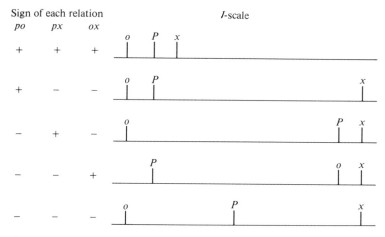

Figure 2.3 Representation of triads in a unidimensional preference space.

would hate each other). With this single special exception, imbalanced triads cannot be represented unidimensionally. The 'preference space' required to map imbalanced situations would require more than one dimension.

This approach carries a number of important implications. First, the preference for balanced structures is a preference for cognitively simpler structures which can be represented in terms of a single evaluative dimension. Second, imbalanced situations require more than one dimension for their representation, but if an individual is prepared to use more than one dimension (base his evaluations of different entities on independent criteria) he can conceptualize such situations quite adequately. A person may be aware that his friend does not share his taste in books without regarding this as something which in any way mars their friendship. The concept of balance therefore only applies to cases where the individual sees all three relations of a triad as interdependent and relevant to each other; where, in other words, he is disposed to make his evaluations in simple unidimensional terms (Stroebe, Thompson, Insko, and Reisman, 1970). Finally, the above definitions of balance and imbalance apply only where the individual evaluates himself positively (i.e., close to his ideal point). In other words, the basic formulation of balance theory assumes a positive self-concept, and the hypothesized preference for balance may be viewed as a preference for situations in which this positive self-concept is unchallenged.

Balance theory, then, has very little to do with any preference people may have for strict *logical* consistency. Instead it implies that people are *biased* towards perceiving their social environment in such a manner that they can make simple evaluative judgements in terms that enable them to maintain a positive view of themselves. Consistency in this sense is primarily a form of cognitive bias, rather than the achievement of perfect rationality. The main empirical questions to be asked therefore concern the relative strength of this bias compared with *other* biases which may also influence a person's perceptions of his social environment, and the extent to which this bias may be dependent upon the stimulus context and the particular mode of response employed. Indeed, even some of the earliest research in this area contained strong hints of the presence of biases other than balance.

Jordan (1953), for example, presented subjects with simple verbal descriptions of different triads, e.g., 'I like o, I dislike x, o dislikes x', and obtained ratings of the 'pleasantness' of each triad. As predicted, balanced triads overall were rated as more pleasant than imbalanced ones. However, Jordan also noticed a preference for positive sentiment relations (a 'positivity bias'), particularly between p and o. That is, situations in which the interpersonal relationship was one of liking rather than disliking tended to be rated as more pleasant, irrespective of any effects due to the presence or absence of balance.

In view of the importance of the po relation, Newcomb (1968) proposed a modification of Heider's theory, based on the assumption that the balance principle applies only when the po relation is positive. Newcomb suggests that the individual does not feel 'engaged' in situations where the po relation is negative, and therefore the issue of a preference for balance does not arise. This accords with findings that balanced triads do not tend to be rated as more pleasant than imbalanced ones if the po relation is negative, particularly when the third entity is another person (poq triads) rather than an impersonal object or issue (Price, Harburg, and Newcomb, 1966; Rodrigues, 1967).

Other evidence has pointed to the importance of an *agreement* bias, whereby situations in which p and o agree are preferred to situations in which they disagree (Gerard and Fleischer, 1967; Rodrigues, 1967; Whitney, 1971; Zajonc, 1968b). Crockett (1974) found consistent evidence of an agreement bias when subjects were required to rate the pleasantness of situations where the third entity was a political issue, regardless of whether or not p liked o. This argues against Newcomb's approach, since no such effects should occur if subjects were only 'engaged' in those situations where the po relation was positive. Crockett also found that balanced situations tended to be those which subjects rated as having a higher likelihood of occurrence, suggesting that pleasantness ratings may not always be the best test of Heider's theory.

Other studies have asked subjects to predict which relations, if any, between the entities in a triad are likely to change over time. Burnstein (1967) found that such predictions tended to be in the direction of balance, i.e., imbalanced situations were predicted to change so as to become balanced. In addition, negative relations between p and o were predicted by the subjects to change so as to become positive. Where subjects have to predict the value of a missing relation in a triad, balance effects have been shown by Rodrigues (1968) and Mower White (1974). Additional evidence of a positivity bias was demonstrated by Mower White, but in the Rodrigues study, presumably because of instructions that may have emphasized the importance of agreement in the hypothetical situations described, an agreement bias was found to be more influential than balance.

Studies on the learning of balanced and imbalanced situations, however, have not produced consistent evidence that balanced structures are easier to recall (Cottrell, Ingraham, and Monfort, 1971; Gerard and Fleischer, 1967; Rubin and Zajonc, 1969; Zajonc and Burnstein, 1965; Zajonc and Sherman, 1967), although these studies have generally shown that positive relations are more easily recalled than negative ones.

Mower White (1974) has also pointed out that an important prerequisite for the occurrence of balance effects may be that the subject identifies with, or takes the role of, the entity p in the triad (as in studies by Aderman, 1969; Jordan, 1953; and Rodrigues, 1967) as opposed to viewing the triad from the standpoint of an uninvolved observer (as in studies by Rubin and Zajonc, 1969; Whitney, 1971; and Zajonc and Sherman, 1967).

Three decades after it was first proposed, the notion of cognitive balance remains an important principle of attitude organization. However, it is clearly not the only principle, nor is it equally important in all situations. As Crockett has appealed (1974, page 110), 'we ought to ask no longer whether one principle or another predominates in people's constructions of social situations. Instead, let us begin to map out how balance, agreement, positivity, and other principles operate with respect to different dimensions of judgment, in different circumstances, and for different kinds of people.'

OTHER CONSISTENCY THEORIES

Although he introduced the concept of cognitive consistency into theories of attitude organization, Heider did not remain exclusively concerned with attitude research, but turned his attention increasingly towards problems in the field of interpersonal perception (Heider, 1958), and in so doing, laid the foundation for the research on interpersonal attribution to be considered in Chapter 4. Further developments of the basic concept were therefore left to other writers. These all accept Heider's notion that individuals are motivated to reduce inconsistency in their attitudes and beliefs, but differ either in the predictions which they derive from this notion, the specific situations to which they apply it, or the criteria they use for defining a structure as consistent or inconsistent.

The most distinct and important of these, Festinger's (1957) theory of *cognitive dissonance*, will be described in Chapter 5. The most similar of these to Heider's own, that proposed by Newcomb (1968), has already been briefly described. The divergence between Newcomb's predictions and those of Heider depends upon the idea that a positive *po* relation may be a necessary condition for the applicability of a balance principle, and this idea in turn reflects Newcomb's interest in the question of attraction and 'symmetry' in interpersonal relations. Balance theory is in fact basic to the hypothesis that similarity of attitudes is an important determinant of interpersonal attraction (see Chapter 6). There have also been attempts to restate balance theory in more precise mathematical terms (e.g., Cartwright and Harary, 1956). The main emphasis in later research, however, has been to use the notion of consistency to predict changes in people's attitudes, and in this context, two of the most important contributions are the theories of 'affective-cognitive consistency' proposed by Rosenberg and Abelson (1960), and of 'congruity' proposed by Osgood and Tannenbaum (1955).

Affective-Cognitive Consistency Theory (Rosenberg and Abelson, 1960)

This theory deals specifically with the question of consistency between an individual's evaluations of attitude objects or 'elements' and his beliefs concerning the relations between them. A 'cognitive unit' or 'band' consists of two evaluated 'elements' connected by a 'relation'. Elements are treated as either positive $(+)$ or negative $(-)$, relations as either positive (p), negative (n), or null (o). In many cases, Heider's 'triads' can be translated into Rosenberg and Abelson 'bands' and vice versa. For instance, the situation, 'My friend disapproves of my political party', could be represented in Heider's terms by treating 'myself' as p, 'my friend' as o (with the implication of a positive po relation), and 'my political party' as x (with the implication of a positive px relation). My perception of my friend's disapproval would then constitute a negative ox relation and the triad would be imbalanced. Rosenberg and Abelson would treat this situation as a band consisting of two positive elements (my friend and my political party) connected by a negative relation $(+n+)$. Heider's distinction between balanced and imbalanced triads is accepted, but expressed differently so that a balanced band is one in which either:

1. two elements of identical sign are believed to be positively related $(+p+$ or $-p-)$; or
2. two elements of opposite sign are believed to be negatively related $(+n-$ or $-n+)$.

An imbalanced band is one in which either:

1. two elements of identical sign are believed to be negatively related $(+n+$ or $-n-)$; or
2. two elements of opposite sign are believed to be positively related $(+p-$ or $-p+)$.

Bands containing a null relation are neither balanced nor imbalanced.

One of the most important differences between this theory and that of Heider is in the way Rosenberg and Abelson use the term 'relation'. Null relations express more or less what Heider referred to as 'negative unit relations' (e.g., 'is indifferent to', 'is not responsible for', 'does not affect'), whereas positive and negative relations express not only positive and negative sentiment (e.g., 'likes–dislikes') but also facilitatory and inhibitory causal relations (e.g., 'helps–hinders', 'brings about–prevents'). Balanced bands thus also include situations in which positive agents are seen as *instrumental* in producing positive consequences or negative agents in producing negative consequences. Positive agents should similarly be seen to inhibit negative consequences and negative agents to inhibit positive consequences. Thus, 'My friend gave me a winning tip for the 3.30 at Doncaster', would be an example of a $+p+$ band [My *friend* $(+)$ *helped* (p) my *winning* $(+)$].

Rosenberg and Abelson predict 'as a major consequence of imbalance (when the person is *attending* to that imbalance) that the cognitive band will be unstable: that it will be comparatively likely to undergo change in a balancing direction' (1960, page 120). They are thus concerned mainly with predicting changes in a person's evaluations of elements or in his perception of the relation between elements, as a consequence of imbalance. At the same time, however, they are well aware that the person has other available strategies for coping with imbalance (Abelson, 1959). He may simply not attend to the imbalance, or he may differentiate or redefine the concepts or elements, e.g., 'Smoking $(+)$ may damage (n) my health $(+)$' can become differentiated into '*Lifelong-heavy-smoking* $(-)$ causes (p) cancer $(-)$, but *smoking-the-way-I-do* $(+)$ has no effect (o) on my health $(+)$', or he may attempt to 'bolster' his existing attitude by relating one or other of the elements in a balanced way to other valued elements, e.g., 'Smoking $(+)$ may damage (n) my health $(+)$, but it improves (p) my concentration $(+)$'.

The translation of triads into bands allows also for the easy description of more complex 'structures' containing numbers of interconnected bands. Such larger structures can themselves be thought of as balanced or imbalanced, depending on whether the component bands are consistent or inconsistent. Rosenberg and Abelson (1960) hypothesized that, when subjects are presented with an imbalanced structure, they will tend to follow the 'least effortful' path towards the restoration of balance, that is, they will try to keep the number of changes in their evaluations of individual entities and relations to a minimum. This hypothesis received support in an experiment which Rosenberg and Abelson report. Additional aspects of the data, however, which were very similar to the 'positivity bias' findings in the tests of Heider's balance theory, led them to conclude: 'In resolving cognitive discrepancies of the sort represented by our materials, subjects seek not only the attainment of cognitive balance and consistency, but they seek also to alter their beliefs and evaluations in ways that will maximize expected gain and minimize expected loss' (page 145).

As in the case of Heider's theory, however, a fuller development of the notion of affective-cognitive consistency would seem to require not only an acknowledgement of the presence of 'forces' or biases other than balance, but also a means of predicting their relative importance in different situations.

Congruity Theory

Osgood and Tannenbaum's (1955) congruity theory is an application of the consistency principle to the specific question of how a person's attitude may change if he is exposed to a persuasive message or communication. The variables considered are, (1) the individual's initial attitude towards the *source* of the message, (2) the individual's initial attitude towards the *concept* evaluated by the source, and (3) the nature of the evaluative *assertion* about the concept contained in the message. Both (1) and (2) are defined in terms of a single evaluative scale of approval–disapproval from $+3$ to -3, which is essentially the 'good–bad' scale of the semantic differential (Osgood, Suci, and Tannenbaum, 1957). The assertion is treated simply as either *associative* (the source approves of the concept) or *disassociative* (the source disapproves of the concept). These three variables are analogous to the three relations of a Heider triad, corresponding respectively to the *po*, *px*, and *ox* relations. Whereas Heider treated all three relations as dichotomies, Osgood and Tannenbaum treat the first two, but not the third, as continua. The fact that the value of the assertion is treated as a simple dichotomy indicates that congruity theory applies strictly only to those cases where the source advocates full, unambiguous, approval or disapproval of the concept. The theory is not concerned with changes in a person's perception of the content of the message, but is concerned with changes in how he evaluates the concept and the source.

The basic congruity principle is that 'changes in evaluation are always in the direction of increased congruity with the existing frame of reference' (Osgood and Tannenbaum, 1955, page 43). If there is an *associative* bond between source and concept, maximal congruity obtains if both occupy the same position on the evaluative scale. If the bond is a *disassociative* one, maximal congruity obtains if source and concept occupy symmetrical positions on opposite sides of the neutral point on the evaluative scale, e.g., if the source is evaluated at $+2$ and the concept at -2. In a state of incongruity, the person's evaluations of *both* source *and* concept are predicted to change in the direction of increased congruity. Osgood and Tannenbaum also assume that the amount a person's evaluation of either source or concept will change will be inversely proportionate to the extremity of that evaluation. This is compatible with the notion that extreme judgements are made with greater confidence and therefore less liable to change.

For example, if a highly regarded source $(+3)$ recommends a concept towards which the person initially held a somewhat negative attitude (-1), four scale intervals separate source and concept according to the person's initial evaluations. However, since source and concept have now become positively associated, they should ideally receive the same evaluation; in other words, they need to move towards each other along the evaluative scale. To predict the separate changes for source and concept, one distributes the initial difference of four scale points in the proportion $1:3$ for source and concept respectively. Since the initial position of the source was three times as extreme as that of the concept, it moves only one-third of the distance moved by the concept. Thus the source moves down one scale interval to $+2$ and the concept up three scale intervals to $+2$. If the source had initially been at $+3$ and the concept at 0, there would have been a difference of three scale intervals to distribute in the proportion of $0 : 3$. Thus, the source would not move at all and the concept would move the total distance of three intervals to $+3$. If the source had initially been at $+3$ and the concept at $+1$, the initial difference of two scale intervals would be distributed in the proportion $1 : 3$, so that the source moved down half an interval to $+2\cdot5$, and the concept up one-and-a-half intervals to $+2\cdot5$.

In the case of a disassociative assertion, one calculates the 'total pressure toward congruity' not from the initial difference in evaluation, but from the sum of the initial evaluations of source and concept. Thus, with a $+3$ source derogating a concept at -1, the total pressure is $+3 - 1 = 2$ scale intervals. These are distributed in the proportion $1 : 3$ so that the source moves down half an interval to $+2\cdot5$, and the concept down one-and-a-half intervals to $-2\cdot5$. With a $+3$ source derogating a concept at $+1$, the total pressure is $+3 + 1 = 4$ scale intervals. Distributed in the proportion $1 : 3$, this means that the source should move down one interval to $+2$, and the concept down three intervals to -2.

In the basic formulation, both source and concept are referred to simply as 'objects of judgement' and are treated as equivalent as far as predictions of change are concerned. Thus, one could interchange source and concept in all the examples above and the same predictions would apply. However, since the attitude change effects observed in empirical studies did not show a perfect correspondence with the predictions of this model, Osgood and Tannenbaum introduced two modifications. The first of these is a 'correction for incredulity', based upon the assumption that 'the amount of incredulity produced when one object of judgement is associated with another by an assertion is a positively accelerated function of the amount of incongruity which exists' (1955, page 47). For example, if a highly positive source praised a highly negative concept, the person might regard the communication as so incredible that he would feel under no pressure to change his attitude towards source or concept. ('Incredulity' is used as a blanket term in this context, and can best be regarded as a general resistance to communications which are incompatible with one's previous beliefs about the relation between source and concept.) The second modification is an 'assertion constant' which embodies the prediction that, over and above any effects due to the person's evaluation of the source, the concept will become slightly more positively evaluated if praised and slightly more negatively evaluated if denounced by the source.

Osgood and Tannenbaum are careful to point out that their model does not attempt to account for all the variables which could produce or inhibit attitude change. To consider the function of a persuasive communication merely to be that of establishing an associative or disassociative bond between source and concept, is clearly an oversimplification. The model establishes a conceptual bridge between the notion of cognitive consistency and the associationist learning principle that stimuli come to take on the valence of other stimuli with which they are associated. At the same time, the predictions of congruity theory apply only to attitude change which occurs within 'the existing frame of reference'. How such a frame of reference becomes established is an important question which the theory leaves unanswered.

THE SUBJECT-VERB-OBJECT APPROACH

A notable recent development in the field of consistency theory is the subject-verb-object approach of Gollob (1974). The basic ideas of affective-cognitive consistency theory and congruity theory are incorporated in a much more generally stated framework, which allows for an easier conceptualization of biases other than balance. Gollob starts by pointing out that the cognitive structures dealt with by the different consistency theories, such as Heider's triads, Rosenberg and Abelson's bands, and Osgood and Tannenbaum's structures of source, assertion, and concept, can be expressed as sentences consisting of a subject, verb, and object. An evaluative sign can often be attached to each of the three parts of the sentence, so that, for example, a sentence like, 'My friend praised my favourite musician', which would constitute a $+p+$ band in the Rosenberg and Abelson notation, is treated by Gollob as consisting of a positive subject, a positive verb, and a positive object.

Heider's balance principle is a statement about the relationship between all three parts of the subject-verb-object (SVO) structure. Gollob therefore refers to Heiderian balance as *SVO balance*. This applies when any two of the three sentence components are negative, and the third is positive, or when all three are positive. In addition, though, Gollob identifies three more 'balance' biases, and three 'positivity' biases. *SV balance* applies when both S and V have the same evaluative sign, in other words, when a good person does something good, or a bad person something bad, regardless of the object or target of such behaviour. This can be thought of as a 'character balance' in that it may reflect an expectation for people to act 'in character'. *SO balance* applies when S and O have the same evaluative sign, reflecting a bias of which Gollob concedes there has been little direct evidence in previous research. *VO balance*, on the other hand, is more recognizable as a 'justice' bias, with good things happening to good objects or people, and bad things being done to bad objects or people. Finally, the three positivity biases refer to preferences for S, V, and O considered singly to be positive rather than negative in evaluation.

Probably the best developed aspect of Gollob's approach is its application to tasks where one of the sentence components has to be inferred from the other two. To deal with this situation, Gollob proposes what he calls the 'relevant bias hypothesis', according to which 'an inference will be affected *only* by those cognitive biases which include the component which is to be inferred' (page 290). So, for instance, if one has to infer O from S and V, the relevant biases are SVO (Heiderian balance), SO (O will be expected to have the same evaluative sign as S), VO (O will be expected to have the same sign as V), and O (O will be expected to be positive). Thus, if S and V are both positive, all four biases predict that O should be inferred to be positive also. On the other hand, if S is positive but V is negative, SVO balance and VO balance lead to an inference that O should be negative, whereas the other two biases lead to an opposite inference. The strength of any given inference is assumed to be a weighted sum of the relevant biases.

Rossman and Gollob (1976) used the SVO approach to predict not only inferences but also pleasantness ratings of structures in which information about all three sentence components was given. Across four types of structures (with the object being a real or abstract person or issue), the two biases which made the most contribution to rated pleasantness were SVO and VO balance. Of these, VO balance was more important than SVO balance in three of the four types of structures; in other words, the rated pleasantness of a structure seemed to depend most on the presence of evaluative congruity between V and O (a kind of 'justice' effect), and after that on the presence of Heiderian balance. When inferences were required from incomplete structures, however, the single most important bias was that of SVO balance.

The three positivity biases and four balance biases can be thought of as the three main effects and four interaction terms of an analysis of variance, with the eight possible triads constituting a 2^3 factorial design. Gollob's weighted summation rule incorporates the assumptions of the analysis of variance model: 'Since the seven biases are mutually orthogonal to each other, the combined sum of squares accounted for by several biases can be obtained by addition' (1974, page 293). This position has been criticized by Anderson (1977), who points out that it involves the following possibly questionable assumptions. The first is that each of the effects in the analysis of variance design corresponds to a single distinct and psychologically real cognitive bias. The difficulty of interpreting SO balance in a meaningful way suggests that this may be problematic. The second is that the different biases are combined additively, rather than integrated by some non-additive rule. The third is that each bias should be constant over all eight types of triads. In other words, the strength of, say, S positivity should be independent of the values of V and O. An apparent violation of this assumption is Newcomb's (1968) hypothesis that Heiderian balance should apply only if the *po* relation is positive. Rossman and Gollob (1976, page 380) relate Newcomb's distinction between levels of balance to their prediction of the importance of SVO and VO balance in pleasantness judgements. However, the more direct implication would seem to be that SVO balance is *not* independent of S positivity. This is because a positive *po* relation ('I like Bill') corresponds to a positive S

('My friend Bill') in Gollob's system. Finally, Anderson objects to the implicit assumption of Gollob's analysis of variance model that one is dealing with responses that can be measured on a interval scale (of perceived likelihood or pleasantness), rather than simply with ordinal scores.

CONSISTENCY AND COGNITIVE SCRIPTS

Like affective–cognitive consistency theory, the SVO approach treats consistency as a bias or heuristic which influences how individuals process information and draw inferences. The extent to which individuals' ways of structuring their attitudes embody rules of formal logic has been explored by McGuire (1960) and more fully by Wyer (1974). As such research shows, however, the interesting thing about a principle such as balance is not so much whether it leads people to make logically valid or invalid inferences, but that it is *used* by individuals as a device for coping with complex social information. This information is typically presented to experimental subjects in the form of language, and the kinds of responses required also tend to be linguistic. It therefore becomes important to ask how a cognitive bias such as balance may be verbalized or represented linguistically.

Gollob's approach assumes a correspondence between the attitude structure of a *pox* triad and the linguistic structure of a SVO sentence. His concern, though, remains primarily with structure rather than with content, i.e., the meaning of the sentence. Meaning, however, is of central importance to the approach proposed by Abelson (1973, 1976). Abelson regards the structure of beliefs as depending on 'implicational molecules', or sets of sentences which are bound together by psychological implication. Although the perceived consistency between sentences may be compatible with the SVO approach (as pointed out by Wyer, 1974), it is not generally predictable from that approach in that it depends on the semantic classes of persons, actions, and objects referred to in the sentences and not just on their evaluative sign. For example, if one has an actor (A), an act (X), and an outcome (Y), an implicational molecule could be formed by the three sentences: A does X. X causes Y. A wants Y. This is a type of 'consistency' that makes sense in terms of the simple rule that people may act in certain ways to produce desired outcomes. Certainly one would expect this to be an important rule in influencing the inferences we draw about one another's behaviour and attributing intentionality (see Chapter 4). Nonetheless, even though it is a highly general rule, it is still an empirical one, rather than one based on *a priori* formal principles.

In his more recent development of this approach, Abelson (1976) uses the term 'cognitive script' instead of 'implicational molecule'. A script is defined as a 'coherent sequence of events expected by the individual, involving him either as a participant or as an observer' (page 33). The basic element in a script is a 'vignette', defined as 'an encoding of an event of short duration, in general including both an image (often visual) of the perceived event and a conceptual representation of the event' (page 34).

The level at which both vignettes and scripts (chains of vignettes) are processed can progress from the 'episodic' level of concrete single experiences, through a 'categorical' level at which events are grouped together on the basis of similarity, to an 'hypothetical' level when they are encoded in terms of more general semantic features. The more a script approaches this 'hypothetical level', the more it gives *guidance for action* which is generalizable to new situations. Abelson proposes that 'cognitively mediated social behaviour depends on the joint occurrence of two processes: (a) the selection of a particular script to represent the given social situation and (b) the taking of a participant role within that script' (pages 42–43).

This represents a simple but vitally significant insight into the relationship between cognitive organization and social behaviour. The rules of cognitive organization which Abelson refers to as scripts are not simply descriptive, or even evaluative, formalizations of information; they are gerundive guides to the action called for by the social circumstances. The kind of reasoning they portray is the reasoning of the *practical* syllogism, the choice of action that is appropriate in the light of informational premises. They allow for interaction with the environment since it is from such interaction that they are learnt.

COGNITIVE COMPLEXITY

The basic assumption of consistency theories is that people are motivated to reduce inconsistency, particularly in their evaluative impressions of others. No mention is made of possible differences between individuals in the strength of this motivation, although it seems more than reasonable to suppose that such differences exist. In fact, a number of researchers have found fairly reliable differences between individuals in the extent to which they will make fine or gross distinctions in their judgements of others, will use simpler or more complex ways of categorizing, and will consider a smaller or greater number of attributes or dimensions simultaneously. On the basis of these findings, various tests have been devised to measure a construct (or set of constructs) known generally as *cognitive complexity–simplicity*. It should be stressed that these tests do not all necessarily measure exactly the same tendency or trait, nor are they based on exactly the same theoretical assumptions (Streufert and Streufert, 1978; Vannoy, 1965).

Whatever the precise definitions and measures employed, however, a common prediction is that balance theory and its derivatives should more adequately describe the behaviour of cognitively simple than of cognitively complex individuals. Support for this prediction comes from a number of studies. Press, Crockett, and Rosenkrantz (1969) found that cognitively simple subjects were quicker at learning balanced than imbalanced structures when presented with a set of like–dislike relationships among groups of four hypothetical persons. Cognitively complex subjects showed no consistent differences in the speed with which they learned the two kinds of structures. Similar results were obtained by Delia and Crockett (1973). Ware and Harvey (1967) found that cognitively simple subjects were more prepared to make generalizations about a person's behaviour, and were more certain of their impressions, when presented with evaluatively consistent information about the stimulus person. Cognitively complex subjects were more prepared to generalize when the information contained evaluative inconsistencies. Similarly, Harvey, and Ware (1967) presented subjects with information about a stimulus person, indicating that his present behaviour was apparently inconsistent with his previous behaviour. When asked to write explanations for this inconsistency, cognitively simple subjects seemed more troubled by it, and tended to explain it away as due to a temporary change in the person. In comparison, cognitively complex subjects were more likely to try and make sense of the inconsistency in terms of an integrated account.

Cognitive complexity can also be viewed, not just as an individual difference variable, but as a motivation in its own right, reflected in tendencies to seek out novelty and variety, and explore unfamiliar situations (e.g., Berlyne, 1960; Maddi, 1968). Although this seems to be a direct contradiction of balance theory, there seems reason to suppose that both the motive to seek out incongruity and the motive to reduce it may co-exist (McGuire, 1968). The need to view one's world as relatively stable and predictable seems basic to any behavioural decision, but the need to find out more about one's world also would seem to have obvious survival value. An organism that expected the environment to be *completely* predictable would be as poorly adapted to the needs of survival as one that expected the environment to be completely unpredictable. The real issue seems to be one of the *level* of congruity or incongruity a person will tolerate or seek to attain.

Streufert and Streufert (1978) have attempted to integrate the different findings in this area through the use of a concept which they term the 'general incongruity adaptation level', or GIAL. (The concept of adaptation level will be discussed in detail in the next chapter.) Broadly, what they propose is that individuals form, on the basis of experience, certain expectations about the level of incongruity they are likely to encounter in any given area. If an individual experiences incongruity above his GIAL, he will act in accordance with the precepts of consistency theory, and seek to reduce the incongruity (though he will not necessarily go so far as completely to restore balance). On the other hand, if he experiences less incongruity than he expected, i.e., below his GIAL, he would actively search out incongruity. An example of this could be when a person is described to us so as to be 'too good to be true' and our suspicions are aroused as a result.

Streufert and Streufert allow for the fact that individuals may have different GIALs for different areas of their experience. For instance, a person might have learned to expect considerable unpredictability in the performance of his favourite sports team, but still expect highly predictable relationships between, say, the political attitudes and patterns of friendship among his neighbours. It remains a possibility, though, that some individuals may have generally higher GIALs across different areas than other individuals. Indeed the notion of cognitive complexity-simplicity as a stable personality characteristic implies just this. At present, though, the measures used provide only a weak basis for any such generalizations beyond the area of interpersonal judgements.

ATTITUDES AND BEHAVIOUR

At the beginning of this chapter, I said that the study of attitudes is a dangerous starting point for a book on social psychology. Probably the greatest danger concerns the predictive utility of the attitude concept. Sophisticated techniques of attitude measurement can be devised, impressive theories of attitude organization can be proposed, but if, at the end of it all, we are no more able to predict what a person will or will not do in a given situation, what use are our measurements and theories?

Some of the most disturbing studies in social psychology, therefore, are those that have claimed to find little or no relation between people's behaviour and their verbally expressed attitudes. Logically we need to assume some kind of correspondence between what people say and what they do, or expressions of preference would be simply unintelligible. A situation in which there was *no* correspondence between people's expressed attitudes and their behaviour, therefore, would not simply be a situation in which people did not act out their beliefs, it would be a situation in which they *could not communicate their preferences* through language at all. The intelligibility of evaluative language is a fact, so the question is not whether there *is* a correspondence between attitudes and behaviour, but *what kind* of correspondence there is, and what are the factors that affect it.

When one looks at those studies that have attempted directly to compare verbal expression of attitude towards a group or issue with other attitude-relevant behaviours, a rather confused picture emerges. Sometimes the verbal measures provide quite good predictors of the specific kinds of behaviour under investigation, but very often they seem to allow no such prediction at all. In his review of such research, Wicker (1969) concluded that only in a minority of cases was a close relationship found between verbally expressed attitudes and overt behaviour, the typical result being one of only a slight association, or no association at all. The classic study in this field is that by LaPiere (1934) who travelled across the United States over a period of two years accompanied by a Chinese couple, and noted the reactions of hoteliers and restaurateurs. During the course of their travels, 'we met definite rejection from those asked to serve us *just once*. We were received at 66 hotels, auto camps and "Tourist Homes" .... We were served in 184 restaurants and cafés . . . and treated with . . . more than ordinary consideration in 72 of them' (page 232). This apparent lack of prejudice at a behavioural level, however, contrasted sharply with the responses of the managers of the same establishments to a questionnaire sent out by LaPiere six months later, which asked the question, 'Will you accept members of the Chinese race as guests in your establishment?' Of the 81 restaurants and 47 hotels that replied, 92 per cent said 'No', the remainder saying, 'Uncertain, depend upon circumstances.'

A similar pattern of results was found by Kutner, Wilkins, and Yarrow (1952). Their study involved two white women entering a restaurant and shortly after being joined by a black woman. In the 11 restaurants visited, the black woman was never refused admission, and the service was completely satisfactory. Later, the same restaurants received a letter asking for a reservation for a racially mixed group and when none had replied 17 days later, all received telephone calls making the same request. Only five of the restaurants then accepted the reservation (reluctantly) and six gave clear refusals. Somewhat more positive results were obtained by DeFleur and Westie (1958), who obtained verbal indices of white college students' racial attitudes during the course of an interview, and then asked them if they would be willing to have their photographs taken in the company of a black person of the opposite sex, for a range of specified purposes. Of the 23 subjects classified as 'prejudiced' on the basis of their verbal attitudes, 18 refused to be photographed, while 14 of the 23 'unprejudiced' subjects agreed to be photographed. Thus, a clear association was found between the verbal and behavioural indices of prejudice, but there were still 14 subjects (30 per cent of the sample) whose behaviour appeared discrepant from their verbally expressed attitudes.

THE THREE-COMPONENT VIEW OF ATTITUDES

There have, therefore, been many examples where measures of attitude and behaviour fail to correlate, or where correlations are found which are ambiguous with respect to the direction of causality. Nonetheless, such results have generally failed to shake the conviction on the part of most attitude theorists that attitudes are an important, if not the major, cause of the kinds of behaviour which interest social psychologists. The most common defence is that embodied in the *three-component* view of attitudes. According to this view, 'attitudes are predispositions to respond to some class of stimuli with certain classes of responses' (Rosenberg and Hovland, 1960, page 3), the three major types of response being defined as affective (evaluative feelings and preferences), cognitive (opinions and beliefs), and behavioural or conative (overt actions and statements of intent). The relationship between these three components is represented in Figure 2.4.

Assuming that the arrows in Figure 2.4 denote the direction of causality (although the *kind* of causality that is at issue here is rarely discussed), it can

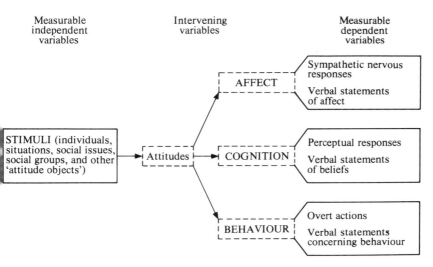

| Measurable independent variables | Intervening variables | Measurable dependent variables |

Figure 2.4 Schematic conception of attitudes. (Reproduced with permission of the Yale University Press, from M. J. Rosenberg *et al.*, *Attitude Organization and Change: An Analysis of Consistency Among Attitude Components*, Yale University Press, New Haven, 1960.)

be seen that the concept of attitudes is being used to intervene between observable antecedent stimuli and observable subsequent responses. 'Attitude', according to this view, is not simply a construct employed to describe the stimulus-response relationship in summary form, nor is it just the individual's own interpretation of the stimuli which he experiences. Instead it is ambiguously situated in the middle of the causal chain, simultaneously an *effect* and a *cause* of external observable events. The most ambiguous part of the diagram is the set of three arrows leading from the box labelled 'attitudes' to those labelled 'affect', 'cognition', and 'behaviour'. It is unclear whether the same set of 'attitudes' simultaneously causes specific affective, cognitive, and behavioural effects; whether affect, cognition, and behaviour are separate components of the 'attitudes' box (i.e., the arrows should be replaced by brackets) simultaneously caused by the same antecedent stimuli; or whether affect, cognition, and behaviour are separate components caused by separate antecedent stimuli. Finally, nothing is implied in the diagram about how affect, cognition, and behaviour may directly influence one another.

The appeal of this ambiguity is that it allows attitude theorists, as the mood may take them, either to treat attitudes as internally consistent structures, or as conglomerations of essentially distinct components. If one finds an apparent discrepancy between verbal attitudes and overt behaviour, this is because one is dealing with distinct components, and any complete description of a person's attitude requires that one should obtain measures of all three classes of responses, and not simply infer attitudes from the affective component alone. On the other hand, if one succeeds in predicting behaviour from a person's statements of affect or opinion, this just goes to show how closely the three components of attitudes are related to one another. In fact, it is difficult to imagine *any* kind of data that could not somehow be made to fit the three-component view of attitudes, and this, of course, is its great weakness as an explanatory model.

Thus, research on the three-component view of attitudes has alternatively emphasized the independence and interdependence of the different components. Triandis (1967) has proposed that instruments of attitude measurement should incorporate indices of all three components, and has also argued, with the support of factor-analytic data (Triandis, 1964), that the behavioural component may itself be multidimensional. For example, personal attributes that might lead others to exhibit 'friendship' towards one, would be distinct from those attributes which would elicit 'respect', 'marital acceptance', or 'deep emotional involvement'.

Ostrom (1969) constructed three types of attitude scales (Thurstone, Likert, and Guttman) from each of three sets of statements concerning attitudes towards the Church, which had been previously categorized by judges as referring primarily to either affect cognition or behaviour. A three-item self-rating scale was also incorporated, with one item representing each component. In comparing the responses of subjects to the different parts of the questionnaire, Ostrom noted that the correlations between the *different* measures of any *single* component were higher than the correlations between the measures of the three *different* components by any *single* method, implying that somewhat different areas of content were being tapped by the different components (see Campbell and Fiske, 1959, for a discussion of the rationale behind this kind of analysis). For each scaling method, however, the correlations between the three components were still high (averaging approximately 0.6, 0.8, 0.5, and 0.7 on the Thurstone, Likert, Guttman, and self-rating scales respectively, for a sample of 189 subjects). In addition, Ostrom asked subjects to indicate their own behaviour towards the Church in terms of seven separate criteria, which were then intercorrelated with the 12 previously derived attitude scores.

The attitude-behaviour correlations were almost all positive but generally very low. The only behaviour that could be predicted from the attitude measures with reasonable confidence was the number of days per year on which subjects attended church services, and even this was not appreciably more predictable from the verbal measures of the behavioural component than from the other verbal measures. Thus, although this study is frequently cited as support for the three-component view of attitudes, it in fact demonstrates that this approach cannot explain the low relationships between verbal attitudes and overt behaviour found in previous studies, since Ostrom also found low attitude-behaviour relationships, having already shown high intercorrelations between the affective, cognitive, and behavioural components. Such research shows that it is one thing to incorporate into one's theoretical definitions distinctions that appear quite plausible on *a priori* grounds, and quite another thing to show that *these* distinctions, rather than any others one could think up, have any major heuristic or explanatory value. The so-called 'attitude-behaviour discrepancy' remains mysterious so long as we are committed to a view of attitudes which assumes that attitudinal continua, such as those of favourability-unfavourability towards Chinese, blacks, or the Church, exist 'out there', and that these continua define an *objective* psychological space in which different individuals, statements, and behaviours can be mapped. Therefore, before asking, 'Why don't attitudes predict behaviour?', we need to ask if our concept of attitude is adequate to the explanatory task which we have demanded of it. As with almost every psychological dimension of individual difference, the best way to remove the mystique surrounding the concept of attitude is to look at the way that generalized attitudinal dimensions are in fact measured.

GENERALITY VS. SPECIFICITY

As has already been pointed out, most attitude scales consist of numbers of separate statements, or items. But what do these items look like? A glance at the impressive collection of attitude scales compiled by Shaw and Wright (1967) can be quite revealing. Suppose we were interested in designing a research project around a title such as 'Attitudinal factors influencing law-abidance and law-breaking'. We might not feel able to design our own scale, and so might select the Rundquist and Sletto (1936) 'Law Scale' (Shaw and Wright, 1967, page 253)—a scale with quite respectable levels of reliability. We could then ask our subjects how much they agreed or disagreed with statements such as: 'The Law protects property rights at the expense of human rights'; 'On the whole, policemen are honest'; and 'A hungry man has a right to steal'. Using this scale, we might then find that right-wing students scored more 'pro-law' than left-wing students; police constables more 'pro-law' than croupiers; and magistrates more 'pro-law' than second-hand car dealers (with apologies to all honest croupiers and car-dealers). At one level, such data (of which there is a considerable amount in the early attitude scaling studies) could be taken as evidence that the scale *did* discriminate between groups of people who exhibited different kinds of behaviour. In other words, one might well discover differences in very *general* kinds of law-related behaviour which were not too unrelated to the *general* measure of attitude employed. But suppose one set oneself a different kind of task. Suppose one had in mind, not law-breaking in general but a *specific* form of law-breaking, say drunken driving. It is more than likely that one would find *no* relationship between people's attitudes towards the law, as measured by this scale, and their tendency to drive when drunk. Why not?

Many of the explanations may by now have a familiar ring. It might be said that a measure of attitudes towards the law is incomplete without items of a more behavioural nature. To compensate for this, we might return to

Shaw and Wright, turn over three pages (page 256), and find the Gregory (1939) 'Law-Abidingness Scale', which contains 14 items designed to measure people's indulgence in various kinds of minor illegal activity, including traffic offences. Out goes the new questionnaire, but still it fails to discriminate drunken drivers from anyone else. So we start thinking about the behaviour a little more directly—suppose law-abidingness is only one of the relevant variables, and not nearly as important as people's attitudes towards the possibility of inflicting physical injury on oneself or others. Back to Shaw and Wright we go, and on page 481 we find the Yuker, Block, and Campbell (1960) 'Attitude toward Disabled People Scale'. With this we can ask our subjects how far they agree with statements like, 'Disabled people are often unfriendly', or 'Most severely disabled people are just as ambitious as physically normal persons'. Still no luck, so still the search can continue, leading us further and further away from where we started. Finally, frustrated and fatigued, we might take the trouble actually to read the attitude scales we have been using. Then, probably for the first time, it might strike us that nowhere, in any of the scales, was there any specific mention of drunken driving.

Does this mean that the scales we used were invalid? Not necessarily, since they were never intended to be *specifically* concerned with drunken driving. It was merely an assumption on our part that a more positive evaluation of the law in general would be predictive of an avoidance of this particular kind of law-breaking. In choosing to use the scales in question for purposes of this kind of prediction, we implicitly reified the construct of a generalized attitude-towards-the-Law dimension. We proceeded as though everyone possessed such an attitude at some level of favourability or unfavourability, and this attitude motivated their specific actions.

But where did this construct of generalized attitude-towards-the-Law come from? From people's behaviour, or researchers' presuppositions? If from people's behaviour, 'attitude-behaviour discrepancies' of the kind we have been discussing would have to be the exception rather than the rule. But if from researchers' presuppositions, how can such a subjective factor still be influential after the rigorous procedures of item selection and scale construction have been scrupulously completed? The answer is that it is precisely these procedures which serve to reify the construct in question. Items which yield responses which are compatible with the assumption of a general unidimensional attitude continuum may be selected for inclusion in the final scale. Items which yield responses incompatible with the unidimensional assumption will not be selected, but this does not mean that these latter responses are random or meaningless. It just means that they come between the researcher and his presuppositions, and are therefore simply removed.

Even so, this does not mean that scales so constructed are necessarily invalid. They can provide perfectly adequate measures of *those aspects* of attitudes towards the Law or any other such issue which *can* be treated in terms of a generalized unidimensional continuum. It is then an empirical question how many specific aspects remain which cannot be treated in this way. Thus, if we found that generalized attitudes towards the Law did not predict drunken driving, this would *not* entitle us to speak of a discrepancy between attitudes and behaviour. If we took the trouble specifically to measure attitudes towards drunken driving, we might well find much higher levels of predictability of behaviour. If this were so, we would have to say, not that we could not predict behaviour from attitudes, but that we could not predict a specific attitude from a more general attitude which we had *presumed* encompassed it.

If we reconsider the literature in this area, it is apparent that most studies have used relatively specific indices of behaviour and relatively general indices of attitude (Ajzen and Fishbein, 1977). The host of studies in which college students were assessed along a *general* attitudinal dimension of prejudice against blacks, and then presented with a specific behavioural option involving interaction with one or more black persons, exemplify this problem to a marked extent. This is even more unfortunate in view of the proportion of the total number of attitude-behaviour studies for which they account (Wicker, 1969). Even in the LaPiere (1934) study, which is by no means the most transparent from this point of view, the hoteliers and restaurateurs may have seen the choice before them as that of whether or not to create a scene by refusing custom to a specific, well-dressed, well-behaved, middle-class Chinese couple (no doubt quite unlike their stereotype of the 'typical' Chinese), who were obviously not out to make trouble, were just passing through, and were in the company of a non-Chinese American, and had also actually arrived at their establishment and so could not be politely diverted with: 'Sorry, we're fully booked tonight'. The measure of 'attitude' used by LaPiere, however, involved a commitment to serve 'members of the Chinese race' in unspecified numbers, at unspecified times, for unspecified periods, and regardless of whether they presented themselves in a socially accommodating manner, even assuming that this attitude measure was elicited from exactly the same individuals whose behaviour had been recorded. The method of measuring attitudes in this study may well have involved just the kind of situation which would maximize the effect of the respondents' stereotypes about Chinese, and the method of assessing behaviour may have involved just the kind of situation in which the effect of these stereotypes would be minimal.

Fishbein (1967) and Fishbein and Ajzen (1975) have emphasized an important distinction between attitudes towards a specific object, and attitudes towards specific behaviour performed with respect to that object. According to Fishbein, a person's intention to perform a particular action will be a joint function of his own evaluation of the action (attitude towards the behaviour) and his impressions of how other people of importance to him will evaluate him if he performed such behaviour (subjective norms concerning the behaviour). Attitudes towards the object will influence behaviour only indirectly, through influencing a person's attitude towards the behaviour, which in turn will influence intention only in combination with relevant 'subjective norms' concerning the behaviour. Often people may make these 'subjective norms' explicit in order to avoid personal (attitudinal) responsibility for their behaviour, by stating that they behave in the way they do to satisfy *other people* on whom they are dependent, whom they represent, or whose feelings they wish to protect. Whether or not such protestations are sincere is not at issue. The point is that they are an intelligible part of behavioural decisions. In more general terms, a large part of what we call 'socialization' involves the learning of norms and rules which define which classes of behaviour are, or are not, appropriate within certain classes of situations. Such norms and rules are likely to have a profound influence on almost any behaviour one might care to imagine, without needing to assume the presence of any specific 'significant other' whose approval the actor is anxious to obtain.

The implication of this is that there is no more reason to assume a one-to-one relationship between a person's general attitude on some issue and his performance of any specific act, than there is to assume such a relationship between his general attitude and his endorsement of any specific attitude statement. Many statements of apparent relevance to a given issue are not suitable for inclusion in an attitude scale in that they do not discriminate between people with different positions on the attitude continuum measured by the researcher. This could be because of the base rate of agreement to the statement in question. The statement could be so implausible or offensive that everyone would reject it, or so obvious that everyone would accept it. Alternatively, the statement could yield a range of responses which was not predictable from subjects' responses to other items in the scale. This would be taken to imply that it was affected by factors other than those which the attitude scale was designed to measure. So much is well-known with respect to verbal indices of attitude. Exactly the same argument, however, can be applied to *behavioural* indices of attitude. One can imagine many specific acts which might be supposed to reflect a person's attitude on a particular issue, but which do *not* in fact discriminate between people with different 'attitudes', either because of response base rates, or because they are affected by factors other than the people's positions on the attitude continuum measured by the researcher.

The 'attitude–behaviour discrepancy' is essentially an artefact of the haphazard selection of specific behavioural indices which researchers have tried to relate to general verbal measures of attitudes. If the selection of specific verbal indices (for inclusion in an attitude scale) were as lax and arbitrary, we would quickly have a situation in which we had to talk of an 'attitude–attitude discrepancy': attitudes would not simply fail to predict behaviour, they would have to be considered self-contradictory even at the level of verbal expression. On the other hand, if we are as selective in our choice of behavioural indices as we are at present in our choice of verbal indices, the 'attitude–behaviour discrepancy' disappears as a substantive problem.

Fishbein and Ajzen (1974) have demonstrated that it is possible to construct 'behavioural' attitude scales by applying the same scaling and item selection procedures to series of behavioural criteria as are conventionally applied to verbal expressions of sentiment and approval. Using the issue of religious behaviour, they had subjects complete both 'behavioural' and standard attitude scales. Their most important finding was that the standard attitude scales, designed to measure whether people were generally favourable or unfavourable towards religion, correlated quite highly with the overall behavioural scores, which indicated how favourably or unfavourably subjects said they behaved or would behave *in general* with respect to religion. At the same time, there was considerable variability in the extent to which specific acts could be predicted from scores on the verbal attitude scales, and Fishbein and Ajzen discuss possible reasons for this.

The question, 'Do attitudes predict behaviour?', is therefore not one which allows any single or simple answer. It depends on the precise content of such attitudes and behaviour—on the subtle distinctions of meaning inherent in what a person says and what he does.

CONCLUSIONS

This brings us back to what has been the central theme of this chapter. A person's attitude is the true meaning of his expressive behaviour. If the *only* important distinctions within such expressive behaviour were ones that could be completely dealt with in terms of a single continuum ranging from overall positive to overall negative affect, we could all communicate our attitudes perfectly adequately through a combination of gurgles, grunts, and growls, without any need for language. Such distinctions, however, have been the major focus of social psychological research on attitudes. The reason for this has been that researchers have seen it as their task to make comparisons between the attitudes of different individuals or of the same individuals on different occasions.

To make a complete comparison of two people's attitudes would be as Herculean a task as to give a complete description of the similarities and differences between two novels, or two works of art. It is just not a practicable possibility. The alternative is to simplify, but inevitably this must involve making assumptions concerning one's subject matter which may appear crude, distorted, and perhaps sometimes even downright wrong. However, if one is lucky or prudent and finds an issue where these assumptions do not appear too crude, one can apply powerful techniques of numerical measurement and analysis which enable one to assign scores or labels to individuals which will have at least some degree of reliability and predictive validity. If one is not so lucky, one will still get scores which one can assign, but these will mean very little. The problem is not with the measurement techniques themselves, but with the assumptions upon which they depend. Sometimes these will be valid, sometimes they will not, but in all cases it is essential to remember that *an assumption has been made*. Attitudes are not simply quantities of mental energy to be read off on some magic meter, even though such an analogy may be temptingly convenient to the researcher.

Nor is it just the researcher who seeks to simplify his conception of the relation between the individual and the attitude object. The individual himself does so as well, through attempting to construct and maintain internally consistent cognitive structures. A world in which persons and objects and the relations between them can be thought of in *unambiguous* evaluative terms, is a world which can be conceptualized much more clearly and succinctly than one where most things are a messy mixture of both good and bad. A 'balanced' world is one where it is simple to say what is good and what is bad, and what should be done and what should not be done, and even if such simplicity has no more reality than a fairy-tale, it still exerts a powerful appeal for many people. To another person, an individual's attitude is the sense that can be made of what he says and does. To the individual himself, his attitude may be his way of making sense of his environment, and of how he decides to react to the events around him. Attaching labels and summary descriptions to objects and people is not just the prerogative of the researcher. Ordinary people do it too, and, as I shall argue in the next chapter, the way in which they do so can directly reflect the attitudes which they hold.

SUMMARY

* An attitude is not a 'thing' inside one's head. It is an explanatory concept used to summarize the meaning of expressive behaviour.
* Techniques of attitude measurement summarize this 'meaning' quantitatively, typically on a scale from extremely unfavourable to extremely favourable towards an issue.
* Thurstone, Likert, and Guttman scales provide unidimensional measures of a person's attitude, derived in different ways from his acceptance/rejection of attitude statements, selected so as to vary in favourability/unfavourability towards the issue. Of the three techniques, Guttman's specifies the most, and Likert's the least, stringent criteria for statement selection.
* An unobtrusive measure of a person's attitude may be derived in certain situations where one can record an aspect of his behaviour known, or presumed to be, systematically related to the attitude in question.
* Multidimensional techniques allow for a richer description of a person's attitude than a simple unidimensional measure of favourability. However, they may sometimes make assumptions concerning the stability of dimensional structures over different persons, issues, and scale items, which are not necessarily valid.
* Theories of attitude organization describe how individuals perceive and infer the interrelationships between their evaluations of objects, issues, and

other people, and their perceptions of others' attitudes towards these objects, etc.

* Balance theory and other consistency theories presume that people seek simple evaluative structures in which similarly evaluated people and objects are seen as associated with each other.

* Balance is not the only principle influencing people's perceptions of the relationship between elements in an attitude structure. Other important principles include a preference for positive evaluations and relationships, and a reliance on situationally relevant 'scripts', or sets of simple implicational rules and causal hypotheses.

* Research on cognitive complexity stresses individual differences in people's tolerance for ambiguity and apparent need to resolve inconsistency. Cognitively more complex individuals may be motivated to seek novel and potentially inconsistent information if the ambiguity in a situation is below their preferred level.

* A number of studies have failed to predict behaviour presumed to be relevant to people's attitudes (e.g., racial or religious) from verbal measures of such attitudes.

* One proposed explanation for this is the 'three component' view, according to which attitudes comprise distinct affective, cognitive, and behavioural components. It is argued that this approach fails to specify how and when these distinct components should be related or unrelated to each other.

* A promising solution is seen to be that one should attend to the levels of generality/specificity of both one's behavioural and verbal attitude criteria. When these levels are matched, verbal and behavioural indices are more closely related.

CHAPTER
THREE

SOCIAL JUDGEMENT

BASIC PRINCIPLES OF JUDGEMENT

The question of how people judge stimuli is one of the oldest in psychology, and its importance to general cognitive psychology can hardly be over-estimated. Any task which requires a subject to decide whether a stimulus is present or absent, or similar to or different from other stimuli, is a judgement task. In attempting to answer this question, researchers have tended to use stimuli of little intrinsic interest to the social psychologist, such as lights of varying brightness, cylinders of varying weight, or lines of different length. Generally, therefore, social psychologists have felt neither inclined nor obliged to relate their own theories and methods to work in this area. Judgemental theorists, however, have chosen to use particular kinds of stimuli mainly on grounds of convenience, and of comparability with previous work. Their aim has been to discover basic principles of judgement which may hopefully apply to *any* kind of stimuli, including those in which the social psychologist is more interested.

Although the search for such basic principles has been a long one, there has by no means been universal agreement as to the kind of principles one should be looking for, or even how judgement itself should be conceptualized. There have been two distinct approaches to this problem. The first, which I shall refer to as the *psychophysical* approach, has been concerned with identifying lawful relationships between the physical magnitude or intensity of any given single stimulus, and the magnitude or intensity of the sensation which it produces. The central dilemma of this approach is that stimulus magnitude cannot be directly related to sensation magnitude. All one can do is relate the physical magnitude of a stimulus to how bright, heavy, or long a person will *judge* it to be, and hope that this judgement will accurately reflect his inner experience.

The second, which may be called the *integrationist* approach, is not specifically concerned with the attempt to measure inner experience, but treats a person's judgemental responses as of central interest in themselves. By comparison with the first approach, there is less concern with the single stimulus, and more with how a given distribution of stimuli will be judged. Judgements are seen not just as mirrors of sensation, but as the end-product of a person's attempt to integrate relevant information about the stimuli, both within and across modalities, to enable him to make the required discriminations.

THE PSYCHOPHYSICAL APPROACH AND THE CONCEPT OF ADAPTATION

The classic achievement of the first approach was the Weber-Fechner law. Nearly 150 years ago, Weber proposed that the detectability of any change in a stimulus was a simple logarithmic function of its initial magnitude. For a stimulus of small size or low intensity, a relatively small change would be noticeable, whereas, for a larger or stronger stimulus, any change would have to be larger in order to be noticed. In other words, the size of the just noticeable difference (JND) is directly proportionate to the size of the stimulus. Fechner (1860) extended his notion in order to relate differences in stimulus magnitude to differences in sensation, by assuming that each JND corresponded to a subjectively equal difference in sensation.

Fechner's principle received little serious challenge for the best part of a century. Although his own work was concerned mainly with refining methods for measuring JNDs, it provided the starting point for Thurstone's work on attitude measurement, and also for Helson's (1947, 1964) theory of adaptation level. Stevens (1957, 1975), however, challenged Fechner's assumption that the perceived distance between two stimuli was a simple function of the number of JNDs between them, and proposed that the logarithmic law should be replaced by a power law, in terms of which 'equal stimulus-ratios produce equal sensation-ratios' (Stevens, 1958, page 636). He also claims that this principle is applicable to symbolic and social psychological continua such as perceived social status, seriousness of offences, and national.power (Stevens, 1966).

For both Fechner and Stevens, the main aim was to discover a stable psychophysical law to relate psychological magnitude, or sensation, directly to physical magnitude. Helson (1947, 1964), on the other hand, was far more concerned with explaining why variations in response to the same stimulus tended to occur when it was presented under different conditions, and to this end proposed his theory of adaptation level (AL). According to AL theory, whenever a person is presented with a stimulus, he compares it with a subjective average or neutral point. Thus, if we are dealing with judgements of people's height, someone might consider a height of 5ft 6in to be average. If he then saw someone of 5ft 9in, he would probably judge him to be fairly tall, whereas someone of 5ft 3in would be judged as fairly short. In Helson's terms, this person's AL for judgements of people's height would be 5ft 6in, and the two people whose height he judged would be respectively above and below his AL. A straightforward extension of this notion is that, if different people have different ALs for judging the same stimuli, their judgements will also differ. Someone whose AL is 5ft 9in will judge more people to be short than will someone whose AL is 5ft 3in. Similarly, a person's AL for a given stimulus dimension may change over time (indeed, it is predicted to do so as a result of a variety of conditions), and where this happens, his judgements will change accordingly: as his AL becomes higher, his judgements of a given set of stimuli will become lower, and vice versa.

How such changes will occur is implied by Helson's definition of AL as a weighted logarithmic mean of all past and present stimulation on a given dimension. As each new stimulus is presented, it will be averaged into the computation of a new AL. Thus, with every new stimulus above the prevailing AL, AL will rise, and with every new stimulus below the prevailing AL, AL will fall. For example, if a subject is judging the heaviness of a series of weights and the experimenter intersperses a new, very heavy weight after each of the original stimuli, the original stimuli would be judged as lighter than they were before. Alternatively, if this new stimulus (conventionally termed either an 'anchor', comparison, or standard stimulus) was much lighter than the other stimuli, the other stimuli would be judged heavier than before. This phenomenon, known as a *contrast effect* is the single most important prediction of AL theory.

Experience of stimuli prior to the judgement task is also predicted to lead to similar contrast effects. Tresselt (1948) presented the same series of weights to a group of professional weightlifters and a group of watchmakers. At least in the earlier stages of the experiments, the professional weightlifters judged the stimuli to be lighter than did the watchmakers. The direction of this effect is consistent with AL theory, although it is uncertain whether its magnitude could have been predicted.

Helson goes further than just saying that stimuli are judged relative to their prevailing context and that changes in this context tend to lead to contrast effects in judgement. In addition, he makes a number of contentious assumptions. First, in the Fechner tradition, he uses a logarithmic mean formula in his definition of AL. This has been challenged by Stevens (1958). Next, he insists that he is dealing with changes not merely in the labels which subjects ascribe to stimuli, but in the intensity of the sensations which these stimuli produce. Judgemental contrast effects, to Helson, are essentially perceptual contrast effects produced by processes at least analogous to those of physiological adaptation. True perceptual contrast effects undoubtedly occur (as can easily be demonstrated by putting your left hand in a bowl of cold water and your right hand in a bowl of hot water, and then, after a minute or so, putting both hands together into a bowl of tepid water—it will feel hotter to your left hand than to your right). It is Helson's assertion that such perceptual shifts are the basis of all contrast effects in judgement.

The objection to this is that generally the same results could be predicted on the basis of the more parsimonious assumption that the subject is attempting to apply an arbitrary response language to a novel and restricted range of stimuli. If the stimulus distribution changes, as with the introduction of a new anchor stimulus, he may change his ideas of what kind of weight it is *appropriate to call* heavy without necessarily *perceiving* the stimulus weights any differently. There have been occasional, rather inconclusive, attempts to isolate the influence of such 'semantic' shifts from 'true perceptual' shifts (e.g., Campbell, Lewis, and Hunt, 1958; Krantz and Campbell, 1961), but in the absence of any pure measure of sensation which by-passes the judgement scale, more prudent researchers have not seen this as a question to be resolved by a single 'crucial' experiment. The most persuasive objection is that contrast occurs not only in the situations which Helson takes as support for his theory, but also in many instances where the idea of perceptual adaptation seems less plausible (e.g., in judgements of whether three-digit numbers are large or small).

A further implication of Helson's reliance on the notion of perceptual adaptation is that *all* stimuli on a given dimension within a given modality should influence AL, including those that are irrelevant to the judgement task. The difficulty with this is that it is quite clear that we use words like 'heavy' and 'light' differently depending on the kind of object we are describing. A light suitcase, for instance, would probably weigh considerably more than a heavy book. Helson (1964, page 126) struggles to deal with this problem by suggesting that it is all a matter of the number of muscles involved—he refuses, in other words, to allow a cognitive principle such as the notion of perceived relevance into the formulation of his theory. The experimental evidence is quite clear, however. Anchor stimuli, which are made to seem relevant to the other stimuli being judged, produce the contrast effects predicted by Helson's model. Stimuli of the same physical magnitude as these anchors, presented in such a way that they seem to be irrelevant to the judgement task, have no such effects (Bevan and Pritchard, 1963; Brown, 1953).

THE INTEGRATIONIST APPROACH AND THE CONCEPT OF FRAME OF REFERENCE

Whereas theorists such as Helson seem to assume that the perceiver takes an essentially passive role *vis-à-vis* incoming stimulation, the integrationist tradition treats the perceiver as a far more active processor and interpreter of stimulus information. The roots of this approach can be traced back to the

Gestalt concept of a frame of reference. Instead of assuming that each stimulus is judged singly in relation to a single standard, be it AL, an absolute threshold value, or a comparison stimulus, the assumption is that perceivers categorize stimuli as belonging to a particular class, and then, if required to judge them, do so in relation to the implicit or perceived distribution of stimuli within that class. An early model in this tradition was that proposed by Volkmann (1951) who claimed that judgements of stimuli were largely predictable from a knowledge of the stimuli at either extreme of the stimulus distribution. Thus, if a subject had to judge a series of lines in terms of a scale from 'very short' to 'very long', he should judge a line of 12 inches as 'very long' if the lengths ranged from 2 inches to 12 inches, but as 'medium' if they ranged from 2 inches to 22 inches. (See Figure 3.1.) In many situations, this model makes much the same prediction as AL theory on the basis of fewer assumptions.

Although adding extra stimuli beyond the end of the stimulus range will generally alter the predicted AL as well as the end-points of the range, it is possible to devise stimulus distributions which differ on a number of parameters but share the same AL according to Helson's formulation. If one wanted a predictor of the stimulus value judged as medium, the *mean* (or logarithmic mean in Helson's formula) is only one of a number of plausible alternatives. If Volkmann's model were correct, the *midpoint* between the two end-stimuli would be the better predictor. Or again, if subjects were to employ an ordinal principle, so as to make the number of stimuli they judged as greater than medium equal the number they judged as smaller than medium, the *median* stimulus value would become the best predictor.

Pointing out that, for typical stimulus distributions, the mean will tend to lie between the midpoint and the median, Parducci (1963) proposed that one could account for the predictive success of Helson's model by assuming that subjects' judgements reflect a compromise between two distinct tendencies. The first is a tendency to use each category of the judgement scale to cover a fixed proportion of the range between the two end-stimuli. The second is a tendency to use each category to cover a fixed proportion of the total number

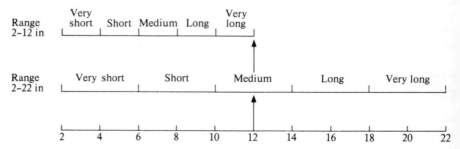

Figure 3.1 Shift in judgement resulting from extension of stimulus range. Arrow indicates predicted rating of a stimulus of 12 in. within two stimulus ranges. [*According to Volkmann's (1951) model.*]

of stimuli. There is by now a considerable body of evidence establishing the predictive superiority of the 'range-frequency compromise' over AL theory (Birnbaum, 1974; Parducci, 1974; Parducci and Perrett, 1971).

Largely for simplicity of exposition, Parducci formulated his original model in terms of a proposed tendency to use categories to cover equal proportions of the range, or equal frequencies of stimuli. More recently, Anderson (1975) has incorporated Parducci's ideas into a more generalized 'functional measurement' approach, which does not require that such ranges or frequencies should be equal. Anderson goes on to challenge the basic tenet of the psychophysical approach, that the judged magnitude of a stimulus is a single direct function of its psychological magnitude, i.e., the intensity of the sensation it produces. Instead he argues that judgements obey a simple 'cognitive algebra', in terms of which a response to any stimulus is the outcome of a process of averaging the available relevant information about that stimulus. Thus, the range-frequency compromise is incorporated by assuming that the subject averages information about the relative location of each stimulus within the range, with information about its rank-order position. The range-frequency compromise is thus the integration of range and frequency information.

Anderson's approach not only frees judgement theory from dead-end arguments over the role of physiological adaptation, or the relative contributions of perceptual and semantic shifts, it also provides a far sounder basis than do the approaches of Helson and Stevens for applying judgemental principles to social psychology and related areas. There already exists a large literature examining the applicability of such notions to impressions of hypothetical personalities based on the integration of information from verbal descriptions (Anderson, 1965), and more recently Anderson (1976) has examined judgements of equity within a similar framework. For the moment, the important conclusion of the integrationist approach is that judgements represent the outcome of an active process of integrating relevant information concerning the stimuli presented to the subject. The integration of information concerning the relative location and rank-order of a stimulus within a series leads to the phenomenon of judgemental contrast as a function of changes in the stimulus distribution, but it is not the only judgemental effect that can be produced by integrating different kinds of information. Another example, of particular relevance to social psychology, will be discussed in the next section.

CATEGORIZATION AND THE EFFECTS OF VALUE ON JUDGEMENTS OF PHYSICAL STIMULI

In their concern with finding conditions in which judgements could be taken as relatively unbiased measures of sensation, traditional psychophysicists have been meticulous in their attempts to use stimuli which differ from each other only in terms of the *single* attribute which subjects are required to judge.

In social psychology, however, we are constantly coming across multi-attribute stimuli. Indeed, even when social psychologists attempt to devise stimuli which differ only in terms of a single attribute, they fail to do so. This is so especially in the case of attitude measurement, where attitude statements are constructed, and judgements typically obtained, along a single pro-anti continuum. Consider, for example, the following two items from a scale to measure attitudes towards birth control devised by Wang and Thurstone in 1930 (Thurstone, 1931): 'The practice of birth control evades man's duty to propagate the race.', and 'Uncontrolled reproduction leads to over-population, social unrest, and war.' Nobody could seriously claim that these two items differed *only* in terms of the degree to which they express favourable or unfavourable attitudes towards birth control, even though judges may be asked to conceptualize the differences between them in terms of such a construct. Even the simplest of social psychological dimensions are already simplifications of something much more complex.

It is therefore very important to know how judgements of a stimulus in terms of one attribute or dimension may be influenced by its other, unjudged, attributes. Researchers in the psychophysical tradition, such as Helson, are quite unable to offer predictions of any such effects, since these are precisely the kinds of undesirable biases that their procedures were designed to eliminate. To researchers in the integrationist tradition, however, the question of how different kinds of stimulus information, both within and across modalities (e.g., Anderson, 1970), are combined to produce composite impressions, is an issue of fundamental theoretical significance.

Some of the earliest research relevant to this question stems from the 'New Look' hypothesis of the 'forties that basic processes, such as perception and memory, are susceptible to influence by emotional and motivational factors. In accord with this approach, Bruner and Goodman (1947) proposed that physical objects associated with some kind of emotional significance or value should be seen as larger than physical objects of the same size without such associations. To test this hypothesis, they presented 10-year-old children with a series of coins (1¢, 5¢, 25¢, and 50¢) and obtained size estimates by means of a piece of apparatus which projected a circular spot of light from behind a ground-glass screen. By turning a knob, subjects could adjust the diameter of the light spot until it appeared to match each of the coins. Compared with a control group, who were presented with grey cardboard discs of equivalent size, subjects overestimated the sizes of the coins, particularly those of greater value.

This effect was broadly replicated by Carter and Schooler (1949) and by Bruner and Rodrigues (1953), with more marked overestimation again being found in the case of the more valuable, i.e., larger, coins. A more recent, and particularly well-controlled, study by Holzkamp and Perlwitz (1966) shows that the *same* stimulus may be judged differently, depending upon assumptions about its value. They glued a circular disc to the back of a ground-glass screen, and illuminated this from behind so that all that subjects saw was its silhouette. Using similar apparatus to that in the Bruner and Goodman study, subjects then adjusted a circular light spot until it seemed to match the silhouette. Subjects who were told that the silhouette was made by a 5 Dm. coin (the largest German coin) gave significantly larger estimates than those who were told that it was made by a cardboard disc.

Additional support for the Bruner and Goodman position comes from the prediction that individuals who differ in the value they place upon the same object should also differ in their estimates of its size. Bruner and Goodman found greatest overestimation in the case of children from poorer backgrounds—a result confirmed by Holzkamp (1965); and Ashley, Harper, and Runyon (1951) found that subjects hypnotized to believe that they were very poor gave larger estimates of the sizes of coins than when hypnotized to believe that they were very rich. The argument is that money has greater subjective value if one is poor than if one is rich, and this greater subjective value should produce greater overestimation.

Although coins have been the stimuli most frequently used in such experiments, Bruner and Postman (1948) found discs bearing a dollar sign were overestimated; so too were discs bearing another 'emotionally relevant' symbol—a swastika—but less reliably. Two later studies failed to confirm these results in the case of discs bearing a swastika (Klein, Schlesinger, and Meister, 1951; Solley and Lee, 1955). On the other hand, Lysak and Gilchrist (1955) found that the sizes of dollar bills were not reliably overestimated in comparison with rectangles of the same size.

Tajfel (1957) was able to synthesize these and other experimental data by pointing out that those studies which showed overestimation effects used stimuli, such as coins, where size and value were explicitly or implicitly correlated, so that the larger stimuli also tended to be those of greatest value. In other cases, where the size of a stimulus was irrelevant to its emotional significance, as in the case of the swastika, reliable overestimation was not observed. Moreover, where overestimation occurs, it is by no means constant over the continuum, but increases steadily as one moves up the scale of size and value. Thus, for stimuli where size and value are correlated, one finds an *accentuation of the judged differences* between adjacent stimuli in the experimental as compared with the control series. This, Tajfel argues, is nothing to do with the effects of value as such, but is part of a more general principle concerned with what happens when stimuli vary concurrently on more than one dimension. If a subject is required to judge a series of stimuli along a single 'focal' dimension, but the stimuli presented also vary along a second 'peripheral' dimension which is correlated with the focal dimension, he may use the perceived position of each stimulus on the peripheral dimension as a *cue* to its position on the focal dimension. He thus has additional information on the basis of which to discriminate it from the other stimuli in the series, which he would not have if such peripheral variation had been eliminated by experimental control, or was only randomly related to the positions of stimuli on the focal dimension.

This notion is discussed more fully by Tajfel (1959) and by Eiser and Stroebe (1972). For the present, it is enough to view this as part of the more general integrationist position, that judgements are the product of a systematic combination and integration of relevant available stimulus information. The visual angle subtended by a coin is only one piece of information relevant to a judgement of its size. If it can also be seen to be a coin of higher value, this also is a piece of information which can be taken into account so as to make a more definite inference that the coin is large, provided that one has learned that size and value are predictably related to each other in the case of coins.

A special case of this phenomenon is where stimuli can be separated into distinct classes or categories in terms of some peripheral attribute. If the class-membership of a stimulus is predictably related to its position on the focal continuum, an accentuation of the judged interclass differences is predicted. To test this hypothesis, Tajfel and Wilkes (1963) required subjects to estimate the length in centimeters of eight lines of different lengths. In the experimental condition each of the four shortest lines had a large A printed above its centre, while each of the four longest lines had a B (the labelling being reversed for half the subjects). The labels A and B constituted what Tajfel and Wilkes call a 'superimposed classification'. As predicted, this produced an accentuation of the judged differences between the two classes (i.e., the interval between the fourth and fifth longest lines was overestimated) as compared with estimates by control subjects, who judged the lines either in the absence of any alphabetic labels, or with the labels being randomly associated with the lengths of the lines.

Similar results are reported by Lilli (1970) and Marchand (1970). In none of these three studies, however, is there significant confirmation of an additional hypothesis proposed by Tajfel and Wilkes that stimuli belonging to the same class should be judged as closer to each other: in other words, that the accentuation of *inter*class differences should be accompanied by a reduction of *intra*class differences. On the other hand, an earlier study by Campbell (1956) on memory for the visual position of two classes of stimuli found a reduction of intraclass differences, as well as a reduction in the perceived overlap between the classes, without the two classes *on average* being seen as further apart.

AN INTEGRATION THEORY INTERPRETATION OF ACCENTUATION EFFECTS

It is not immediately obvious why the reduction of intraclass differences should be more reliable in some cases than in others. Perhaps the most useful way to consider this problem is to speculate about the kind of 'cognitive algebra' a person might be using to incorporate information about the class-membership of a stimulus to produce a judgement of the position of each stimulus along a defined focal dimension. Let us suppose that the individual is presented with two distinct or partially over-lapping classes of stimuli (a_1, $a_2 \cdots a_{na}$, b_1, $b_2 \cdots b_{nb}$), and that his judgement of each stimulus is a function of sensory information concerning the actual position of each individual stimulus on the focal dimension, and of the position that the subject would predict on the basis of the class-membership information alone. By definition, this latter position would be the same for all members of a given class, so in our example it can take only two values (A or B, for the two classes respectively). For present purposes, it does not matter whether this predicted position is a result of unsubstantiated prejudice, or experimental learning. In either case, we can express the response R to each stimulus as a weighted sum of the experienced position of each stimulus and the predicted position of the 'class-type'. Thus:

$$Ra_i = w_1 a_i + w_2 A$$

and
$$Rb_i = w_3 b_i + w_4 B$$

If the weights w_1 and w_3 both equalled 1 (and w_2 and w_4 were both greater than 0) the outcome would be an accentuation of interclass differences, but no change in the size of the intraclass differences. If w_1 and w_3 both exceeded 1, the outcome would be an accentuation of both interclass and intraclass differences. If one assumed that $w_2 = 1 - w_1$ and that $w_4 = 1 - w_3$, one would have an averaging model of the kind discussed by Anderson (1970). A variety of effects could then be predicted, depending on the size of weights, and on the values taken by A and B relative to the individual stimuli within each class. If A equalled the mean of the stimuli in class a and B the mean of the stimuli in class b, there would be a reduction of intraclass differences and a consequential reduction in overlap (or increase in the separation of adjacent stimuli) at the boundary between the classes, but without the two classes *on average* being judged as further apart (e.g., Campbell, 1956). The larger the weights w_2 and w_4, the more pronounced would be these effects. Any differences between w_2 and w_4 would result in asymmetrical reductions of intraclass differences (as may happen in interpersonal judgements of members of one's own and an alien group).

If A and B were further apart than the means of classes a and b, the outcome would be the commonly observed accentuation of interclass differences, together with a reduction of intraclass differences. At the same time, the possibility of a reduction of interclass differences, though not commonly reported, is not precluded, since A and B could be closer together than the means of classes a and b. Thus, changes in interclass and intraclass differences would depend on the extremity of the 'class-types' A and B, and their relative weights.

It is a short step from here to the more general case of stimuli which vary concurrently along two or more correlated dimensions. (Class-membership as described above can be thought of simply as a dichotomous peripheral attribute.) If s_i represents the experienced position of a stimulus i on the focal dimension, and t_i the position that would be inferred from its other (peripheral) attributes, then we have the following general formula, which is equivalent to that presented by Anderson (1970, page 155).

$$R_i = w_1 s_i + w_2 t_i$$

Assuming again that $w_2 = 1 - w_1$, the judgements given to each stimulus would depend on the value of t_i compared with s_i. If the t values had a wider range than the s values, the outcome would be accentuation of each interstimulus interval, as seems to occur with estimates of the size of coins. Anderson assumes that the weights w_1 and w_2 should remain constant for all stimuli in a series, but no such assumption is made here.

COGNITIVE ASPECTS OF STEREOTYPES

The question of the reduction of intraclass differences was one of wider significance for Tajfel, since his more general concern was with laying a foundation for a cognitive approach to the study of stereotypes and prejudice (Tajfel, 1969). According to Tajfel, one aspect of prejudice is a tendency to react to members of an alien group simply in terms of group membership, without due regard to individual differences within the group. Thus, an individual's group membership is analogous to a classification superimposed upon the particular focal dimension one is judging—be it educability, trustworthiness, arrogance, skin colour, or whatever. When this happens, the outcome is predicted to be a subjective accentuation of the difference between the alien group and one's own (usually involving devaluation of the alien group) and a subjective minimization of individual differences within the alien group (so that such devaluation applies more or less without exception). Such a way of dealing with interpersonal perceptions has precisely the same appeal that cognitive consistency has as a way of dealing with interpersonal and other attitudes—it maximizes the chances for positive self-regard and minimizes the need to make complex differentiations.

Evidence from interpersonal judgements, in fact, shows more positive support for the hypothesis of a reduction of intraclass differences. Judgements of photographs of people who are labelled as belonging to particular ethnic groups show a failure, at least among more prejudiced subjects, to distinguish adequately between members of the alien group (Secord, 1959; Secord, Bevan, and Katz, 1956). The same has been found for facial recognition, with white subjects being much poorer at distinguishing between black faces than between white faces (Malpass and Kravitz, 1969). Using a group discussion situation, Hensley and Duval (1976) led subjects to believe that their co-discussants fell into two subgroups, whose opinions were respectively similar or dissimilar to their own. The greater the supposed difference between the subgroups, the smaller were the perceived differences within each subgroup.

What seems crucial for stereotyped judgements to occur is that the attribute being judged should be *believed* to be distinctively associated with the group in question. Tajfel, Sheikh, and Gardner (1964) compared subjects' ratings of two Indians and two Canadians on a number of scales. The two Indians were judged to be more similar to each other on traits which formed part of the Indian stereotype, and the two Canadians on traits which formed part of the Canadian stereotype. But how do beliefs in the association of particular attributes with particular groups come about? Obviously this is a very broad question, and if one demands an explanation for the content of *specific* stereotypes, it is unlikely that one will be satisfied without a sociological and historical, as well as a social-psychological, analysis of the relationships between the groups in question. At a general level, however, two suggestions seem reasonable. The first is that stereotypes exaggerate differences that actually exist between an alien group and one's own, although these differences may be slight and involve a great deal of overlap between the groups. This is plausible enough when one is considering relatively easily observed characteristics such as skin colour (though even in this case it is unnecessary to assume that a person has to have 'observed' a representative sample, or indeed *any* member, of another group before he can form or accept a stereotyped view of the group as a whole), but less plausible when one considers other components of the stereotype, such as personality and intelligence. The second possibility is that stereotypes at least partly reflect an illusion of difference, that is, a bias towards attributing distinctive characteristics to an alien group, more or less regardless of validity.

These two possibilities are not necessarily incompatible. However, whereas any 'kernel of truth' in a stereotype may be difficult to verify (Brigham, 1971), the cognitive processes implied by the latter interpretation are amenable to experimental investigation. Hamilton (1976) has argued that stereotyping may reflect a cognitive bias termed 'illusory correlation'. Chapman (1967) used this term to refer to certain systematic biases he found in his subjects' responses on a paired associate learning task. Subjects overestimated the frequency (in the experiment) of co-occurrence of pairs of words whose meanings were strongly associated (e.g., lion–tiger, bacon–eggs), and also overestimated the co-occurrence of the longest word in one list with the longest word in the other list. It is suggested that stimuli which are distinctive within their respective sets are more likely to be seen as paired with each other. Hamilton extends this notion to suggest that people are biased towards seeing an illusory correlation between uncommon or distinctive attributes and membership of a distinctive group.

Hamilton and Gifford (1976) report two experiments in support of this interpretation. In the first of these, subjects were presented with a series of statements describing behaviour performed by a male member of either Group A or Group B, and were told that 'In the real-world population, Group B is a smaller group than in Group A' (page 395). Two-thirds of the statements referred to a Group A member, and one-third to a Group B member. The desirability of the behaviours described was also varied, and the statements were distributed so that, within both Group A and Group B, there was a 9 : 4 ratio of desirable to undesirable behaviours. Thus Group B was more distinctive than Group A, and undesirable behaviours were more distinctive than desirable behaviours, but there was no *actual* correlation between group membership and desirability in the statements presented. However, when asked to recall how many statements concerning members of each group had described undesirable behaviours, subjects overestimated the co-occurrence of distinctive attributes, i.e., they recalled Group A members as having performed more of the desirable behaviours and Group B members as having performed more of the undesirable behaviours. In their second study, Hamilton and Gifford used a similar procedure, but with two-thirds of the statements describing undesirable behaviours. Since desirable behaviour was now more distinctive, their hypothesis was supported by the finding that subjects overestimated the frequency with which desirable behaviours were performed by Group B and undesirable behaviours by Group A.

These findings provide a basis for explaining not only negative, but also positive, stereotypes. There are a number of reasons, though, for expecting that the characteristics people attribute to alien groups will tend not only to be distinctive, but negatively so. If one were to adopt an adaptation-level theory approach, one would argue that distinctiveness depends on distance from prevailing AL, which will itself reflect the preponderance of one's familiar experiences. As the Hamilton and Gifford experiments assume, therefore, distinctiveness and statistical infrequency should go together. There is evidence that increasing the frequency of occurrence of certain stimuli experimentally (at least under non-aversive conditions) can lead subjects to evaluate such stimuli more positively (Zajonc, 1968a), and in everyday language there is an association between frequency of usage and positive evaluative meaning (Boucher and Osgood, 1969).

In many ways, Hamilton's work represents a rediscovery of concepts and issues that have received relatively little attention from American social psychologists since the 'fifties. The intervening years have witnessed the rise of attribution theory (see Chapter 4) to a dominant position in the field of social perception research. During this same period, however, categorization and accentuation processes have remained a major concern of European social psychologists, particularly with regard to such issues as the perception of group membership and intergroup relations (see Chapter 9), and it is only recently that these traditions have started to come together.

An important example of this rapprochement is a paper by Taylor, Fiske, Etcoff, and Ruderman (1978). Its theoretical contribution consists, partly at least, of a restatement of the ideas contained in Tajfel's (1959, 1969) earlier writings, for which more explicit acknowledgement might have been appropriate, even though the experiments by Tajfel and Wilkes (1963) and Tajfel *et al.* (1964) are described. Taylor *et al.* start from the assumption that '. . . there is no theoretical or empirical reason to assume that forming generalizations about ethnic groups is radically different from forming generalizations about other categories of objects' (page 778). They then develop the following seven hypotheses:

1. People use physical and social discriminators such as race and sex as a way of categorizing people and organizing information about them.
2. As a result of this categorization process, within-group differences become minimized and between-group differences become exaggerated.
3. As a result of this categorization process, within-group members' behaviour comes to be interpreted in stereotyped terms.
4. The social perceiver pays more attention to, and makes more discriminations within, a subgroup, the fewer members of the subgroup there are.
5. The social perceiver pays more attention to, and makes more discriminations within, more familiar subgroups, such as those of which he is himself a member, than less familiar ones.
6. Group members are stereotyped depending on the number of other members of the subgroup present.
7. Social units are stereotyped as a function of the proportion of different subgroup members.

This approach, therefore, incorporates the accentuation principles proposed by Tajfel (1959), as well as the notion of the salience or distinctiveness of statistically less frequent classes of persons and events, emphasized by Hamilton and Gifford (1976), and elsewhere by Taylor and Fiske (1975, 1978).

The experimental situation used by Taylor *et al.* involved subjects listening to a sound recording of a group discussion between six people, synchronized with a slide projector so that, as each voice spoke, a picture (supposedly) of the speaker was projected onto a wall. Subjects were then asked to recall which suggestions had been made by which participants in the discussion, and the main dependent variable was the pattern of errors obtained. In the first of their experiments, three of the participants were presented as white, and three as black. As predicted, it was found that intraracial confusion was higher than interracial confusion. In other words, a suggestion actually made by one of the black participants was more likely to be misattributed to one of two other blacks than to one of the three whites, and vice versa for the suggestions of the white participants, after correcting for the fact that interracial errors would be expected to exceed intraracial errors in a 3 : 2 ratio on a chance basis. All subjects were white, but, contrary to prediction, were no more likely to confuse the contributions of the different blacks with each other than those of the different whites.

A second experiment found essentially the same results, this time using sex rather than race as the basis for categorization, with three males and three females in the recorded discussion group. Again, proportionately fewer of the errors than would be expected by chance involved misattributing a suggestion to a participant of a different sex, but subjects were no better at recalling the contributions made by members of their own than of the opposite sex.

In a third experiment, the sex composition of the group was varied continually from all male to all female, and the dependent variable consisted of ratings of the individual group members, rather than accuracy of recall. The results of this last experiment were somewhat mixed, but there was a tendency for female participants to be rated as more stereotypically feminine, and male participants as more stereotypically masculine, the fewer the other members of their own sex taking part in the discussion. At the same time, both male and female participants were seen as more assertive and influential in the discussion, the fewer the other members of their own sex in the group. Throughout the three experiments, the content of the discussion, and the intonation, speed of speech, and, as far as possible, attractiveness of the different participants were carefully controlled.

These results, therefore, reinforce the view that characteristics such as race and sex can function as a basis for categorizing information about other people, and support a cognitive interpretation of stereotyping. In contrast to many other studies, however, no support was found for the prediction that people are better at discriminating among members of their own than among members of another group. One factor not included in this study was the personal emotional significance or 'salience' of the classification for the individual subjects. According to Tajfel (1959), accentuation effects should be more pronounced on more personally salient dimensions (cf. Tajfel and Wilkes, 1964). If, as one suspects, the Harvard students who served as subjects were neither particularly racist nor sexist, the tendency to stereotype members of another race or sex would not be expected to be very strong.

THE JUDGEMENT OF ATTITUDES

Just as research on the judgement of physical stimuli started from a concern with questions of the validity and reliability of psychophysical measurement, so a concern with equivalent questions in the field of attitude measurement gave rise to research on the judgement of attitudes. Most of such research has been concerned with Thurstone's method of equal-appearing intervals. As will be remembered from Chapter 2, this method is aimed at selecting a series of short attitude statements, varying along an interval scale from extremely unfavourable to extremely favourable towards a given issue. The 'scale value' of each item, or statement (i.e., its assumed position on the scale of favourability) is calculated from the ratings of a group of independent 'judges', who are required to say how favourable or unfavourable towards the issue they consider the item to be, typically in terms of an 11-point scale. When proposing this method, Thurstone and Chave (1929, page 92) stated boldly that 'if the scale value is to be regarded as valid, the scale values of the statements should not be affected by the opinion of the people who help to construct it'. In other words, different judges should agree with each other as to the degree of favourability expressed by each statement, even if their own personal attitudes on the issue are different. The majority of research in this field has therefore been concerned with whether judges' own attitudes affect their ratings, and if so, how.

The first test of Thurstone's assumption was by Hinckley (1932), using what has become the classic issue in such research, that of 'attitude toward the Negro'. Hinckley presented a series of statements on this issue to three groups of college student judges; whites with pro-Negro attitudes, whites with anti-Negro attitudes, and blacks. On the basis of a 0·98 correlation between the scale values obtained from the ratings of the two white groups separately, and a 0·93 correlation between the scale values of the blacks and anti-Negro whites, Hinckley concluded that his scale was 'not influenced in its measuring function by the subjects used in the construction' (page 203). There followed a number of studies on different attitude issues, which found the same kind of high correlations between the ratings of different judges, and drew essentially the same conclusions (Beyle, 1932; Eysenck and Crown, 1949; Ferguson, 1935; Pintner and Forlano, 1937). Hinckley's conclusion thus remained essentially unchallenged for twenty years, even though during this period increasing evidence was being accumulated which pointed to the effects of attitudes and values on the perception of physical stimuli.

Struck by the paradox that perceptions of physical stimuli were supposedly influenced by perceivers' attitudes, but perceptions of attitudes were not, Hovland and Sherif (1952) conducted an extended replication of Hinckley's study. At the same time, they examined the effects of a methodological device, suggested by Thurstone and used by Hinckley, called the 'carelessness criterion', according to which judges who lumped together too many items in a single response category were excluded for presumed 'carelessness'. Analysing their data without the use of this criterion, Hovland and Sherif found that both black and pro-Negro white judges lumped a large proportion of the items together close to the 'unfavourable' extreme of the scale, with a small minority of the items being judged as 'extremely favourable', and with the intermediate scale categories used only very occasionally. The ratings of the anti-Negro group were distributed more evenly over the scale, with a higher proportion of items being judged as close to the 'favourable' extreme. The 'average' white judges (students from various colleges in south east Oklahoma) sound from the description given by Hovland and Sherif to have been likely to have held fairly anti-Negro attitudes, and their ratings in fact correspond quite closely with those of the anti-Negro group. Using the same 'carelessness criterion' as that employed by Hinckley had the effect of excluding a disproportionate number of pro-Negro subjects, and of producing scale values closely resembling those obtained by Hinckley (see Figure 3.2).

Although Hovland and Sherif were concerned mainly with demonstrating that judges' attitudes could have an effect, and less with describing the precise

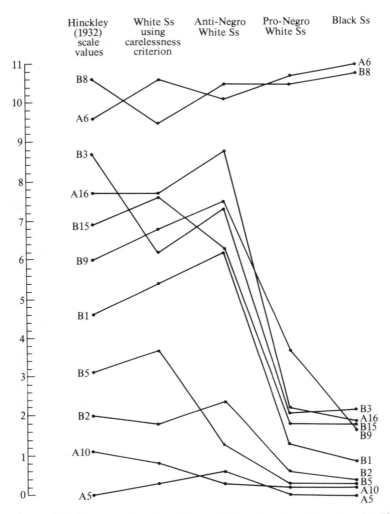

Figure 3.2 Scale values for selected items obtained from the ratings given by different groups of subjects. [*Adapted from Hovland and Sherif (1952)*.]

kind of effect involved, an impressive feature of their data is the apparent tendency of judges to 'displace' large proportions of the item series towards the extreme of the scale opposite to their own position. In other words, favourable judges tended to rate more of the statements as 'unfavourable' and unfavourable judges more of the statements as 'favourable'. The apparent similarity of this phenomenon to the kind of contrast effects found in judgements of physical stimuli did not escape notice, and in subsequent research both the terminology and theoretical explanations of psychophysics were eagerly adopted.

The ability of AL theory to explain such contrast effects was asserted by Helson (1964), on the assumption that more favourable judges have ALs closer to the more favourable extreme. This could either be because they may have had more experience of statements congruent with their own attitude, or because they use their own attitude as a kind of 'anchor' or subjective comparison stimulus. One implication of this is that the effects of judges' own attitudes on their ratings should be comparable to the effects that might be produced by varying the distribution of items presented to the judges. A statement presented in the context of a predominantly favourable series should be judged as less favourable than if presented in the context of more unfavourable statements. Although general evidence exists for such effects (Fehrer, 1952; Segall, 1959; Upshaw, 1962), in none of these studies are the contrast effects obtained as a function of variation in the distribution of statements precisely of the form which AL theory would predict (Eiser and Stroebe, 1972).

THE ASSIMILATION-CONTRAST MODEL

The best-known theory of attitude judgement has been the 'assimilation-contrast' model proposed by Sherif and Hovland (1961). There are two distinct, but supposedly related, parts to their theory, which I shall consider in turn. The first relates to how a judge's own opinion will influence his ratings of the favourability of attitude statements, and the second relates to how a person's opinion will change as a function of the discrepancy between his own position and that advocated in a persuasive communication. The basic assumption is that the individual uses his own attitude as an 'anchor' or comparison stimulus, with the result that statements of attitude not too divergent from his own will be 'assimilated' and those further away will be 'contrasted'.

Thus, in the context of attitude judgement, instead of the unilateral shifts predicted by AL theory, Sherif and Hovland predict a bilateral increase in the use of the extreme categories of the scale, that is, greater *polarization* of judgment, for judges with more extreme, as compared with more moderate, attitudes. Two questions therefore need to be asked about this model. First, does it adequately *predict* the effect of judges' attitudes on their ratings of attitude statements? Second, does it constitute an adequate *explanation* of the effects obtained?

If the Hovland and Sherif (1952) study were the only one to find differences in polarization as a function of judges' attitudes, it is doubtful whether one would need to take the 'assimilation' part of the assimilation-contrast model very seriously. Although the blacks and pro-Negro whites appear to assimilate a few pro-Negro statements, the number of such statements is not particularly large. This objection, however, can be quickly dismissed by inspecting some of the items actually used (Shaw and Wright, 1967, pages

360–362), and comparing them in terms of the selected scale values shown in Figure 3.2. The two examples, in this fugure, of items already very favourable in terms of their original (Hinckley) scale values, which become rated as even more extremely favourable (i.e., are 'assimilated') by blacks and pro-Negro whites, in fact read as follows:

Item A6: 'The Negro should be given the same educational advantages as the white man.'

Item B8: 'I believe that the Negro is entitled to the same social privileges as the white man.'

Historical and cultural relativity notwithstanding, this is enough to lead one to question how extremely favourable the supposedly 'extremely favourable' items really were. Other items yield a similar picture. *Item A16*, with an original scale value of 7·7 (i.e., to the favourable side of neutral) expresses a straight segregationist position: 'The Negro should have the advantage of all social benefits of the white man but be limited to his own race in the practice thereof.' Similarly, *Item B3*, which is even more favourable in terms of its original scale value (8·7) reads: 'Although the Negro is rather inferior mentally, he has a fuller and deeper religious life than the white man, and thus has an emphatic claim upon our social approval.' Both these items are 'contrasted' by pro-Negro and black judges, so as to be judged as fairly close to the unfavourable extreme. For comparison purposes, it is also worth citing the two most extremely anti-Negro items listed in the same figure. These are:

Item A10: 'No Negro has the slightest right to resent, or even question the illegal killing of one of his race.'

Item A5: 'I place the Negro on the same social basis as I would a mule.'

There seems every reason to suppose, therefore, that if the item pool had contained a higher proportion of clearly favourable statements, the assimilation effects found for subjects with pro-Negro attitudes would have been far stronger—perhaps even as strong as the contrast effects found with the less favourable statements. Yet curiously this very asymmetry in the strengths of the assimilation and contrast shifts, which may be more than an artefact of a biased item pool, becomes for Sherif and Hovland an integral part of their model, and particularly of its extension to the field of attitude change. According to them, the relative strengths of assimilation and contrast effects depend upon the relative sizes of a person's 'latitudes of acceptance, non-commitment, and rejection'. A person's latitude of acceptance is simply the range of opinions he will accept, and his latitude of rejection the range of opinions he will reject, with the latitude of non-commitment containing attitude positions which he neither accepts nor rejects. Basically, Sherif and Hovland assume that statements which fall within a person's latitude of acceptance will tend to be assimilated and others will tend to be contrasted. They also assume that people with extreme opinions will tend to have narrow latitudes of acceptance (i.e., agree with very few opinions at all different from their own) and hence will tend to assimilate relatively few items.

Another feature of the Hovland and Sherif data is less easy to reconcile

with their assimilation-contrast model. Although judges with pro-Negro attitudes seem to show the predicted polarization effects, the same effect should
also occur in the cases of extremely anti-Negro judges: they should assimilate
unfavourable and contrast favourable statements and so show greater polarization than more moderate judges. There is no evidence that this occurred,
and in fact all that seems clear is that the 'average' and anti-Negro whites
gave less polarized ratings than the blacks and pro-Negro whites. The similarity in the ratings given by the former two groups could mean that no *really*
anti-Negro subjects were included in the sample, and that those labelled
anti-Negro were in fact really moderate. If this were so the data would not
allow a test of the assimilation-contrast model for judges with opinions at the
unfavourable extreme.

With a changing cultural context, the difficulty of finding really anti-
Negro judges within a random sample of college students cannot be entirely
ruled out as a contributory factor, and Manis (1964) used this argument in
order to defend the assimilation-contrast model against the results of a study
of Upshaw (1962), which also found that anti-Negro judges polarized less
than neutral judges. Manis himself (1960, 1961) found results more supportive
of the assimilation-contrast model when using the issue of fraternities. Two
further studies on the issue of attitudes towards Negroes, however, by Zavalloni and Cook (1965) and Selltiz, Edrich, and Cook (1965), again found that
anti-Negro judges gave the least polarized ratings, after apparently being
careful to find some who were 'really' anti-Negro. The second of these studies
also added new items at the pro-Negro end of the scale to compensate for the
bias in the original Hinckley pool.

One study on this issue (Ward, 1966) failed to show a polarization effect,
finding instead only an overall contrast effect which is interpreted in terms of
AL theory. The results of this study, however, can be completely discounted
as far as the effects of judges' attitudes are concerned, owing to large numbers
of subjects being excluded for apparent confusion of the ends of the rating
scale on the basis of a dubious criterion non-randomly related to judges'
attitudes (Eiser, 1971b).

To summarize these studies, then, there is fair evidence of a tendency for
more favourable judges to rate statements, on average, as more unfavourable
than do unfavourable judges. This overall contrast effect, however, is very
much a function of where the statements fall on the pro-anti continuum. The
evidence on polarization of judgement seems to point to a direct relationship
between polarization and favourability of attitude on this issue, with pro-
Negro judges giving the most, and anti-Negro judges the least, polarized
ratings (see Figure 3.3).

As far as the explanatory value of the assimilation-contrast model is
concerned, I have already mentioned that Sherif and Hovland based their
predictions on the assumption that judges use their own position on an issue
as an 'anchor'. The more conventional (e.g., AL theory) application of this
notion would be that judgements should be inversely related to the position

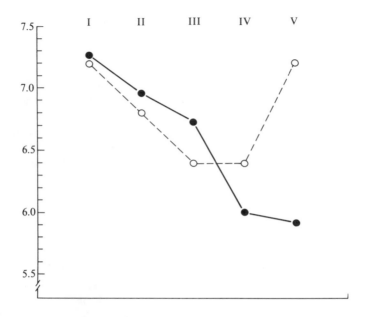

Figure 3.3 Relationship between judges' attitudes and polarization (mean differences between ratings of favourable and unfavourable items). ●———● Relationship observed by Zavalloni and Cook (1965); ○- - - - -○ Approximate form of relationship predicted by Sherif and Hovland (1961). Attitude groups: I. Negro students, actively involved. II. Pro-Negro white students, actively involved. III. Pro-Negro white students, not actively involved. IV. Anti-Negro white students, not actively involved. V. Anti-Negro white students, actively involved.

of the anchor, and so contrast effects should be observed for *all* items in a series. Sherif and Hovland, however, claim to use this same principle to predict that items near to the judge's own position (anchor) will be assimilated and items further away will be contrasted. In other words, within the *same* item series, the *same* anchor can produce judgemental shifts in *opposite* directions.

Sherif and Hovland do not discuss this discrepancy between their own predictions and the typical findings in psychophysical judgement, but instead cite a single study of their own judgements of the heaviness of lifted weights (Sherif, Taub, and Hovland, 1958). In this study, they found the typical contrast effects in conditions where a series of weights was judged in the context of an anchor stimulus lying outside the range of the original series. In one condition only, where the anchor was of exactly the same weight as the heaviest stimulus in the original series, assimilation and not contrast occurred: in other words, *all* the stimuli were judged as somewhat heavier than when they were presented without the anchor. No comparable assimilation occurred to an anchor equal in weight to the lightest of the other stimuli. The possible influence of non-standard features of the experimental procedure in producing the exceptional assimilation effect in the one condition has been discussed by Parducci and Marshall (1962).

Even if we take these results as completely reliable, however, they bear absolutely no resemblance to the 'assimilation-contrast' effects observed, or at least predicted, in attitude judgement. The hypothesis, which Sherif *et al.* interpret their results as supporting, is that anchor stimuli at, or near to, the extreme of a stimulus series will produce assimilation *of the total series*, and that anchors further away will produce contrast *of the total series*. What matters, therefore, is the relation between the anchor and the series as a whole, not that between the anchor and each stimulus taken by itself. There is simply no way in which these results, concerning shifts of the total series as a function of *different* anchors, can be used to generate the prediction of simultaneous assimilation and contrast of different stimuli within a single series as a function of a *single* anchor.

The transition from the attitude judgement to the attitude change part of the assimilation-contrast model is also beset by difficulties. The attitude change effect that the model attempts to explain is that a person exposed to a communication advocating a position somewhat discrepant from his own may change his viewpoint in the direction of that advocated, i.e., he will be persuaded by the communication to a greater or lesser extent. On the other hand, if the advocated position is extremely discrepant from his own, an opposite 'boomerang' effect may sometimes occur. Sherif and Hovland bridge the gulf that separates such results from the attitude judgement data by treating normal persuasion effects as equivalent to 'assimilation' and 'boomerang' effects as equivalent to 'contrast', but the bridge they build is perilously unsteady. As before, the individual's own position is his anchor, whereas the persuasive communication takes the role of the attitude statement in the judgement task, but now, instead of predicting changes in the judged favourability of the statement, the model starts trying to deal with changes in the actual favourability of the anchor. Moreover, whereas in attitude and certainly psychophysical judgement, contrast is the typical effect and assimilation the exception, in attitude change 'boomerang' effects generally occur only under fairly exceptional conditions of extreme discrepancy between a person's initial attitude and that advocated by a communicator.

This last point is troublesome for one of the substantive predictions of the model, namely that the direction of any attitude change effects will be determined by whether a communication falls within a person's latitude of acceptance or rejection. As in the judgement situation, 'assimilation' should only occur to communications which advocate positions within, or just beyond, the latitude of acceptance. Communications which a person would definitely reject should make him more extreme in the direction contrary to that advocated. This model has some merit in helping to explain the resistance to persuasion often observed among people whose initial attitudes are extreme. According to Sherif, Sherif, and Nebergall (1965), such people will tend to have high 'ego-involvement' with regard to the issue in question, and hence will have relatively narrow latitudes of acceptance (Hovland, Harvey, and Sherif, 1957). In other respects, though, its contribution is very limited. It takes no account of the possibility that the discrepancy of an advocated position from a person's own may be taken as a cue to the credibility of the communication, and that it may be credibility rather than discrepancy *per se* which is important. In addition, when the direction of attitude change effects can be related to an individual's latitudes of acceptance and rejection, direct persuasion effects have been found as a result of communications well within the latitude of rejection (e.g., Dillehay, 1965). Also Miller (1965) failed to decrease the width of subjects' latitudes of acceptance by experimentally increasing their levels of involvement.

THE VARIABLE PERSPECTIVE MODEL

Although it is completely established that Thurstone and Chave were incorrect in their assumption that judges' ratings would be unaffected by their attitudes, it does not necessarily follow that this invalidates Thurstone scales as a measure of *relative* differences along a specified attitude continuum. Upshaw's (1962) main aim was, therefore, to show that the scale values obtained by the Thurstone method could still be regarded as constituting an interval scale, even though they were clearly influenced by judges' attitudes. Comparisons between ratings obtained from different attitude groups, and between conditions in which the range of items presented was experimentally varied, revealed significant differences in the derived scale values, but these differences did not lead to significant departures from linearity when the different sets of scale values were correlated with each other. Upshaw infers from these results that the basic function of an interval scale, that of comparing the relative sizes of differences in different parts of the continuum, is still fulfilled by Thurstone scales, even though no *absolute* meaning can be attached to the scale value of any item considered singly.

Upshaw (1965) interprets the high linear correlations between different sets of scale values as evidence against the assimilation-contrast model. Sherif and Hovland predict that statements near the centre of the scale will show the greatest shifts, on the assumption that these statements are the most 'ambiguous' and hence the most liable to biased or distorted interpretation when presented to judges with strong emotional involvement in an issue. If this were so, the relationship between the scale values obtained from judges with different attitudes would be less than perfectly linear.

While this argument is correct, it is still possible that departures from linearity might occur, but have little effect on the value of the correlation coefficient. As Ager and Dawes (1965) have pointed out, as long as two sets of values have a high rank order correlation with each other, the product-moment correlation coefficient tends to be very insensitive to departures from linearity. Assuming that the relationships are in fact linear, however, Upshaw proposes that differences in judgement can be conceptualized in terms of differences in 'perspective'. The concept of perspective is essentially the same as that of 'frame of reference' in the sense it was used by Volkmann (1951). In other words, the judge anchors the two ends of his judgement scale to two subjective values, the one corresponding to his perception of an extremely unfavourable position, and the other to his perception of an extremely favourable position. His perspective—the distance between the two end anchors—is then divided up between the different categories of the judgement scale into what normally can be assumed to be equal intervals. The width of each interval—in Torgerson's (1958) terms, the width of the scale 'unit'—will then be *inversely* related to the degree of polarization, since the wider each interval or unit, the more items will fall within fewer scale categories (see Figure 3.4).

In his 1962 paper, Upshaw predicts that a judge's perspective will correspond to the range of items presented for judgement, plus the judge's own position. As can be seen from Figure 3.4, this implies that a judge's attitude will alter his perspective so as to produce a contrast effect in judgement *only* when it lies beyond the range of items presented. This last prediction is not supported by the many studies in which fairly moderate differences in judges' attitudes have produced significant judgemental shifts. One has to conclude that, if such shifts are to be thought of as resulting from changes in perspective, perspective must be determined by factors other than simply the range of items presented, plus own position.

Another implication of Upshaw's variable perspective model has received more support, however. This is that the way a judge rates his *own* position will depend not only on the 'content' of his attitude (where it falls on the underlying continuum), but also on his perspective, that is, how he applies the

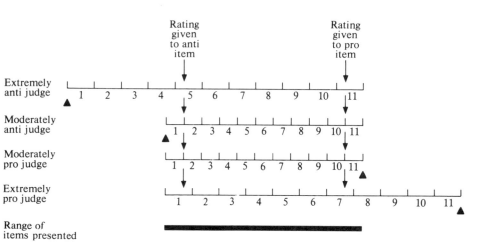

Figure 3.4 Perspective as a function of judges' own position. Upshaw's (1962) variable perspective model. △ indicates own position.

response language. In other words, self-ratings should be liable to context effects following changes in perspective in the same way as ratings of any other item (Ostrom and Upshaw, 1968). Thus, if something happens to make a judge extend his perspective at the pro extreme on some issue, he will then rate his own attitude as more anti, even though the content of his attitude (the position he endorses) may not have changed at all. This prediction is supported in studies by Ostrom (1970) and Upshaw, Ostrom, and Ward (1970), in which subjects' perspectives were changed by giving them differing information concerning the expected range within which their own positions might fall. A more recent study by Kinder, Smith, and Gerard (1976) is presented as inconsistent with this prediction, but, as Upshaw (1976) points out, fails to operationalize the crucial variables, such as perspective, in a way that provides an adequate test of his model.

An interesting question raised by the distinction between attitude content and self-rating is whether, in certain circumstances, individuals may not be even more committed to a particular self-label, such as 'unprejudiced', 'fair-minded', 'radical', or whatever, than to any *specific* position or policy. This leads on to the evaluative and persuasive role of language as applied to attitudinal issues, which I shall consider in the next section.

ACCENTUATION THEORY

Although a number of related explanations have been suggested for the overall contrast effects first noted by Hovland and Sherif (1952), the polarization effects found in a number of studies are not predicted at all by AL theory, and are only partly predicted by the assimilation-contrast model. Although describable in terms of differences in perspective, they are not specifically predicted by Upshaw's (1962) model either. In all these approaches, some kind of continuity has been assumed between psychophysical and social judgement, but in none has attention been paid to those physical judgement effects which might seem to correspond most closely to the polarization effects observed in judgements of attitude statements. These are the accentuation effects produced by peripheral stimulus attributes, discussed earlier in this chapter.

In a study designed to demonstrate that comparable accentuation effects could be produced in judgements of attitude statements (Eiser, 1971c), students were presented with a series of 64 statements concerned with the non-medical use of drugs, which had to be rated in terms of an 11-point scale from 'extremely permissive' to 'extremely restrictive'. The study was presented as to do with the role of the mass media in shaping attitudes, and subjects in the control condition were informed that the statements were 'drawn from newspapers'. In the experimental condition, subjects were (falsely) told that all the statements in fact came from two newspapers, and each statement was presented in quotation marks with one of two newspaper names (*The Gazette* and *The Messenger*) typed underneath it on the questionnaire. Subjects were told that these fictitious names were substitutes for the real names of the two newspapers ('to control for any personal biases'). In fact, the 32 more permissive items were attributed to *The Gazette* and the 32 more restrictive to *The Messenger*. This manipulation is thus a direct analogue of the superimposed classification used in the Tajfel and Wilkes (1963) study.

The results showed a clear-cut accentuation of interclass differences, as well as a nonsignificant reduction of intraclass differences, in the experimental as compared with the control condition. This accentuation principle is then used to re-interpret the effects predicted by the assimilation-contrast model. If judges assimilate items within their latitude of acceptance and contrast items within their latitude of rejection, this need not have anything to do with the supposed anchoring effects of their own attitudes. Instead what may be happening is that judges use their own acceptance or rejection of the items as an additional cue superimposed upon the focal dimension of favourability towards the issue. Judges with, say, extremely favourable attitudes will tend to agree with favourable items and disagree with unfavourable items, so, for them, the subjective acceptable-unacceptable distinction will be superimposed on the favourable-unfavourable distinction and should lead to an accentuation of the judged differences between favourable and unfavourable items—in other words, *increased polarization* in comparison to more neutral judges for whom the acceptability and favourability of the items are unlikely to be monotonically related.

Up to this point, this interpretation makes basically the same prediction as the assimilation-contrast model, and so is open to the same empirical objections. Most importantly, in the previous studies on attitudes towards Negroes, it can still only account for the ratings of the more pro-Negro judges. Like the assimilation-contrast model, it fails to explain the fact that anti-Negro judges give less polarized judgements than neutral judges. Moreover, when the subjects in the Eiser (1971c) study were split into a 'permissive' and a 'restrictive' group in terms of their own attitudes on the drug issue, it was found that polarization was directly related to permissiveness of own position, with no evidence that the most restrictive subjects gave more polarized ratings than more neutral judges. Figure 3.5 shows the mean differences between the two item groups as a function of judges' attitudes and the superimposed classification.

To account for these results, as well as those of the previous studies mentioned, an additional principle is introduced. This relates to the *value connotations* of the words used to label the response scale. It is that terms such as 'anti-Negro' and 'restrictive' may carry relatively negative value connotations for most of the subjects used. In other words, even a person who endorsed anti-Negro statements might be reluctant to describe such statements (or himself) as 'anti-Negro', since he would still recognize this as a term which implied a negative evaluation. Thus, for pro-Negro judges, but not for anti-Negro judges, the value connotations of the response language would be *congruent* with the acceptability and unacceptability of the items to

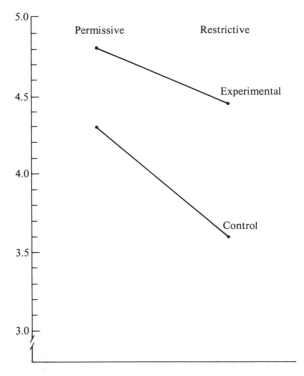

Figure 3.5 Mean item group differences (polarization of judgement) as a function of judges' attitudes (permissive vs. restrictive) and superimposed classification (experimental vs. control). [*Data from Eiser (1971c).*]

the judges personally. If a pro-Negro judge were to rate an anti-Negro statement as 'extremely anti-Negro', he would be attaching a 'bad' label to a statement with which he disagreed—something which he presumably would be only too happy to do. The anti-Negro judge, on the other hand, would be in the position of having to attach a 'bad' label to statements with which he agreed, and a 'good' label to statements with which he disagreed. This presumably would be something he would *not* be happy to do, so he might try to avoid making extreme discriminations on the particular scale provided. The same argument should apply to the Eiser (1971c) data, if one can assume that 'restrictive' was a relatively 'bad' label and 'permissive' a relatively 'good' label for most subjects.

 This gives rise to a revised accentuation principle that 'only insofar as the judge's own evaluations of the items are congruent with such connotations will he tend to accentuate the differences between the items which he accepts and those which he rejects' (Eiser, 1971c, page 10). In other words, more extreme judges should *not* give more polarized ratings if their 'own end' of the scale is defined by a label with evaluatively negative connotations. The observed effects of judges' attitudes on the polarization of their ratings are thus a function of experimenters unwittingly requiring responses to be made in terms of a judgemental language which was evaluatively biased so as to accord more with the attitudes of judges on one side of the issue than the other.

EVALUATIVE LANGUAGE AND DIMENSIONAL SALIENCE

This leads to the prediction that changing the judgemental language may alter the relationship between judges' attitudes and polarization of judgement. In a further study on the drug issue (Eiser, 1973), students rated a modified series of 30 items on five scales. These included the permissive-restrictive scale, which showed the same relationship between judges' attitudes and polarization which had been found in the previous study. The same relationship was also found on two other scales (liberal-authoritarian and broad-minded–narrow-minded) where the more pro-drug term was more positive in connotation and the more anti-drug term more negative. However, this relationship was reversed, with the more anti-drug subjects giving more polarized ratings, on two scales (immoral-moral and decadent-upright) where the anti-drug term was the more positive.

Even more clear-cut results were obtained in a subsequent study (Eiser and Mower White, 1974a) in which 14- to 15-year-olds judged 10 short communications, supposedly comments made by young people concerning the issue of adult authority, in terms of ten scales in which an attempt was made to balance the implicit evaluative connotations of the judgement scale labels. Five of the statements, which were longer and more informally worded than conventional attitude scale items (see Eiser and Stroebe, 1972, pages 159–160, for the complete text), represented positions broadly favourable towards the idea that parents and teachers should have authority over teenagers, for example:

> I think life can be just as exciting if you do what you're told. Teachers and parents generally know best and they often have good ideas. Also if you're polite and do what they say you usually come off best in the end. I think you should support them because they've probably done quite a lot for you.

The remainder were chosen to represent broadly anti-authority positions, for example,

> Nobody has the right to tell anybody else what to do with their lives. It's up to each individual to decide what he wants to do, and what he wants to be, and to discover life in his own way. You have to break free from authority if you want to discover your true self, even if this means offending people in the process. If you think your parents or teachers are wrong, you shouldn't be afraid of saying so.

The ten scales included five which were chosen so that the pro-authority extreme would be the more positive in connotation (e.g., disobedient-obedient), and five chosen so that the anti-authority extreme would be the more positive (e.g., adventurous-unadventurous). Subjects were split into three attitude groups on the basis of their agreement with the ten statements. Taking as a measure of polarization the mean difference between the two groups of five statements, the results showed that the pro-authority judges gave more polarized ratings than the anti-authority judges on scales such as disobedient-obedient, but less polarized ratings than the anti-authority judges on scales like adventurous-unadventurous. In other words, judges seem to try to maintain evaluative consistency between their ratings and their agreement with the items.

A further study by Eiser and Mower White (1975) was designed to look for more general evidence, not restricted to the case of *evaluative* consistency, for the hypothesis that 'polarization of judgement depends both on the correlation between the focal and peripheral continua and on the degree of congruity between the peripheral cues and the response scale labels' (page 770). To this end, a peripheral cue was superimposed on the same series of ten statements, consisting of the supposed sex of the young person by whom each statement was made, resulting in three conditions. In the *direct* condition, the five pro-authority statements were presented as having been made by girls (with a different girl's name printed under each of these statements), and the five anti-authority statements were presented as having been made by boys. In the *reverse* condition, the pro-authority statements were presented as having been made by boys, and the anti-authority statements as having been made by girls. In the *control* condition, the statements appeared without either boys' or girls' names attached. Subjects were also split into three attitude groups (pro, neutral, and anti) on the basis of their agreement with the statements.

Subjects had to rate the statements on eight scales, chosen to produce a 2×2 design. The effects of the value connotations of the scales were determined by comparing four scales where the pro-authority extreme was the more positive (P scales) with four where the anti-authority extreme was the more positive (A scales). Figure 3.6 shows the predicted interactive effect, on polarization, of judges' attitudes and value connotations of the scales, replicating the main finding of Eiser and Mower White (1974a).

Independently of value connotation, four of the scales ('marked' scales) were chosen, on the basis of a pilot study, so that the anti-authority term was seen as more applicable to boys, and the pro-authority term as more applicable to girls. For instance, boys were seen as more likely to be 'bold', and girls to be 'timid'. The remaining four ('unmarked') scales were chosen so that neither term would be perceived as more applicable to boys or to girls. The hypothesis was that subjects in the direct condition should show more polarization than the control subjects on both types of scales, but those in the reverse condition should do so only on the unmarked scales. On the unmarked scales, the question of the congruity between the response language

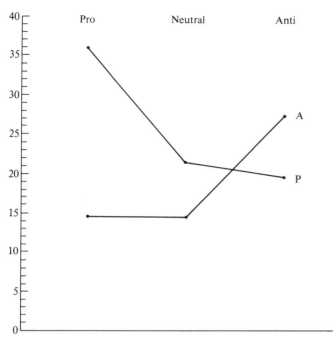

Figure 3.6 Mean item group differences (polarization of judgement) as a function of judges' attitudes (pro, neutral, anti) and value connotations of scales (P scales: pro end positive vs. A scales: anti end positive). [*Data from Eiser and Mower White (1975).*] Ratings of items scored from 0 (anti end) to 100 (pro end).

and the superimposed classification does not arise, so both direct and reverse conditions should show more polarization. 'The terms used to label the marked scales, on the other hand, would be congruent with the superimposed classification in the direct condition but incongruent for the reverse subjects; on these scales, therefore, only the direct subjects should show greater polarization than the control subjects.' (Page 772.)

As can be seen from Figure 3.7, this hypothesis was confirmed, although the data also show an unpredicted effect of greater polarization on the marked than unmarked scales. The situation of the reverse subjects using the marked scales is comparable to that of the pro-subjects using A scales, or anti-subjects using P scales. The direct subjects, on the other hand, believed the authors of the pro statements to be girls, and the authors of the anti statements to be boys, and so could attach feminine and masculine labels to each respectively without incongruity.

The main thesis of the Eiser and Mower White (1975) paper is that the two principles of categorization and cognitive consistency should be regarded as alternative ways of conceptualizing the same fundamental process. The central notion of cognitive consistency theory is that individuals attempt to

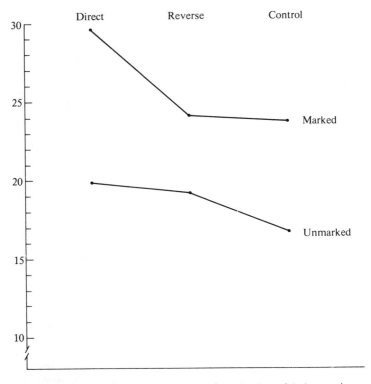

Figure 3.7 Mean item group differences (polarization of judgement) as a function of super-imposed classification (direct, reverse, control) and congruency of scales with classification (marked vs. unmarked scales). [*Data from Eiser and Mower White (1975)*.]

organize their cognitions and evaluations, as Osgood and Tannenbaum (1955, page 43) put it, 'in the direction of increased congruity with the existing frame of reference'. In other words, there is a search for a subjective representation of reality in terms of which objects, people and events can be evaluated with maximal simplicity and minimal ambivalence. Similarly, throughout the literature on accentuation and categorization processes (e.g., Bruner, Goodnow, and Austin, 1956), there has been an equivalent acknowledgement of people's need to simplify their perceptual and social environment so as to make it conceptually manageable. Such simplification is achieved primarily through an exploitation of the redundancy which one learns to recognize in one's perceptual experience, so that a conglomeration of a multitude of separate items of stimulus information come to be treated as a single object or category.

Normally, the presence of a clearly detectable peripheral attribute which is correlated with the focal attribute will lead to greater accentuation of inter-stimulus differences. In terms of an integrationist approach (see pages

65–66), the extent to which one stimulus will be rated higher on a given scale than another stimulus (i.e., the $R_i - R_j$ difference) will be a joint function both of the perceived difference on the focal attribute $(s_i - s_j)$, and of the differences which would be predicted on the basis of peripheral stimulus information $(t_i - t_j)$. However, it may be the case that the sign of the $t_i - t_j$ difference is opposite to that of the $s_i - s_j$ difference, which is precisely what happens if there is incongruity between the peripheral cue and the response language.

There is likewise no reason to suppose that the principle of cognitive consistency is independent of the language in terms of which an individual expresses and conceptualizes the relationship between different attitude objects. It is all very well to talk of 'increased congruity with the existing frame of reference', but how is this frame of reference to be defined? The implication of the Jaspars (1965) interpretation of balance theory is that this frame of reference consists, in the case of a typical balanced state, of a unidimensional preference space in terms of which the perceiver is also able to evaluate himself positively. The hypothesized motivation towards balance may be interpreted, therefore, as a search for cognitive dimensions in terms of which attitude objects can be appraised in a way which presents the least challenge to a positive self-evaluation.

Stemming probably from the factor-analytic and multidimensional scaling traditions, but preserved also within the methodology of work on personal construct theory (Kelly, 1955) and cognitive complexity (Crockett, 1965), the conventional definition of a cognitive dimension is based heavily on correlational techniques. If different rating scales are highly intercorrelated, they are generally taken to represent the same underlying dimension, factor, or construct. In terms of this general approach, what is crucial is the question of which *attributes* a person uses to distinguish between different objects in his experience.

In the studies described in this section, however, the different scales tend to be very highly intercorrelated, in spite of being chosen so as to differ in this implicit value connotation. In a strictly positivistic sense, these scales may reflect the same underlying dimensions, but they are nonetheless used very differently by judges with different attitudes. Intuitively, it appears that some judges 'prefer' to use some scales, and others 'prefer' to use other scales.

The basis for this intuition is the extent to which a judge seems prepared to commit himself to extreme discriminations along a given scale, or alternatively clusters his ratings around the more neutral categories. In short, polarization may be a sign of *preference*. This would be broadly consistent with the view that greater extremity of response is an index of greater confidence (Cantril, 1946), or of greater salience or personal relevance to the individual of the judgements he is required to make (Bonarius, 1965; Cromwell and Caldwell, 1962; Landfield, 1968; Tajfel and Wilkes, 1964). Salience is certainly not the most clearly defined of concepts (Eiser, 1971a), but it seems to have much in common with the Sherif notion of ego-involvement—the idea that one's self-esteem has been brought into play and may require protection.

Recently, van der Pligt and van Dijk (1979) have provided evidence for the relationship between polarization and preference for particular labels. When subjects were given a choice of labels with which to describe statements on the drug issue, the labels they chose were evaluatively congruent with their own positions. Also, when these same labels were combined in the form of rating scales, greater polarization was again shown by judges whose own positions were closer to the positively labelled extreme. This demonstrates the limitation of the conventional 'positivistic' definition of a cognitive dimension in terms of an underlying *attribute*, rather than the individual's own *description* of such an attribute. Even in situations where the individual has little or no control over the stimulus variation he experiences, language may allow him many ways of describing, interpreting, and evaluating such variation. It is therefore only to be expected that, when it comes to attitudinal issues, the individual will prefer to use language which is evaluatively congruent with his own attitude. It is such language, rather than the underlying attribute *per se*, which defines the 'existing frame of reference' in terms of which congruity is achieved.

VALUE AND EXTREMITY

Although most research stemming from the assimilation-contrast and accentuation theory approaches has been concerned with differences in polarization, changes in overall mean judgement (what Upshaw calls changes in scale origin rather than scale unit) can also be observed as a result of manipulations of response language. It may be useful to think of these in terms of differences in perspective, even though they are not specifically predicted by Upshaw's (1962, 1969) model.

In particular, there was a very clear 'positivity' effect in the Eiser and Mower White (1974a, 1975) studies for judges' ratings of the series of statements as a whole to be 'displaced' towards the evaluatively positive extreme of each scale. A possible interpretation of this effect is that judges tend to use the different scales to cover different regions of the underlying attitude continuum. Evidence in the field of personality trait inferences (Peabody, 1967, see Chapter 4) implies that more extreme positions on a given trait tend to be evaluated negatively, and more moderate positions positively. This notion in fact dates back well over two thousand years, and Aristotle gives an excellent example in Book Two of his Nicomachean Ethics: 'In agreeableness in social amusement, the man who hits the mean is "witty" and what characterizes him is "wittiness". The excess is "buffoonery" and a man who exhibits that is a "buffoon". The opposite of the buffoon is the "boor" and his characteristic is "boorishness".' (Translation by Thomson, 1955, page 70.)

In the Eiser and Mower White studies, therefore, a statement would not have to be particularly extreme on the pro-authority side to be rated as 'obedient', but would have to be quite extreme on the anti-authority side to be rated as 'disobedient'. Similarly, a moderately anti-authority statement could be rated as 'adventurous', but only more extremely pro-authority statements would be rated as 'unadventurous'.

This 'positivity' effect is an instance of how scale origin can depend on the value connotations of the response language. However, such connotations may also influence scale unit, i.e., polarization of judgement, in a manner that does not depend cn judges' own positions. The scales used by Eiser and Mower White (1974a, 1975) were all ones where the value connotations of the two extremes were opposed, or asymmetrical; in other words, one extreme was relatively negative in connotation. Eiser and Osmon (1978), however, compared scales where both extremes were evaluatively negative (EN) with those where both extremes were evaluatively positive (EP). The same 10 statements concerned with adult authority used in the Eiser and Mower White studies were presented to a final sample of 60 13-to-14-year-olds for judgement on four EN and four EP scales. An example of an EN scale was resentful-timid, and of an EP scale, bold-polite.

The hypothesis was that, if evaluatively negative labels tend to denote more extreme positions on a descriptive continuum, the EN scales should cover a wider perspective, and hence show less polarization, than the EP scales. This can be seen from Figure 3.8, which shows the hypothetical differences in perspective and judgement that could be expected between EN and

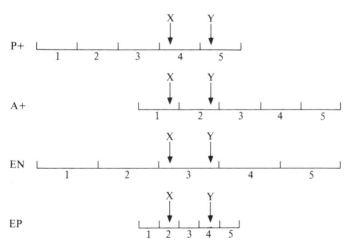

Figure 3.8 Differences in item ratings as a function of the value connotations of the response scale: hypothetical example to show ratings given to a relatively anti-authority item X and a relatively pro-authority item Y on four five-point scales assumed to represent different regions of the underlying continuum from anti- to pro-authority. P + Asymmetrical value connotations, pro end positive (e.g., disobedient-obedient); A + Asymmetrical value connotations, anti end positive (e.g., adventurous-unadventurous); EN Symmetrical value connotations, both ends negative (e.g., resentful-timid); EP Symmetrical value connotations, both ends positive (e.g., bold-polite). Reproduced from J. R. Eiser and B. E. Osmon, 'Judgemental perspective and the value connotations of response scale labels', *Journal of Personality and Social Psychology*, **36**, 494, 1978, with permission of the American Psychological Association.

EP scales, as well as on scales of the kind used by Eiser and Mower White (1974a, 1975), viz.: P + scales where the pro-end was the more positive (e.g., disobedient-obedient) and A + scales where the anti-end was the more positive (e.g., adventurous-unadventurous). As can be seen, the difference in connotations between P + and A + scales should produce the 'positivity effect' observed by Eiser and Mower White (1974a, 1975), whereas the EN and EP scales should differ in terms of polarization. This last prediction was strongly supported by the Eiser and Osmon results, the effect being independent of judges' own positions.

This interpretation could also be applied to the results of a study by Dawes, Singer, and Lemons (1972). Using the issue of the Vietnam war, they found in one experiment that 'hawk' statements were judged as more extreme by 'hawks' than by 'doves'. In a second experiment, students had to write statements which they considered to be typical of 'hawk' and 'dove' positions. 'Hawk' statements written by students who were in fact 'doves' were rejected by genuine 'hawks' as too extreme, and similarly 'dove' statements written by 'hawks' were rejected as too extreme. Dawes et al. interpret these findings as instances of 'contrast effects' which are *not* dependent on changes in perspective, that is, in how judges interpret descriptive labels. However, a semantic interpretation is clearly applicable if one assumes that extremity is negatively evaluated and hence that, in the first experiment, negatively evaluated positions were judged as more extreme than positively evaluated positions and, in the second experiment, labels which subjects evaluated negatively were seen by them as applicable to more extreme positions.

CONCLUSIONS

Social judgement is much more than the study of how individuals locate the positions of attitude statements and similar stimuli along arbitrarily prescribed dimensions. It is not a reductionist attempt to dismiss as troublesome or irrelevant anything intrinsically social about our appraisals of social objects and events, nor is it just a technological appendage to the field of attitude measurement which may serve to enhance the reliability of conventional instruments. Instead, it asks fundamental questions not only about how individuals categorize social stimuli along given dimensions, but also about how they choose and symbolically define the dimensions in terms of which to categorize. It is this element of choice and symbolic definition which is of greatest theoretical significance to the social psychologist, and which is the basis of the constructive role of individual judgements in social interaction.

SUMMARY

* How people compare different stimuli with each other is of importance, not only to general experimental psychology, but also to social psychology.

* Psychophysics has traditionally been concerned with deriving measures of sensation from judgemental responses. Adaptation-level theory interprets judgemental contrast effects (e.g., when a weight is judged to be lighter in the context of other heavier weights) as reflecting a change in sensation, such as may result from processes of perceptual adaptation.
* The integrationist approach stresses the individual's capacity to define the judgemental language in a manner appropriate to the stimuli being judged, and postulates processes whereby separate items of stimulus information are combined cognitively to yield a judgemental response, without assuming that a change in sensation must necessarily underlie any change in judgement.
* Judgements of stimuli along a physical dimension such as size may be influenced by other, unjudged, attributes of the stimuli. Notably, the judged differences between stimuli may be accentuated when the stimuli differ systemically from each other on a dimension other than that being judged (as when coins which differ in size differ also in value), so that the subject has additional cues on which to base his discriminations.
* Such accentuation effects are a special case of information integration.
* These processes also seem to be involved in the tendency to stereotype members of distinctive or alien groups.
* Thurstone's method of attitude scale construction requires judges to rate series of statements in terms of their favourability/unfavourability towards the issue in question. Such ratings are influenced by judges' own attitudes on the issue.
* Sherif and Hovland proposed that this effect results from subjects using their own attitude as an 'anchor' and assimilating statements which they accept, and contrasting statements which they reject. The main empirical weakness of this proposal is that it predicts that judges with extreme attitudes at either end of the scale will give more polarized (bilaterally extreme) ratings than more neutral judges. Studies using the issue of attitudes towards black people have confirmed this prediction in the case of judges with favourable, but not unfavourable, attitudes.
* Upshaw's variable perspective model attributes changes in judgement to judges' redefinitions of the response language with which they are provided. Judges' self-ratings of their own attitude may be similarly subject to judgemental shifts. However, there is only weak support for predictions of the model concerning the effects which should result from changes in the range of statements presented for judgement.
* Accentuation theory predicts that judgements of attitude statements will be more polarized when the statements are distinguishable from each other in terms of an additional unjudged attribute, correlated with the judged dimension of favourability/unfavourability. It is assumed that, for more extreme judges, the acceptability/unacceptability of the statements can constitute such an additional cue.
* It is predicted that judges will only tend to accentuate the differences between more and less acceptable statements when using a response langu-

age which is evaluatively congruent with their own attitude, i.e., which allows them to attach a 'good' label to statements of which they approve. This prediction is supported by studies which have manipulated the value connotations of the response scales which judges are required to use.

* Evaluatively negative labels may also be seen as more appropriate descriptions of more extreme positions on the attitude continuum.

PERCEPTIONS OF PERSONALITY
AND CAUSALITY

NAIVE PSYCHOLOGY

To ask the question of how people perceive one another, one has first to make explicit one's assumptions concerning the process of perception itself. In many instances, the approach to this question has taken the form of an attempt to identify the physical features, postures, and movements which serve as cues to a person's mood, character, or intentions. The emphasis in such work has typically been on non-verbal cues, such as forms of facial expression (e.g., Ekman, 1971) or eye-contact (e.g., Exline, 1971). The search for similarities and differences in such forms of expression across different cultures has produced fascinating evidence (Ekman, 1971; Ekman and Friesen, 1970), as has the comparison between such forms of expression in human beings and other primates (Vine, 1970). Occasionally, researchers in this field have argued that non-verbal cues are more 'basic' and hence more influential than verbal cues (Argyle, Alkema, and Gilmour, 1971). There is also the appealing, if rather circular argument, that the relationships conveyed by non-verbal cues, such as affiliation, antagonism, dominance, and submission, should be considered the 'basic' building-blocks of social interaction, both human and non-human.

Throughout such work, however, the emphasis has been on specifying the nature of the perceptual *input*, rather than the perceptual *process*. This is not by any means a criticism, but it implies that there will be important questions which such an approach is not, by itself, equipped to answer. The emphasis of a cognitive social psychology, however, is unashamedly concerned with process rather than input. This is not to say that input is unimportant, nor that attention to cultural variation or universality in input may not lead to the discovery of greater cultural variation or universality in process than might otherwise be recognized. What is implied instead is simply the conviction that, at the present time, the important unanswered theoretical questions in social psychology are those concerned with how individuals deal with the information which they receive, whatever this information may be.

As was seen in the last chapter, people's judgements of even very simple stimuli, such as weights and lines, require a view of the judgemental process which places the perceiver in an active and constructive role, attempting to interpret and integrate the information which he receives. Judgements of physical stimuli are not simply a function of passive physiological adaptation, but reflect the judge's cognitive appraisal of the stimulus context.

With judgements of attitude statements, this process of active construction is carried even further, in that the individual needs not only to decide upon the relative positions of the statements along a given dimension, but also upon the appropriateness of the judgemental language he is to use. I argued that the individual's choice of a particular judgemental language may reflect an attempt to construe attitudinal issues in a manner consistent with a positive self-evaluation. Such a way of appraising attitudinal issues fulfils an important function for the individual in enabling him to acknowledge the existence of opinions which differ from his own, but remain relatively uninfluenced by them. The attaching of negative labels to opposing positions does not just enable the individual to say 'Those who disagree with me are bad'. It enables him to draw the far more comforting conclusion that 'Those who disagree with me do so *because* they are bad and I am good'. Judgements of attitudes thus reflect individuals' *explanations* of attitudinal differences.

Balance theory, and related theories of cognitive consistency, thus attempt to describe how individuals try to explain their social environment. As descriptions of 'objective' reality, such theories are obviously gross over-simplifications—but that is precisely their point. In their attempt to explain and interpret their social environment, individuals *do* grossly over-simplify the information they look for and receive. Theories of attitude organization and judgement are thus theories about people's theories—their explanations of attitudinal differences. In the same way, when one looks at how people perceive one another, one is in fact looking at people's theories about people; that is, at their explanations of individual differences. The study of person perception is thus the study of 'naive psychology'—the study of people's preconceptions about why they, and others, act the way they do. The focus of the research to be described in this chapter is therefore the *subjective* fabric of social relationships and individual differences.

IMPRESSION FORMATION

In social psychological jargon 'impression formation research' refers less to research on a single psychological process than to studies involving a specific set of experimental paradigms. The hallmark of these studies is their use of 'personality trait adjectives' as stimulus material. The phrase 'personality trait' is not restricted to technical terms such as neurotic or introvert, such as one would find in personality or clinical psychology textbooks, but is taken to include any description which one person could make of another's character. The proportion of our language given over to such descriptions is truly immense. Allport and Odbert (1936) identified around 18 000 'trait names' in a standard English dictionary, of which 4504 were seen as descriptions of 'consistent and stable modes of an individual's adjustment to his environment' (Allport, 1937, page 306). More recently, Anderson (1968b) has presented a list of 555 such adjectives, ordered in terms of 'likeableness'.

Impression formation studies typically present subjects with such trait adjectives, either singly or in combination, and require responses either in the form of ratings or inferences. When ratings are required, subjects are essentially asked to obey instructions of the form 'Imagine someone who is (e.g.) honest, and rate this person on this scale from (e.g.) not at all likeable to extremely likeable'. When inferences are required, subjects are essentially asked, 'How probable is it that someone who is (e.g.) honest would also be (e.g.) likeable?' There seems little reason to suppose that these different response modes reflect any fundamental differences in the way subjects deal with the stimulus information presented to them.

The first systematic exploration of this paradigm was by Asch (1946). The best-known feature of his data was a comparison of subjects' impressions of a hypothetical person on the basis of a list of trait adjectives, of which one 'central' trait was varied between experimental conditions. Thus, 91 per cent of subjects said that they thought someone whom they heard described as 'intelligent, skilful, industrious, warm, determined, practical, and cautious' would also be 'generous', whereas only 8 per cent did so in another condition where the trait 'cold' was substituted for 'warm'. Asch's interpretation of these findings was that subjects were attempting to build the separate items of information (the different adjectives) into a coherent impression, or *Gestalt*, and that inferences to other traits were then made on the basis of how well they fitted this established impression. He also introduced a distinction between 'central' traits, such as 'warm-cold' which had important effects on global impressions, and 'peripheral' traits, assumed to have less effect. The importance of the pattern of intercorrelations between different trait descriptions as a determinant of the centrality of any given trait was later demonstrated by Wishner (1960).

Asch's research raises the question of whether different traits are seen to imply each other because they describe similar characteristics, or types of behaviour (e.g., honest, truthful), or because they are consistent at a purely evaluative level (e.g., honest, generous). In many studies of impression formation, however, it is impossible to determine the separate influences of descriptive and evaluative similarity.

To deal with this problem, Peabody (1967) proposed the following scheme for constructing sets of traits in which the roles of descriptive and evaluative similarity could be unconfounded. First, one decides on the particular behavioural attribute in which one is interested, for example, a disposition to take risks. Next, one chooses two different terms to denote this attribute, one of which is positive (e.g., bold) and one of which is negative (e.g., rash) in evaluation. Then one chooses two further terms to denote the opposite extreme of the descriptive continuum, of which again one must be positive (e.g., cautious) and one negative (e.g., timid). One can then compare the similarity of inferences from descriptively similar, but evaluatively dissimilar, traits with those from evaluatively similar, but descriptively dissimilar, traits.

On the basis of results obtained with this paradigm, Peabody (1967) initially concluded that evaluative similarity had little importance, other than as a by-product of descriptive similarity. Rosenberg and Olshan (1970), however, pointed out the presence of an artefact in Peabody's factor analysis which precluded the emergence of any simple evaluative factor. In response to this criticism, Peabody (1970) conceded that both evaluative and descriptive similarity have important independent influences. A similar conclusion was also reached by Felipe (1970), who argued that there is a definite sequence in the way in which subjects seek to achieve descriptive and evaluative similarity. First, 'traits similar in such descriptive attributes regardless of their evaluative contents, are judged to have more likelihood of occurring together in a person than traits that are evaluatively similar, but descriptively different'. Next, once the criterion of descriptive consistency has been satisfied, 'traits which are both descriptively and evaluatively balanced have a greater likelihood of occurring together than traits which are only descriptively, but not evaluatively, balanced'. (Page 635.)

Evidence for the independent importance of evaluative and descriptive aspects of personality descriptions is also provided by a study conducted by Peabody (1968) in the Philippines. Ratings of four ethnic groups, i.e., Chinese living in the Philippines, Filipinos, Americans, and Japanese, were obtained from members of the first two groups. There were 14 pairs of scales, each pair being constructed according to the scheme described above for unconfounding evaluative and descriptive similarity. Thus, one pair of scales was 'thrifty-extravagant' and 'generous-stingy'. The results showed that the two groups of judges tended to disagree about their evaluations of each other's group, but agree about the descriptive attributes which they considered to be characteristic of each group. Thus, for example, both groups agreed that the Filipinos were more generous/extravagant than the Chinese. However, whereas the Filipinos preferred to label themselves as generous and the Chinese as stingy, the Chinese preferred to label themselves thrifty and the Filipinos as extravagant.

The largest body of research generated by Asch's (1946) paradigm, however, has been that concerned with the question of how different items of information, i.e., separate traits, are combined to form a composite inference or impression. Bruner, Shapiro, and Tagiuri (1958) compared the inferences made on the basis of single traits with those made from the same traits in combination. Where all separate traits in a combination were seen as implying another attribute, this attribute tended also to be inferred (typically with an enhanced degree of certainty compared with the average of the inferences from each trait singly) from the trait-combination. In situations where the implications of each separate trait were inconsistent with each other, the composite inference would be generally determined by the inferences that could be drawn from a majority of the separate traits, or, if there was no majority, from the traits carrying the most definite implications.

Attempts to describe this process in more quantitative terms led to a controversy between additive (Triandis and Fishbein, 1963; Fishbein and Hunter, 1964) and averaging (Anderson, 1962) formulations. A synthesis of these two positions is represented in Anderson's (1965) weighted average model, which allows for different stimulus items having different degrees of influence on the final impression, and deals with the data presented by supporters of the additive models by assuming the final impression is a weighted average both of the information actually presented (the set of traits) and of an 'initial impression' which the subject has before being given any information, which is expected to be neutral. Although alternative models have comparable predictive power (Warr and Smith, 1970), Anderson's weighted-average formulation has remained the most influential and heuristic in this area, and has proved capable also of generating useful hypotheses with regard to other areas of research, such as those dealt with in the last chapter.

Anderson's model of impression formation, particularly in its more recent developments and extensions, is both precisely stated and highly adaptable. This adaptability, however, is achieved primarily through the assumption that different items of information (or attributes of a given stimulus) may be weighted differently in a composite impression. This assumption makes good intuitive sense, but in situations (of which there are a great number in social psychology) where the precise weights attached to the different items of information cannot be predicted with any confidence before the composite impression is known, its effect is to protect the model, for the time being at least, from serious empirical challenge.

One field of research that bears directly on the question of the weights attached to different items of information is that concerned with order effects in impression formation. Jones and Goethals (1971) point out that the literature contains examples both of primacy, in which information presented earlier in a temporal sequence has greater weight than that presented later, and recency effects, in which later information has more weight.

In Anderson's own studies, primacy effects are the more typical, and there is reason to suppose that a mediating factor may be a tendency for subjects to pay less attention to later traits or information items. When subjects receive instructions designed to make them attend equally to the whole list of traits, primacy effects disappear (Anderson and Hubert, 1963; Stewart, 1965; Hendrick and Constantini, 1970). Anderson and Jacobson (1965) argue that this decrement in attention may lead subjects to attach less weight to later items, thus incorporating primacy effects into the weighted-average formulation.

As Jones and Goethals argue, however, Anderson rarely makes any pretence of encouraging his subjects to believe that the traits in a list refer to a real person, or that the order of presentation of the traits has any special significance. In one study, however, Anderson (1968a) presented subjects with lists of traits which showed a gradual transition through the list from either extremely favourable to moderately favourable traits, or from extremely unfavourable to moderately unfavourable traits. Thus the traits were in a definite sequence, and the degree of inconsistency among the different traits in a single list was far less than in the other studies. Also, Anderson explained the serial presentation procedure to his subjects 'by analogy to real life in which one customarily gets to know a person step by step' (page 365). As a consequence, recency effects were demonstrated. A mediating factor here might be that later information is better recalled, but it also seems that the instructions may have encouraged subjects to view the later information as analogous to judgements based on a longer period of acquaintance with a person, and more valid for that reason.

Such procedural variations are by no means the only factors relevant to the primacy-recency issue. Another was demonstrated by Thibaut and Ross (1969), who showed stronger primacy effects when subjects were made to feel committed to their initial impressions. The main point to emerge from these studies, however, is that even an apparently simple problem such as the effect of order of presentation turns out on closer inspection to be a complex function of factors that may influence subjects' interpretations of the task they are asked to perform, or, as Jones and Goethals put it: 'the information conveyed by the order of events itself is contingent on the context in which these events unfold and on the nature of the entity being considered as an attributional target.' (1971, page 28.)

Other research relevant to the question of the different weights that are to be attached to different kinds of information has concentrated on what happens when such information is inconsistent or contradictory. There is evidence that evaluatively negative information about a person can carry greater weight than positive descriptions (Kanouse and Hanson, 1971; Warr and Jackson, 1975). This may be because negative attributes are perceived as having a lower likelihood of occurrence, and therefore as carrying more information value (Boucher and Osgood, 1969), or conversely because people do tend to evaluate more positively traits of greater familiarity or subjective frequency (Zajonc, 1968a). Of major importance, however, may be the question of how subjects attempt to deal conceptually with the inconsistent information presented to them.

Cohen (1971) has argued that the weighted-average approach may only predict subjects' responses to inconsistent trait combinations when one forces subjects to make their responses in terms of the dimension which contains the inconsistency. Thus, a typical situation might involve selecting two evaluatively negative traits (e.g., dishonest, arrogant), and then asking subjects a question of the form, 'How *good* or *bad* is someone who is dishonest, clever, affectionate, and arrogant?' In such a situation, the subjects will generally give relatively neutral responses in terms of the good-bad dimension. On the other hand, if subjects were simply asked, 'How would you describe someone who was dishonest, clever, affectionate, and arrogant?', they might well be able to report quite definite impressions, but not ones which could be adequately conceptualized in terms of the good-bad dimension. As Cohen has put it:

> Only when one forces a judge—we assume—to give an estimate, say, of the intelligence of a student who does excellently on written exams but dreadfully on orals, or to rate the aggressiveness of a murderer who happens to be a pacifist as well: only in such cases will the judge, of necessity, make his judgement on that contradiction-laden dimension. If, however, he were allowed the opportunity to express himself freely, a large portion of the variance of his judgements would fall on dimensions other than the contradiction-laden one .... Further, it appears reasonable to assume that under conditions of free expression the subject will interpret the contradiction itself as an item of *further* information and as a signal to switch his judgments to a dimension which is independent of that on which the contradictions exist. (1971, pages 476–477.)

In support of this position, Cohen reports the results of an experiment in which subjects were required to make ratings of consistent and inconsistent pairs of traits in terms of a large number of rating scales (36 in all). Factor analyses revealed that the majority of the variance of ratings of consistent trait combinations fell on the same dimension as that which accounted for most of the variance of the ratings of the single traits in isolation. Combining consistent information, therefore, does not require major cognitive restructuring. However, for ratings of contradictory trait combinations, most of the variance fell on dimensions other than that which accounted for most of the variance of the single trait judgements. These results were confirmed in later studies using more realistic behavioural descriptions as stimulus information.

Cohen's study has a number of important implications. On the question of general research strategy, it points to the dangers of drawing simplistic conclusions about cognitive processes from situations in which the forms of response open to a subject have been artificially restricted. The quantitative sophistication of models such as Anderson's is bought at a price—and the price is the assumption that the specified response continuum has psychological significance for the subject, not only because the experimenter has decreed that it should be the continuum that is used, but because it allows the subject to interpret the information presented, and express his interpretation, in what he considers to be a meaningful way. This is similar to the assumption one makes when one uses standardized measures of favourability towards an issue as *the* measure of a person's attitude. In situations where such simplifying assumptions are correct, as Coombs (1964) would put it, we have a bargain. Cohen's results suggest that in situations where inconsistent information is combined, we may not have such a bargain—we may buy the simplicity which Anderson's algebraic solution provides at the cost of ignoring the most informative part of what subjects would be prepared to say about such information, if we allowed them to do so.

Another important feature of Cohen's data is that, when subjects 'switch dimensions' in response to contradictory information, they tend to show considerable agreement among themselves over which dimensions they should switch *to*. In other words, the qualitative changes in impression generated by such trait combinations are consistent across subjects. What experimenters have defined as contradictory information is in fact information that is contradictory in terms of the specified response dimension (e.g., likeableness), but which need not necessarily be inconsistent in terms of some other dimension. Osgood and Tannenbaum (1955) predicted that changes in evaluation should be such as to produce increased congruity within 'the existing frame of reference'. An alternative strategy open to subjects, rather than compromise on a neutral impression as both Anderson's model and congruity theory suggest, is to find *another* dimension, or frame of reference, in terms of which the information is not contradictory. The need for cognitive simplicity implied by cognitive consistency theory might, therefore, lead, in such situations, to a search for an appropriate cognitive restructuring.

The question of how individuals form impressions and integrate information about other people is only worth asking as long as we do not lose sight of the more fundamental question of *why* they do so. This is the importance of the concept of 'naive psychology'. People's judgements of each other reflect their own theories of human behaviour. They are not reflex reactions to stimulus input, but attempts at explanation. Inconsistent trait combinations pose a problem for models of impression formation, for the simple reason that inconsistency is more problematic to explain. At the same time, if the important questions are those about how individuals *interpret* information, there is little value in putting all one's eggs in the basket of a single research paradigm, in which subjects' interpretations of the experimental situation itself may well be an important mediating factor in many circumstances.

ATTRIBUTION THEORY

One of the major criticisms that can be made of the impression formation literature is that very little attempt is made to present subjects with the kind of information which they would be likely to receive about real people in real life. Although assumed to reflect 'lay conceptions of personality', subjects' ratings might reflect little more, in many instances, than their appreciation of conventional linguistic usage. Such usage could, of course, reflect culturally shared assumptions about 'human nature', but the worry may remain that the impression formation paradigm provides at best a very indirect way of looking at how people try to explain one another's behaviour.

The problem is not just that such studies provide subjects with minimal information on which to base their ratings, it is that the kind of information provided has already been linguistically structured. Every personality trait adjective is in itself already an attempt at explaining behaviour. We cannot *observe* traits, we can only observe behavioural and physical cues and then, if we wish, summarize our impressions in words which *purport* to describe personality traits. We cannot observe arrogance, we can only observe people behaving in ways which we may choose to label arrogant. Alternatively, we may hear one person describing another as arrogant, but here we are only receiving impressions at second hand. To assume that person perception is the perception of personality traits (with traits assumed to be observable entities) is to beg so many questions that it is doubtful whether any remain that are really worth asking.

Attribution theory is distinguished from the research tradition just described by treating trait descriptions as a possible output from, rather than as a possible input to, the person perception process. It is concerned explicitly with how people try to find appropriate causal explanations for one another's behaviour, and more generally for any event in their social environment. Its origins can be traced to Heider's (1944, 1958) work on the notion of phenomenal causality. Heider assumes that individuals are motivated to see their social environment as predictable and hence controllable, and that they apply the same kind of logic to the prediction of social events as to the prediction of physical events: they look for the necessary and sufficient conditions for such events to occur. Such conditions may either be situational or impersonal factors, external to the person whose behaviour one is trying to predict and explain, or factors regarded as internal to the person, such as his ability or personality. In Heider's words, 'Attributions in terms of impersonal and personal causes, and with the latter, in terms of intent, are everyday occurrences that determine much of our understanding of a reaction to our surroundings.' (1958, page 16.)

Heider goes on to stress the importance of the concept of intentionality, arguing that behaviour should only be attributed to personal causes if its outcome is seen to have been intended by the actor (1958, pages 101–102). There is assumed to be a kind of 'trade-off' relationship between the assumed influence of personal and impersonal factors, so that attributions to a person's character will not be so likely to be made if the behaviour is seen to be under the control of external constraints. Personality-trait descriptions are thus an attempt to explain behaviour which cannot be clearly attributed to external conditions. Even so, Heider argues, the effect of such environmental conditions may not be fully taken into account: 'It seems that behaviour in particular has such salient properties it tends to engulf the total field rather than be confined to its proper position as a local stimulus whose interpretation requires the additional data of a surrounding field.' (1958, page 54.) In other words, we may be biased towards explaining behaviour in terms of personal factors—a bias which may be reflected in the readiness to treat problematic behaviour as a disorder of *individual* personality.

On the basis of these notions, Jones and Davis (1965) propose a model of how individuals make inferences about a person's dispositions or character, which they explain as follows:

> It is assumed that the perceiver typically starts with the overt action of another; this is the grist for his cognitive mill. He then makes certain decisions concerning ability and knowledge which will let him cope with the problem of attributing particular intentions to the actor. The attribution of intentions, in turn, is a necessary step in the assignment of more stable characteristics to the actor. (Page 222.)

Ability and knowledge are relevant in that it is assumed that the actor must be seen as knowing that his action could have the consequences produced, and being able to produce these consequences intentionally by his action, before an attribution can be made to his intentions. When the perceiver infers that the actor's behaviour is 'in character', he is said to have made a *correspondent inference*. For example, if the actor shows aggressive behaviour, the most 'correspondent' inference is that he does so because he is an aggressive person, which also involves the assumption that he intended to act aggressively.

At a conceptual level, there are a number of serious difficulties with this model. At its most mechanistic, it implies that personality causes intentions and intentions cause behaviour. Yet we do not assume that stupid people necessarily *intend* to act stupidly, or that forgetful people necessarily *intend* to forget things. Nor can we assume that just because a person adapts his behaviour to the constraints of external circumstances, he has acted unintentionally. Nor again, in the absence of external constraints, can a person be said to have acted unintentionally just because his action produces unintended consequences. As Anscombe (1963) has argued, to say that a person acted intentionally does not entail that he acted with the intention of bringing about any of the actual consequences of his action.

Notwithstanding these difficulties surrounding the concept of intentionality, the Jones and Davis model contains empirical predictions concerning the conditions most likely to lead to correspondent inferences. The likelihood of a correspondent inference is assumed to be less if the consequences of the actor's behaviour are high in 'social desirability': unusual or deviant behaviour is more likely to lead to inferences about an actor's personality. Also correspondent inferences are more likely if an action produces a larger number of consequences ('noncommon effects') which would *not* have been produced if the actor's traits or intentions had been different. For instance, if we had to decide whether a new acquaintance was 'shy' or 'unfriendly', there would be no point in just considering behaviour which could be interpreted as a sign of either characteristic.

The important question thus appears to be that of the _distinctiveness_ of the behaviour on the basis of which a perceiver bases his attributions. This notion is developed more explicitly by Kelley (1967, 1971), who assumes that attributions are based on a 'naive version' of J. S. Mill's method of differences: the effect is attributed to that condition which is present when the effect is present and absent when the effect is absent. This is most easily understood if we take as the 'effect' the specific impression that a perceiver has formed concerning an actor on the basis of his behaviour. This effect could be said to lack distinctiveness if the perceiver described almost everyone in the same way, so that if we heard person A described by person B as 'unfriendly', we could assume nothing about person A's real personality if it turned out that person B described everyone as unfriendly. The question of _consensus_ is also important, in that we would be more likely to accept person B's assessment if it were shared by persons C, D, E, etc. In this example, one can thus think of one effect (the impression 'this person is unfriendly') and two sets of conditions (the person being perceived, and the person doing the perceiving). One will attribute the impression to the true characteristics of the target person, if different target persons are perceived differently, and if different perceivers report the same impressions.

Other criteria dealt with by Kelley are those of _consistency over time_, and _consistency over modality_. If continued observation of the target person over time confirms the same impression, it is more likely to be regarded as accurate. On the other hand, if the target person sometimes appears friendly and sometimes unfriendly, his occasional 'unfriendliness' cannot be attributed to a characteristic of 'unfriendliness', but instead to whatever _external_ condition is seen to covary with such changes in behaviour over time. The criterion of consistency over modality can be interpreted literally in terms of sensory modalities, in the case of simple perceptual judgements (e.g., for an object to be round it must both look round and feel round), or metaphorically in terms of the kinds of information one considers about a target person.

Attribution theory therefore assumes that individuals attempt to weigh up different kinds of explanations for behaviour by looking for covariation between presumed causes and effects. For behaviour to be seen as reflecting stable characteristics of the actor, the perceiver has to feel able to assume that others would share his impression, that his impression would be confirmed by varied and repeated observations, and that he might have formed a different impression if the actor had behaved differently.

BASE-RATE PROBABILITIES, STATISTICAL REASONING, AND ATTRIBUTIONS

One of the difficulties that teachers and students often have with attribution theory, particularly as formulated by Kelley (1967, 1971), is that it appears so 'logical' as to be little more than a statement of the obvious. Kelley's 'analysis of variance' model of the attribution process does indeed seem to be a statement of the normative rules describing how statistical inferences *should* be derived from a given data set. However, Kelley certainly would not claim that attributions always, or generally, make optimal use of the information presented, nor that the various criteria of consensus, consistency, and distinctiveness are afforded equal attention. His model, therefore, is intended as, and should be interpreted as, a framework for empirical research rather than a set of empirical predictions.

One of the most important questions which has been asked within this framework is whether individuals in fact attend to consensus information. Much of the impetus for this research comes from the increased attention which is being paid by attribution theorists to work by cognitive psychologists such as Tversky and Kahneman (1974) on statistical reasoning and judgement under uncertainty. As mentioned in Chapter 1, this work shows that base-rate information concerning the probability that a particular event will occur, or that an object or person belongs to a particular category, is largely ignored in favour of a number of simplifying, but misleading, heuristics or biases. In terms of Kelley's model, base-rate information, such as 'Almost all people act in this way in this situation', is information which is relevant to the criterion of consensus. If one extrapolates from the Tversky and Kahneman work, however, such information should have little influence on attributions.

There is evidence which suggests that this is indeed the case. McArthur (1972, 1976) presented subjects with brief verbal descriptions of hypothetical behaviour, varied in order to manipulate levels of consensus, consistency, and distinctiveness, and found that the consensus information had little influence on their ratings. More realistic situations were used by Nisbett and Borgida (1975) and by Nisbett, Borgida, Crandall, and Reed (1976), and the same conclusion was supported. Nisbett and Borgida presented students with detailed descriptions of an experiment designed to determine the willingness of individuals to endure painful shocks, or their promptness at intervening to help another person in an emergency. The students then had to predict how individually identified subjects in the experiment had in fact responded, as well as how they themselves would respond in the same situation. These predictions remained essentially unaffected by 'consensus' information, concerning how the sample of subjects as a whole had supposedly responded in each experiment. In the shock experiment, this information indicated that the most frequent response was to endure the maximum level, and in the helping experiment to fail to help at all. This information should have made the observer-subjects more likely to predict that individually identified subjects would endure higher levels of shock, or be slower in giving help, as compared with a condition in which no consensus information was given. It had no such effect, suggesting that subjects disregarded base-rate probabilities in favour of their intuitive impressions of the individual target cases.

Nisbett *et al.* present additional data to show that those suffering from negative mood states, such as 'Sunday blues', chronic depression, or work anxiety, do *not* have their feelings alleviated by 'consensus' information that their reactions are very typical of people in their situation. They also investigated how students' choices between different course options were affected by either 'abstract' statistical information in the form of mean course evaluations by all students who were in the class the previous term, or 'concrete' information in the form of face-to-face contact with a panel of individual students who had supposedly taken the courses. The face-to-face information had a much stronger effect, even though it was arranged so that the mean evaluation of each course given by the panel was the same as in the 'abstract' condition.

Other researchers have attempted to discover conditions under which base-rate information is more fully utilized. Although Nisbett and Borgida report that telling subjects that the individual target cases were selected at random from the experimental sample had little effect, Wells and Harvey (1977) replicated their experiments with some modifications, and reported greater use of consensus information when subjects were told that the experimental sample as a whole had been randomly chosen so as to be representative of the population. Borgida (1978), however, has argued that even these data can be interpreted as showing that consensus information in underutilized. Work on 'actor-observer differences' (see below) also suggests that base-rate information, combined with assurances about random sampling, may affect the attributions which subjects make for another's behaviour, but has little influence on how subjects explain their own behaviour (Hansen and Donoghue, 1977).

A particularly constructive approach to this issue has been made by Ajzen (1977). He argues that base-rate information tends to be neglected when it has no apparent causal relationship to the attribute being judged or predicted. For example, in an experiment described by Kahneman and Tversky (1973), subjects had to predict whether a given individual was an engineer or a lawyer, having been told that 70 per cent of the sample were engineers and 30 per cent were lawyers, or vice versa. This base-rate information was almost totally ignored when subjects were given brief character sketches of the individual target cases. Ajzen argues that this base-rate information, though statistically informative, was not *causally* relevant, in that the different proportions would not have caused an individual to become a lawyer or engineer. Even the most randomly constructed character description, however, might encourage subjects to look for causal antecedents of occupational choice. To complement the heuristics identified by Tversky and Kahneman (1974), therefore, Ajzen proposes what he calls a 'causality heuristic':

> When asked to make a prediction, people look for factors which cause the behavior or event under consideration. Information that provides evidence concerning the presence or absence of such causal factors in therefore likely to influence predictions . . . . Statistical information is used mainly when no causal information is available (Page 304).

This is supported by evidence that, when asked to predict the academic performance of students, subjects took account of their IQ's and of the number of hours per week spent studying, both of which were intuitively expected to affect academic performance, but ignored information that appeared causally irrelevant, such as amount of money earned in part-time jobs or living distance from campus, even though this last information was presented in a form which would have allowed an equally powerful statistical inference. Also, information about examination pass rates influenced predictions of the performance of a particular candidate, when calculated on the basis of all those taking the examination, but not when based on a non-random sample (cf. Wells and Harvey, 1977). Ajzen interprets the former type of base-rate information as causal, in that it allows inferences to be drawn about the difficulty of the examination, which in turn will be a causal factor influencing each candidate's success.

Ajzen's contribution is especially valuable in reasserting the central and original theme of attribution research—the search for causal explanations. Statistical prediction and causal explanation are not always equivalent, and it is with the latter process that the research to be described in the remainder of this chapter is mainly concerned. One of the features of this process most commonly investigated in experimental studies is the influence of situational factors which might be seen to facilitate or inhibit the behaviour in question. A small sample of these studies is described in the next section.

INTERNAL VS. EXTERNAL ATTRIBUTIONS

An experimental situation commonly used by attribution theorists involves presenting subjects with a description of some behaviour by another ('target') person, together with additional information which implies that the target person stood either to gain, or to lose, by such behaviour, or that he chose freely, or was compelled, to act the way he did. Subjects' assessments of the intentions or character of the target person are then the dependent variable.

An early study within this tradition was that by Jones, Davis, and Gergen (1961), in which student subjects listened to a tape-recording of a simulated job interview, where it was clear which characteristics would, or would not, be desirable in the candidate. They were then asked what they felt the interviewee was 'really like as a person'. When the behaviour shown by the interviewee was such as to imply that he was suitable for the job in question, he received only moderate ratings on the relevant attributes, and subjects expressed little confidence in their judgements. However, when the interviewee responded so as to imply that he was unsuitable for the job, subjects made more extreme and confident inferences, since his behaviour could not be attributed to an attempt to create a favourable impression in terms of the criteria specified by the interviewer. In terms of the Jones and Davis (1965) model, this is an example of more 'correspondent inferences' occurring where the target person's behaviour has fewer 'noncommon effects', i.e., where there would be little reason for him to behave in such a way if it did not correspond to what he was 'really' like. All this, of course, assumes that the candidate was seen as supposedly trying to get the job, and Messick and Reeder (1972) have shown, not too surprisingly, that the results of this study can be reversed if subjects are led to assume that the candidate is trying to avoid getting the job.

A related procedure is involved in studies where subjects are presented with statements about some controversial issue made by the target person, and are asked to infer the target person's true attitude, in the light of additional information concerning the circumstances under which such statements were supposedly elicited. Jones and Harris (1967) report two experiments using the issue of attitudes towards Cuba, and a third using the issue of segregation, in which the target person was supposedly either free to choose what side of the issue to support, or was instructed to defend a specific point of view (by a course instructor, or as part of a debating contest). As predicted, the target person's real opinions were seen as being more in line with those he expressed under the former, 'free-choice', conditions. Even under 'no-choice' conditions, however, there was a tendency to assume some degree of correspondence between real and expressed attitudes, particularly when the expressed attitudes were in line with subjects' prior expectations. This may be thought of as an example of what Heider (1958, page 54) meant when he talked of behaviour 'engulfing the field'.

Jones, Worchel, Goethals, and Grumet (1971) followed up this study with an experiment in which subjects were presented with an essay that was either strongly favourable, moderately favourable, moderately unfavourable, or strongly unfavourable towards the legalization of marijuana, supposedly either by someone who had been allowed a free choice over what position to support, or had been specifically instructed to write on the side he did. Subjects were also given aditional information about the writer's supposed attitudes on other issues, so constructed as to give an impression of someone with clearly radical or conservative views, which could be expected to generalize to the issue of marijuana. The results for the strongly favourable and strongly unfavourable essays were in line with those of the Jones and Harris (1967) study. The moderate essays were seen as corresponding to the writer's real opinion under 'free choice' conditions, but a moderately favourable essay written in response to instructions calling for a favourable essay was seen as reflecting a moderately unfavourable attitude, and a moderately unfavourable essay in response to instructions calling for an unfavourable essay was seen as reflecting a moderately favourable attitude. Apparently, these moderate essays were seen as a sign of 'foot-dragging' under 'no choice' conditions.

A more subtle manipulation of apparent freedom of choice was involved in a study by Kruglanski and Cohen (1973), in which subjects were presented with an essay arguing either for, or against, the broad issue of cooperation 'in human affairs'. This essay had supposedly been written in response to a request by a survey worker that allowed the writer free choice as to whether to argue for cooperation or competition, but at the same time made it clear that an essay supporting one side of the issue (depending on the condition) would be preferred 'because we are particularly interested in the kinds of argument people bring up on this side of the issue'. Subjects thus rated either a pro-cooperation or a pro-competition essay which either conformed to, or deviated from, the preferences supposedly stated by the survey worker, and they were also provided with background information about the target person which would lead them to expect either a pro-cooperation or a pro-competition essay to be 'in character'. When the essay was 'in character', it was assumed to reflect the writer's true opinion, regardless of the survey worker's preference. When the essay was 'out of character', it was more likely to be seen as reflecting the writer's true opinion when it went against the survey worker's preference.

The persuasiveness of a message has also been shown to depend on the attributions subjects make about the communicator and the situational constraints under which the message is delivered. From an attributional perspective, the perceived truth, and hence persuasibility, of a message should depend on its content being seen as 'caused' by external reality, rather than by the personal biases of the communicator or his intended audience. The less predictable a message is from these latter factors, therefore, the more persuasive it should be.

Support for this hypothesis was found by Eagly and Chaiken (1975) and by Eagly, Wood, and Chaiken (1978). In the first of these studies, students listened to a recorded interview, supposedly with a university employee, who was made to seem either attractive (pro-student) or unattractive (anti-student), and who then argued in favour of either a desirable or undesirable attitudinal position. Ratings indicated that the more attractive communicator was seen as more likely to support the desirable position, and the unattractive comunicator the undesirable position. Although the more attractive communicator produced much more attitude change when the advocated position was undesirable, this difference in persuasiveness was eliminated when the position was desirable. In the second study, students read a transcript of a defence of an environmentalist position in front of what was supposedly a pro-business or pro-environment audience, and were given information about the communicator suggesting that his own background was pro-business or pro-environment. Again, support was found for the prediction that the message would be more persuasive when it went against the subjects' prior expectations, regardless of whether these expectations were based on the presumed bias of the communicator, of his audience, or of both combined.

ATTRIBUTION OF RESPONSIBILITY

The manipulation of perceived freedom of choice has also been central to those studies which have looked at attributions of responsibility for behaviour. Much of this research has stemmed from Walster's (1966) hypothesis that the more serious the consequences of a person's behaviour, the more likely it is that he will be seen as 'responsible', even if these consequences were unintended. Walster found support for this prediction by asking subjects to make judgements about the central character in a story involving a car accident. Later research, however, has generally failed to confirm the simple relationship predicted by Walster (Shaver, 1970a,b; Shaw and Skolnick, 1971; Walster, 1967), and, as pointed out by Wortman and Linder (1973), there has generally been insufficient care taken to unconfound severity and perceived likelihood of consequences.

A more general criticism of the attribution of responsibility literature is that the dependent variables (e.g., responses to questions like, 'To what extent is this person responsible?') are an uncertain mixture of causal inference and moral judgement, and differences in response may largely reflect differences in the sense in which the experimenter's questions are interpreted under different conditions. Fishbein and Ajzen (1973) point out that researchers in this area (with the exception of Shaw and Sulzer, 1964) have often ignored the distinctions recognized by Heider (1958) between different 'levels' of responsibility. At the first level, a person might be said to be responsible for all effects with which he was associated (*Association*); at the next level, only for effects he was instrumental in producing (*Commission*); at the next level, only if he could have foreseen the effects (*Foreseeability*); at the next level, only if the effects were foreseen and intended (*Intentionality*); and, at the final level, only if his intended behaviour was not constrained by external factors beyond his control (*Justification*). Just asking subjects to say whether a target person was responsible, without stating the level of responsibility with which one is concerned, is to ask a question which different subjects are likely to interpret in different ways. A person could be responsible for the effects of a car accident at the level of commission, but presumably not at the level of intentionality, and differences in response may simply reflect differences in the level chosen. In most of these studies, there is no implication that the consequences were *intended* by the target person. What seems to be mainly at issue is whether the consequences could have been foreseen and prevented. Thus, any value that these studies have for an understanding of attribution processes is with respect to inferences concerning the knowledge and ability of the target person, not inferences about intentions.

In spite of these conceptual difficulties, an attempt to impose some order on the attribution of responsibility literature has been made by Brewer (1977). Starting from what she calls an 'information-processing' approach, she suggests that attribution of responsibility (AR) is related to just two independent subjective probability estimates: 1. the *prior expectancy* (PE) that the outcome would have occurred anyway without any action by the target person, and 2. the *congruence* (C) between the action and its outcome, i.e., the expectation that the action would lead to the outcome without any prior knowledge of the situation. AR is assumed to be inversely related to PE, but directly related to C.

Walster's (1966) findings can be fitted into this interpretation, if it is assumed that the more severe consequences had a lower PE. The failures to replicate Walster's findings may also be interpreted, albeit *post hoc*, if it is assumed that different outcomes varied not only in PE but also in C. For example, part of what Shaw and Skolnick (1971) found was that a description of a low PE positive outcome led to a *lower* AR than a higher PE positive outcome (respectively a major discovery or a pleasant smell accidentally produced by a chemistry student). It seems plausible that there would have been an even larger difference in C between these outcomes, with the former being seen as a very unlikely result of the student's behaviour.

Regarding the issue of levels of responsibility, Brewer treats the levels not as qualitatively different, but simply as 'determinants of judgements made along a continuous dimension, that of the degree of congruence between action and outcome' (page 60). Essentially, the more intended the consequences, the higher should be C and hence AR. However, Brewer does not really deal with the Fishbein and Ajzen (1973) point that subjects may give different AR ratings depending on the level of responsibility they *consider relevant*. This implies that subjects may require different 'threshold levels' of C before making positive AR ratings, depending, for example, on their interpretations of the experimenter's instructions. At the very least, this seems to require a modification of Brewer's position.

Perhaps the crux of the difficulty, though, is Brewer's attempt to equate 'responsibility judgements with *cause*, rather than praise or blame' (page 63). *If* all that subjects were asked in these studies was whether the actor 'caused' the outcome, Brewer's analysis might be perfectly adequate. However, subjects are asked to assign *responsibility*, and so what matters is not how responsibility is defined in terms of an information-processing model, but how the concept is used by the subjects. The fact is that the concept of responsibility, as ordinarily used, is *not* completely synonymous with causality, and *does* carry evaluative connotations of praise and blame. It is precisely for this reason that attribution of responsibility can be so difficult to interpret.

Another problem with such studies is that the stimulus information presented to subjects is typically not behaviour *per se*, but an *account* of behaviour constructed by the experimenter. That subjects are able to pick out the explanation implicit in such accounts does not by itself entail that they would produce the same explanation in an actual interaction. The conceptual merit of attribution theory in comparison to earlier approaches to person perception is its emphasis on the role of the perceiver as an active interpreter of events. The theory makes its best contributions where subjects are actually involved in the situations which they attempt to explain, and are not mere receptacles for second-hand accounts.

SELF-ATTRIBUTION

The central tenet of attribution theory—that interpersonal descriptions are the outcome of an attempt to explain observable behaviour, applies just as much to the descriptions one may make about oneself as those one may make about others. The information on the basis of which we make self-descriptions may be somewhat different from that to which we have access when judging others, but, according to attribution theory, the processes of inference are essentially the same. In other words, the same criteria of consensus and distinctiveness, the same assumption of a trade-off relationship between internal and external factors, should operate when we are judging ourselves as when we are judging others.

Some of the earliest work relevant to this hypothesis was concerned with the self-attribution of emotion. One might suppose that we 'know' how to describe our own emotional states simply through some process of introspection, or that emotional states are a direct result of internal physiological conditions, unmediated by any cognitive interpretation, but the results of a number of studies have shown that situational factors can influence how we choose to describe the way we feel. The classic study in this field is that of Schachter and Singer (1962), in which subjects had to fill out a questionnaire containing a number of potentially offensive questions in the presence of another person (supposedly another subject, but in fact a confederate of the experimenters) who either behaved increasingly angrily as the session progressed, or behaved in an increasingly lighthearted fashion, practising basketball shots with balls of paper, and such like. Cross-cutting this manipulation, some subjects had been injected with epinephrine (a synthetic form of adrenalin), a drug which causes general physiological arousal, but were *not* led to expect that they would feel aroused. Another group received the same injection, but were forewarned about its effects, and a control group received a placebo injection. Subjects in the first group behaved more emotionally than those in the other two groups, but the form of their behaviour, and the way in which they labelled their emotions was determined by the behaviour of the other 'subject'. When he behaved angrily, they did so also, and when he behaved in a lighthearted fashion, so did they. Schachter and Singer interpret these results as showing that subjects labelled their emotional states in terms of the situational cues provided by the other 'subject's' behaviour—they were aroused because of the offensive or farcical nature of the task, and hence either angry or euphoric—but only when they could not explain their arousal as the normal expected result of the injection which they had received. Subjects who were told to expect to feel aroused could *explain* their arousal as a drug effect without having to label it as anger or euphoria.

The design of this study unfortunately fails to control for an alternative interpretation; namely, that, provided the stooge's behaviour is seen as a genuine reflection of his mood, what is happening is a kind of 'contagion' effect, whereby the subject's own mood is *directly* influenced by the other's behaviour. Such contagion could well be enhanced by physiological arousal, but this does not mean that the subject is necessarily using the other's behaviour as a cue to help explain his own arousal.

This distinction between internal (physiological) and situational cues has remained an important theme in Schachter's subsequent work. Applied to the problem of obesity, it is used to generate the prediction that obese people overeat because situational cues, such as the availability of food, the sight of other people eating, or the passage of time (Nisbett, 1968; Schachter and Gross, 1968) are more likely to make them feel hungry (i.e., label their emotional state as 'hunger') than in the case of less obese people, whose appetites tend to be more regulated by physiological cues. Thus, fat Jews were found to be more likely to fast on Yom Kippur, and the less exposure they had to food-relevant cues during this period (specifically, the longer the time they spent in the synagogue), the less unpleasant they found the fasting. As another example, overweight pilots working for Air France were less likely than those who were not overweight to complain about 'jet-lag' disrupting their eating habits, suggesting that 'internal clocks' were less important in comparison to 'local time' as cues for eating in the case of the former rather than the latter group of pilots (Goldman, Jaffa, and Schachter, 1972). Tom and Rucker (1975) also found that obese students in comparison with those of normal weight ate more crackers, and intended to buy more crackers, after viewing slides of food dishes as opposed to slides of scenic views. Also, obese subjects ate *more*, and intended to buy more, if they had been 'preloaded' with ham sandwiches at the start of the experiment than if they had not eaten, the reverse being true for those of normal weight.

More recently, Schachter, Silverstein, Kozlowski, Perlick, Herman, and Liebling (1977) have suggested a contributory reason for the fact that many cigarette smokers claim that smoking 'steadies their nerves' by arguing first that heavy smokers tend to regulate their smoking so as to maintain a relatively constant level of nicotine in their bloodstream (Russell, 1976), and second that stress alters the pH balance of the urine so that more nicotine is excreted (without reaching the brain). In stressful situations, therefore, the heavy smoker will attempt to compensate for the resultant fall in blood-nicotine level by smoking more, but this change in behaviour will be interpreted as a means of coping with the stressful situations, rather than a compensation for loss of nicotine. This, of course, does not preclude the possibility that nicotine may have pharmacological effects of the kind which smokers claim, so that any such misattributions may simply enhance the perceived effects of a cigarette.

Other studies have used false feedback concerning a person's state of arousal as a means of influencing self-attributed emotion. Valins (1966) showed male students film slides of a number of *Playboy* nudes, while they were connected to an apparatus that supposedly amplified the sound of their own heart-beat. In fact, the sound of the heart beat was pre-recorded so that each subject appeared to hear his heart-beat change on half the slides (determined at random), remaining constant on the other half. Subjects tended to judge the nudes that had apparently produced a change in heart-beat as more attractive, and these tended to be those most frequently chosen when subjects were told that they could take some away to keep for themselves. In a later study, Valins (1972) showed that such preferences persisted even after the full details of the experimental deception were disclosed, interpreting this finding as implying that subjects looked harder at those slides which produced an apparent change in heart-beat to discover what was so special about them!

Another way of influencing self-attributions of emotion was employed by Laird (1973), who recruited subjects for an experiment on 'the activity of facial muscles under various conditions', attached dummy electrodes to different parts of their faces, and asked them to hold their facial muscles in certain fixed positions when viewing a number of pictures. After the presentation of each picture, subjects had to report their emotional reactions. In fact, the fixed positions in which subjects had to hold their facial muscles were a smile and a frown, though the words 'smile' and 'frown' were not used when instructing subjects to adopt either expression. Subjects tended to report that they felt happier when they had been smiling and angrier when they had been frowning, and in another experiment reported finding cartoons more amusing when they were smiling rather than frowning.

ATTRIBUTION FOR SUCCESS AND FAILURE

A question of major theoretical importance for attribution theory, and of great practical relevance in the fields of education and of clinical psychology, is that of how people explain the achievement, or lack of achievement, shown by themselves and others. If one succeeds, is it because the task was easy, because one was lucky, because of superior skill, or because of extra effort? The answer is likely to affect how much personal credit one should be given for such success, and whether one would expect such success to be repeated.

The question of whether success or failure should be internally or externally attributed is basic to social learning theory approaches to personality (Rotter, Chance, and Phares, 1972). According to Rotter (1966) individuals differ in the extent to which they expect 'reinforcements' to occur, as a function of their own behaviour ('internal control'), or as a function of luck or forces beyond their personal control ('external control'). The I-E scale devised by Rotter to measure individuals' positions on this dimension of 'locus of control' consists of pairs of statements such as, 'Becoming a success is a matter of hard work, luck has little or nothing to do with it' *vs.* 'Getting a good job depends mainly on being in the right place at the right time', subjects having to indicate which statement in each pair is closer to their own opinion. (In this example, endorsement of the first alternative would be taken as indicative of an internal orientation.)

Although attempts have been made to develop comparable measures for use with younger subjects (e.g., Crandall, Katkovsky, and Crandall, 1965; Gammage, 1975), most of the large literature on locus of control has used college students as subjects (Lefcourt, 1972). The most common research strategy has been to look for differences between 'internals' and 'externals' in their responses on a variety of judgement and performance tasks. For example, Jones, Worchel, Goethals, and Grumet (1971) found that 'internals' were more sensitive than 'externals' to whether essays on a controversial issue had been supposedly elicited under free choice or no choice conditions, when asked to assess the real attitudes of the writers of the essays. With very few exceptions (e.g., McArthur, 1970), there has been little attempt to relate changes in an individual's generalized expectancies for locus of control to specific learning experiences. Mirels (1970) has since disputed the unidimensionality of the I-E scale, distinguishing items concerned with personal control from those concerned with potentiality for influence in a political context. There have also been attempts to identify 'defensive externals' who adopt external attitudes so as to protect themselves from the implications of accepting personal responsibility for failure, but may be rather similar to internals in other respects, such as motivation for academic achievement (Prociuk and Breen, 1975).

A closely related notion is that of 'learned helplessness'. The origin of this notion can be seen in an experiment by Seligman and Maier (1967), who found that dogs who had received a series of shocks from which they were unable to escape, later failed to learn a simple operant response for avoiding shock in a different situation. The interpretation is that the dogs develop an expectancy that responding will be ineffective and so fail to initiate new behaviours that may lead to the termination of shock, or, if they make an occasional response that turns off the shock, fail to repeat it. Seligman has since argued (1972, 1975) that this situation may be analogous to depression in humans: an inability to respond effectively may reflect a learned expectancy that any response will be ineffective.

Hiroto and Seligman (1975) found that exposing human subjects to inescapable aversive stimuli, or presenting them with insoluble discrimination problems, produced deficits in subsequent performance at tasks involving avoidance behaviour or anagram solving, analogous to the 'learned helplessness' effects found with dogs. Benson and Kennelly (1976) have pointed out that these results show only that uncontrollable *negative* reinforcements can produce learned helplessness in man. In a modified replication of the Hiroto and Seligman study, they failed to find deficits in performance following uncontrollable *positive* reinforcements, which, according to Seligman, should produce similar feelings of helplessness.

Seligman's approach implies that one way of 'curing' depression may be to lead individuals to make different kinds of attributions for failure and success. For example, Dweck (1975) found that, among a group of extremely 'helpless' schoolchildren, aged 8 to 13 years, those who were given only success experiences continued to show a deterioration in performance after failure on a later task, whereas those who were taught instead to take responsibility for failure and attribute it to their own lack of effort were better able to cope with later failure. In the light of the Benson and Kennelly data, one would not confidently attribute the children's helplessness to earlier experiences of success not 'earned' by performance, but this study at least suggests that such experiences do not help alleviate helplessness, once it has been learned.

Klein, Fencil-Morse, and Seligman (1976) showed that patterns of behaviour similar to those shown by depressives could be produced in subjects who underwent the sort of learning experiences assumed to underly the development of depression. In other words, helplessness can be taught as well as learned. Depressed and non-depressed college students were recruited to take part in a problem-solving experiment. In the first phase, subjects performed a discrimination task consisting of a series of either four soluble or four insoluble problems, a control group receiving no problems. Among those who received insoluble problems, some received no instructions on how to attribute their failure, some were told, 'most people are able to get three or four of the problems correct' ('internal attribution for failure' instructions), and the remainder were told, 'the problems are very difficult and almost no one has been able to solve them' ('external attribution for failure' instructions). All subjects were then given an anagram task, at which depressed subjects performed worse than non-depressed subjects, and those who had been given insoluble problems in the previous phase performed worse than those who had been given soluble problems. The performance of non-depressed subjects given insoluble problems in the previous phase resembled that of depressives who had been in the control or soluble problem groups. The instructions on how to attribute their failure on the insoluble problems had little effect on non-depressed subjects. However, depressives given instructions which allowed them to attribute their failure externally to the difficulty of the task performed much better than depressives who were given insoluble problems but were led to expect that the problems would be easy, or were given no such instructions.

Considered simply in terms of the internal-external distinction, these last two studies might appear to contradict one another. In the study by Dweck, learned helplessness appeared to be alleviated by attributing failure to an internal factor (lack of effort), whereas in the Klein *et al.*, study, it was alleviated by attributing failure to the external factor of task difficulty. Weiner (1970; Weiner and Kukla, 1970), however, has pointed out that an equally important distinction, cross-cutting that between internal and external factors, is that between causes which are presumed to be stable over time, and those that are presumed to be unstable. Thus, a person's ability would be an internal factor stable over time, the amount of effort expended on a task would be an internal but unstable factor, the difficulty of the task would be both external and stable, and luck would be external and unstable. The difference between the two internal factors, ability and effort, is important when evaluating other people's performance. Weiner and Kukla (1970) found that subjects, instructed to play the role of school-teachers giving rewards and punishments for pupils' examination performance, rewarded pupils more for greater effort than for greater ability, and where pupils of different ability achieved the same level of performance, the one with less ability received the greater reward.

In the context of attributions for one's *own* success or failure, Weiner incorporates these distinctions to revise Atkinson's (1957) concept of achievement motivation. According to Atkinson, the amount of 'pride' obtained from the attainment of some goal is related to the subjective difficulty of the task, so that success at a more difficult task leads to a greater sense of achievement. In terms of the attributional model of achievement motivation (Weiner and Kukla, 1970; Weiner, Frieze, Reed, Rest, and Rosenbaum, 1971), what is crucial is the degree of perceived personal responsibility for success or failure. Thus individuals high in achievement motivation are assumed to be attracted to achievement-related activities, which allow the attribution of success to ability and effort; persist in the face of failure, which they tend to attribute to lack of effort rather than ability; select tasks of intermediate difficulty (since too easy a task will give no sense of achievement, but too difficult a task is likely to lead to failure); and tend to try hard, in accordance with their assumption that success is at least partly a function of effort. By comparison, individuals low in achievement motivation are assumed to be less attracted to achievement-related activities, since they would tend to attribute success externally even if they succeeded; give up in the face of failure, which they are more likely to attribute to lack of ability than to lack of effort; select either extremely easy or extremely difficult tasks, since these provide the least information on which to base a self-evaluation; and tend not to try hard, since success, particularly at the kinds of tasks they choose, is assumed to be largely unrelated to effort.

In contrast to Atkinson, therefore, who defines achievement motivation as 'capacity for experiencing pride in accomplishment' (1964, page 214), Weiner distinguishes the affective component of achievement motivation (e.g., pride in success or shame at failure) from expectancy for future success or failure. Whereas, the affective component is seen to depend primarily on attributions to internal vs. external causes, expectancy is seen to depend primarily on attributions to stable vs. unstable causes. A number of studies have lent support to this two-dimensional interpretation where attributions for one's own success or failure are concerned (Meyer, 1970; Weiner, Heckhausen, Meyer, and Cook, 1972; McMahan, 1973). In addition, the attributions to stable or unstable causes which others make for their success or failure can affect one's own expectancy of success on a similar task (Fontaine, 1974; Pancer and Eiser, 1977).

In the context of attributions for failure, Weiner and Sierad (1975) argue that high achievement needs lead to an ascription of failure to lack of effort, which leads in turn to an increase in performance (greater effort). By comparison, low achievement needs lead to an ascription of failure to a lack of ability, which leads in turn to a decrease in performance. In support of this interpretation, they report an experiment in which subjects received a placebo pill before performing a task involving the substitution of symbols for a group of numbers. The pill was described as likely to interfere with hand-eye coordination, and the experiment was explained as being concerned with assessing the extent of this interference. Subjects were then randomly assigned either to a 'pill' or 'no pill' (control) condition, unless they objected to taking the pill. All subjects who refused to take the pill were assigned to the control condition but excluded from subsequent analysis. Subjects had previously completed a measure of individual differences in achievement motivation (Mehrabian, 1969), and on the basis of this measure were divided into those 'low' and 'high' in achievement motivation. As predicted, those low in achievement motivation performed better in the 'pill' than the 'no pill' condition (since they did not have to attribute their failure to lack of ability), whereas those high in achievement motivation performed worse in the 'pill' condition (since they did not have to attribute their failure to lack of effort).

Individual differences in achievement motivation are thus assumed to influence behaviour through the kinds of attributions which individuals make for success and failure. Also, from a similar standpoint, learned helplessness is a function of attributing failure to lack of ability. If one attributes failure internally to lack of effort (as the children in Dweck's study were taught to do), one can expect improved achievement by trying harder. If one attributes failure to task difficulty, one can still expect success at easier tasks, and if the task is portrayed as so difficult that most people like oneself would fail at it (as in the Klein *et al.* study), failure need not be attributed to lack of ability. The essence of learned helplessness is not just the internal attribution of failure, but attribution of failure to a factor which the person feels he can do nothing to change.

SELF-SERVING ATTRIBUTIONS

Research of this kind is also important when it comes to evaluating the assumption, originally made by Heider (1958), that, for an event to be seen as attributable to a given reason, 'the reason has to fit the wishes of the person'—in other words, individuals generally appear to be biased towards explaining events in a manner congruent with a positive self-evaluation. This assumption is in accordance with research on cognitive consistency theories of attitudes, and also social judgement, but has in fact received only qualified support from studies more directly within the attribution theory tradition. A study frequently cited as support for Heider's assumption is that by Johnson, Feigenbaum, and Weiby (1964), who examined the attributions made by student teachers in a simulated teaching situation. When a child performed badly at a task over two sets of trials, the student teachers blamed the child and denied personal responsibility for his lack of improvement, but when he improved from the first set to the second, they saw this improvement as due to the success of their teaching. Schopler and Layton (1972) found a similar effect when student subjects evaluated the simulated performance of a fellow-student. Subjects were more likely to see themselves as having influenced the other's behaviour when his performance improved over two sets of trials, and also when it remained at a high level over both sets of trials, as compared with a condition where the other's performance started at a low level, and failed to show improvement.

Reviewing these and other similar studies, Miller and Ross (1975) argue that it is important to distinguish between 'self-protection' effects, or attributions which involve denying responsibility for negative consequences, and 'self-enhancement' effects, or attributions which involve claiming responsibility for positive consequences. Miller and Ross conclude that there is only minimal evidence in the literature for self-protection effects. Schopler and Layton (1972), for instance, included a condition in which the target person's performance started at a high level, and then deteriorated over the two sets of trials. There is no evidence that subjects in this condition were inclined to deny responsibility for the target person's decline in performance. The evidence for self-enhancing attributions is more consistent with Heider's assumption, but even here, according to Miller and Ross, there is no general need to favour a motivational orientation. Kelley's (1967, 1971) formulation of attribution theory assumes that individuals will attribute effects to causes which are seen to covary with changes in such effects. In other words, a change in the target person's behaviour over time is likely to be attributed to a factor which also is seen to change over time. In studies such as those by Johnson et al. (1964), the influence of the subjects' instruction of the target person would be assumed to increase over time, and hence would covary with any increase (or decrease) in the person's performance. Conversely, if the target person's performance shows no change (for the better or the worse), Kelley's covariation principle would imply that subjects should look for a cause which could be assumed to remain constant over time, such as the target person's lack of ability.

Bradley (1978), on the other hand, has argued against the 'non-motivational' interpretation proposed by Miller and Ross. He points out that studies which show evidence of self-serving biases in attribution use situations where subjects' performance is publicly observable, and hence where one might expect motives of self-esteem maintenance to be operative. Emphasizing subjects' observability (i.e., increasing their 'objective self-awareness'—see Chapter 6) can increase their tendency to make self-serving attributions. This was shown by Federoff and Harvey (1976) who had subjects attempt to give therapy to another person, the success or failure of which was indicated by supposed feedback concerning the person's state of muscular relaxation. Subjects were more likely to see themselves as responsible for the outcome of the therapy when they appeared to succeed in relaxing the client than when they failed, but only in a 'high self-awareness' condition in which they administered the therapy in front of a camera.

Why should the tendency to disclaim responsibility for failure be less consistent than the tendency to claim responsibility for success? Bradley's suggestion is that subjects realize that their own 'interpretative activities' are also being observed and evaluated, and so they will be less likely to deny responsibility for failure if such a denial would appear implausible. If there is a plausible alternative reason for failure, responsibility may be denied. Thus Snyder, Stephan, and Rosenfield (1976) report that players in a competitive game attributed their outcomes more to bad luck if they lost, and more to skill or effort if they won. However, subjects may sometimes attribute their failure to bad luck even in conditions where such denials are barely plausible, for example, when one repeatedly fails at a task at which others succeed (Stevens and Jones, 1976).

Rather less direct evidence of self-enhancement comes from studies concerned with the issue of how individuals evaluate others who yield to their point of view in an argument. Cialdini (1971) and Lombardo, Weiss, and Buchanan (1972) produce evidence that individuals report greater liking for others whom they manage to persuade to come round to their own point of view. Also, when an attempt is made to hold subjects' liking for the other person constant, subjects tend to rate someone who yields to their point of view as more intelligent than someone who does not, whereas observers of the subjects' attempts at persuasion rate those who yield to persuasion as *less* intelligent than those who do not (Cialdini, Braver, and Lewis, 1974).

Cialdini and Mirels (1976) have examined such effects in relation to individual differences in attributional style. Student subjects were classified as high or low in ' personal control' on the basis of their scores on the nine items of Rotter's (1966) I-E scale which were differentiated by Mirels' (1970) factor analysis. Those subjects who were high in ' personal control' (responded more ' internally' on these items) rated a target person who yielded to their arguments as more intelligent and attractive, and one who did not yield as less intelligent and attractive, than did observers of their influence attempts. However, for subjects low in personal control, these differences were completely reversed.

ACTOR-OBSERVER DIFFERENCES

Another important source of ' bias' in the attribution process relates to the differences between attributions made by ' actors' and by ' observers '. According to Jones and Nisbett (1971, page 80), 'there is a pervasive tendency for actors to attribute their actions to situational requirements, whereas observers tend to attribute the same actions to stable personal dispositions.' Put another way, one is less inclined to account for one's own behaviour in terms of underlying personality traits, and more inclined to see oneself as responding to circumstantial factors, whereas one is more likely to see other people's behaviour as emanating from aspects of their personality than as contingent upon transient features of the situation.

In support of this hypothesis, Nisbett, Caputo, Legant, and Maracek (1973) asked people to predict the future behaviour of subjects whom they observed responding to a request to volunteer for a social service task. These observers were relatively willing to generalize from what they saw to predict how the subjects (actors) would react to a similar request in the future, thus making an implicit assumption that the actors' behaviour was indicative of stable dispositions. The actors themselves, when asked to make the same prediction about their *own* behaviour, made no such assumption of cross-situational consistency. In addition, Nisbett *et al.* found that students tended to ascribe more personality trait descriptions to others than to themselves, and that when asked to account for their own, and their best friend's, choice of girl friend, they would tend to concentrate on the girl friend's attributes when considering their own choice, and on their best friend's attributes when describing his choice. The same bias was observed in accounts which students gave for their choice of major course subject: comparatively speaking, one chooses one's own course because of what the course has to offer, whereas other students choose their courses because of the kind of people they are.

Differences between attributions of freedom made by actors and observers have also been reported by Gurwitz and Panciera (1975). Their experiment involved testing subjects in pairs, with one subject in each pair taking the role of a 'teacher' and the other subject taking the role of a 'student'. Depending on the 'student's' performance on an anagrams task, the 'teacher' either rewarded him by giving him money, or punished him by taking money away. Both 'teachers' and 'students' viewed their partner's behaviour during the experiment as more indicative of their behaviour in general than they viewed their own, and the 'students' saw the 'teachers' as having more freedom than the 'teachers' saw themselves. Similarly, Harvey, Harris, and Barnes (1975) employed a situation in which subjects either had to play the part of a 'teacher', supposedly having to give mild electric shocks to another person (in fact an accomplice of the experimenters) whenever he made a mistake on a paired-associate learning task, or alternatively were assigned to an observer condition, in which case, they sat alongside the 'teacher' and observed his behaviour. The more the apparent distress caused by these punishments, the greater was the amount of freedom and responsibility attributed by the observers to the 'teacher'. However, the 'teachers' attributed less freedom and responsibility to themselves, the more severe the apparent consequences of their behaviour.

The Jones and Nisbett hypothesis was also supported by West, Gunn, and Chernicky (1975), who employed what must rank as one of the most extreme forms of deception in the history of social psychology. A random sample of criminology students were approached by the experimenter, 'who was known to most of the subjects as a local private investigator', with news that he had 'a project you might be interested in'. All those approached agreed to a later meeting to discuss the project, which in fact turned out to be a proposal to burgle a local advertising firm, for which the experimenter had produced elaborate plans. Subjects were then each given one of four different justifications to entice them to agree to take part in the burglary. In the first two conditions, they were told that the burglary was to be committed for a government department (the Inland Revenue Service) for the purpose of microfilming an allegedly illegal set of accounting records which would provide evidence of a large tax fraud by the firm. The microfilm was supposedly required so that a search warrant and subpoena could be obtained and the original records seized. In the first condition, subjects were told that the government would guarantee their immunity from prosecution if they were arrested, while, in the second condition, they were given no such promise of immunity. In the third condition, they were told that another local advertising firm had offered $8000 for a copy of a set of designs prepared by the first firm, and that their own fee would be $2000 if they participated. Finally, in the fourth condition, subjects were told that the only purpose of the burglary was to see if the plans the experimenter had devised would work, and that nothing would in fact be stolen.

Subjects were told that the burglary team would consist of four people, including themselves, the experimenter, a confederate present at the meeting, and a lock-and-safe expert, not present at the meeting, but described as having an extensive background in military intelligence. Subjects were then shown elaborate plans for the burglary, and were encouraged to ask questions (most of these were concerned with technical details of the plan). They were then asked to come to a final planning meeting at the experimenter's office. If they refused, they were asked to reconsider their decision, and if they refused again, the experiment was terminated. The confederate recorded the subject's decision to take part or not, and his expressed rationale for doing so. The percentages of subjects agreeing to take part in each condition were 45 per cent, 5 per cent, 20 per cent, and 10 per cent respectively. Clearly, the promise of immunity from prosecution had a powerful effect.

These results were then compared with the responses made by a group of 238 psychology students, who were each given a mimeographed booklet which described one of the four conditions in great detail, and were asked to say how many students out of 100 they thought would agree to participate (this yielded no significant differences between conditions), and whether they themselves would do so, responses being in the form 'Yes', 'No', or 'Maybe'. West et al. take both 'Yes' and 'Maybe' responses as indicative of self-estimated compliance, and report rates of 28·1 per cent, 14·0 per cent, 12·2 per cent, and 18·2 per cent for the four conditions respectively. In addition, subjects were asked to give reasons for why another student might have agreed or refused to participate after hearing the proposal. The reasons attributed by these subjects (observers) were then compared with the rationales offered by those who had actually been confronted with the proposal (actors), and were coded in terms of whether they emphasized the attitudes or personality of the actor, or in terms of an environmental factor, such as the justification or inducement given. As predicted, observers made more dispositional attributions than did the actors themselves.

West et al. present their study as relevant to an understanding of phenomena such as the Watergate break-in, which sections of the American press attributed to such factors as, 'the paranoid style of the Nixon administration, and the recruitment of an amoral staff of non-political administrators'. In other words, such 'observers' of the event sought to explain it in terms of the internal characteristics of those who perpetrated it. On the other hand, members of the Nixon administration, the 'actors', were more inclined to see the break-in as necessitated by circumstances. The results of this study imply that normally law-abiding citizens may be more likely than might be supposed to commit illegal activities in the name of a government agency when offered the safeguard of immunity from prosecution. Cook (1975) rightly draws attention to the serious ethical considerations involved in this study, since subjects were not simply asked to indulge in some mildly counter-attitudinal behaviour, but actually enticed into what, for all they knew, was a conspiracy to commit a criminal offence. Whether the 'real-life relevance' of these results justifies the means by which they were obtained, is a matter of opinion.

If the research of West *et al.* implies that actor-observer differences in attribution can occur outside the experimental laboratory, a much more experimentally oriented study by Storms (1973) contributes more directly to an understanding of the cognitive processes underlying the phenomenon. Before labelling actor-observer differences as a manifestation of a 'bias' with a presumably motivational rather than rational basis, it needs to be asked whether actors and observers do in fact make their inferences on the basis of the same information. At the simplest level, the actor knows more about how he has behaved in the past in similar and dissimilar situations than does the observer, who has typically nothing else to go on apart from what the actor's present behaviour implies if taken in isolation. The actor is therefore in a far better position to assess the extent of any covariation between his own behaviour and features of the external situation, and hence make a situational rather than an internal dispositional inference. By comparison, the observer has to take what he sees in the here and now as being typical. (For, also, if it were atypical, why should the experimenter be interested in his impression of the actor's personality?) In addition, and it is this aspect of a difference in available information to which Storms' experiment is more directly addressed, the actor cannot see himself in the same literal, physical, sense that he appears to others. Actors see the situation as more important because it is the situation which they are looking at, whereas observers see the actor himself as more important since he is the focus of their attention. The same behaviour, therefore, will be perceived from different physical perspectives by actors and observers.

Storms was able to overcome this physical constraint by the simple device of videotaping two-person conversations simultaneously through two separate cameras, positioned so as to record the interactions from the physical perspectives of each of the two participants. When the actor was allowed to view the recording of the conversation from what had been the other person's (the observer's) orientation, he became more 'internal' in his attributions to himself—in fact even more than the observer had been. Similarly, when observers viewed the conversations from the actors' orientation, they attached far more importance to the situation in explaining the actors' behaviour. Another study by Regan and Totten (1975), which also used videotape recording of a two-person conversation (though with less clear-cut results as a function of a different kind of camera-position manipulation), managed to elicit more situational and less dispositional attributions from independent observers who were not themselves participants in the conversation, but were instructed to 'empathize' with one of the participants in particular.

Taylor and Fiske (1975, 1978) have also shown that those participants in an interaction who are most 'salient', i.e., attract most attention, whether because of the position in which they are seated, or because of some distinctive characteristic, such as race or sex, tend to be seen as disproportionately 'causal' or influential—in other words, attract particularly internal attributions. Such results reinforce the viewpoint that actor-observer differences may be a function of differences in the kind of information available to, or attended to by, actors and observers respectively.

Research on actor-observer differences also has implications for the question of how individuals process information concerning base-rate probabilities, which I discussed earlier in this chapter. If actors see their own behaviour as more situationally appropriate, rather than personally distinctive, they should attach a relatively higher probability to others behaving in the same way as themselves, than should independent observers of their behaviour. Ross, Greene, and House (1977) found that students overestimated the commonness of their own responses on a number of criteria (from questionnaire items, to compliance with a request to walk round the campus wearing a sandwich board). In other words, whatever their own responses, they tended to believe that the 'typical' student would respond in the same way as themselves. Similar conclusions were reached by Hansen and Donoghue (1977). This tendency, which Ross *et al.* call a 'false consensus' effect, may have implications for processes of stereotyping discussed in Chapter 3, and for intragroup and intergroup relations, to be discussed in Chapter 9.

It is also interesting to set this finding alongside that of McGuire and Padawer-Singer (1976), who found that children tended to describe themselves more often in terms of those traits which served to distinguish them from their classmates. Also, in a subsequent study, ethnicity was mentioned more by children whose own ethnic group was in a minority (McGuire, McGuire, Child, and Fujioka, 1978). Distinctive, rather than normative, characteristics are thus regarded as more personally informative, even though individuals may underestimate their own distinctiveness.

When combined with a possible bias towards self-enhancement, actor-observer differences in attribution may raise important methodological problems in other areas of psychology, whenever individuals are asked to offer explanations for life-events—particularly good and bad events considered in contrast to one another. Farr (1977a, 1977b) has recently argued that Herzlich's (1973) analysis of conceptions of health and illness, according to which the self is seen as the source of health and the environment as the source of illness, may be an 'attributional artifact' whereby good events are attributed internally and bad events externally, and that same 'artifact' may be present in the two-factor theory of work motivation proposed by Herzberg, Mausner, and Snyderman (1959), according to which the self is seen as the source of job satisfaction and the environment as the source of job dissatisfaction.

CONCLUSIONS

Research on person perception in general, and attribution theory in particular, is currently one of the most prolific areas of experimental social psychology, and it would be rash to try and predict with any confidence what new avenues of enquiry may be opened up even in the time between the writing of this chapter and the date this book is published. Nonetheless, looking back over the past fifteen to twenty years, a number of consistent trends can be identified. The first seems to be a relative decrease in emphasis on the identification of interpersonal 'cues', and a relative increase in emphasis on the question of how such cues, whatever they may be, are combined by the perceiver to form a meaningful and integrated impression. The second, arising from much the same considerations that have led people to question the validity of trait-theoretical approaches to personality generally (Mischel, 1968), is a disenchantment with the view that interpersonal perception consists of the perception of personality traits, conceived of as objective attributes of the target person. With this disenchantment has come a relegation of such questions as the accuracy of person perception and the 'centrality' of certain traits over others. Associated with it also has been a move away from the use of personality trait adjectives as the basic stimulus material for studies in this field.

In contrast to earlier approaches, attribution theory views 'traits' not as objective attributes of people, but as naive explanations of interpersonal behaviour. In other words, to understand how people come to label one another in the way they do, one must start by looking at the 'lay conceptions of personality' held by the perceiver, rather than searching in the personality of the perceived for stable dispositions corresponding to every separate verbal tag attached to him. Just as with attitudes, one is dealing with explanations and interpretations, not with objects and entities, and, just as with cognitive consistency theory, attribution theory is an attempt to describe how individuals try to simplify their experience to the point at which it can appear interpretable and explicable. By now, however, we have reached the stage at which it is no longer useful, if indeed it ever was, to try and 'prove' attribution theory, any more than it would be useful to try and 'prove' balance theory or any of its derivatives. That is not to say that predictions cannot be derived from one or other version of the theory and submitted to empirical test, but rather that attribution theory has made its most useful contribution to social psychology by providing a working heuristic framework for defining the cognitive processes involved in interpersonal perception. The aim of empirical research should be to identify the situational and individual factors by which such processes are affected.

SUMMARY

* People's perceptions of one another's attitudes or character imply assumptions about the reasons for their behaviour.
* Many studies have tried to examine such perceptions by seeing how subjects respond to personality trait adjectives, such as might be used to describe another person. The two main questions have been how individual traits are seen to imply each other, and how sets of traits combine to yield a composite inference or impression. Special problems concern the need to distinguish evaluative from descriptive similarity, and the processing of inconsistent trait combinations, where subjects may resolve the inconsistency by restructuring the information in terms of a new dimension.
* Despite this difficulty, Anderson's weighted-average model of information integration provides a generally viable interpretation of how trait information is processed in terms of a single cognitive dimension.
* Attribution theory places more explicit emphasis on people's causal explanations for one another's behaviour. Such explanations may be liable to a number of biases, which produce departures from perfect rationality.
* In many situations, individuals pay little attention to statistical information concerning the base-rate probability of an actor behaving in a certain way (i.e., whether the behaviour is common or uncommon), unless such information is interpretable in terms of an intuitive causal theory.
* Attributions concerning a person's attitudes or personality tend to be affected by situational factors perceived to facilitate or inhibit his behaviour.
* Studies concerned with when a person will be seen as responsible for certain consequences have been beset by difficulties due to ambiguities in the concept of 'responsibility', which may be interpreted differently in different experimental conditions.
* Inferences concerning the reasons for one's own behaviour may reflect similar processes to those underlying inferences concerning other people.
* Success and failure may be attributed to different kinds of stable or unstable, personal or situational, factors. Individual differences exist in people's tendencies to see their own (failure or) success as attributable to their own (lack of) effort or ability, which have implications for their feelings of control or helplessness.

* Attributions may often be biased by a tendency to defend or present a relatively positive self-image. There is controversy over whether this tendency requires a 'motivational' interpretation.
* In a variety of contexts, an actor may be more likely to attribute his behaviour to situational factors, whereas an observer may be more likely to attribute the same actor's behaviour to aspects of the actor's personality. This tendency may reflect differences between actors' and observers' foci of attention.

CHAPTER
FIVE

INCENTIVE, DISSONANCE, AND JUSTIFICATION

INTRINSIC AND EXTRINSIC MOTIVATION

A central place in psychology has always been accorded to the study of the effects of reward and reinforcement on behaviour. The 'law of effect', that the probability of a response being emitted varies as a function of its consequences for the subject, is one of psychology's most basic postulates. But does this 'law' adequately describe the effects of rewards and incentives on more complex forms of human social behaviour? Is a simple manipulation of reward and punishment, incentive and deterrent, all that is required to change people's behaviour in a 'desired' direction? The answer to this question has profound implications for educational, clinical, criminological, industrial, and marketing psychology, and indeed for any applied area of psychology one could think of. It also raises more general issues concerning the potential abuse of psychological techniques for political purposes. It is not just an abstract theoretical question. Nonetheless, it is in research on attribution processes and attitude change that some of the clearest evidence can be found concerning the limiting conditions of this principle.

As we saw in the last chapter, an important part of attribution research is concerned with individuals' explanations for their own behaviour. The basic question for a subject in a self-attribution experiment is: 'Am I behaving this way because of the sort of person I am, or because of the situation I am in?'

Confronted with incentives and deterrents, the individual might similarly ask himself: 'Am I behaving this way because of my own feelings towards what I am doing, or because of what I hope to get out of it?' Many of the same considerations that apply to the distinction between 'internal' (personal) and 'external' (situational) attributions can be translated into the distinction between 'intrinsic' and 'extrinsic' motivation. A person who performs a task because he finds it interesting or enjoyable in itself is said to be 'intrinsically' motivated, whereas someone for whom the task is merely a means of achieving some ulterior goal or reward is said to be 'extrinsically' motivated.

How do these two types of motivation affect each other? In the last chapter we saw that there seems to be a kind of 'trade-off' relationship between internal and external attributions, so that people are less likely to explain their own, or another person's, behaviour in terms of internal personal factors when the behaviour can plausibly be attributed to external features of the situation. On the basis of such evidence, it might be expected that a similar trade-off relationship would operate between intrinsic and extrinsic sources of motivation, so that an individual may be less likely to find an activity intrinsically motivating if there are strong extrinsic reasons (such as a large monetary reward, or the threat of punishment) for him performing the activity. Extrinsic rewards, in other words, may undermine intrinsic interest, at least if one is dealing with behaviour which the individual might have been happy to perform *anyway*. Offering the individual an excessive incentive to perform such behaviour may make him feel 'I'm just doing this for the money', or 'I have to do this or else I'll get punished', rather than 'I'm doing this because I want to'. If this happens, then one would expect that the individual would stop performing the activity as soon as the extrinsic rewards or threats were withdrawn.

A number of studies have supported this 'overjustification hypothesis'. Deci (1971) had college students play with a commercially produced puzzle during each of three experimental sessions. During the second of these three sessions, the experimental group received payment for their solutions to the puzzle, while the control group did not. Deci found, as predicted, that the experimental group spent less time playing with the puzzle of their own free choice in the third session when the incentive for performance had been removed, whereas the control group spent slightly more time.

Kruglanski, Friedman, and Zeevi (1971) found that high school students who were unexpectedly promised a tour of the university psychology laboratory after volunteering for a problem-solving task showed less intrinsic motivation for the task than a group who received no such promise, as reflected by a number of measures of performance, including the strength of the Zeigarnik effect (the tendency to recall interrupted problems more than completed ones). Calder and Staw (1975) had male undergraduates solve a series of 15 easy jigsaw puzzles, designed so as to be either fairly interesting (consisting mainly of pictures from *Life* and *Playboy* magazines) or fairly boring (of exactly the same shape, but without any pictures), under conditions where they either received no payment, or collected $1 which was left for them beside the last of the puzzles. When subjects were asked to rate their enjoyment of the task, those who had solved the blank puzzles gave higher ratings when they had received payment, whereas those who had solved the more interesting picture puzzles rated their enjoyment less when they had been paid.

Similar effects have been found using much younger subjects. Lepper, Greene, and Nisbett (1973) had nursery school children (aged three to five years) draw with felt-tip pens either under a 'no award' condition, or an 'expected award' condition where they were promised a 'Good Player Award' (a brightly decorated certificate) for drawing pictures, or an 'unexpected award' condition where they received the same award, but had not been promised it beforehand.

One or two weeks later, independent observers counted the time spent by the children playing with the felt-tip pens during a free-play period. The amount of time so spent by subjects in the 'expected award' condition was approximately half that spent by those in the other two conditions. In terms of attribution theory, the interpretation is that subjects in the 'expected award', but not the 'unexpected award', condition could attribute their interest in the drawing activity to their eagerness to obtain the promised reward, rather than to the enjoyability of the task itself.

Lepper and Greene (1975) found a similar difference between unexpected and expected award conditions, with an interesting puzzle as the experimental activity, and access to a variety of toys as the reward. Children who had been promised a reward showed less subsequent interest in the puzzle, as did another group who were told that their activity was being monitored by a television camera.

In the two experiments just described, subjects who expected a reward also knew what that reward would be. An experiment by Ross (1975) compared instead a no reward condition with a 'non-salient' reward condition in which nursery school children were promised a reward, but not told what it would be, and a 'salient' reward condition, in which a box was put in front of them throughout their performance of the experimental activity (beating a drum) with the unknown reward underneath. Subsequent measures showed that intrinsic interest in the drum-beating was lowest in the salient reward condition. In a second experiment, Ross established that decrease of intrinsic motivation as a result of expected rewards is not simply due to the possibility, suggested by Reiss and Sushinsky (1975), that the thought of reward might distract subjects from the experimental activity. In the experimental conditions of this second study, subjects were all told the reward that they would receive (some marshmallows). The crucial comparison was between a 'think-reward', condition, in which subjects were told to 'think about the marshmallows' while they were playing the drum, and a 'distraction' condition, in which they were told to 'think about snow'. Subjects who had been in the distraction condition on average spent more than twice as much time as those who had been in the 'think-reward' condition playing with the drum in a later free-play period.

A more recent study by Ross, Karniol, and Rothstein (1976) examined the possibility that the apparent decrease in intrinsic motivation in conditions where subjects anticipate a reward for performing the experimental task might be due to the frustration of having to wait for the reward making the task itself, by association, seem more unpleasant. This suggestion is very plausible in view of the relative lack of tolerance by young children for delayed gratification (Mischel, 1974). As in previous studies, Ross et al. found that an anticipated reward reduced subsequent intrinsic motivation, but only when subjects were told that the reward depended on them performing the activity in the absence of the experimenter. When the reward was dependent only on their waiting for the experimenter's return, intrinsic interest in the activity was actually enhanced. Delay of gratification should produce frustration, regardless of whether the reward was dependent on performance. From an attributional perspective, however, the reward should undermine intrinsic motivation only when it was made contingent on performance, which is what happened.

Reiss and Sushinsky (1975, 1976), however, have raised a more basic objection to this body of research, on the grounds that it is frequently unclear exactly what is being rewarded in the 'reward' conditions of the experiments just described. It would presumably make a difference if subjects felt that they had to show special care rather than creativity, or creativity rather than persistence, to obtain the reward. Also, it is possible that the rewards given might reinforce responses other than those in which the experimenter was interested. There is, however, no consistent evidence that the quality of subjects' performance during the experimental sessions as opposed to subsequent free-play periods is typically any worse under reward than no reward conditions (though obviously this may sometimes be difficult to measure). In other words there is no consistent evidence that subjects are being reinforced for 'low quality play'.

Another criticism is that there is little direct evidence that subjects verbalize their reasons for performing the rewarded task by saying, 'I did it to get the reward'. Bearing in mind both the age of the subjects in most of these studies, as well as possible demand characteristics of the experimental situation, such lack of evidence should not be regarded as crucially damaging for an attributional approach. In view of the arguments put forward by Nisbett and Wilson (1977, see Chapter 1), it remains an open question how far the cognitive processes posited by attribution theory, if indeed they exist, are typically available to introspection, and hence identifiable through verbal self-reports. A study by Kruglanski, Alon, and Lewis (1972), which showed decreases in reported task enjoyment after subjects (10- to 11-year-olds) had been *unexpectedly* rewarded for winning a team game, showed that a proportion of those who had been rewarded misattributed their reasons for participating in the game to the prize of which they had been unaware at the time.

One of the main reasons why Reiss and Sushinsky object so strongly to the overjustification hypothesis seems to be their interest in defending the use of behaviour modification techniques, such as token economies. One of the most important points that they make is that the experiments described have used single-trial reinforcements, whereas behaviour modification techniques rely generally on a *series* of reinforcements for continued performance of the activity which the experimenter wishes to produce. Somewhat belatedly, perhaps, Greene, Sternberg, and Lepper (1976) have attempted to deal with this objection by demonstrating overjustification effects following multiple-trial reinforcements of an intrinsically interesting activity. However, as Lepper and Greene (1976) point out, there remains an equally important difference between the situations studied in the behaviour modification and the overjustification literatures. This is, that the former body of research is primarily concerned with influencing subjects to acquire and maintain *new* patterns of behaviour which they would *not* have consistently performed of their own accord without such intervention. Whereas the effects of such treatments may not always generalize to other forms of behaviour or necessarily survive for long after the complete withdrawal of reinforcement, at least they provide many psychiatric patients, autistic children, and other groups of clients, with much-needed success experiences (and presumably subsequent gains in self-esteem) which they would otherwise not have had. By contrast, the overjustification literature is concerned explicitly with undermining motivation for behaviour in which the subject is *already* keen and able to engage, before any experimental intervention. Ross (1976) has also made a very important distinction between extrinsic rewards that are made contingent simply on the *performance* of an activity, and those that are made contingent on the *quality* of the performance. The evidence seems to be that rewards for success, i.e., for quality of performance, do *not* undermine intrinsic motivation.

A study by Miller, Brickman, and Bolen (1975) provides evidence that subjects' intrinsic motivation can be *increased* by influencing their self-attributions. In the first experiment which they report, classes of pupils around ten years of age were submitted to schedules designed to make them be tidier and clean up litter in their classroom. One class was assigned to an 'attribution' condition, in which their teacher repeatedly told them how neat and tidy they were. Another class was assigned to a 'persuasion' condition, in which the teacher continually told them that they *should* be neat and tidy. Pupils in the 'attribution' class were considerably tidier than both the 'persuasion' class, and a control class who received no special treatment, as assessed by the percentage of litter put into a waste paper basket rather than left on desks or on the floor, shortly after the training phase had been completed. A delayed assessment two weeks later (after the period in which no further mention was made of tidiness by the teacher) showed the 'attribution' group at least as tidy as on the previous assessment, but the 'persuasion' group had returned to the level of the control group.

In their second experiment, Miller *et al.,* generalized this approach to performance at mathematics among pupils about seven years old. Pupils who received comments from their teacher such as: 'You are doing very well in arithmetic' or 'You really work hard in arithmetic', showed sustained improvement as compared with those who were told: 'You should be good at arithmetic' or 'You should work harder at arithmetic'. Miller *et al.* suggest that 'persuasion often suffers because it involves a negative attribution (a person should be what he is not), attribution generally gains because it disguises persuasive intent' (1975, page 430). It may be that 'overjustification' procedures similarly imply negative attributions, such as, 'I know that you wouldn't want to do this for nothing, so this is what I'm offering you'.

COGNITIVE DISSONANCE THEORY

In between those kinds of behaviour in which a person would be eager to engage spontaneously, and those which he would refuse, or feel unable, to perform except in the presence of powerful and consistent reinforcements, there lie a large number of behaviours which a person might be prepared to undertake, but still have doubts about whether he was doing the right thing. It is this last category that has been the prime focus of probably the most influential theory in social psychology, Festinger's (1957) theory of cognitive dissonance. According to this theory, any decision between alternative courses of action will lead to a state of psychological tension or 'dissonance' to the extent that the net attractiveness of the two alternatives is similar. This state of dissonance, moreover, does not immediately dissipate once the individual has embarked on his chosen course of action. For it to do so, he must usually engage in some 'cognitive work' which will lead to a re-evaluation of the relevant 'cognitive elements'.

To see how this might apply, imagine the case of a student (male for purposes of this example) who finds that yet another week is staggering to its close, and he has to make a decision as to how he is going to spend his Saturday evening. Being someone of fairly simple tastes, at least by Saturday evening, his choice boils down to one between just two alternatives: either his peak experience of the evening is going to be watching the football match on the college television, or he could go off to a party that some friends of his are having. Whichever way he decides, there is always the risk that the next morning someone could greet him with 'You missed a great party last night' or 'Wasn't it a fantastic match last night? What? Didn't you see it?'. Any doubt that he might feel as to whether he made the right choice would be an example of what is meant by cognitive dissonance. Any reassessment that convinced him that he had chosen rightly after all would provide a means of resolving such dissonance.

Since this example assumes that the choice is initially one between two attractive alternatives, it can be seen that dissonance will increase to the extent that our student learns about positive aspects of the rejected alternative or negative aspects of the chosen alternative. Similarly, any negative aspects of the rejected alternative, or positive aspects of the chosen alternative would allow him to reduce dissonance. The main game might have been a goalless draw between two inferior teams in which he had no interest, rather than the five-one victory by his favourite team that he had hoped to see. Or he might find out the next day that a girl he had been quietly fancying had been at the party unaccompanied and had been asking after him—until she went off with someone else.

In terms of dissonance theory, the cognition that he stayed behind to watch the football is inconsistent with other cognitions that the match was dull, or that he missed a good party. In much the same way that balance theory predicts that individuals will be motivated to resolve cognitive imbalance, dissonance theory predicts that he will be motivated to resolve this inconsistency. Since he is stuck with the fact that he did stay behind (cannot change the cognition that he behaved in such a way), he therefore has to try and justify his decision. There are any number of ways in which he could do so, and dissonance theory *as such* (i.e., as opposed to experimental tests of the theory) does not require that any single method of dissonance resolution should be preferred over others. Indeed, it is likely that a person might use any number of strategies in combination with each other. Most strategies we could imagine, however, relate to central concepts of the theory, and there is a large body of experimental research that testifies to their importance.

One strategy would be to *re-evaluate the two alternatives*, so that the chosen alternative (the football match) appeared, on reconsideration, even more positive than the rejected one (the party). This might take the form of either a more positive evaluation of the chosen alternative, or a more negative evaluation of the rejected alternative, or both. In the first case, our student could convince himself that he really found the game quite exciting. In the second case, he could convince himself that the party would not really have been worth going to after all—it would have a meant a long cold walk in the rain, then having to talk to all those boring people, and he didn't really fancy her anyway. Experimental evidence for this kind of process of re-evaluating alternatives to reduce any doubt about the correctness of one's choice was found by Brehm and Cohen (1959) in a situation which involved children having to choose between toys of comparable attractiveness. The data suggest an increase in the relative perceived attractiveness of the chosen toy, after the choice was made.

Another strategy would be to *recall selectively* those aspects of the chosen alternative which were compatible with the decision, and suppress the more negative aspects ('I know there weren't any goals, but there was some superb defensive play'). Although not researched as fully as some other aspects of the theory, this is again a process that has received some experimental support. Brehm (1962) had pairs of friends (college students) perform a rating task, and then compare their completed questionnaires with each other. (In fact, the experimenter did not show subjects their friends' actual questionnaires, but ones which were specially completed so as to be the same as the subjects' own on 30 out of 40 responses, but discrepant on the remaining 10). The assumption was that the information that one's friend had responded differently on certain items would be relatively dissonance-arousing. As predicted, these discrepant responses were less accurately recalled when subjects were re-tested one week later.

Another strategy would be to deny *freedom of choice*. It is conceivable that our student could say to himself, 'I heard about the party, but no-one really invited me, so I didn't think I could go.' In such a situation, he can admit that the football on the television was really boring, and that he would have really enjoyed the party, but such feelings of envy or whatever do not constitute a state of dissonance—a feeling that his decision needed justification—since he is perceiving the situation as one in which he did not have a decision to make. Possibly this may be a very common dynamic in situations where a person can say fairly plausibly that he 'can't help himself'. One such instance might be that of the large proportion of cigarette smokers who claim that they would like to give up smoking if they could do so easily, but see themselves as 'addicts' who are unable to do so (Eiser, 1978). Such smokers also tend to be those most prepared to acknowledge the health hazards of smoking, but it cannot necessarily be concluded that such fears for their health, however distressing, constitute a state of dissonance. Rather, it may be that the self-attribution of addiction—the denial that one could stop smoking of one's own free choice—provides a mode of dissonance *resolution*.

Finally, another strategy to be considered is that of denying the *foreseeability of the consequences* of the decision. He could say to himself, 'I never thought it would be such a dreadful match'—but in this case it would have to be considerably worse than he expected, or was entitled to expect, for this justification to be plausible, as he should have been aware of *some* risk of disappointment when he made his decision. (It would be more plausible to use this strategy, for instance, if the television broke down in the middle of the game.) A more promising application of this strategy in this instance would be along the lines of, 'I never thought *she'd* have been at the party'. As Wicklund and Brehm (1976) have pointed out, the foreseeability of consequences of one's decision, the perceived freedom of that decision, and one's personal responsibility for it, are some of the most crucial variables shown by more recent research to govern the occurrence of cognitive dissonance phenomena.

FORCED COMPLIANCE

The term 'forced compliance' is that given to the most common of the wide range of experimental situations to which cognitive dissonance theory has been applied. Such experiments involve 'compliance', in that a crucial part of the procedure involves inducing the subject to comply with some request.

Such compliance is said to be 'forced' in the sense that it is assumed that subjects would not normally wish to undertake the requested behaviour of their own free will. Specifically, it is assumed that the decision to comply with the experimenter's request arouses dissonance, in that the behaviour requested is designed to run counter to the subject's pre-existing attitudes. Whereas, the example in the previous section was a choice between two fairly attractive alternatives, here the individual has to choose what he sees to be the lesser of two evils. Either he must refuse what is an unusual, but typically polite, request and risk the embarrassment of appearing antagonistic to the experimenter, or he must commit himself to behaving in a way which he knows to be inconsistent with his true feelings. In fact, the situations devised are ones in which a practised experimenter can elicit almost universal compliance. (Where this is not so, one needs to be very cautious over interpreting any results. Obviously, if a substantial number of subjects refused to perform the counter-attitudinal behaviour requested of them, the pressures towards compliance would have to be assumed to be rather weak, and hence one could be less sure that those subjects who did comply were in fact behaving counter-attitudinally.) The experimenter's main interest, therefore, is not just in whether the subject will comply, but in the conditions that enhance or minimize any dissonance associated with such compliance, and in how such dissonance will be resolved.

To take the last point first, it has already been mentioned that dissonance theory does not require that any specific mode of dissonance reduction be employed by all individuals in a given situation. (Götz-Marchand, Götz, and Irle, 1974, provide a delightful demonstration of how subjects' choice of a mode of dissonance reduction can be influenced by the order in which alternative modes are presented.) However, the situations are so devised that a possible means of resolving dissonance is to *change one's attitudes so as to be more consistent with the way in which one has behaved*. Thus, someone induced to deliver a speech against his previously held beliefs *could* resolve such dissonance by changing those beliefs. In formal terms, if a person holds the two cognitions, 'I have argued in favour of X' and 'I am opposed to X', one way of resolving the dissonance that this typically produces is by changing the latter cognition to, 'I am now in favour of X'. This prediction that attitudes can change as a *consequence* of behaviour is the vital intuitive step that separates cognitive dissonance theory from other formulations of the consistency notion. It does not follow from the theory that dissonance *has* to be resolved in this way. Hence, subjects who do not show such attitude change cannot necessarily be said to be acting in a manner contrary to the tenets of the theory—a consideration which has prompted some critics (e.g., Chapanis and Chapanis, 1964) to regard the theory as incapable of disproof. A more constructive point of view, however, is that any experiment that tests the prediction of the theory for any specific single effect, such as a change in post-compliance attitudes, provides a conservative test of the theory: the predicted effect could fail to occur even if the theory was correct, but would *not* occur (according to dissonance theorists) if the theory was wrong. Suffice it to say that a large number of studies have succeeded, as will be seen, in producing changes in post-compliance attitudes, and the more serious challenges to dissonance theory have been in terms of the interpretation of such effects, rather than over the question of their occurrence.

With regard to the conditions that are assumed to enhance or minimize dissonance, one of the variables most commonly considered is the monetary or other incentive that the subject is offered for performing the counter-attitudinal task. As in the over-justification literature, it is assumed that a large extrinsic incentive, such as money, may provide a justification for behaviour so that it need not be regarded as attractive for any other reason. In terms of the theory, performing the counter-attitudinal task will arouse dissonance, but this dissonance can be largely resolved if doing so produces adequate extrinsic rewards for the individual. With such dissonance reduced there is then less pressure to change the cognition concerning one's initial attitude. Although the cognition 'I have argued in favour of X' is still inconsistent with the cognition 'I am opposed to X', it is consistent with the cognition 'I have been very well paid for arguing in favour of X'. The point is simply that the amount of dissonance a person will experience is assumed to be a function of the strength and/or frequency of cognitions under the heading of 'What is bad about my decision' *minus* that of cognitions under the heading of 'What is good about my decision'. The fact that the behaviour was counter to one's attitudes comes under the first heading, but the resulting dissonance can be cancelled out by the fact that the behaviour produced a large reward, which comes under the second heading. The intriguing implication, therefore, is that, since it is predicted that dissonance from counter-attitudinal behaviour can motivate the individual to change the cognition concerning his attitude, and since large incentives will reduce this dissonance, *there will be less attitude change when the individual is given a large, rather than a small, incentive for performing the counter-attitudinal behaviour.*

A classic study by Festinger and Carlsmith (1959) was the first to test this prediction directly, and is worth describing in some detail. Subjects, male introductory psychology students, volunteered for a two-hour experiment on 'measures of performance' from among other options open to them to enable them to fulfil a course requirement, which meant that they had to spend a specified total number of hours as experimental subjects. It was explained that the psychology department was also conducting a study to evaluate these experiments with a view to their future improvement, and that a sample of the students would be interviewed independently after they had served as subjects. On arrival at the laboratory, subjects were all told that the experiment for which they had volunteered, although scheduled for two hours, would in fact take only slightly over one hour, so that they would possibly be in the sample to be interviewed afterwards ('Since we have that extra time, the introductory psychology people asked if they could interview some of our subjects . . . . I gather that they're interviewing some people who have been in experiments. I don't know much about it. Anyhow, they may want to interview you when you're through here' [page 204]). For one hour, the subject was then required to perform what was designed to be an extremely boring task.

At the end of this period, the experiment was ostensibly over from the subjects' point of view, the experimenter then continued with what seemed to be a full explanation of the purpose of the study. Subjects were told that there were two conditions to the study. In the condition to which they had been assigned, subjects performed the tasks with no prior expectations—

> But in the other group, we have a student that we've hired that works for us regularly, and what I do is take him into the next room where the subject is waiting—the same room you were waiting in before—and I introduce him as if he had just finished being a subject in the experiment. That is, I say, 'This is so-and-so, who's just finished the experiment, and I've asked him to tell you a little of what it's about before you start.' The fellow who works for us then, in conversation with the next subject, makes these points: (The E then produced a sheet headed 'For Group B' which had written on it, 'It was very enjoyable, I had a lot of fun, I enjoyed myself, it was very interesting, it was intriguing, it was exciting . . .') Now, of course we have the student do this, because if the experimenter does it, it doesn't look as realistic, and what we're interested in doing is comparing how these two groups do on the experiment—the one with this previous expectation about the experiment, and the other, like yourself with essentially none. (Page 205.)

Subjects in the control condition were then told that, 'that fellow from the introductory psychology class' was due to arrive to interview them, and were asked to wait for him. For subjects in the two remaining conditions, however, the experimenter then continued, with much hesitation and embarrassment:

> Now, I also have a sort of strange thing to ask you. The thing is this. The fellow who normally does this for us couldn't to it today—he just phoned in, and something or other came up for him—so we've been looking around for someone that we could hire to do it for us. You see, we've got another subject waiting who is supposed to be in that other condition. Now Professor _____, who is in charge of this experiment, suggested that perhaps we could take a chance on your doing it for us. I'll tell you what we have in mind: the thing is, if you could do it for us now, then of course you would know how to do it, and if something like this should ever come up again, that is, the regular fellow couldn't make it, and we have a subject scheduled, it would be very reassuring to us to know that we had somebody else who we could call on who knew how to do it. So if you would be willing to do this for us, we'd like to hire you to do it now and then be on call in the future, if something like this should ever happen again. We can pay you _____ for doing this for us, that is, for doing it now and then being on call. Do you think you could do that for us? (Page 205.)

In one of the conditions the amount offered was one dollar. In the other condition it was twenty dollars. Subjects were then taken in and introduced to the 'next subject' (a female undergraduate hired for the role), and were left to tell her how interesting and enjoyable the tasks had been. When they had finished, they were told that, 'that fellow from introductory psychology' was probably waiting to interview them, and on the way to find this interviewer, the experimenter thanked them, as he had the control subjects, with the words, 'Thanks very much for working on those tasks for us. I hope you did enjoy it. Most of our subjects tell us afterwards that they found it quite interesting. You get a chance to see how you react to the tasks and so forth.' (Page 206.)

In the post-experimental interview, subjects in the $1 condition rated the tasks as significantly more interesting and enjoyable than subjects in either of the other two conditions. A similar, but less statistically reliable, pattern of results was evident in responses to a question concerning willingness to participate in a similar experiment in the future.

Although this experiment is one of the most frequently cited of all dissonance studies, I have described it in such detail because it both provides the archetype for many subsequent experiments, and contains a number of important subtleties that would be missed in a more cursory account. First, what produces the hypothesized state of dissonance? Although the task itself was boring, this boredom in itself was not assumed to be a source of dissonance. Although it was boring, the 'performance' task in fact lasted only slightly over half the time they had initially anticipated. The experimenter then appears to be concerned, through the debriefing, to provide the subject with some kind of learning experience. So far so good. The subject is now ready to leave the experiment after a less than fruitful experience, but one that at least provided him with a credit towards his course requirement. But then (except in the control condition), the experimenter asks him, as a special favour, if he would be willing to help him stand in for the missing assistant. Note that the experimenter has now (1) told the subject the supposed design of the study, together with details of the assistant's task, (2) told the subject that the assistant would get paid for what he did (but not how much), (3) appealed to the subject to help him out in an emergency, (4) implied that this was the first time he had made such a request of a subject, and (5) put the request on a contractual basis through the mention of money and through asking for a fairly open-ended commitment on the part of the subject to be available to stand in, in any future emergency, until the completion of the study. Note also that the experimenter has *not* said that he suspects the task was in fact very boring, and so does *not* put the request in terms of explicitly asking the subject to tell the girl something which, in the experimenter's eyes, would be untrue. Boredom, after all, is pretty relative, and social psychologists have rarely had difficulty in devising 'boring' tasks which are still credible as procedures within the range of general psychological practice.

In fact, it is an interesting speculation what response such a request might have had if subjects had been promised no money whatsoever. It is quite possible that the apparent confidence of the experimenter in the subject's ability to play the role might have been flattering enough to elicit substantial compliance without any further inducement. What would seem to militate against this is the fact that subjects know 'They normally pay someone to do this', so that once the question of payment is introduced, they can then ask themselves whether they consider this payment to be equitable, bearing in mind the continuing nature of the commitment.

In terms of the theory, dissonance is produced by virtue of the inconsistency between the cognition 'I found the tasks boring' and the cognition 'I told the girl the tasks were interesting'. How should such dissonance be resolved? By avoiding the latter cognition? Apart from a few discarded subjects, this cognition *within this situation* can be assumed to be fairly resistant to change. The open-ended commitment to repeat such action in the future is also extremely relevant here (and not just as a variable influencing the perceived adequacy of any reward). Even when he leaves the experiment proper, and is being interviewed by the 'fellow from introductory psychology', he has not fulfilled his commitment. On the contrary, for all he knows, he could be called in the next day to play the same role again. So, the choice for him is either to find compensating elements in his contract with the experimenter, or to change his cognition that the tasks were boring. The plausibility of this latter alternative is increased by the fact that the experimenter himself seems genuinely to regard the tasks as quite interesting, and tells the subject after his role-playing, but before the post-experimental interview, that previous subjects found the experiment quite enjoyable. By implication, the experimenter is saying, 'You told the girl the truth'. Subjects in the $1 condition, without any other obvious way of justifying their recent action and future commitment turn out to be comparatively willing to accept this construction of events. Subjects in the $20 condition, however, can regard their sizeable monetary bonus as adequate compensation for the otherwise negative aspects of their contract with the experimenter. They are thus prepared to give the *independent* interviewer a different account of their experience than they gave to the girl 'subject'. Thus we have the paradoxical, but predicted, finding that larger rewards for counter-attitudinal role-playing produce *less* change in independently measured attitude.

THE MAGNITUDE OF INCENTIVE

A number of experiments have been designed to test the prediction that attitude change following counter-attitudinal role-playing will be inversely proportionate to the size of any incentive or payment for such role-playing, within the context of attitudinal issues that might be assumed to have greater personal significance than the situation used by Festinger and Carlsmith (1959). Typically, these have capitalized on actual issues of topical significance to their subject populations.

The first of these was conducted by Cohen (1962) at Yale, at a time when the students there were accusing the New Haven police of brutality in quelling a recent campus demonstration. The experimenter approached subjects individually, explained that he was a student doing a research project in 'human relations' on the issue of the police action, hinted that he assumed the subject was opposed to the police action, but explained that, in trying to study this problem, it was important to obtain a full list of possible arguments on both sides of the issue. He went on to explain that an ample number of anti-police arguments had already been collected, but that there was a need for more pro-police arguments. The subject was therefore asked to write the 'strongest, most forceful, most creative and thoughtful essay you can, unequivocally against your own position and in favour of the police side of the riots'. (Note that, unlike the Festinger and Carlsmith study, the subject is aware that the experimenter knows that compliance with this request would indeed be counter-attitudinal.) The experimenter then said he could pay the subject a specified amount (ranging from $0·50 to $10) for doing so, but that it was entirely their own choice whether or not they were willing to take part in the study. (There is no report of how many refused in the different conditions. Hopefully this was not a function of the size of the incentive.)

Immediately after they had written the essay, subjects were asked, by the same experimenter, to complete a questionnaire which included a critical item on how much they felt the police action was justified. It was suggested to subjects that they might like to look at the issue 'in the light of' the reasons they had just considered. As predicted by dissonance theory, the larger the monetary incentive, the less justified they rated the police action.

The Cohen study has been severely criticized by Rosenberg (1965), who sees its results as running counter to his own application of cognitive consistency theory (Rosenberg and Abelson, 1960). His major argument is that the 'dissonance' effect reported by Cohen could be a function of either, or both, of two research contaminants, which he labels 'evaluation apprehension' and 'affect arousal'. The first of these refers to the possiblity that the subject could have been nervous about the conclusions the experimenter might draw about his honesty and integrity: 'They probably want to see whether getting paid so much will affect my own attitude, whether it will influence me, whether I am the kind of person whose views can be changed by buying him off.' (Rosenberg, 1965, page 29.) The second, related, possibility is that large rewards might make the subject suspicious of the experimenter and for that reason resentful towards him, with the consequence that the subject might 'find emotional release' for such resentment in refusing to show the change in attitude which he sees the experimenter as trying to achieve. Rosenberg's argument, therefore, is that Cohen's results reflect experimenter bias (cf. Orne, 1962) rather than dissonance reduction, and that the so-called 'dissonance' effect should disappear if the source of such bias, specifically the fact that the same experimenter elicits both the counter-attitudinal behaviour and the final attitude measure, is removed. Rosenberg does not explain how this would apply to the Festinger and Carlsmith (1959) study, in which these two phases were separated as he recommends.

Rosenberg, therefore, attempted a modified replication of the Cohen study. As before, the issue was one of topical significance for the student subjects—whether the university governing body would allow the university football team to enter a national competition. Subjects arrived as scheduled at the experimenter's office to find him still busy with another 'student'. At this point, the experimenter apologized that they would have to wait 15 or 20 minutes, but then 'remembered' that he had had a call from a graduate student in the education department, who needed some subjects in a hurry for 'some sort of study he's doing—I don't know what it's about exactly except that it has to do with attitudes and that's why he called me, because my research is in a similar area as you'll see later . . . . I gather they have some research funds and are paying people.'

Having agreed to go over to investigate this 'second' experiment, subjects were put through a procedure very similar to that used by Cohen, with the 'education graduate student' appealing for an essay opposed to the university team's participation in the competition. They were then paid $0·50, $1, or $5, and returned to the first experimenter, who explained that the purpose of his study was a continuing survey of student attitudes, and then administered a questionnaire which included an item on the critical issue. As predicted by Rosenberg, subjects in the $0·50 condition showed the least, and those in the $5 condition the most, shift in favour of a ban on the team's participation (the position for which they had argued) as compared with a base-line control condition.

However, there are a number of difficulties with Rosenberg's explanation. From a design point of view, he only shows that, with 'evaluation apprehension' removed, dissonance effects did not occur. He does not show that Cohen's results would have been replicated if evaluation apprehension had been reintroduced into his situation. In other words, since he did not manipulate what he considered to be the most important variable differentiating his own study from Cohen's, he cannot be certain that this variable was responsible for the difference in the pattern of results. Or perhaps Rosenberg actually did collect data on this point, but did not see fit to mention them in his discussion. This is Nuttin's (1975, pages 228–230) interpretation of an oblique reference by Rosenberg (1966, page 154) to additional conditions 'run as part of his study'. Also, as Wicklund and Brehm (1976, page 40) note, the essays written by Rosenberg's subjects were later scored for persuasiveness, and those by the $5 group were rated as most persuasive. Since writing a persuasive essay against one's own position should give rise to greater dissonance than writing an unpersuasive essay, it could be that subjects in the $5 group thereby experienced greater dissonance than the other subjects. If this were so, the greater attitude change shown by this group would not be incompatible with dissonance theory.

Rosenberg's argument is also disputed by Nuttin (1975) who attempted a conceptual replication of his study in the context of Belgian students' demand for reform of the university examination system. Nuttin obtained results in the contrary direction, that is, consistent with dissonance theory, with those students who composed a speech in favour of the traditional system for a small reward showing more attitude change towards the position which they had advocated than those who did so for a large reward. Also, when Nuttin added a large reward condition in which the two phases of the experiment (the speech-writing and the final attitude measure) were *not* separated, the results were almost identical to those of the large reward condition where the possibility of 'evaluation apprehension' was removed. Nuttin reports a great deal more evidence of relevance to this discussion, and this will be considered shortly. However, on this specific point, it seems safe to conclude that the inverse relationship between attitude change and incentive magnitude of the kind first predicted and observed by Festinger and Carlsmith (1959) is not likely to be a mere artifact of evaluation apprehension or some similar bias.

CHOICE, FORESEEABILITY, AND RESPONSIBILITY

A number of researchers have approached the problem of the relationship between incentive magnitude and attitude change by viewing it as dependent on other variables which may be crucial for the occurrence of the hypothesized state of dissonance. Essentially, the argument is that one should only expect the inverse relationship between attitude change and incentive magnitude predicted by dissonance theory if indeed the counter-attitudinal behaviour was elicited in such a manner as to produce dissonance in the first place. If, for any reason, such behaviour did not produce dissonance, it would be reasonable to expect a direct relationship between incentive magnitude and attitude change in accordance with straightforward principles of reinforcement.

Linder, Cooper, and Jones (1967) reasoned that a necessary condition for the arousal of dissonance should be that a person can construe the situation as one in which he chose *freely* to perform the counter-attitudinal behaviour. If 'forced' compliance was perceived by subjects to be truly forced, it should not produce dissonance. In other words, dissonance is not dependent on the cognition, 'I did X' (where X is a counter-attitudinal act), but on the cognition, 'I *chose* to do X'. If this is so, one would expect an inverse relationship between attitude change and incentive magnitude under conditions of perceived freedom of choice. In the first of two experiments, they performed a modified replication of the Cohen (1962) study, using the issue of proposed legislation in the state of North Carolina which would have forbidden Communists and similar groups from addressing meetings at state-supported institutions. The subject population (psychology students at Duke University) were strongly opposed to this legislation. Subjects arrived individually at the laboratory to meet the experimenter, who asked them to write essays in favour of the proposed legislation, but before making the request, said to subjects in the 'free-decision' condition, 'I want to explain to you what this task is all about. I want to make it clear, though, that the decision to perform the task will be entirely your own.' To subjects in the 'no-choice' condition, however, he merely said, 'I want to explain to you what this task that you have volunteered for is all about.'

After explaining the purpose of the task, the experimenter told subjects in the free-decision condition that the association that was supposedly sponsoring the research would pay them either $0·50 or $2·50 for writing the essay, over and above their experimental course credit, but stressed again that the decision was entirely the subjects' own, and that they would not forfeit the credit if they refused. In the 'no-choice' condition, subjects were simply told in an off-hand way that the association would be paying them either of the two amounts. In both choice conditions, the money was then paid to the subjects before they started to write. As predicted, the results showed that the free-decision subjects who received only $0·50 subsequently indicated, on a brief questionnaire administered by the experimenter, a more favourable attitude towards the legislation than those who had received the $2·50 payment, whose responses were close to those of control subjects who did not perform the essay-writing task. In the no-choice condition, however, the results were reversed, with subjects who received the low reward giving responses close to those of the control group, and those who received the larger amount showing more favourable attitudes towards the legislation.

In their second experiment, Linder *et al.* applied the same notions to an interpretation of the Rosenberg (1965) results. If a direct relationship between incentive magnitude and attitude change applies under no-choice conditions, perhaps Rosenberg's finding of such a relationship was due to his procedure having somehow reduced subjects' perceived freedom of choice. Although Rosenberg did not pressurize his subjects to go and help out the 'other' experimenter, subjects might well have found it difficult to refuse by the time they had gone to the trouble of finding their way to this 'other' experiment, and had received fairly obligating instructions as to what they then had to do. The procedure for this experiment closely followed that of Rosenberg, with subjects being asked if they were willing to help out 'some graduate student in eduation' while they were waiting. In the 'prior-commitment' condition, subjects went off to find this second experimenter without any extra comment by the first experimenter other than what was said in the Rosenberg study. In the 'free-decision' condition, however, the first experimenter added: 'All I told this fellow was that I would send him some subjects if it was convenient but that I couldn't obligate my subjects in any way. So, when you get up there, listen to what he has to say and feel free to decide from there.' On arrival at the 'second' experiment, all subjects then received identical instructions, up to the mention of either a $0·50 or $2·50 payment, for writing an essay in favour of university regulations to which they were strongly opposed. As predicted, subjects in the prior commitment condition subsequently indicated more favourable attitudes on this issue after receiving the larger rather than the smaller reward, thus replicating Rosenberg's finding. In the free-decision condition, however, the results were in the reverse direction, in accordance with dissonance theory.

The implication of this last experiment is that Nuttin's finding of a 'dissonance' rather than an 'incentive' effect in his attempted replication of

Rosenberg's study might have been due to his presenting the possibility of participation in the 'second experiment' rather less coercively. One can only speculate about differences in the non-verbal aspects of experimenter-subject communication in the two studies, but two more tangible differences might have been crucial. First, Rosenberg's subjects were obliged to participate in what was ostensibly the 'proper' experiment of his study as part of a course requirement, whereas Nuttin's subjects attended entirely voluntarily, and without expectation of credit or payment. Second, there are slight differences in the wording of the instructions. After mentioning the 'second' experiment, Rosenberg told his subjects, 'So if you care to go down there you can', whereas Nuttin said to his subjects, 'Perhaps you would like to help him'. (Nuttin, 1975, page 29.) Nuttin's 'second' experimenter was also presented as a graduate in *psychology* (hence there was less commitment involved in a journey to another location), and seems to have reassured subjects that their choice was still a free one: 'Of course, I do not want to force you to write the essay, but you certainly would do me a favour . . . .' (Nuttin, 1975, page 31).

In case such differences in instructions are considered too subtle to influence perceived decision freedom, it is worth mentioning a study by Holmes and Strickland (1970). Subjects were instructed in groups to write a counter-attitudinal essay for a reward of either one or two experimental credit points under either 'free' choice, ('. . . we'd like your discussion group to write . . .') or 'no-choice', ('. . . we're going to have your group write . . .') conditions. The results confirmed the interaction found in the Linder *et al.* study, free-choice subjects showing a 'dissonance' effect, no-choice subjects an 'incentive' effect.

Research has also shown that an important prerequisite for dissonance arousal is that the individual should be aware of possible negative consequences of his decision at the time the decision was made. In an early study in this tradition, Freedman (1963) investigated the effects of giving subjects high or low justification for performing a boring task before or after the task was performed. In one of the experiments he reports, subjects had to spend some time writing a long sequence of numbers in a random order. Those in the high justification condition were told that the data from their class would be extremely useful in allowing the experimenter to complete his study on people's implicit assumptions about the number system. In the low justification condition, they were told that the data from their class would be of no use, since all the necessary data had been collected the previous week, and that they had simply been put through the procedure in accordance with a previously arranged schedule. When subsequently asked to rate their enjoyment of the task, those subjects who received high justification before the task rated it as less enjoyable than those who received low justification before, whereas those who received high justification afterwards rated it as more enjoyable than those who received low justification afterwards. The implication is that the dissonance analysis of the effects of differential levels of justification (or reward) is relevant only to cases where subjects are aware of such justification at the time they commit themselves to the behaviour. Unexpected consequences of one's behaviour seem to operate more in accordance with reinforcement theory assumptions—more positive consequences producing more positive evaluations of the behaviour.

A number of subsequent studies have produced results consistent with this conclusion. Two such experiments are reported by Cooper and Brehm (1971). In the first of these, female undergraduates arrived to take part in a study advertised as 'Art Judgment', but then described in a way designed to appear boring (one hour of verbal analogy items to provide normative data). Half the subjects (high deprivation condition) were told that most subjects would receive one hour's credit for their participation, but some people, randomly selected, would not receive any credit points. In all cases, the instruction letter to the subjects indicated that they were in this deprived group. In the low deprivation condition, subjects were told that the standard credit given would be only for half-an-hour. Cross-cutting this manipulation, subjects were either given no choice over whether to perform the task, but were told about the credit system beforehand, or were given a letter implying that they had the right to refuse, and were again told about the credits beforehand; or were given the same letter, but with no mention of the credits until after they had performed the task ('*fait accompli*' condition). When required afterwards to rate their satisfaction with the task, those who had the right to refuse and knew about the credits beforehand gave more positive ratings when they thought that they were more deprived relative to the other subjects. Those who had been given no choice, or who were not told about the credits until after the task, rated it (nonsignificantly) more negatively when they felt themselves to be more relatively deprived.

The second experiment reported by Cooper and Brehm employed a similar design, but this time involved male students having to provide 'normative data on a particular type of hand-eye co-ordination' (threading 150 sewing needles). Relative deprivation was manipulated through informing subjects that most of the others were supposedly receiving either $2 or $0·50 for their participation. The task was again rated significantly more positively by subjects who were given the right to refuse and were told about the money beforehand under the condition of greater relative deprivation. However, greater relative deprivation led to significantly more negative ratings in the no-choice and *fait accompli* conditions.

Closely related to this line of research are studies that have manipulated the extent to which subjects might feel responsible for persuading others through advocating a position with which they personally disagreed. Cooper and Worchel (1970) conducted an experiment based on that of Festinger and Carlsmith (1959), which involved male student subjects performing a dull task (actually, one of those used by Festinger and Carlsmith) and then being induced, for either an extra half-hour or one hour experimental credit, to tell the 'next subject' how interesting it had been. This 'next subject' (a male confederate) then either played the part of becoming increasingly persuaded that it would indeed be interesting, or remained unconvinced. Subjects who felt that they had convinced the 'next subject' through the false information they had given him showed more positive evaluations of the task. Also, the difference between the two levels of incentive, which was in the same direction as that found by Festinger and Carlsmith, came out clearly only when the confederate appeared to be persuaded.

Subsequently, Cooper and Goethals (1974) showed that what is important is whether subjects *expect* their counter-attitudinal advocacy to lead others to change their views. Subjects who expected a recording of their counter-attitudinal advocacy to be played to another group still changed their attitudes in spite of later news that the recording would not be used after all. Collins and Hoyt (1972) also manipulated subjects' feelings of personal responsibility for the consequences of their counter-attitudinal behaviour through the simple device of having subjects sign a receipt for their payment (either $0·50 or $2·50) for writing an essay. For half the subjects, this receipt stated, 'Responsibility for its contents is mine'; for the remainder, it stated, 'I am in no way responsible for its contents'. The perceived importance of the consequences of their behaviour was also varied. Both immediately after writing the essay, and also two weeks later, the only subjects to show a strong shift in attitude were those who felt that their essay could have important consequences, had received only the low ($0·50) payment, and had accepted responsibility for its contents.

Within the forced compliance paradigm, therefore, attitude change occurs only if the subject sees himself as having chosen to perform the counter-attitudinal task with reasonable foreknowledge of its likely negative consequences, and hence with personal responsibility for his decision.

SELF-PERCEPTION THEORY

Self-perception theory is the name given to an alternative interpretation of cognitive dissonance phenomena proposed by Bem (1965, 1967). Essentially, it is a straightforward application of notions of self-attribution of the kind discussed in the last chapter. According to Bem, any self-report of attitude is an *inference* from observation of one's own behaviour, and, as with any other attributional inference, it takes account of the situational constraints, if any, under which such behaviour occurs. If the attitude-relevant behaviour occurs under situations of minimal constraint, an individual will infer that his attitude corresponds to the way in which he behaved. On the other hand, if the behaviour occurs under conditions when it can be attributed to situational constraints, no such correspondent inference will be made.

General support for the notion that attitudinal responses may be influenced by processes of self-observation comes from a number of sources. For instance, Ross, Insko, and Ross (1971) had subjects complete a questionnaire requiring ratings of agreement or disagreement with a large number of statements on a number of issues, and then at a later session returned these initial questionnaires to the subjects, but with some of the statements replaced by new ones, and with fictitious responses marked in against these, so as to appear to the subjects as though they were ratings that they themselves had made. When their attitudes on these new items were then assessed, subjects behaved as though the ratings assigned to them accurately reflected their 'true' opinions. Also, Kiesler, Nisbett, and Zanna (1969) found that subjects who had committed themselves to trying to persuade passers-by to sign a petition against air pollution, using arguments prepared by the experimenter, expressed attitudes more strongly against air pollution when the relevance of their own attitudes to such behaviour was emphasized, as compared with when they were led to believe that the reason for their commitment was a concern for the scientific value of the study. This was achieved by having a confederate agree immediately beforehand in the subject's presence to a similar request to present arguments on the topic of road safety by saying, in the first condition, 'Okay, I wouldn't mind convincing people about something I really believe in', and in the second condition, 'Okay, it would be good to be in a study that really shows something.'

Applied to the forced compliance paradigm, Bem's argument is that conditions which are designed to compensate for the dissonance supposedly incurred in any counter-attitudinal act, the prime example being the provision of a large incentive, are just the conditions which would allow an external attribution by the individual to situational factors ('I decided to do it for the money'), rather than an internal attribution to this attitude ('I decided to do it because that's what I believed'). The prediction is therefore that high dissonance (e.g., low incentive) conditions lead to more 'correspondent inferences', and hence to subjects reporting attitudes more closely in line with their behaviour.

Bem presents his proposition, however, in a very extreme form. He does not simply say that dissonance-reduction may be a special sub-class of self-attribution. Instead, he says that the attributions a person will make concerning his own attitudes are *the same* as those that would be made by an independent observer with access to the same information. To substantiate this thesis, Bem (1965, 1967) presents evidence from a procedurally novel set of experiments, which he calls 'interpersonal simulations'. Such simulations typically take the form of presenting observer-subjects with a summary description of the experimental situation used in a well-known study supporting dissonance theory, telling them of the agreement by an individual subject to perform the counter-attitudinal act requested by the original experimenter, with information about the incentive provided in a given condition, and then asking them to predict the original subject's final attitude response. Among the studies so simulated are those by Cohen (1962) and by Festinger and Carlsmith (1959). Superficially, the results seem to offer good support for Bem's position, with the predictions of the observer-subjects closely paralleling the responses of the actual subjects in the original experiments.

Before one hastens to commend such simulations as an easy, cheap, and non-deceptive method of testing social psychological theories, two questions need to be asked. The first is simply: *so what?* Even if exact simulations produce exact replications of results, does this discriminate between different theoretical explanations? Not at all—it is quite conceivable that states of dissonance arousal and reduction could be experienced vicariously by empathic observers if the simulations were at all realistic, just as we may experience other emotions vicariously whenever we watch a convincing film. Second, do *exact* simulations in fact produce exact replications? Jones, Linder, Kiesler, Zanna, and Brehm (1968) point out that Bem's (1965) observer-subjects, for instance in the simulation of the Cohen (1962) study, were told of the agreement of just one actual subject with the experimenter's request, and so may have concluded that many of those approached may have refused. They may thus have concluded that any subject who did agree to write a pro-police essay *already* had pro-police attitudes, especially where there would have been no other obvious reason, such as a large monetary reward, for doing so.

Jones *et al.*, therefore, compared the results of a replication of the Cohen study (with $0.50 and $1 incentives) run with Bem's instructions (where observer-subjects were told that the 'actual' subject had been selected at random) with conditions where observer-subjects were told that the original experimenter had contacted a number of students, *all* of whom had indicated negative attitudes towards the police. The idea behind this was to prevent observer-subjects from inferring that an accident of random sampling had given them an exceptional case who was pro-police and agreed to write the essay. When Bem's instructions were used, the same pattern of results was obtained as in Bem's and Cohen's original study. However, with these new instructions, the results were reversed.

Jones *et al.* also included conditions which included fuller details of the instructions given to subjects in the Cohen study (which enumerated a variety of reasons for writing the essay) than the more abbreviated summary used by Bem. Here again, Bem's findings were not confirmed—observer-subjects gave, on average, the same estimate of the actual subject's attitude response regardless of the level of incentive that had supposedly been offered. An even more complete simulation of Cohen's procedure by Piliavin, Piliavin, Loewenton, McCauley, and Hammond (1969) again found no differences among observer-subjects' estimates as a function of incentive level ($0.50, $1, and $5).

The implication of these findings seems to be that observer-subjects do not generally reproduce the responses of actual subjects when the conditions of the original experiment are replicated precisely. Bem's results appear to be the product of the deletion of details from the original procedures that were judged by him to have been non-essential, on intuitive rather than empirical grounds. An important deletion seems often to have been anything that allows the observer-subjects to infer what the actual subject's attitude was prior to the act of compliance, and this might lead one to expect that self-perception theory generally will only be able to predict attitude change in forced compliance situations when subjects ignore, or are unaware of, their initial attitudes.

A small number of experiments have therefore attempted to contrast dissonance and self-perception theories by investigating the effect on subjects' attitudes of making their initial attitudes prior to compliance more salient. The argument as put forward by Bem and McConnell (1970), is that stressing the counter-attitudinal nature of any essay-writing or similar task, by reminding subjects of their prior attitudes, should lead to greater dissonance and hence *more* attitude change according to dissonance theory, but to *less* attitude change from a self-perception theory point of view, since subjects would be more likely to use this extra information as a basis for 'inferring' their true beliefs. Implicit in this position is the notion that subjects in a typical forced compliance study are not normally too attentive to what their prior attitudes may have been, unless the experimenter goes out of his way to make these salient.

Bem and McConnell had subjects write counter-attitudinal essays on the issue of student control of curricula under conditions of apparent freedom or absence of choice. After writing the essay, half the subjects were simply asked to record their final attitudes, whereas the remainder were asked to say what their previous attitudes had been prior to the experiment, before they recorded their final attitudes. (Actual measures of subjects' initial attitudes had been obtained one week earlier.) The results showed clearly that subjects' estimates of their initial attitudes were practically the same as their ratings of their final attitudes and were more highly correlated with final attitudes than with actual initial attitudes.

Two subsequent studies employed the same issue and basic procedure as Bem and McConnell, but with an additional manipulation to increase the salience of prior attitudes for half the subjects. Snyder and Ebbesen (1972) accomplished this by telling some of their subjects, prior to 'choice' or 'no choice' instructions to write a counter-attitudinal essay, to 'take a few minutes to think about and organize your thoughts and views on the issue'. Their results showed more attitude change under 'choice' than 'no choice' instructions, except when subjects were made to think about their own views beforehand. The choice manipulation had no reliable effect after their initial attitudes had been made salient in this way. Ross and Shulman (1973) instead contrasted a 're-instatement' condition, in which subjects re-read a questionnaire they had completed one week earlier and which contained a response to the critical issue now singled out for special attention, with a 'non-re-instatement' condition in which subjects were not allowed to examine their previous responses. The results of this study showed more attitude change under choice than no-choice conditions, regardless of the reinstatement manipulation. Although subjects in the reinstatement condition, as was intended, were able to recall their prior attitudes significantly more accurately than those in the non-reinstatement condition, they showed no less attitude change as a result.

But would these studies have allowed a crucial test to be made of the two theories, whatever the results had been? The finding that subjects do not accurately recall their earlier attitudes *after* engaging in counter-attitudinal behaviour (Bem and McConnell, 1970) *may* show that such initial attitudes are irrelevant to later responses, or it may reflect the selective forgetting of dissonant cognitions. Shaffer (1975) has since found greater error in recall of prior attitudes following counter-attitudinal rather than pro-attitudinal advocacy. Moreover, dissonance theory predicts attitude change as a function of counter-attitudinal advocacy only to the extent that cognitions concerning one's attitudes are less resistant to change than other relevant cognitions. Making initial attitudes more salient might simply make them more resistant to change and hence, according to dissonance theory, impel the subject to explore alternative modes of dissonance reduction other than a change in attitude. Greenwald (1975) has even proposed that self-perception theory could be used to predict greater 'attitude change' following increased salience of initial attitudes. Essentially, the argument is that an observer of a person's counter-attitudinal behaviour could interpret the emphasis on the person's previous attitudes as a 'situational demand' which should militate *against* the occurrence of the behaviour—in Kelley's (1971) terms, it would count as an inhibitory condition. Under such circumstances, the observer might infer that the person's *present* attitude corresponded even more closely with his behaviour, and the same should apply to self-attribution of attitude.

Greenwald's intention is to show that a truly crucial test of the two theories is impossible. However, if we allow Bem to derive his own specific predictions, the balance of evidence shows that these are not confirmed as convincingly as those of dissonance theory. Yet these specific predictions are not required by any *general* attributional approach to cognitive dissonance phenomena. For instance, Bem's assumption that self-attributions of attitude should be exactly the same as those that would be made by an outside observer would no longer seriously be entertained by most attribution theorists, in view of the work on actor-observer differences in attribution (see Chapter 4). Even if Bem's procedures and predictions have met with only mixed success, therefore, the viability of an attributional interpretation of cognitive dissonance phenomena remains an open question.

Rather than assuming that attribution theory and cognitive dissonance theory *are* fundamentally different, that is, that they posit different psychological processes and/or make different predictions about how these processes operate, it may be more fruitful to view these theories as describing essentially the same processes, but in terms of different conceptual language. This does not necessarily mean that no choice between them is possible, but rather that the choice is unlikely to be made on the basis of some 'crucial' empirical data consistent with one of the theories but not the other. Instead, the relevant criterion would seem to be the power of each theory (that is, each conceptual language) to relate the phenomena under consideration, within a changing scientific and cultural content, to other knowledge that has been acquired concerning the ways in which individuals operate psychologically in their social environment.

From this perspective, the choice is one between a theory that has as its central concept a notion of tension reduction, and one that has in its place a notion of rational inference. In a sense, the choice may come to depend on how useful these concepts respectively prove to be in *other* fields of psychology, but such a line of reasoning would lead us beyond the scope of this volume. Bem unequivocally regards the notion of internal motivational states as implied by dissonance theory to be irrelevant or even non-existent, and is happy to label himself as a 'radical behaviourist' for doing so. Instead, he argues that statements of attitude should be seen as observable responses contingent on observable stimuli (specifically, attitude-relevant behaviour within specific situations). As I argued at the start of Chapter 2, such talk about stimuli and responses does not get one very far. To be sure, attitude statements must refer to observable phenomena in order to be intelligible, but this entails nothing about any feelings of tension the individual may, or may not, be experiencing.

Is there any direct evidence for such a tension as a function of dissonance arousal? It is a fair criticism of much of the cognitive dissonance literature that researchers have rarely attempted to measure their central construct, but have instead inferred its existence from predicted changes in their dependent variables. Festinger and Bramel (1962) have even suggested that there may be an overlap between states of cognitive dissonance and states of psychoanalytic (i.e., *un*conscious) conflict. However, a study by Zanna and Cooper (1974) provides some important information on this point. They had subjects write a counter-attitudinal essay under conditions of high or low perceived choice (hence, high or low dissonance), but in addition gave all subjects a placebo pill before they wrote the essay. Subjects were either told that it would make them feel tense, that it would make them feel relaxed, or were given no information. The results are shown in Table 5.1.

When subjects were not led to expect any side effects from the drug, the typical dissonance result was obtained (with the important additional information that these subjects reported greater feelings of tension under high

Table 5.1 Mean agreement with the position defended in the counter-attitudinal essay in each condition of the Zanna and Cooper (1974) study

	Potential side-effect of the drug		
	Tenseness	None	Relaxation
High choice	3·4	9·1	13·4
Low choice	3·5	4·5	4·7

Note: Higher scores indicate greater agreement, 31-point scale, $n = 10$ per cell.

choice instructions). However, this effect was eliminated when subjects were able to attribute any experienced tension to the drug, and significantly enhanced when they were given 'relaxation' instructions, the effect of which was intended to make them think, 'If I'm feeling this tense writing the essay after taking a drug to make me relaxed, I must be *really* tense'.

These findings are complemented by a more recent study by Cooper, Zanna, and Taves (1978). Again, subjects had to write a counter-attitudinal essay (defending President Ford's pardoning of Richard Nixon) under high or low choice instructions. There were also three drug conditions, with the difference that this time one-third actually received a tranquilizer (phenobarbital), one-third amphetamine, and one-third a placebo, but *all* subjects were told that the pill they had taken was in a fact a placebo. Subjects given amphetamine, therefore, should feel most aroused, but not attribute their arousal to the drug. On the other hand, the tranquilizer should suppress any dissonance-produced arousal, and subjects should not attribute such lack of arousal to the drug. The results are shown in Table 5.2. As can be seen, the results confirmed the predictions, with the additional finding of a change in the low choice amphetamine condition. It should be noted that in this same condition, possibly because they felt so aroused, subjects (wrongly) reported that the choice to write the essay had been a free one.

It is fascinating that these two studies not only provide evidence for the central tenet of dissonance theory, that attitude change is mediated by arousal, but do so by means of a classic technique used in studies of the self-attribution of emotion (e.g., Schachter and Singer, 1962). This argues forcibly for the compatibility of the dissonance and attribution approaches. Dissonance research has for some time been paying increasing attention to variables that may mediate the arousal of dissonance, and these variables—perceived freedom of choice, perceived responsibility, foreseeability of consequences—turn out to have a great deal in common with the central concern of attribution theorists. Attribution theory assumes that individuals are motivated to find explanations for events, and that apparent anomalies, or

Table 5.2 Mean agreement with the position defended in the counter-attitudinal essay in each condition of the Cooper, Zanna, and Taves (1978) study

	Type of drug administered		
	Tranquilizer	Placebo	Amphetamine
High choice	8·6	14·7	20·2
Low choice	8·0	8·3	13·9

Note: Higher scores indicate greater agreement, 31-point scale, $n = 10$ per cell.

unexplained occurrences, will 'engage the attribution process'. Dissonance has been particularly, though not exclusively, concerned with explanations, or justifications, for decisions taken, and makes the additional assumption that an individual who sees himself as having taken an important decision for no reason will experience tension. This hypothesized state of tension, however, is still essentially cognitive in nature, and is derived from the same 'motivation' proposed by attribution theorists—the need to explain one's environment.

A question which remains is whether the attribution process will become 'engaged' in situations where there is no apparent anomaly or experienced tension. Fazio, Zanna, and Cooper (1977) have suggested that self-perception theory may be more applicable to behaviour which is congruent with a person's attitude, and dissonance theory to counter-attitudinal behaviour. However, there may still be situations when having to defend one's own position produces tension of a kind, or when counter-attitudinal behaviour prompts changes in self-attributions.

WHAT IS 'DISSONANCE'?

Recently, an important challenge to cognitive dissonance theory has been published by Nuttin (1975). In what he calls a 'response-contagion' theory of persuasion, Nuttin argues that so-called 'dissonance' effects (specifically, within the forced-compliance paradigm) do not arise from any strictly *cognitive* dissonance, but are to be attributed to the general arousal effects of any novel or unusual situation. The first part of his argument is to deny that varying levels of incentive work in the manner that dissonance theory assumes. According to dissonance theory, the performance of counter-attitudinal acts arouses dissonance by virtue of the inconsistency between cognitions of the form, 'I have argued in favour of X' and, 'I am opposed to X'. The provision of a large, but not a small, incentive is then assumed to cancel out, or compensate for, this inconsistency (what Nuttin calls 'central dissonance'), so that the motivation for attitude change is removed in the former, but not the latter, case. The assumption is that low incentives are *just sufficient* to elicit the subjects' compliance, but are not large enough to provide a *justification* for such compliance.

Nuttin argues that this last assumption is essentially devoid of empirical support. Dissonance researchers have repeatedly found attitudinal shifts in low, as compared with high, incentive conditions, but have *not* compared low reward with *zero* reward conditions. What might we expect to happen in a zero reward condition? The accepted rationale for low incentive conditions implies that, without a 'just sufficient' incentive, subjects would refuse to comply with the experimenter's request. Yet the decision on what constitutes an appropriate low incentive has been made generally on the basis of intuition or precedence, rather than any systematic attempt to reduce the level of incentive to the minimum. It might well be the case that the removal of all incentives would *not* lead to a marked fall in the rate of compliance. Even though it is difficult, if the assumption of 'central dissonance' arousal is correct, to see why *any* subjects would comply, there is now ample evidence of subjects' willingness to perform considerably more bizarre and threatening activities rather than confront the experimenter and deny his right to make a request (Milgram, 1974, see Chapter 8). It is thus possible that subjects would often be prepared to oblige the experimenter *anyway*. If so, what happens to 'central dissonance'? According to dissonance theory, it should be even greater among compliant subjects in a zero than a low reward condition, so that subjects who are given *no* reward should show even greater attitudinal shifts in the direction of the position they are required to advocate than those who receive low rewards.

Apparently, things are not so simple. In one of a number of experiments reported by Nuttin (1975), Belgian students were approached by a female experimenter, who posed as a reporter from the national broadcasting company, and complied with her request to record arguments, for use in a radio programme, against reform of the university examination system. This, of course, was directly contrary to their own position. The experiment included two conditions comparable to the low and high incentive conditions of other dissonance experiments (20 Belgian Francs and 200 Belgian Francs), and measures of subjects' attitudes after they had recorded their speech revealed the expected 'dissonance' result, with those who received the smaller reward showing the greater shift, in favour of the traditional examination system. However, the experiment also included a zero reward condition. Here, subjects failed to show the shift found in the 20BF condition, giving instead a mean response which was almost the same as that in the 200BF, as well as that in a control condition, where subjects were given no reward, but argued in favour of their own position (Nuttin, 1975, page 87). Thus we have the paradoxical result, apparently inconsistent with dissonance theory, that a low reward leads to more attitude change (presumably as a result of greater dissonance arousal) than no reward at all.

Another condition of the same experiment brings us a little nearer to an explanation. This was a 'relative deprivation' condition, in which subjects were told that those students who had taken part so far (among whom, by implication, there would be many who would have been allowed to argue in favour of reform) had been paid for doing so, but that the broadcasting company's funds allocated for these payments was now used up, so that they themselves would not receive any payment. These subjects showed the most anti-reform attitudes of any of the groups, even more than those in the 20BF condition. As in the Cooper and Brehm (1971) study already discussed, not being paid for a task for which others have been paid arouses dissonance, or, less interpretatively, can lead to 'dissonance-reducing' attitude change. But this suggests a crucial departure from the assumptions of earlier studies such as that by Festinger and Carlsmith (1959). *It is not that a large reward necessarily reduces dissonance, but that the inequitable withholding of a reward gives rise to dissonance.* If the subject is not led to expect that the task is one for which he should be paid—if, in other words, the question of payment never arises—he may well show no evidence of 'central dissonance' or consequential attitude change. Presumably, in such cases he construes his behaviour as a personal favour, or as a contribution to scientific enquiry, but its *counter*-attitudinal aspects, according to Nuttin, are essentially irrelevant. If, however, the question of payment arises, the subject then has to assess whether the payment is appropriate or equitable. Such an assessment of 'appropriateness' may depend on many factors—how difficult the task was (which may be related to whether pro- or counter-attitudinal advocacy was required), how much other participants were paid, as well as the resources of the person who gives the payment. What would be appropriate as a token of appreciation from a fellow-student might be seen as quite derisory from a national broadcasting company, and it is an interesting speculation how many student experimental projects, aimed at replicating standard dissonance results, may have 'failed' because 'low' rewards were seen by subjects as all that the experimenter could afford. Thus, whereas the dissonance theory account is that large rewards compensate for 'central dissonance', but small rewards leave it unaffected, Nuttin argues that so-called large rewards are typically not too much more than the subjects would expect, granted that they are to be paid for the task at all, but that small rewards are perceived as inappropriately low. It is, according to Nuttin, this inappropriateness of the *reward*, rather than the counter-attitudinal nature of the *task*, that produces whatever psychological tension or arousal may be experienced, and that leads to the observed changes in attitudinal responses.

Nuttin goes on to provide additional data aimed at clarifying this notion of 'inappropriateness'. In these later experiments, the same female experimenter, now in the true role of a junior member of staff in Nuttin's department, elicited counter-attitudinal arguments from male psychology students on the same general issue of examination reform, under conditions which departed from subjects' expectations in a number of ways.

In the first of these experiments (Nuttin, 1975, page 119), very marked 'dissonance-reducing' shifts were produced when the experimenter supposedly altered the rather bad mark obtained by the student in a recent examination in the student's favour—clearly a most unusual but very welcome reward. This effect was even stronger when the experimenter did this (offering the student money as an alternative) before the student prepared the counter-attitudinal speech. So here a reward which was probably inappropriately *generous*, and certainly violated role expectations in the kind of generosity involved, produced shifts of the same order as those produced by an inappropriately low, or inequitably withheld, reward in the previous experiment.

Next, Nuttin added a condition which was inappropriately aversive from the subjects' point of view. Here the experimenter unjustly accused the student of disrupting a lecture she had recently given, before he started on the counter-attitudinal task. Again, a shift was found in the direction of making subjects' final attitude responses more consistent with the speech they had produced (Nuttin, 1975, page 136). This result is reminiscent of a finding by Zimbardo, Weisenberg, Firestone, and Levy (1965), that students and army reservists who were asked to 'volunteer' to eat grasshoppers subsequently rated grasshoppers as less unpleasant to eat when the experimenter had made the request in an unfriendly, as compared with a friendly, manner.

Finally Nuttin (1975, page 150) found comparable shifts following a very different kind of 'inappropriateness', which he terms the '"dissonant" dress' condition. This involved the student, on arrival at the experimental room, finding the experimenter, his lecturer, 'dressed in very short hot-pants and an exceptionally low-necked T-shirt'—definitely *not* the normal outfit for a Belgian lady academic!

Nuttin argues that what all the experimental conditions which produce shifts in the 'dissonance-reducing' direction have in common is that they confront the subject with a novel or incongruous situation, and that it is *this* incongruity or novelty, rather than the presumed inconsistency between initial attitudes and compliance with the experimenter's request—the so-called 'central dissonance'—which produces the arousal that is the precursor of changes in attitude response. This analysis, however, does not so far explain why such arousal should lead to attitude change rather than any other response, since it is difficult to see how changing one's attitude reduces the incongruity of the experimental situation. Nuttin's answer is an intriguing one—arousal does *not* lead to a change in attitude response unless the response is elicited.

The main evidence for this assertion comes from a comparison between conditions where subjects' post-advocacy attitudes were measured first at the time of the original experimental session, and then again about five weeks later, and conditions where the first of these measurement phases was omitted. The stability of the shifts produced in the first set of conditions after this intervening period is impressive (Nuttin, 1975, page 169). Where the first measurement phase was omitted, however, subjects' responses, assessed for the first time five weeks after the experiment, showed no evidence of any shift. '*There appears to be no trace of any attitude change effect in a situation where the attitude response was not emitted in close temporal contiguity with the ongoing counterattitudinal verbal responses.*' (Nuttin, 1975, pages 170–171.)

On the strength of these data, Nuttin puts forward his purportedly *non-cognitive* interpretation of cognitive dissonance phenomena. Arousal tends to stabilize ongoing behaviour, so that when a person is induced to produce particular verbal responses, such as a counter–attitudinal plea, under highly arousing conditions, there is an increased probability of his making a qualitatively similar response on a verbal rating scale if questioned about his attitude immediately afterwards. This is derived from the notion that arousing conditions [e.g., social facilitation (Zajonc, 1965)] tend to increase the probability of a response that is 'dominant' in an individual's repertoire, i.e., one that already, as a function of previous learning, has a high probability of occurrence. Whether this derivation is authentic depends on whether one accepts that what normally applies to dominant responses also applies to ongoing responses, since the subject's counter–attitudinal behaviour would *not* have had a high probability of occurrence prior to the experiment. Nonetheless, it is interesting that arousing conditions, all involving some violation of expectations, but not all intentionally related to the manipulation of *cognitive* dissonance, may produce shifts that appear at least as stable as those resulting from more conventional manipulations.

At the same time, it would be premature to regard Nuttin's results as damaging dissonance theory beyond the point of repair or compromise. Nuttin succeeds in demonstrating that subjects' attitudes, as measured by verbal response scales, change in the direction of the position they were induced to advocate if they either received an inequitably low reward, received a large but unethical reward (the extra examination marks), were confronted by an unjustly accusing and hostile experimenter, or had to prepare and present their speech with the experimenter dressed in such a way that it must have been very difficult for them to give their full attention to the task in hand. In addition to the studies already mentioned, unethical counter-attitudinal behaviour has been claimed to be particularly dissonance-arousing (Aronson, 1969), and the effort of performing a task is supposed to be directly predictive of the magnitude of dissonance produced (Aronson and Mills, 1959; Lawrence and Festinger, 1962). Nuttin's manipulations, therefore, need not be regarded as necessarily beyond the scope of a dissonance framework. There are also other manipulations, notably the perception of decision freedom, which certainly are predictive of the magnitude of 'dissonance' effects, but which seem less obviously interpretable within Nuttin's approach. Finally, Nuttin deals only with the forced compliance paradigm, and it remains to be seen if his theory can account for different paradigms, such as the free decision situation when an individual has to choose between attractive alternatives.

In a direct attempt to compare dissonance and response contagion interpretations, Verhaeghe (1976) has shown that situations may be emotionally arousing but still not lead to the attitude change effects predicted by Nuttin. In a variation on the Festinger and Carlsmith (1959) study, subjects were induced to persuade two stooges to spend an extra amount of time performing a boring task. In addition to replicating the standard dissonance effect with a low incentive and a high incentive condition, Verhaeghe introduced a 'compensation' condition and a 'retaliation' condition. In the first of these, each subject was given the opportunity, after he had apparently successfully persuaded the stooges, of compensating them for the deception. In the second, the stooges had acted unpleasantly towards the subject during the period between his counter-attitudinal advocacy and the elicitation of the final attitude response. In other respects these two conditions followed the procedure of the 'low incentive' condition and, therefore, should have produced the same degree of emotional arousal at the time subjects performed their counter-attitudinal behaviour, and hence the same amount of attitude change according to response contagion theory. In fact, no attitude change was produced in either of these two conditions—a result which Verhaeghe interprets as showing that dissonance was reduced through the cognitions that the stooges would be compensated for the aversive consequences of the subjects' deception of them, or that they had acted in such a way that they deserved these consequences.

The most important conclusions to be drawn from Nuttin's results at the present time relate to the denial of the concept of 'central dissonance' and the specificity of the kind of 'attitude change' produced. It does seem that we should move away from a concept of dissonance as aroused by counter-attitudinal behaviour *per se*, but compensated for by high rewards or the denial of personal responsibility, and think instead of dissonance as produced only under specific conditions. Also, one should hesitate before assuming that one is witnessing changes in general social attitudes rather than specific expressive responses. As Nuttin points out (1975, pages 178–179), there is evidence from other studies (Festinger and Carlsmith, 1959; Carlsmith, Collins, and Helmreich, 1966) that 'dissonance' effects may only be found on scales that incorporate the *specific words* used in the counter-attitudinal argument.

LABELLING, JUSTIFICATION, AND ATTITUDE CHANGE

As was discussed in the chapter on social judgement, an important feature of the way in which individuals seek to justify their own standpoints on an issue may be the particular words they use to label different positions. Specifically, there seems to be a general preference for descriptive language that allows one to label one's own position positively and opposing positions negatively. What implications might this have for attitude change? The literature on forced compliance shows that, under certain conditions, a person induced to engage in a specific kind of expressive behaviour will change his response on a linguistically appropriate measure of attitude, so as to reduce the inconsistency between the expressive behaviour and the attitudinal response. Such 'expressive behaviour' consists of the presentation of *arguments* of the kind that one would normally expect of someone who was genuinely for or against the issue in question. But what would happen if such expressive behaviour consisted of the use of particular evaluative *labels* congruent with either a favourable or unfavourable attitude on the issue? This was the question examined in studies by Eiser and Mower White (1974b), Eiser and Ross (1977), and Eiser and Pancer (1979).

The hypothesis of these studies was that, if people prefer to use evaluative language which enables them to label their own position positively, then inducing people to construe, or discuss, an issue in terms of specific evaluative labels should predispose them to adopt a position more congruent with the implicit value connotations of such labels. In other words, if pro-authority teenagers prefer to construe the issue of adult authority over young people in terms of labels such as disobedient-obedient rather than adventurous-unadventurous, then inducing teenagers to apply labels such as disobedient-obedient to the issue should make them more pro-authority, whereas inducing them to apply labels such as adventurous-unadventurous should make them more anti-authority. Thus, the use of evaluative language may affect attitudes, just as attitudes affect the use of evaluative language.

The Eiser and Mower White (1974b) study involved three parallel classes of 12- to 13-year-olds who were presented with the 10 statements concerning adult authority used in the studies by Eiser and Mower White (1974a, 1975) discussed in Chapter 3. Subjects in the class serving as the *control* condition were simply instructed to rate their agreement with the statements. The *pro-bias* condition, however, were first told that the questionnaire was 'a survey designed to find out if you are the kind of person who is obedient, helpful, polite, and cooperative as opposed to the sort of person who is disobedient, unhelpful, rude, and uncooperative'. In the *anti-bias* condition, subjects were told instead that the questionnaire was, 'a survey designed to find out if you are the sort of person who is bold, adventurous, creative, and with-it, as opposed to the sort of person who is timid, unadventurous, uncreative, and old-fashioned.' As predicted, subjects were able to discern the kind of attitude which would be 'socially desirable' in terms of the instructions, giving more pro-authority attitude scores in the pro-bias, and more anti-authority attitude scores in the anti-bias, condition.

The main experiment reported by Eiser and Ross consisted of a comparison between a *pro-bias* condition, in which subjects were induced to use words consistent with a pro attitude, and an *anti-bias* condition, in which they were induced to use words consistent with an anti attitude. The prediction was that those in the former condition should shift their attitudes in a more pro direction, as compared with those in the latter condition, who should shift their attitudes in a more anti direction. The subjects for this experiment were Canadian introductory psychology students, who had completed a questionnaire during a lecture period to measure their attitudes on a number of topics including the critical issue, capital punishment. About one week later, they were contacted by telephone and asked to take part in an ostensibly unconnected experiment in psycholinguistics. On their arrival, they were instructed to write an essay on the topic of capital punishment, incorporating as many words as possible from a list of 15, the supposed aim being to see how this affected the 'stylistic structure and verbal fluency' of their essays. In the pro-bias condition, all the words in the list implied a negative evaluation of the abolitionist position (e.g., over-sentimental, starry-eyed). In the anti-bias condition, they all implied a negative evaluation of capital punishment (e.g., callous, sadistic). Subjects were *not* told to write either for or against capital punishment, but only to use the words provided.

After writing the essay, subjects had to rate their own opinion towards capital punishment. They were also divided into a pro and anti group on the basis of their attitudes towards capital punishment expressed in the previous questionnaire. As can be seen from Table 5.3, the pro group rated themselves much more pro than the anti group in both conditions, indicating that their attitudes on this issue were reasonably stable. Nonetheless, the predicted effect for the self-ratings to be more positive in the pro-bias condition achieved significance. Table 5.3 also shows the mean number of words out of 15 incorporated in the essays by each group of subjects, and, as can be seen, subjects used more words if they were given a list which was evaluatively congruent with their own attitude.

Eiser and Pancer used a similar design, with British teenagers as subjects, and the issue being that of adult authority over young people. The attitude shifts found by Eiser and Ross were replicated with biased word lists which included both evaluatively positive and evaluatively negative labels. No change in attitude was observed in a control condition, who also wrote an essay but were given no words to incorporate. However, one week later it was found that these shifts had largely disappeared. Thus, although the initial changes were consistent with prediction, it is doubtful whether this kind of manipulation (or at any rate a single trial of it) can produce long-term shifts in attitudinal responses as stable as those found by Nuttin (1975) and others who have used more typical 'dissonance' procedures.

An additional question concerns the relationship between evaluative language and what Abelson (1976) has referred to as 'scripts' (see Chapter 2). The idea that individuals organize their cognitions in terms of interrelated propositions which may be expressed linguistically could imply that changes in such organization, and hence in attitude, would follow if individuals were led to use particular kinds of scripts, or to modify their existing scripts in particular ways. It is possible that repeated exposure to (and/or use of) evaluatively biased language might have this effect, but when Eiser and Ross

Table 5.3 Mean self-ratings of attitude following essay-writing, and mean number of words from list of 15 incorporated by each group of subjects, in the Eiser and Ross (1977) study

Initial attitude	Pro-bias		Anti-bias	
	Pro	Anti	Pro	Anti
Self-rating	88·5	29·3	61·0	19·6
Number of words	11·0	8·3	8·7	11·3

Note: 0 = extremely unfavourable, 100 = extremely favourable.

required subjects to incorporate short arguments (e.g., 'Capital punishment is primitive') instead of single words, no attitude change was observed.

There is considerable evidence of a less experimental nature, however, that points to the fact that evaluatively biased labels or slogans are used to change people's attitudes. Even if the claimed effectiveness of such techniques may sometimes be exaggerated, the concept of a product's 'image' is basic to most commercial advertising. What is being communicated is typically a positive evaluation. There are clearly hosts of possible examples, but perhaps one of the more ironic is the name of a brand of cigarettes currently on the market in West Germany—*Life*.

Political propaganda contains many examples of slogans whose purpose is hardly to convey 'information', but rather to suggest a way of categorizing uncertain events and situations. For evidence of the explicit assumptions behind one of the most obscene, but effective, campaigns of political persuasion in recent history, we need look no further than the following remarkable passage by Hadamovsky (1933), a deputy to Goebbels:

> The unsophisticated man, and even more so the broad masses, will almost invariably yield to the power of the word, without concern for its inner truth. It is not the truth inherent in the word itself which gives the lie to what has been said, but rather a new word pitted against the old. . . . Politics avails itself of the technique of creating expressions to win over the masses and to hold new followers forever within the spell of a definite conception and *Weltanschauung*. . . . The French revolution set in motion the era of the struggles of the masses. . . . The refined old language of diplomacy yielded to the earthy and impetuous terminology of political mass propaganda. . . . Liberty, equality, fraternity, capitalism, socialism, communism, profit, surplus value, proceeds, world economy, Soviet Germany, nationalism, blood, soil, race, autarchy, the Third Reich, these are some of the slogans of this language, slogans which by themselves as well as in their derivations encompass entire *Weltanschauungen*. They beat down on the adversary, pound him, create doubt, fear repulsion and agreement. To those who believe in these slogans they appear as positive promises of a brighter future. . . . The political layman is suddenly confronted by an enigmatic linguistic ogre, a flood of alien concepts through which he receives a strictly one-sided impression of a world mysteriously confined and stupefying. Thus he is faced by a linguistic monster manifesting itself through words—recruiting and organizing.

CONCLUSIONS

The consequences of such 'recruiting and organizing' are only too familiar, but what is even more frightening is the extent to which Hadamovsky's 'political laymen' felt *justified* in their atrocities and acts of aggression. The empirical research reviewed in this chapter has provided many examples of, mercifully, less dramatic conversions. Such research does not, however, provide us with conclusive instances of changes in 'generalized social attitudes' as conventionally defined. All that can be said with confidence is that changes in specific evaluative responses can be reliably and predictably produced. Does this mean, as Nuttin (1975) argues, that attitude change in the conventional sense is an illusion? One of the major arguments of this book is that 'generalized social attitudes' are constructs of the psychologist rather than measurable entities in the heads of one's subjects. If something does not exist, any feeling that it changes must be illusory. But to dismiss changes in evaluative responses as *mere* linguistic effects runs counter to the observation, if we believe Hadamovsky, that linguistic processes can produce changes in entire *Weltanschanauungen,* or world views, changes that in turn may lead to violent changes in behaviour. Psychologists should not blindly impose their own general constructs on the psychological processes of their subjects, but each individual is entitled to choose his *own* general interpretative framework to explain and justify his own experience. The motivation to see one's own behaviour as justified, and to see it as intrinsically motivating even in the absence of external justification, is one of the most important principles of human social behaviour, and to study it properly, we cannot ignore the language in which such justification is expressed.

Because of this, there are definite limits to the applicability of any simple principle of reinforcement to the area of attitude change. Whatever one wants to make of the periodic fluctuations in the popularity of cognitive dissonance theory, it is quite clear that changes in attitude can be observed which go directly counter to such a reinforcement principle, at least as it pertains to incentives offered in advance of the behaviour. Such 'dissonance' effects are themselves contingent on a number of conditions, of which the most important are that the subject can see himself as having chosen freely, and having taken the consequences of his action into account at the time he made his choice. Similar considerations apply to the research on 'overjustification' effects, where individuals can lose interest in a task as a result of being given excessive extrinsic rewards, provided the task is one which they would normally find attractive, provided they are aware of the extrinsic rewards when performing the task, and provided such rewards are given irrespective of the quality of performance.

SUMMARY

* A number of studies have found that subjects' apparent 'intrinsic' wish to perform an activity for its own sake may be undermined by the provision of additional 'extrinsic' incentives. However, intrinsic motivation does not seem to be undermined by rewards which are made contingent on the quality of subjects' performance. Also, these studies do not permit an extrapolation to situations where the activity in question would not be performed in the absence of any incentive.
* Cognitive dissonance theory predicts a variety of attitudinal and behavioural consequences of people's presumed need to see their decisions as reasonable and justified.
* In the 'forced compliance' paradigm, subjects comply with an experimenter's request to behave in a way that is contrary to their own attitudes.

* Support has been found for the dissonance theory prediction that, following such counter-attitudinal behaviour, subjects will change their reported attitudes so as to be more in accordance with how they have behaved if they receive only a small reward for their behaviour. Less attitude change occurs if the reward is large.
* Limiting conditions for such effects include that subjects should see their compliance with the experimenter's request as a free choice, that the consequences of their choice could reasonably have been foreseen by them at the time, and that they see themselves as responsible for such consequences.
* Bem's self-perception theory reinterprets such effects in terms of self-attribution processes, without postulating a noxious internal state of dissonance, which individuals are motivated to reduce. However, there is only mixed support for his prediction that 'observer-subjects', provided simply with a description of the experimental procedures, can predict the responses of actual subjects undergoing the same procedures.
* There is evidence that physiological arousal may be a consequence of, as well as a factor which mediates the effects of, conditions hypothesized to be dissonance-arousing.
* Other evidence suggests that *inappropriately* low *or* high rewards may produce dissonance, but that compliance with a request to act counter-attitudinally need not do so, if the question of reward does not arise.
* Attitude change produced by forced-compliance procedures seems rather specific to particular verbal expressions used in defense of the counter-attitudinal position, and incorporated in the verbal measures of subjects' attitudes.
* If individuals are led to construe an issue in terms of language which implies a clear evaluative bias, they may change their attitudes in the direction of the more positively labelled extreme.

PART
THREE

PEOPLE AS PARTICIPANTS

INTERPERSONAL ATTRACTION

ATTRACTION RESEARCH AND COMMON SENSE

The question of how people become attracted to one another and form bonds of love and friendship is one to which everyone has their favourite answer, and experimental social psychologists have been no exception. Yet it is a question with so many facets that anyone who expects from social psychology—or from any other discipline or source—anything more than the most partial of answers, is in for a disappointment. Such a disappointment would be additionally acute for anyone who held the expectation that the answers which psychological 'science' has to offer must necessarily be new and surprising. This field is one where the dangers of misconstruing the purpose of social psychological research, and the relation between social psychological 'knowledge' and common sense, become particularly acute. It may be useful, therefore, to consider this relation briefly, before looking at the work of researchers in this field.

First of all, there is no need to assume that common sense notions concerning the bases of love and friendship bear no correspondence to reality. On the contrary, the 'reality' in question is a social reality, constructed from these self-same notions. People behave towards each other in a manner which reflects their subjective theories about what makes people do what. Individuals' accounts of their own relationships are thus not a source of information to be derogated in any way. On the contrary, where such information can be systematized, it is of very real value. From individual accounts to common sense notions, however, one has to cross a bridge from the particular to the universal, and in so doing so, one frequently loses the basis for any insight into individual or situational variation. Common sense notions, such as the proverb, 'Birds of a feather flock together', are verbalized at such a high level of generality that they give no glimpse at all of answers to questions of when, where, for whom, and to what extent. Yet these are precisely the questions that social psychological research is best equipped to answer.

Also, even when a finding seems obvious or commonsensical, it is not always obvious *why* it is obvious. If it is the case that people tend to prefer others whose attitudes are similar to their own, why is this so? If parental opposition can intensify a romantic attachment, why does this occur? Much of the endeavour of researchers in this field, therefore, has been to bring general explanatory principles to bear on the specific phenomena of interpersonal attraction, rather than to set about 'discovering' new phenomena. It is with these hypothesized explanatory principles—consistency, the need for consensual validation of one's beliefs, self-esteem, and reinforcement, the cognitive labelling of emotions, interdependence, and complementarity—that this chapter is concerned.

BALANCE AND SIMILARITY OF ATTITUDES

One of the first attempts to develop a social theory of attraction was made by Newcomb (1956). Newcomb's theory, for most relevant purposes, may be considered a restatement of Heider's (1946) theory of cognitive balance (see Chapter 2), applied to the specific issue of the prediction of positive and negative interpersonal attitudes from agreement and disagreement about an attitude object and vice versa. At its simplest, Newcomb's theory predicts that, if a person A perceives that another person B shares his opinion (whether positive or negative) about an object X, he will like B more than if he thinks B disagrees with him. In addition, if A likes B, he will be more likely to perceive B as liking him, as well as more likely to agree with him. An important difference between Heider's and Newcomb's formulations is that there will be little motivation to reduce imbalance, according to Newcomb, in situations when A dislikes B. Whereas Heider does not differentiate systematically between the three relationships of the *p-o-x* triad in terms of their importance for balance or imbalance, Newcomb places especial emphasis on the interpersonal link: if A likes B, he will be concerned that their attitudes should be in agreement, but if A dislikes B, B's attitudes will have little or no psychological significance for B, and will not, as Newcomb puts it, induce any 'strain toward symmetry'. Heider, however, would predict that people would be just as motivated to disagree with others whom they dislike, as to agree with others whom they like.

Much of the evidence reviewed in Chapter 2, which points to the importance of 'cognitive biases' other than balance, e.g., the importance of positivity and agreement, is directly relevant to the evaluation of Newcomb's theory at a formal level. An important difference between Newcomb and Heider, however, is that Newcomb does not claim to derive his theory from any *Gestalt* principle, but rather from a consideration of the conditions which facilitate interpersonal communication. Thus, one may avoid communicating with others whom one dislikes, or choose to communicate with others whom one likes, as a means of reducing the 'strain' produced by disagreement.

This difference is reflected in the kind of data Newcomb sought as support for his theory. Rather than the abstract paper-and-pencil tasks used by researchers such as Jordan (1953) to test Heider's theory, Newcomb looked for evidence in the patterns of attitude similarity and friendship which developed as members of 'real-life' groups became acquainted with each other. In an early investigation of this process, Newcomb (1943) described how female students attending a small private college in Vermont in the 'thirties (Bennington College) espoused the liberal attitudes of their lecturers and fellow-students, even though they came from predominantly conservative backgrounds, and stuck to their new attitudes long after leaving college. In another study, the attitudes of male college students who shared a house provided by the experimenter were monitored over a sixteen-week period. As the house-members' acquaintence with each other increased, patterns of friendship became more predictable from similarity of attitudes on various issues, including liking for other house-members (Newcomb, 1961).

There is also evidence from many sources pointing to the interrelationships between friendship and communication. In the classic study of housing communities by Festinger, Schachter, and Back (1950), physical proximity was found to be an important predictor of friendship patterns, with next-door neighbours most likely to become friends. Friendship has also been shown to be predictable from actual (Gullahorn, 1952), and anticipated, (Darley and Berscheid, 1967) amounts of interaction. The converse relationship also holds true, with individuals who are attracted to, or friendly with, each other being more likely to talk to each other in group discussions (Lott and Lott, 1961), keep physically closer to each other (Byrne, Ervin, and Lamberth, 1970), and maintain eye-contact (Exline, Gray, and Schuette, 1965; Goldberg, Kiesler, and Collins, 1969). Although such findings, taken individually, are perhaps not all that surprising, cumulatively they add up to a case for looking at interpersonal liking, not simply as an abstract evaluative response, but as functionally related to processes of communication and cooperative interaction. A large part of 'being friendly' seems to involve putting oneself (or being put) into situations which facilitate communication, the exchange of information, and the mutual transmission and reception of stimulation generally.

In spite of these considerations, a powerful research tradition has attempted to look at interpersonal attraction, and its relation to attitudinal similarity in particular, by using experimental situations which deliberately exclude the possibility of any such interaction or communication. At the centre of this tradition are the studies by Byrne and his associates.

ATTRACTION AND SIMILARITY OF ATTITUDES

In a short research note published in 1961, Byrne first described a procedure which was to serve as a paradigm for a long series of subsequent studies. Students were presented with an attitude scale to measure their positions on 26 different issues (e.g., God, premarital sex relations, classical music, politics). They also had to indicate which of the issues they considered to be the 13 most and the 13 least important. Two weeks later they were told that they had completed the scale as part of a study of interpersonal perception. They were then shown an anonymous questionnaire, supposedly of a student in another class, to 'determine how much they could learn about one another from this information alone' (page 714). This 'other student's' questionnaire was faked so that the responses were (1) identical to the subject's own on all issues, (2) opposite to the subject's own on all issues, (3) similar on important and dissimilar on unimportant issues, or (4) dissimilar on important and similar on unimportant issues.

When the 'other student' held similar as opposed to dissimilar attitudes on all issues, subjects indicated that they felt they would like him more, would enjoy working with him more, and rated him more intelligent, knowledgeable, moral, and well-adjusted. Smaller differences in the same direction were found when comparing the conditions where attitude similarity occurred on important as opposed to unimportant issues.

Since this first experiment, two themes appear to be discernible in Byrne's research. The first is the presentation of the basic relationship between attraction and attitude similarity as a generalized 'law', described in simple mathematical terms. Specifically, it is proposed that the degree of interpersonal attraction towards another is directly and linearly related to the proportion of attitudinal items on which this other holds similar, as opposed to dissimilar, attitudes to the subject (Byrne and Nelson, 1965). The cognitive processes involved here are obviously akin, if not identical, to those involved in studies of personality impression formation and information integration, and debates such as that over the respective merits of averaging and additive models can also be assumed to be applicable to this situation. The observed linear relationship seems to be generalizable beyond paper-and-pencil presentation of the 'other's' attitude to conditions involving sound and/or visual recordings (Byrne and Clore, 1966), and beyond the use of college students as subjects (Byrne and Griffitt, 1966). Nonetheless, the 'other' in these studies remains an object of perception, rather than a partner in any real interaction.

The second theme in Byrne's work is the attempt to offer a motivational interpretation of the effects of attitude similarity. Specifically, the knowledge that another person holds a similar attitude to oneself on a given issue is assumed to be a 'positive reinforcement' and the knowledge that another person holds a dissimilar attitude is assumed to be a 'negative reinforcement' (e.g., Byrne and Nelson, 1965). It is not altogether clear what responses are supposed to be reinforced by attitude similarity. It is plausible that subjects' responses to the original attitude items might be 'reinforced' by the knowledge that someone else (similar to oneself) held the same opinions, but this would mean interpreting Byrne's theory as a theory about attitude stability, rather than interpersonal attraction. Responses in the form of *actual* approach, cooperation, and bond-formation are excluded by virtue of the experimental paradigm employed. This seems to leave the verbal ratings of attraction, which after all are the main dependent variable in these studies, as the most likely candidates for the status of 'reinforced responses'. However, one then runs into the problem that the same information about another's attitudes has to be assumed to be both the *basis* for such an evaluative response, and the *reinforcer* of that response. Perhaps it is fairest to interpret the phrase 'positive reinforcement' as Byrne uses it to mean nothing much more precise than 'something nice', and not to inquire too closely into what is meant to be being reinforced. The question of why similarity of attitudes should be 'nice' and dissimilarity should be 'nasty' still remains, and has not been ignored by Byrne and his colleagues. The answer which he suggests makes assumptions which have much in common with other theories described in this book. 'The motive involved is the learned drive to be logical and to interpret correctly one's stimulus world . . . . The satisfaction of this motive depends primarily on consensual validation, especially with respect to events which constitute social reality.' (Byrne, 1962, page 164.)

Byrne and Clore (1967) claim that, by demonstrating that attitude similarity can lead to attraction for a complete stranger, towards whom one has no pre-existing positive orientation of the kind implicitly required by Newcomb's model, 'it has become possible to place the relationship between attitude similarity and attraction in an antecedent-consequent framework' (page 2). This claim is justified only within the narrowest of contexts. In real life there are still both chickens and eggs, and convergence of attitudes can be both a consequence and a cause of friendship and attraction. In Byrne's experimental paradigm, however, the causal relationship *can* only be one way. The subject's expressed liking or disliking for the other is elicited *in vacuo*, with the possibility of even simulated interaction with the other having been expressly excluded. By definition, the subject's liking or disliking *can have no consequences* for future interaction with the other, as no such interaction can occur.

If one wants to look at attraction and attitude similarity within an 'antecedent-consequent framework', it seems inappropriate, to say the least, to use only those situations in which the possibility of continued interaction between the individuals in question has been excluded. Even if one is interested just in the social psychology of 'first encounters', such encounters in real life derive their significance from the fact that they might lead to more continuous relationships. It is for this kind of reason that the early field studies by Newcomb (1943, 1956) and Festinger *et al.* (1950) are classics in not just an historical sense.

More recently, Duck (1973) has obtained evidence of relevance to the attraction-similarity hypothesis by studying the patterns of friendship that developed among students of the same sex within their first six months at university, who shared the same hall of residence or were taking the same course. Similarity was defined in terms of responses on a Kelly repertory grid test (Kelly, 1955), and in general was positively related to friendship development. However, Duck makes two important points: first, that the *kind* of similarity in the responses of any pair of individuals is more predictive of their relationship than just the *amount* of similarity, with closer personal relationships being associated with greater similarity in the use of 'psychological' as opposed to 'role' constructs—a finding which has parallels to the developmental data on children's interpersonal descriptions reported by Peevers and Secord (1973); and second, that similarity of any kind should not be regarded as a reinforcer, so much as a cue or 'filter' which individuals use as a criterion for selecting potential friends from a wider circle of possible acquaintances. Such 'filtering' is assumed to be continuous, with the implication that different kinds of cues may have different degrees of importance at different stages in the development of a relationship.

REACTIONS TO PERSONAL EVALUATIONS

The notion that individuals seek consensual validation for their attitudes and beliefs implies that other people may also be an important source for the views one holds about oneself. The notion that one tends to perceive oneself as others see one can be traced historically through the writings of James (1968), Cooley (1968), and Mead (1968) to the more recent literature on self-attribution processes. The scope of such self-evaluations may be quite general, e.g., the extent to which one sees oneself as a good and pleasant person, or quite specific, e.g., the extent to which one's most recent essay or course assignment was creative, accurate, or uninspired. In either case, there will be some occasions when other people appear to evaluate one in the same way as one evaluates oneself, and other occasions when other people's evaluations differ from one's own, in either a more positive or more negative direction. When such discrepancies occur, they may provide an impetus for a change in either one's self-concept, or one's attitude towards the other person by whom one has been evaluated, or both. For instance, a student who received a lower mark than he expected for an essay or an examination might respond by lowering his estimate of his own ability or of the adequacy of his preparation, or he might persist in his belief that he had really done a brilliant piece of work, the merit of which his lecturers or examiners were too perverse or stupid to recognize. Either way, it seems reasonable to suppose that some kind of cognitive resolution of the discrepancy would frequently be sought.

It is intuitively highly plausible, therefore, that one's liking or disliking for another person will be influenced by the extent to which one feels this other person regards one's personality, or performance at some task, in a favourable or unfavourable light. But at this point a less obvious question arises: do we prefer others who merely say favourable things about us, or do we prefer others whose views of us coincide with, and hence validate, our own self-perceptions, be they favourable or unfavourable?

The latter view is that held by Secord and Backman (1965) in what they refer to as their 'social congruity theory'. As the name implies, it is a straight application of the principles of congruity and consistency discussed in Chapter 1. Consistency theory predicts that we should evaluate more positively a person who makes a favourable remark about something of which we approve, or an unfavourable remark about something of which we disapprove, than a person who contradicts our own approval or disapproval. The extension embodied in 'social congruity theory' is merely the observation that this 'something' can be oneself, or some aspect of one's behaviour. For someone who evaluates himself positively, that is, has relatively high self-esteem, the theory predicts simple reciprocity of liking: he should prefer others who evaluate him favourably and thus validate his own favourable opinion of himself. On the other hand, someone relatively low in self-esteem, or with a relatively low opinion of himself, or of his performance on some task, should, according to the theory, prefer others who evaluate him negatively. Evaluations by others, in other words, should lead to liking only if they are perceived as accurate.

One of the main studies cited in support of this position is that by Deutsch and Solomon (1959). Subjects in their study were female telephone operators who performed a task individually, but supposedly as members of a team, and were led to believe that they had either done well or poorly at the task. They were then shown an evaluation made of their performance, supposedly by another subject, which was designed to be either very favourable or very unfavourable. Their own evaluations of this 'other subject' on the basis of this feedback were then recorded. When subjects believed that they had succeeded, they clearly preferred others who evaluated their performance positively, whereas this preference disappeared in the condition where subjects believed that they had failed. Deutsch and Solomon interpret these results as indicating both the presence of a congruity effect, or preference for accurate evaluations, and a positivity effect, or preference for favourable evaluations.

Although one might be tempted to ask which of these two 'biases' or preferences is the more important, this is not the kind of question that is likely to yield any sensible answer which is generalizable beyond a specific situation. A more fruitful enterprise is to examine the variables that may make sometimes accuracy, and sometimes positivity, the more important factor. Skolnick (1971) introduced only minor variations into the Deutsch and Solomon procedure but found results that strongly supported the prediction of a positivity effect. Whether subjects were led to believe that they had succeeded, or that they had failed, or if they were given no feedback about their own performance, they clearly preferred a positive to a negative evaluation from the simulated fellow-subject. There was even an interaction of marginal significance ($p < 0.09$) in the direction opposite to that predicted by social congruity theory, indicating that this preference for positivity was strongest when subjects believed that they had failed. On the strength of these results, Skolnick tentatively proposes a viewpoint which he calls 'signification theory', which predicts that individuals will prefer positive to negative evaluations *especially* when their own opinion of themselves is low. Essentially, what is being argued is that positive evaluations from others are welcomed insofar as they boost one's morale, but if one's morale is already high, it is in less need of a boost.

Skolnick goes into some detail discussing the implications of differences between his own procedure and that of Deutsch and Solomon. His subjects were students rather than telephone operators, and may have been more 'ego involved' in the experiment and hence more motivated to believe that they had performed well. He suggests that 'telephone operators may be less likely to become aroused by a test that purports to measure their intelligence and leadership ability than would college students'. This seems a rather patronizing speculation, but perhaps it is not intended to be taken too seriously. Suffice it to say that Skolnick's subjects did appear to him to be highly involved, and it may well be a valuable intuition that more involved subjects are more concerned to protect their self-esteem and to be able to evaluate themselves positively.

Other factors discussed *post hoc* by Skolnick are the stability of subjects' self-concepts, and the credibility of the 'other subject's' evaluation of their performance. It is suggested that the manipulation of subjects' self-esteem through feedback concerning their own success or failure 'would not have as strong an effect on telephone operators, who probably have more stable self-concepts, than on college students, who are very tuned into identity problems and are in the process of modifying their self-image constantly' (page 66). Also, in contrast to the students who were deliberately selected so that they did not know each other, 'the telephone operators might have been friends and/or thought each other unlikely to evaluate them incongruously' (page 66). How idyllic it must be to be an uninvolved, unambitious, simple, stable, non-neurotic, non-introspective, friendly telephone operator!

If Skolnick is right in suggesting that the credibility of incongruous evaluations differed between his own and the Deutsch and Solomon studies, the reason may lie in the task itself, rather than in the subjects' backgrounds. Skolnick used tests of logical reasoning in which it was probably quite difficult for subjects to be absolutely sure how well or poorly they had done. Following up this possibility, Dutton (1972) manipulated both perceived task importance (by telling some subjects that task performance was highly correlated with intelligence, and others that it was not), and stability of positive or negative self-evaluations (by giving subjects feedback indicating they had performed better or worse than the other group-members, with either little or considerable trial-by-trial fluctuation in their supposed levels of performance).

When the task was made to seem important, senders of positive evaluations were preferred in all conditions except when subjects had formed stable negative self-evaluations. When the task was made to seem unimportant, a congruency effect was found, with subjects who had formed positive self-evaluations preferring the positive evaluator, and those who had formed negative self-evaluations (particularly when stable) preferring the negative evaluator. There was no evidence of the processes suggested by Skolnick's 'signification theory'. Dutton's study is valuable in demonstrating the relevance of the attributional criterion of consistency, as well as elucidating the question of task importance.

The importance of attributional processes in reactions to personal evaluations is further stressed in a study by Stroebe, Eagly, and Stroebe (1977). Student subjects were classified as high or low in chronic self-esteem on the basis of a personality test (as opposed to having their self-evaluations manipulated experimentally). Having completed the questionnaire which was to provide this measure, subjects were told that their responses would be shown to another subject, who would be asked to record his impressions. The subjects were told that the other person had either been instructed to record his 'sincere' impressions, or had been acting under 'role-playing' instructions to write a description of the subject's character so as to be convincingly positive or negative. After some delay, subjects were then all given hand-written notes, actually made up by the experimenters. Just two such notes were used, one favourable and one unfavourable in content, and each about 100 words long. Subjects were then asked to say how likely or unlikely it was that the person supposedly evaluating them had produced his description of them under 'role-playing' rather than 'sincere' instructions. The results indicated that high self-esteem subjects felt that the description was less likely to be sincere if it was negative, whereas the low self-esteem subjects felt that it was less likely to be sincere if it was positive. Apparently, therefore, subjects in this study, presented with evaluations of themselves by others which were incongruent with their own self-evaluations, resolved this incongruity by attributing their evaluator's behaviour externally to the experimental instructions.

OBJECTIVE SELF-AWARENESS

In attempting to generalize the results of such studies beyond experimental situations where the subject has no choice but to listen to what others have to say about him, an important factor is likely to be the individual's willingness or unwillingness to seek out information relevant to a self-evaluation. A significant observation by Wicklund (1975) is that individuals may often try to avoid having to focus attention on themselves, or treat themselves deliberately as objects of their own perception. There are obviously a large number of things that we do that we do worse, if indeed we can manage to do them at all, if we try to attend consciously to what we are doing. Apparently simple acts such as walking or running in fact involve such a fine coordination of muscular movements that, if we tried to shut off our ability to perform them automatically, and instead gave conscious instructions (e.g., 'Now shift your weight on to the ball of your right foot just as your left foot leaves the ground, swinging your left arm forward and your right arm back'), we should more than probably fall flat on our faces. We can all also supply many instances from our own experience when 'social skills' can be similarly inhibited by too much self-consciousness. There can also be very few people who have not experienced something little short of blind terror on first entering a new situation, or taking on a new role, and feeling oneself stared at by everyone in sight. Or again, there are moments such as the sudden hush that can suddenly fall upon a party, leaving just one person still shouting to make himself heard.

The 'theory of objective self-awareness' (Duval and Wicklund, 1972; Wicklund, 1975), however, assumes more than that people will be embarrassed by situations which remove their social spontaneity. Rather, the theory assumes that deliberate self-appraisal will generally be avoided in that 'the person in self-reflection will typically find shortcomings in himself' (Wicklund, 1975, page 234). Such 'shortcomings' are conceptualized primarily in terms of discrepancies between one's real and ideal self, or between how one is forced to see oneself and how one would like to see oneself. Occasionally, there may be instances where such discrepancies are 'positive', i.e., where one exceeds one's aspirations, but Wicklund argues—essentially on intuitive grounds—that such instances are comparatively rare.

Evidence from a variety of sources is cited in support of the theory. For instance, Ickes, Wicklund, and Ferris (1973) had female students complete a questionnaire, which allowed for a measure of their real-ideal self discrepancies, either while listening to a tape-recording of their own voice, or of someone else's voice. Subjects forced to listen to their own voice were more self-critical, at least on the earlier items of the questionnaire. Subjects who receive negative evaluations from others will also tend to avoid listening to the tape-recorded sound of their own voice (Wicklund, 1975, pages 250–251). When given positive or negative feedback concerning their performance on a supposed test of creativity, and then asked to fill in the missing pronouns in a piece of prose, subjects performing in front of a camera or a mirror were found to use more self-relating pronouns if the feedback had been positive, whereas the difference between feedback conditions was eliminated if the camera or mirror was absent (Davis and Brock, 1974). The implication is that success experiences may make one more prepared to focus attention on oneself, and that this increased self-focused attention may be reflected in the increased use of first-person pronouns.

There are many aspects of the theory that require further conceptual definition and empirical justification. For instance, the assumption that one's observations of oneself will generally lead to one perceiving oneself as falling short of one's aspirations, is likely to vary in its validity from situation to situation and from individual to individual. In this context, the relation of the theory to research on achievement motivation has yet to be systematically explored. Similarly, the implications of the theory for processes of interpersonal attraction have yet to be made fully explicit. At the very least, however, research on objective self-awareness points to processes that may mediate the influence of interpersonal evaluations. In particular it suggests that attraction towards an evaluator may not simply be a function of the content of the evaluation and of one's own opinion of oneself, but whether it is deemed situationally appropriate for the other to offer *any* evaluation of oneself, and so heighten one's objective self-awareness. Outside specific formal role relationships (e.g., teacher–student, doctor–patient) there are probably few situations in our culture where it is not seen as socially taboo, deliberately rude, or embarrassingly ingratiating for one person to announce what he thinks of another to his face. Such normative restraints will be reduced or absent in more intimate and/or established personal relationships, and in especially contracted relationships of pseudo-intimacy such as those that can occur in encounter groups. It is significant that simple instructions given to subjects who know that they are in a social psychological experiment seem sufficient for the suspension of these norms, and the fact that these norms can be so easily suspended demonstrates at the same time the power and the limitations of such experimental situations for the study of interpersonal attraction.

PHYSICAL ATTRACTIVENESS AND THE 'MATCHING HYPOTHESIS'

Apart from similarity of attitudes, the kind of similarity most often studied in terms of its relation to interpersonal attraction has been similarity along the dimension of physical attractiveness. To talk of physical attractiveness as a single dimension is obviously an oversimplification, as any judgement that a person is physically attractive or unattractive is likely to depend on a large number of distinct physical attributes, as well as on contemporary, subcultural, and cultural norms. The basis for such judgements, however, is not usually directly considered. Whatever the cues may be upon which such judgements are based, people find it reasonably easy to judge others in terms of physical attractiveness, and, within a relatively homogeneous subject population, such judgements show tolerable inter-rater reliability. Unlike some of the other attributes that may make one person more likeable than another (e.g., a 'pleasant personality'), physical attractiveness is something which is quite easy to measure, even though any such measurement relies upon subjective evaluations.

The attention given to physical attractiveness in research also arises from the typical situation in which most social psychology experiments have been conducted. University and college students, particularly those in their first year, are likely to be especially concerned with forming new friendships and sexual attachments. Students' choice of a 'dating partner' provides researchers with the opportunity to look at behavioural consequences of interpersonal attraction, within a context where the course of such behaviour is relatively predictable or interpretable in terms of shared social expectations.

The metaphor that has most influenced theorizing in this area is an economic one. A 'dating partner' may be thought of as an asset to acquire, the desirability of this asset being dependent on how it compares with other available assets in terms of specified criteria. If physical attractiveness is taken as the most easily specified of such criteria, does this mean that the most physically attractive partner will be the one whom everyone wants to 'date'? The answer to this question is complicated by the fact that, where the choice is at all mutual, choosing a partner also involves offering oneself as an asset to one's partner. One's estimate of one's own worth in the eyes of one's chosen partner will thus affect one's confidence that one's overtures will be accepted. This estimate will depend upon a subjective comparison between oneself and one's potential rivals. The quality of any such competition can in turn be assumed to depend on the attractiveness of the partner of one's choice. A highly attractive person should have a wider range of options than a less attractive person.

Following this line of reasoning, Walster, Aronson, Abrahams, and Rottman (1966) likened the choice of a partner in terms of attractiveness to the choice of a task (as in achievement motivation research) as a function of its difficulty. The probability of being accepted by the partner of one's choice may be thought of as analogous to the probability of succeeding at a task, and should be inversely related to the attractiveness of one's partner, and directly related to one's own attractiveness. The higher one aims, therefore, the greater should be the probability of being rejected. As with achievement motivation, there are likely to be wide individual differences in how far people are prepared to put themselves at risk in this context. (See Stroebe, 1977, for a fuller discussion of the influence of self-esteem.) At least as important are likely to be the situational factors that determine the benefits that may accrue from being accepted, and the costs, in terms of loss of face, disruption to existing relationships, etc., of being rejected by the partner of one's choice. With such factors remaining constant, however, one would expect that individuals seeking to maximize both their own chances of being accepted, and the chances that the partner who accepts them will be 'worth having', should choose partners who neither far exceed, nor fall far short of, themselves in terms of estimated attractiveness and desirability. In other words, they should choose others roughly comparable in attractiveness to themselves.

Walster *et al.* (1966) tested this hypothesis by exploiting a popular event in American universities—the computer dance. The procedure involved first year students filling in a questionnaire, the results of which were then supposedly fed into a computer, which matched them with compatible partners of the opposite sex for the dance. Walster *et al.* in fact had the computer generate matchings on a completely random basis. Also, when they arrived to buy their tickets for the dance, all subjects were rated in terms of physical attractiveness without their knowledge by four judges (second year students). The inter-rater reliabilities for these attractiveness ratings were only tolerable, ranging from 0·49 to 0·58. During an intermission in the dance, subjects filled in individual questionnaires, supposedly as an evaluation of the computer selection, which asked them how much they liked their partner and would like to go out with him or her in future. Walster *et al.* found that more attractive participants of either sex were liked more by their partners, but that the partners' own attractiveness had little influence on their ratings. Not surprisingly, subjects' own ratings of the attractiveness of their partner correlated more highly with their liking for their partner than did the ratings of attractiveness by the independent judges. There was some evidence that subjects correctly perceived how much their partners liked them. On the other hand, there was no evidence that subjects liked partners who liked them more. This study therefore failed to provide evidence for reciprocity of liking, or for liking being dependent on matching in terms of physical attractiveness.

A number of reasons may have contributed to the failure by Walster *et al.* to find evidence for the matching hypothesis. One factor may have been that subjects had been given to believe that they had had a partner, selected for them by the computer, who already would be well matched with them— indeed, they paid their money to the dance organizers for this very purpose. Even if they found themselves to be not well matched with their partner in terms of attractiveness, presumably this just meant that the computer, in its wisdom, had placed more emphasis on other kinds of similarity. Moreover, all subjects had been given to believe that they had had a partner, selected for them by the computer, who already would be well matched with them— unattached and looking for a partner. Under such circumstances, the loss of face involved in being rejected might not be especially high.

Stroebe, Insko, Thompson, and Layton (1971) had students rate supposed members of the opposite sex who varied in both physical attractiveness (judged from facial photographs) and similarity of attitudes to themselves (manipulated along the lines of Byrne's 1961 procedure). The ratings included four dependent variables—how much they thought they would like the other person, how happy they would be to work with him/her, whether they would consider him/her for a date, or as a potential marriage partner. Both attitude similarity and attractiveness contributed to more positive ratings on all four measures for both male and female subjects, with some indications of females placing more emphasis than males on attitude similarity, and males placing more emphasis than females on attractiveness. Acceptability as a marriage partner was enhanced by attitude similarity, but less so if the other was unattractive, suggesting that attractiveness might act as a 'filter' in partner selection (cf. Duck, 1973). Subjects' estimates of their own attractiveness were related to the dating, but not the marriage, measure in the manner predicted by the matching hypothesis.

Kiesler and Baral (1970) temporarily raised or lowered the self-esteem of male subjects by having them succeed or fail on a fake intelligence test. After the test, the subject was taken individually to the cafeteria and introduced to a female student, with whom he was left alone. The female student—in fact the experimenter's confederate—was either made up to look very attractive or unattractive, and surreptitiously recorded all attempts at 'romantic behaviour' made by the subject while they chatted for about half an hour. As predicted, subjects whose self-esteem had been raised were more flirtatious when the female student was made to be more attractive, whereas those with lowered self-esteem were more flirtatious when she was less attractive. These results therefore provide support for the matching hypothesis, as long as it is remembered that the subjects' estimates of their own worth, and the worth of the female confederate, were manipulated so as to depend on *different* attributes (intelligence and attractiveness).

Other studies have yielded more ambiguous results. Berscheid, Dion, Walster, and Walster (1971) had subjects choose a dating partner from photographs, informing them that their chosen partner either would, or would not, have the right to refuse them. Berscheid *et al.* reasoned that, if matching depends on the perceived probability of rejection, subjects who were sure that their partner would have to accept them would show no matching tendency but simply go for the most attractive partner available. This manipulation, however, failed to reduce the degree of matching—no doubt because it failed to reduce the perceived probability of being rejected later on by someone whose initial acceptance was made under duress.

Huston (1973) similarly attempted to eliminate the fear of rejection for half his (male) subjects, who were required to choose a dating partner who had already seen the subject's own photograph, and had indicated that they would accept him. As predicted, subjects whose acceptance was assured chose more attractive partners. When acceptance was not assured, subjects who rated themselves as more attractive estimated that they had a higher chance of being accepted by the partner of their choice than those who rated themselves as less attractive. However, this effect on perceived probability of acceptance did not carry over to produce any matching effect when it came to the actual choice of a dating partner. As in other studies of this kind, it is debatable how severe a deterrent would be the loss of face incurred through rejection when the potential partners, whether or not particularly interested in the subject personally, were, by implication, unattached and available to be dated by *someone*.

The matching hypothesis remains, on the basis of these studies, a plausible but not proven possibility. The emphasis on physical attractiveness as the main parameter of a partner's worth is an oversimplification which is understandable in view of its ease of experimental manipulation. No doubt also this emphasis made such studies fun for the experimenters concerned. It is also likely, however, that subjects themselves may have recognized it as an oversimplification, and have looked for additional criteria even where none were deliberately provided. Furthermore, the dating situation employed is highly specific, and inferences from it might not even generalize to more senior students at the same universities, once they have emerged from the hectic bond-forming activities of their first year. If such speculations have any substance, then generalizations of the conclusions of these studies to new situations must rely upon new evidence.

ROMANTIC LOVE

A common reaction to experiments of the kind described so far in this chapter is that, whatever their merits as studies of first impressions, they provide little direct insight into deeper and more involved personal relationships. A number of researchers have gone further, claiming that there are essential qualitative differences, as opposed to mere differences of degree, between romantic love and less intense forms of liking and attraction. Rubin (1970, 1973), for instance, devised a questionnaire to distinguish loving from liking, and found that differences in religious backgrounds—which one would expect to contribute to less liking—were associated with greater expression of love for one's partner in relatively newly formed heterosexual attachments (up to 18 months). In more long-term relationships, however, such differences were associated with fewer such expressions. Berscheid and Walster (1974) have similarly argued that, whereas liking for another person is a straightforward function of the 'positive reinforcements' which the other provides, love often occurs in the face of adversity, and in situations associated with stress and frustration.

Driscoll, Davis, and Lipetz (1972) investigated one such source of stress—parental opposition to the relationship. Their subjects were married and unmarried couples who volunteered for a longitudinal study, and who were 'interested in learning more about their relationships'. The data were provided by a questionnaire administered to both partners in each couple at the start of the study, and then again from 6 to 10 months later. The unmarried sample consisted initially of 49 couples, who had been going out together for a median of 8 months prior to the start of the study, and of whom 18 were living together. Perceptions by these couples of interference by their parents in their relationship were positively and significantly correlated with their expressed love for each other. There were also 91 married couples in the initial sample. For these, the correlation between perceived parental interference and expressed love was near zero. Driscoll *et al.* use the differences between the two groups as the basis for distinguishing romantic from 'conjugal' love. In particular, conjugal love is seen by them as associated with expressions of stronger mutual trust, fewer reports of negative behaviour in the relationship, and fewer criticisms of one's partner, than is romantic love.

One of the most influential attempts to account for such findings is the 'misattribution hypothesis' (e.g., Berscheid and Walster, 1974), which implies that stress and frustration intensify romantic love since individuals misattribute the arousal due to such stress as being the result of their intense attachment to their partner. This hypothesis is based upon the work of Schachter and Singer (1962) on cognitive labelling of emotional states, and is also related to Schachter's earlier work on affiliation. There is evidence that misattributed arousal can increase affiliative behaviour, for instance among groups of male students who were administered caffeine but not informed of its stimulant effects (Mills and Mintz, 1972). However, such affiliation scarcely ranks as romantic love. In fact, the experiments that relate to this hypothesis tend to revert to the study of sexual attraction in first encounters, rather than to more long-term attachments, as studied by Rubin (1973) and Driscoll et al. (1972).

Stephan, Berscheid, and Walster (1971) led male students to expect that, as part of a study of 'the dating practices of college students', they would go on a blind date with a female student who had also agreed to participate, the matching to be done on a random basis. While waiting for the experiment to start, they were asked by a 'graduate student' to rate a passage of prose for its potential for sexual arousal. This passage was either highly arousing or not arousing. Soon after they had read and rated the passage, the experimenter returned with 'background questionnaires', with attached photographs, of the female students who would be taking part. The subjects were then told that they would each have to rate their first impressions, on the basis of this information, of two of the females, one of whom would be their date, and one of whom would not. Half were given their own date's questionnaire to evaluate first, and half the supposed date of one of the other subjects. In fact the experiment was terminated after all subjects had rated only one female at which point they were debriefed. The important findings were that subjects who had read the more arousing passage rated the female as more attractive than did those who had read the non-arousing passage. In addition, the more aroused subjects rated the female as more likely to be sexually receptive if she was supposedly going to be their own date rather than somebody else's. This study does not provide conclusive evidence for a *mis*attribution explanation, however, since subjects had already acknowledged the extent to which they found the prose passage sexually arousing.

Rather more convincing are the results of a study by Cantor, Zillmann, and Bryant (1975), who argued that aspects of the physiological arousal produced by physical exercise decay relatively slowly, so that there is a recovery period after exercise when a person feels he is back to normal but during which he is still relatively aroused. Male students were shown four parts of an erotic film either immediately after, five minutes after, or nine minutes after, pedalling on an exercise bicycle. The middle of these three groups rated the film more sexually arousing, exciting, aesthetic, entertaining, and involving than did the other two groups. The reasoning is that the middle group were in the intervening recovery phase when they viewed the film, whereas the first group still attributed their arousal to the exercise, and the last group were no longer experiencing any residual arousal that could be misattributed to the film.

Among these studies, however, the prize for creativity has to go to Dutton and Aron (1974). The subjects for the first of three experiments they report were male tourists, unaccompanied and appearing to be between 18 and 35 years old, who were visiting a canyon area in British Columbia. The most dramatic condition involved them being approached individually by an attractive young female interviewer who introduced herself as a student who was doing a psychology project on the 'effects of exposure to scenic attractions on creative expression'. The unsuspecting male then had to fill in a questionnaire which contained a Thematic Apperception Test (TAT) item designed to provide a projective measure of sexual arousal. All this took place as subjects were crossing a 5-foot wide, 450-foot long wooden suspension bridge described as having the following features: '(a) a tendency to tilt, sway, and wobble, creating the impression that one is about to fall over the side; (b) very low handrails of wire cable which contribute to this impression; and (c) a 230-foot drop to rocks and shallow rapids below the bridge' (page 511). The control condition consisted of the same interviewer approaching unaccompanied males crossing a shorter, wider, and firmer wooden bridge 10 feet above a small rivulet further up the canyon. These two conditions were also repeated with a male interviewer approaching male subjects.

The results of this first experiment showed that approximately two-thirds of subjects approached by the female interviewer agreed to fill in the questionnaire, as compared with about half those approached by the male interviewer, regardless of the bridge being used as the location. The scores for sexual imagery on the TAT item were low in the male interviewer conditions, higher with the female interviewer on the safe bridge, and highest of all with the female interviewer on the dangerous bridge. To provide an additional measure, the interviewer tore off a corner of each subject's questionnaire, and wrote on his or her name and phone number, and invited the subject to phone, 'if he wanted to talk further'. The rate of acceptance of the phone numbers was more than twice as high when the interviewer was female, and of those subjects who accepted her number, 9 out of 18 subsequently phoned her, if they had been interviewed by her on the dangerous bridge, as compared with 2 out of 16 in the safe bridge condition.

A second experiment was conducted to guard against the possibility that these results were due to different kinds of tourists being attracted to different parts of the canyon. In this experiment, the reactions of males approached by a female interviewer on the dangerous suspension bridge were compared with the reactions of those approached after they had crossed and been sitting or walking for at least 10 minutes afterwards in a small park. As predicted, subjects in this latter group showed less sexual imagery in their tests than those interviewed on the bridge. The rates for accepting the questionnaire, and then the interviewer's phone number, were close to those in the first experiment (there was no male interviewer), and once again, the subjects approached on the bridge were more likely to phone her subsequently (13 out of 20, as compared with 7 out of 23).

The third experiment reported by Dutton and Aron was a more orthodox laboratory study, in which male students were led to believe that they and their 'fellow subject' (an attractive female student) would receive, on the basis of a random allocation, either a weak or a painful electric shock to see how this would influence performance on a learning task. Before this task was to start, the subject and the female confederate were shown into separate cubicles to fill in a questionnaire, which included two questions concerning how attractive the subject found the confederate ('How much would you like to ask her for a date?', 'How much would you like to kiss her?'). Subjects' attraction to the female confederate (measured by the mean of these two items) was significantly higher when they themselves expected a strong rather than a weak shock, but were not significantly influenced by the level of shock they expected the female to receive. The purpose of this last manipulation was to test the suggestion that male subjects were more attracted, in the previous two experiments, to the female interviewer when cast in the role of a 'damsel in distress'.

Imaginative though some of these studies are, they offer only tentative support for the misattribution theory of romantic love proposed by Berscheid and Walster (1974). It should be noted that there is a strong bias towards using males as subjects, and females as the target of attraction. It may be that the same conclusions would hold for females' feelings of attraction towards males, but one would like to have evidence. Second, not all researchers have been as concerned as Driscoll et al. (1972) to distinguish romantic love from other forms of affection or sexual interest, yet the whole point of the misattribution hypothesis is to imply such a difference in process. Third, evidence is scarce, outside the Cantor et al. (1975) study, that arousal is indeed misattributed, or that, even if it is, it is a necessary condition of enhanced attraction that subjects should fail to recognize the cause of their arousal. Indeed, both the field and laboratory experiments reported by Dutton and Aron (1974) include manipulation checks which indicated that subjects were quite afraid about crossing the bridge, or anxious about being shocked. This is quite different from studies in the Schachter and Singer (1962) mould, that have deliberately sought to mislead subjects as to the true cause of their arousal.

For such reasons, Kenrick and Cialdini (1977) have argued in favour of a 'reinforcement view' of the effects of arousal on romantic attraction. 'Lovers not only provide increases in arousal for one another, but they also provide reductions of that arousal . . . it is our major hypothesis that it is more often the reduction of that arousal, rather than its labelling, that intensifies the relationship' (page 385).

Kenrick and Cialdini suggest that the presence of a calm female confederate in frightening situations such as those used by Dutton and Aron (1974) might provide reassurance and hence *reduce* anxiety and arousal. They also mention studies of imprinting in species other than man, which show that the presence of frustration or aversive arousal can intensify the bonds that are formed. Apart from the notion of drive reduction as a reinforcer, an attractive member of the opposite sex may provide a distraction from anxiety. Also interrelated concepts such as partial reinforcement and hedonic contrast effects (see Chapter 3; also Beebe-Center, 1932; Shapiro, 1967) can provide the basis for essentially similar explanations. Passionate love may be more passionate against a backdrop of danger, doubt, or deprivation, and this backdrop may need no disguise.

INTERDEPENDENCE AND SATISFACTION

As we have seen, researchers who have been concerned with interpersonal attraction in first encounters have frequently discussed the 'rewards' or reinforcements that one individual may provide for the other. Often such 'rewards' are defined in terms of specific attributes of the target person, such as physical attractiveness, which contribute to that person's relative 'worth' as an acquaintance or intimate. More rarely has any systematic attention been paid to the questions of reciprocity and stability in more long-lasting relationships, or to the susceptibility of such questions to an analysis in terms of rewards and costs.

Almost as soon as one progresses beyond first encounters, it becomes less viable to define rewards in terms of static attributes of each individual. Instead it becomes important to specify each person's *behavioural* contribution to the interaction. Even with a variable as important as physical attractiveness, the fact that one or both partners *look* sexy does not guarantee a mutually or even individually satisfying relationship over any continuous period of time. If attraction in first encounters is a matter of responding to cues, continued attraction involves discovering whether the expectations one formed on the basis of such cues are in fact correct. Two important and related questions therefore need to be answered: first, how does each partner's satisfaction with the relationship compare with what he or she feels could reasonably be expected; and second, how does each partner's behaviour affect the satisfaction or dissatisfaction of the other?

As in too many other areas of social psychology, the research literature of the 'sixties and 'seventies, with its heavy bias towards experimentation with introductory psychology students within established methodological and conceptual traditions, has provided few instances of attempts to tackle such general theoretical questions head-on. Instead, one has to go back to the 'fifties to find researchers willing to formulate general conceptual frameworks within which such questions may be posed. Moreover, one often finds that such general models bear a curious relationship to subsequent empirical research, in that (with the important exception of dissonance theory) different precepts of the models have been used as the bases for experimental hypotheses in a number of studies, but few attempts have been made to put the general conceptual frameworks proposed to an empirical test.

Pre-eminent among such general models is that proposed by Thibaut and

Kelley (1959). Although their book is entitled *The Social Psychology of Groups*, it is for the most part concerned with dyadic (two-person) relationships, and is thus directly relevant to the topic of this chapter. The two key questions involved in the model are those of each person's satisfaction with the relationship, and of each person's power over, or dependence on, the other. Both these questions are seen to depend on the rewards and costs the two members of the dyad exchange during the course of their interaction. In short, interpersonal relationships depend upon interpersonal *exchange*.

The first important concept which Thibaut and Kelley introduce is that of *comparison level* (CL). This is directly analogous to the concept of adaptation-level (AL) in psychophysical judgement (see Chapter 3), without involving the specific mathematical or physiological assumptions made by Helson (1964). A person's CL is the standard against which he judges his satisfaction with a relationship. If his outcome from the relationship is more positive than his CL, he will be relatively satisfied; if more negative, he will be relatively dissatisfied. The CL is defined as 'some modal or average value of all the outcomes known to the person (by virtue of personal or vicarious experience), each outcome weighted by its salience (or the degree to which it is instigated for the person at the moment)' (page 81). This definition in terms of 'some modal or average value' assumes, as does AL theory, that judgements are made relative to a neutral point, rather than to opposing end-anchors, but it is vague enough to adjust to advances in judgemental theory such as have been proposed by Parducci (1963) and Anderson (1970).

The relation of a person's outcomes to his CL, and hence his satisfaction, is not, however, assumed to be the factor which most directly influences his *comparison level for alternatives* (CL_{alt}). This, it is assumed, 'will depend mainly on the quality of the best of the member's available alternatives, that is, the reward-cost positions experienced or believed to exist in the most satisfactory of other available relationships' (page 22). If a person's outcomes fall below his CL_{alt}, it is assumed that he will leave the relationship. On the other hand, if his outcomes are below his CL, that is, below 'what he feels he "deserves"' (page 21), he will be dissatisfied with the relationship but will remain in it as long as his outcomes still do not fall below his CL_{alt}. People may thus remain in relationships long after they cease to be 'rewarding', either because they do not feel that any alternative relationships are available to them, or because they feel that the costs involved in pursuing such alternatives (e.g., the financial and emotional costs of a divorce) may outweigh the rewards of the new relationship or their current annoyances. It is, of course, likely that a person's CL and CL_{alt} will influence one another. The higher a person's CL_{alt}, that is, the more satisfaction he thinks he could expect from alternative relationships, the more he might feel he deserved from his current relationship. Conversely, 'the more satisfactory any given relationship has been found to be, the higher will be the comparison level for evaluating any new relationship' (page 95).

Thibaut and Kelley go on to distinguish different kinds of power in a

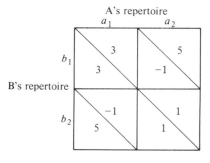

Figure 6.1 An example of a dyad with all outcomes specified.

dyad, depending on the effect that each member's behaviour has on his own and the other member's outcome. Such outcomes are typically represented in terms of a matrix, such as the one in Figure 6.1, which shows a very simple dyadic relationship between person A and person B, in which both A and B have a repertoire of only two possible behaviours. The outcomes that accrue to each member of the dyad are represented numerically, and depend, in this example, on both their own and the other member's behaviour. Within each cell of the matrix, the number above the diagonal represents the outcomes for person A and the number below the diagonal that for person B. The particular relationship shown in this matrix is one that has attracted a very large amount of empirical research, as will be seen in the next chapter. (In fact, it conforms to the rules of a 'Prisoner's Dilemma Game'.) For present purposes, it is enough to notice that A can reduce B's outcome by a difference of four units, whatever B does (by performing a_2 rather than a_1), but in doing so, A cannot necessarily guarantee high outcomes for himself, since B has equivalent control over A's outcomes.

As the numbers in the different cells of the matrix are changed, so are the power and dependence relationships between the two members of the dyad. Figure 6.2 shows a relationship in which B's outcomes are completely determined by what A does, whereas A receives the same outcome whether B performs b_1 or b_2. This is said to be a relationship where A has *fate control* over B. However, B may still not be completely powerless, depending on his own CL_{alt}. Since A derives positive outcomes from any interaction with B, he

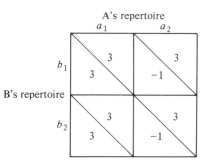

Figure 6.2 An example of a dyad where A has fate control over B.

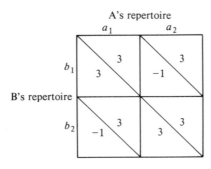

Figure 6.3 An example of a dyad where A has behaviour control over B.

is in one sense dependent on B for those outcomes. If B is able, and chooses, to leave the relationship, these positive outcomes will cease to be available to A. Jones and Gerard (1967) refer to this power that B has to break off the relationship as *contact control*.

Another kind of power distinguished by Thibaut and Kelley is that of *behaviour control*, and is represented in Figure 6.3. By varying his behaviour, A can make it more or less desirable for B to perform b_1 rather than b_2. In this example, if A performs a_1, it will be to B's advantage to perform b_1, whereas if A performs a_2, it will be to B's advantage to perform b_2. Even where A only has fate control over B, however, he can use this fate control in a way that amounts to controlling B's behaviour. Thus, in Figure 6.2, if a A chose to perform a_1 only if B performed b_1, and to perform a_2 only if B performed b_2, it would then become advantageous to B to perform b_1. This use of fate control to influence the other's behaviour is referred to as *converted fate control*.

When one takes into account the fact that there may be more than two options in the participants' behavioural repertoires, that the magnitude of any basis of power can vary with differences in the sizes of the pay-offs, that the different participants may have different kinds of control, as well as amounts of control over each other, that there may be more than two participants, and that they may not share the same CL or CL_{alt}, the relatively simple notions on which the model is based suddenly begin to look very complex. Such complexity, however, is dimensional rather than conceptual. Essentially, the central assumptions of the Thibaut and Kelley approach remain very straight-forward: that satisfaction with a relationship depends, as do other social judgements, on relevant anchors or standards of comparison, and that the satisfying outcomes each participant will receive from a relationship often are jointly contingent on the behaviour of each participant. The description of such interdependence requires attention to be paid to differences in the type and amount of control each participant can exercise over the other. Such differences, it is further assumed, can be represented numerically as in the examples shown. The specific application of this general model to issues such as sexual attraction and marital stability thus demands a definition of the behavioural options open to each partner and of the outcome contingencies. Many of the studies reviewed so far in this chapter cannot meet this demand.

COMPLEMENTARITY AND STABILITY

One assumption of the Thibaut and Kelley model is that 'dyad formation is facilitated by the members being able, at low cost to themselves, to provide their partners with high rewards' (page 45). This implies that interpersonal relationships such as marriages or close friendships are likely to be more stable if the satisfaction of either member does not entail the dissatisfaction of the other. This does not require that both partners enjoy exactly the same activities to exactly the same extent as each other. What is required is that their interaction with each other includes combinations of behaviour which yield pleasure to at least one of the partners without yielding too much displeasure to the other, so that over a sequence of different behavioural combinations, both partners derive more satisfaction from remaining in the relationship than they would from leaving it.

In light of the importance that has been attached to factors such as attitude similarity in experimental research, it should be emphasized that a given behavioural combination (or cell of the matrix) can be mutually reward-ing even if the individual behaviours of the two partners are extremely differ-ent from each other. Take for instance a marriage in which the husband likes playing football on a Sunday, but dislikes his mother-in-law. The wife, on the other hand, has no interest in football, particularly when it requires her shivering on the touch-line watching her husband make a muddy fool of himself, but is fond of her mother and enjoys visiting her. Here both partners have two options, which we can label 'Football' and 'Mother'. The possible behavioural combinations and their respective outcomes are shown in Figure 6.4. The actual numbers, of course are arbitrary, but are chosen to convey some idea of the degree of pleasure each partner achieves.

This matrix shows that there is one combination which both the husband and wife would wish to avoid: the husband goes to see Mother by himself while the wife goes to watch a game of football in which her husband isn't playing! There are then two possible combinations which could give rise to conflict: the husband insists on the wife coming to watch him play, or the wife insists on the husband coming with her to see Mother. In both of these combinations, the partner who derives the greater pleasure could use the argument that 'it won't hurt you too much'. The greatest mutual satisfaction

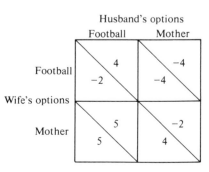

Figure 6.4 Matrix representation of a football-loving husband and a mother-loving wife.

in this example, however, can be achieved by the simple expedient of the two partners doing what they prefer separately, and in fact this may even enhance their individual satisfactions.

A number of researchers have attempted to formulate more general schemes to predict what kinds of behavioural combinations tend to be complementary, that is, to provide mutual (though not necessarily equal) satisfaction for both members of a relationship. As a first step, a common approach has been to use factor analytic techniques to discover the 'basic dimensions' of interpersonal behaviour. This approach is analogous to the search for basic dimensions of individual personality by looking at the inter-correlations between trait descriptions (e.g., Cattell, 1965). The main difference in this case is that the data on which such analyses are based are explicitly descriptions of interpersonal behaviour. There are interpretational problems with any such analysis (Mischel, 1968). For present purposes, though, it is enough to note the consistencies that have been suggested by a number of different studies.

Borgatta, Cottrell, and Mann (1958) collected interpersonal ratings made by graduate students in small discussion groups, and submitted these to factor analysis. The two main factors to emerge were those of individual assertiveness, and sociability. Borgatta (1960) replicated this result with a new sample, finding that the individual assertiveness factor was more important in ratings of males than of females. Borgatta (1964) divided members of college sororities and fraternities into groups of five members who knew each other well and obtained interpersonal ratings. For both sexes, the first two factors were assertiveness and likeability.

Schaefer (1959) analysed records of mothers' behaviour towards their children based on observations and interviews, and found two factors labelled control-autonomy and love-hostility. Slater (1962) inferred two dimensions (warmth vs. coldness and strictness vs. permissiveness) from a cluster analysis of the reports given by male college students about their parents. Becker and Krug (1964) similarly proposed a classification of children's social behaviour in terms of the categories—assertive vs. submissive, and loving vs. distrusting.

Carson (1969) has suggested that these studies point to a common two-dimensional structure implicit in interpersonal behaviour. These dimensions are treated as orthogonal, and referred to as friendly-hostile and dominant-submissive. Since these dimensions are orthogonal, there are possibilities of different degrees of friendly-dominant, hostile-dominant, friendly-submissive and hostile-submissive behaviours. Not all such behaviours will be equally common in all environments, or for all individuals, however. Ratings of the interpersonal behaviour of psychiatric patients, for instance, seem to show an under-representation of more assertive or dominant behaviours (Lorr and McNair, 1965).

Leary (1957) proposed a remarkably sophisticated statement of this two-dimensional scheme of interpersonal behaviour, represented in what he calls the Interpersonal Behaviour Circle (see Figure 6.5). The behaviours in the

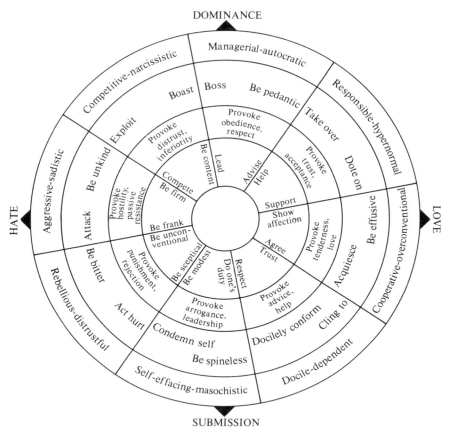

Figure 6.5 Leary's interpersonal behaviour circle. [*Adapted from Leary* (1957).]

different segments of the circle represent different weightings of the two principal dimensions (different loadings on the two factors). In each of the segments there are behaviours assumed to be potentially socially adaptive,
depending on circumstances (managerial, responsible, cooperative, docile,
self-effacing, rebellious, aggressive, and competitive), and more specific instances of these categories of behaviour are listed closer to the centre of the
circle. There are also socially maladaptive versions of these behaviours,
however, (autocratic, hypernormal, over-conventional, etc.) and more specific
instances of these are listed towards the perimeter of the circle. Reliance on
the more extreme forms of behaviour in any single segment is viewed as a sign
of psychological maladjustment. 'In many cases the "sicker" the patient, the
more likely he is to have abandonned all interpersonal techniques except
one—which he can handle with magnificent finesse' (Leary, 1957, page 116).
Possible support for this assumption comes from a study by Moos (1968).

Ratings of the behaviour of psychiatric patients and of hospital staff suggested greater cross-situational rigidity or consistency in the behaviour of the patients as opposed to the staff.

In a discussion that owes much to Sullivan's (1955) interpersonal theory of personality, Leary points out that behaviour in any part of the circle will tend to elicit *complementary* behaviour from the other participant in the relationship. Perfect matching involves the *same* degree of love-hate, but *opposite* degrees of dominance-submission. Friendly-submissive behaviour (e.g., 'trust') would thus tend to elicit friendly-dominant behaviour (e.g. 'support') from the other person. Behaviours engaged in with the purpose of eliciting a desired response from the other person are termed 'security operations'.

Carson (1969) discusses how the four main categories of behaviour which he distinguishes (friendly-dominant, hostile-dominant, friendly-submissive and hostile-submissive) may be thought of as four behavioural options open to each member of a dyad, representable in the form of a complex (4 × 4 rather than 2 × 2) version of the matrices already discussed in this chapter. The outcomes of the different behavioural combinations would depend, in part, on the complementarity of the individual behaviours. Complementary combinations, however, may be mutually damaging as easily as they may be mutually rewarding. Also, even combinations that are mutually rewarding need not be equally rewarding for both members. Nonetheless, other things being equal, one would expect greater mutual satisfaction from complementary interactions towards the 'friendly' extreme of the 'love-hate' dimension, and mutual dissatisfaction towards the 'hostile' end.

Evidence that supports this assumption comes from a study by Lipetz, Cohen, Dworin, and Rogers (1970). Their subjects consisted of two groups of married couples, there being 50 couples within each group in the final sample. The first group of couples were volunteers, none of whom were seeking divorce, or professional counselling for their marriage. The second group consisted of couples currently seeking professional psychotherapeutic help because of marital difficulties. Subjects were required to complete a number of questionnaire measures, including the Edwards Personal Preference Scale (Edwards, 1953), and a specially devised 'marriage-specific need scale'. From these measures, scores were derived which represented the extent to which subjects' general or marriage-specific 'needs' were complementary with those of their spouse.

Complementarity scores calculated on the basis of general needs (the Edwards scale) showed no significant differences between the two groups of couples. The measures of complementarity based on marriage-specific needs, however, showed significantly more complementarity among the stable married couples than among those seeking help, both with regard to a 'total complementarity' score, and with regard to the majority of the specific needs contributing to this total. This study, therefore, provides strong evidence for the complementarity hypothesis in a situation where there is a clear operational definition òf the stability of the relationship. It also demonstrates the importance of using situation-specific measures, whether these be measures of personality (cf., Mischel, 1968), or attitude (cf., Ajzen and Fishbein, 1977), in order to predict behaviour.

CONCLUSIONS

The research reviewed in this chapter has dealt with two main issues. The first relates to individuals' evaluations of others who are potential partners for a future relationship. The second relates to individuals' satisfactions with current relationships. Experimental social psychologists have concentrated to a disproportionate extent on the first of these issues, while the second issue has been primarily the concern of more socially oriented researchers in clinical psychology and personality. Both issues have been analysed in terms of the rewards and costs presumed to accrue to the individuals involved. Research in the first category has attempted to show that certain attributes of the target person, such as attitude similarity or physical attractiveness, are generally rewarding or reinforcing. Explanations of *why* such attributes are rewarding, however, have tended to be more speculative. Research in the second category, by comparison, treats any such rewards or costs as features of the interaction, jointly dependent on the behaviour of both participants. Moreover, it has stressed that outcomes may only be judged costly or rewarding relative to an implicit standard, which may vary from individual to individual, and relationship to relationship. Many kinds of relationship offer the possibility of mutual satisfaction. The mere presence of this possibility, however, does not ensure that it will be achieved, as will be seen in the next chapter.

SUMMARY

* According to balance theory, individuals should be attracted to others with similar attitudes, and should adopt similar attitudes to those of their friends. Support for this prediction has been found both in real-life groups, and in experiments where subjects are shown the questionnaire responses of a simulated stranger.
* Working within the latter of these paradigms, Byrne has argued that attitude similarity constitutes a 'positive reinforcement', and that it is the causal antecedent of attraction. Regarding the first argument, however, it is not clear what is supposedly being reinforced, and the second argument is only trivially true within the context of the paradigm.
* There may be different kinds of similarity, which are important at different stages of a relationship.
* Another prediction of balance theory is that a person should be more attracted to others who confirm rather than contradict his own opinions

about himself, whether positive or negative. This has been tested in experiments where subjects are told how they have supposedly been evaluated by another person. Evidence has been found both for this, and an alternative principle, that a person will tend to prefer others who evaluate him positively, regardless of his self-evaluation. The relative strength of each principle seems to depend on a variety of factors, such as the stability of subjects' self-evaluations.

* Manipulations which lead subjects to focus attention on themselves may make them more self-critical.
* Although subjects tend to express more anticipated liking for physically more attractive members of the opposite sex, there is little experimental evidence that they will prefer partners of comparable physical attractiveness to themselves. However, such experiments have tended to use situations where the implied costs of rejection are small, and the potential partner is unattached.
* Attraction to a member of the opposite sex may be increased under conditions of heightened arousal, but it does not seem necessary for this arousal to be misattributed to the presence of this other person.
* It is debatable how much such experiments tell one about romantic love, as distinct from other forms of attraction. There is relatively little longitudinal research on factors influencing love and attraction within actual relationships.
* In terms of social exchange theory, each partner's satisfaction with a relationship should depend on whether the relationship is seen to provide outcomes which equal or exceed a 'comparison level' (what he or she feels could reasonably be expected) and/or a 'comparison level for alternatives' (outcomes anticipated from available alternative relationships).
* The interdependence of the partners on each other for the provision of outcomes may be conceived of in terms of various combinations of 'fate' and 'behaviour' control.
* Attempts have been made to develop typologies of interpersonal behaviour based on two dimensions of dominance-submission and love-hate. It has been suggested that the stability of a relationship will be greater if the partners behave towards each other in ways which represent opposite positions on the dominance-submission continuum, and similar positions on the love-hate dimension.

SEVEN

STRATEGIC INTERACTION

THE BACKGROUND OF EXPERIMENTAL GAMING RESEARCH

As was seen in the last chapter, interpersonal relationships may involve outcomes that are mutually rewarding, mutually damaging, unilaterally rewarding, or unilaterally damaging. The outcomes achieved depend upon the behavioural options chosen by the different participants. It also seems reasonable to expect the participants to select their options on the basis of the outcomes which they hope to achieve. In simple terms, one might expect individuals to cooperate if it pays them to do so, and compete if their interests are in conflict (Deutsch, 1949).

In practice, however, things are far from being so simple. The mere presence of a common interest does not guarantee cooperation if individuals think that they can achieve short-term gains for themselves at the expense of others. An historical example of this conflict between short-term individual and long-term mutual interest is described by Hardin (1968), in what he refers to as 'the tragedy of the commons'. When villagers in medieval England were given the right to graze their animals on common land, each villager could make a greater personal profit by increasing the number of animals he grazed' there. With more and more villagers attempting to increase their profits in this way, however, the common land ceased to provide adequate pasture, and so the villagers ended up with a collective loss. Comparisons are only too easy to draw with present-day instances of environmental exploitation. Also, as I shall describe, a large body of research has shown an apparently similar disregard of mutual interest by subjects in laboratory experiments.

From the start, the idea that conflict and cooperation could be analyzed in terms of the outcomes or pay-offs to the parties concerned, appealed to social psychologists with a view of human beings as rational decision-makers. To understand this appeal, one has to appreciate the powerful tradition within psychology and related social sciences, according to which, conflict and aggressive behaviour are attributed to essentially irrational drives, frustrations, or instincts (see Billig, 1976). The more rational view of human nature implied by exchange theorists such as Thibaut and Kelley (1959) offered the hope that one could explain why ordinary people might find themselves in conflict with each other as a result of social pressures rather than personality defects. It also offered the hope that such social pressures could be quantified, and if quantified, then simulated in the laboratory.

A whole new experimental tradition therefore sprang up from the mid-'fifties onwards, with the aim of predicting how subjects would behave in simple experimental games, which offered varying incentives for cooperation and competition, depending on the pay-offs specified by the experimenter. In the vast majority of such studies, subjects are allowed only an extremely limited number of behavioural options, with their repertoire typically being restricted to only two possible responses. What is more, these responses tend to involve extremely 'impersonal' operations, such as pressing a button or flicking a switch. There is usually no opportunity for subjects to communicate with each other, and they are generally not led to expect that they will be introduced to each other when the experiment is over. The main purpose of these studies has been to look for the minimal conditions necessary for interpersonal conflict or cooperation, in situations designed to exclude or control the effects of extraneous variables such as antecedent attitudes and prejudices. The experimental game is indeed the archetype of the controlled laboratory experiment in social psychology. As Pruitt and Kimmel (1977, page 370) put it, it is 'a research tradition that is both loved and hated'.

Over the years, critics of this tradition have become increasingly insistent that the external validity of gaming experiments requires explicit demonstration, and cannot be assumed *a priori*. Yet many researchers, notably Rapoport (1970), have expressed little interest in generalizing their results beyond the laboratory. Instead, the primary concern has been with defining the principles which may be used to predict subjects' behaviour under rigidly specified conditions. Others, such as Deutsch (1969, 1973), are much more prepared to extrapolate to wider social issues, but appear less responsive to the conceptual difficulties involved in any such extrapolation. Analogies can be drawn between wider social conflicts and experimental games, but the two situations have not been related to each other in any coherent theory. While a number of extremely reproducible results have been found within the experimental gaming paradigm, it is often a matter of subjective judgement or pure speculation whether or not these same effects will be reproducible outside the laboratory.

There seem to be basically two courses open, therefore. Either one can dismiss this whole area of research as artificial and irrelevant, and say that nothing can be learned from it about real-life interaction. Or one can attempt to define the nature of any such artificiality, so as to understand *why* the independent variables employed in such research have the effects which they do. This question of 'why' is a question about how individuals make decisions in novel, but precisely defined, social situations, and it is a question to which the answer is by no means obvious. As Pruitt and Kimmel have put it: 'We believe that experimental games usually place people in an *unfamiliar strategic environment* and that the findings reflect the limitations of such a setting. The unfamiliarity of this environment means that well-rehearsed habits of analysis and behaviour are not readily available, and subjects must innovate.' (1977, page 370.)

The cognitive processes which such innovations reflect are unlikely to have evolved for the sole purpose of playing experimental games. On the other hand, we cannot assume that such processes will operate in the same way in all experimental situations, or follow the same rules as in more familiar real-life settings. To understand the operation of these processes, we first need to know how subjects respond to situational variations within the laboratory, before we can judge the validity of any extrapolation from laboratory to real-life situations. Subjects' responses, however, are essentially creative, rather than mere passive reactions to pay-off structure. Almost in spite of itself, gaming research has provided evidence of the ability and apparent need of individuals to invest novel situations with evaluative meaning, even where researchers have attempted to remove all such meaning from the experimental context. Gaming research was founded on the assumption that cooperative and competitive behaviour is under the control of outcome contingencies. Yet, paradoxically, it is the gaming literature itself that provides the most direct evidence of the inadequacy of any analysis based purely upon a definition of pay-off structure, without consideration of how that structure, and more general features of the experimental situation, are interpreted by the subjects themselves. First, though, let us look at some of the games that have been used.

COORDINATION GAMES

These involve the different players taking it in turn to perform individually profitable behaviour. Typically the players have to decide amongst themselves how they are going to take turns. Since time is at a premium, the sooner they can work out a satisfactory rule of procedure, the better the joint outcomes of the different players will be.

A study by Mintz (1951) provides an early example of this kind of situation. A number of cones were inserted in a narrow-necked bottle, and subjects were each given a string attached to one of the cones. They were offered small rewards for removing their own cones before they became wet as the bottle was slowly filled with water from the bottom. Although enough time was allowed for everyone to remove their cones one at a time, frequent jams occurred at the neck of the bottle, so that few subjects in any group obtained their rewards. Only when the instructions stressed that they were to compete together as a team against another group did they manage to operate with any efficiency.

The most important experimental game of this type is the Deutsch and Krauss (1960, 1962) trucking game. This involves two players, each of whom takes the part of the owner of a trucking firm. Each player gets paid à fixed sum, minus a variable cost, which depends on the length of time he takes to deliver each load of merchandise to his destination. Each player has two possible routes to his destination, either a short main route including a section of one-lane road (which the two players need to use in opposite directions) or a long alternative route which would involve a small loss. The danger is that both players will attempt to use the shorter route at the same time, and meet head-on in the one-lane road. Until one of the players then backs out, both will lose time and money. The obvious cooperative solution is for the two players to take turns at using the shorter route, but deadlock often occurs instead.

The main issue studied with the help of this game was the effect of threat on the emergence of cooperation—an issue assumed by Deutsch (1969) to have implications for international armed conflict and deterrence. The capacity of either player to threaten the other was achieved by giving him control over a gate situated at the end of the one-lane road nearest his own starting position. When this was closed, the other player's exit from the one-lane road would be blocked. Depending on the condition, both, one, or neither of the players had control of a gate. Cooperation, and with it joint profit, was highest in the 'no-gate' condition, when neither player could threaten the other, and lowest in the 'two-gate' condition.

Other variables that may have an effect in this game are the size of the monetary pay-offs involved (Gallo, 1966)—an issue to which I shall be returning later—and the relative advantage to be gained by taking the shorter route. Deutsch, Canavan, and Rubin (1971) demonstrated that shortening the one-lane road, so that the time saved by using it would be even greater, made it more difficult for players to come to a cooperative solution.

THE MINIMAL SOCIAL SITUATION

A radically different kind of game is the 'minimal social situation' pioneered by Sidowski (1957), and extended by Kelley, Thibaut, Radloff, and Mundy (1962). Two subjects, typically unaware of each other's presence, are seated in separate cubicles and instructed to respond by pressing one of two buttons in front of them, after which they receive either a reward (e.g., points) or a punishment (e.g., electric shock). This continues for a number of trials, during which time each subject has to try and guess which button to press on each trial to receive a reward and avoid punishment. In fact, however, each subject's choice has no effect on his own outcomes, which are entirely dependent on the choice of the other subject. Thus if subject A presses button 1, subject B receives a reward, while if he presses button 2, subject B receives a shock: subject B's behaviour similarly has no effect on his own outcomes, but determines subject A's outcomes in the same way. Thus a situation of mutual reward ('cooperation') would be established when both subjects were pressing the buttons which would reward the *other* person. As defined by Thibaut and Kelley (1959), this situation is one of mutual fate control, as represented in Figure 7.1. The catch is that, since each subject is unaware of the other's presence, he is likely to assume that his outcomes are somehow contingent on his *own* behaviour.

Surprisingly, even in this highly restricted set-up, there seemed reason to suppose that cooperation would be fairly easy to achieve. Applying simple principles of instrumental learning, it would be predicted that whenever a subject received a reward, he would repeat the same behaviour on the next trial, but if he was punished, he would change his behaviour. If both subjects simultaneously operated on this 'win-stay, lose-change' principle, then a situation of stable mutual reward should develop extremely quickly, as in the following exchange:

Trial 1. Person A rewards Person B: Person B punishes Person A
Trial 2. Person A punishes Person B: Person B punishes Person A
Trial 3. Person A rewards Person B: Person B rewards Person A
Trial 4. Person A rewards Person B: Person B rewards Person A

The typical findings are that subjects do in fact show significant improvement over time in their rates of cooperative responding, but 'over time' usually means something in the region of 100 to 150 trials, rather than the two or three trials that would be all that was necessary if both subjects adopted the 'win-stay, lose-change' strategy, and even at the end of this period the level of cooperation is by no means total. Informing subjects of each other's presence, and of the nature of their dependence on one another, leads to noticeable improvements in cooperation.

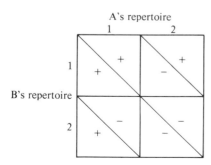

Figure 7.1 The minimal social situation.

Further evidence that subjects do not operate on a simple 'win-stay, lose-change' principle comes from an experiment reported by Kelley *et al.* (1962) using three and four-person groups rather than dyads. In a three-person group, in which A's choices determined B's outcomes, B's choices C's outcomes, and C's choices A's outcomes, the same principle would predict a stable situation of one positive and two negative outcomes, unless all three subjects made the same choice on the first trial. With four-person groups, however, the 'win-stay, lose-change' strategy should again produce stable mutual reward for all members of the group. There is thus a clear prediction that four-person groups should learn to cooperate, whereas three-person groups should not. However, the proportion of positive outcomes remained close to the 50 per cent level (as would be expected if subjects responded randomly) for both three and four-person groups, and showed no significant improvement over 150 trials. In summary, then, the choices of subjects in the minimal social situation cannot be adequately predicted from any notion that they should repeat reinforced behaviour, and avoid behaviour which results in loss.

THE PRISONER'S DILEMMA GAME (PD)

The Prisoner's Dilemma Game is the most frequently used of all experimental games. It owes its name to an imaginary situation in which two prisoners are awaiting trial, and each is considering informing on the other, with the hope of receiving a lighter sentence for himself. If neither of them informs, both their sentences are likely to be moderate: if one informs but the other does not, the informer receives only a light sentence, but the other receives a severe one; but if both inform, they will both receive moderately severe sentences, and so be worse off than if they had both kept quiet. Since they have to make their decisions independently, the dilemma for each of them is whether they can trust the other not to inform.

The laboratory version of this dilemma is a two-person game in which each player has a choice between two alternative responses on each trial, referred to as cooperation (C) and defection or competition (D). The outcomes each player receives on each trial depends both on his own behaviour and on the behaviour of the other player. These outcomes, which often are in the form of small monetary rewards, can be represented in terms of the matrix shown in Figure 7.2, where the number above the diagonal in each cell of the matrix represents the outcomes of person A and the number below the diagonal the outcomes of person B. Thus, if A and B both choose C, both receive x_1; if both choose D, both receive x_4; if one chooses C and the other D, the one who chooses C receives x_2, and the other receives x_3. The PD game is distinguished from other games by the following rules concerning the relative sizes of the respective pay-offs: 1. $x_3 > x_1 > x_4 > x_2$; and 2. $2x_1 > (x_2 + x_3) > 2x_4$. Thus, the matrix shown earlier in Figure 6.3 is in fact

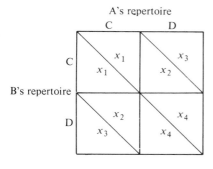

Figure 7.2 General form of the Prisoner's Dilemma Game.

a typical PD, with $x_1 = 3$, $x_2 = -1$, $x_3 = 5$ and $x_4 = 1$. Unlike in the minimal social situation, subjects would typically be shown the matrix, and the extent of their mutual interdependence would be fully explained.

The relative sizes of the pay-offs have important implications for the players' decisions to cooperate or compete. From the point of view of person A's *individual* outcomes, on any given trial he will receive more points for himself if he chooses D rather than C, *whatever person B chooses*. The problem is that if person B thinks the same way, they both are likely to choose D and receive relatively low pay-offs. Even from the point of view of their maximum *joint* outcomes, they should each choose C, but by choosing C they each leave themselves open to exploitation if the other switches to D.

Before considering the experimental findings, one point needs to be made about the games just described. Even though the pay-off structure may be described in matrix form, there is an important difference between these games and the situations discussed in terms of the Thibaut and Kelley (1959) theory in the last chapter. This is that no mention is made of the concepts of CL and CL_{alt}. The attractiveness of any outcome is treated as depending only on the number in the relevant cell of the matrix. In fact, the concept of CL_{alt} is excluded by definition, since the experimenter requires subjects to remain in the relationship. The neglect of the concept of CL is particularly unfortunate, in that subjects may well judge their outcomes against a standard of what they feel they deserve or could reasonably expect.

COOPERATION IN THE PRISONER'S DILEMMA GAME

The single most striking finding of the large body of literature on the PD is the fact that subjects tend to be markedly unsuccessful in achieving mutual cooperation. In coordination games and the minimal social situation subjects often seem inefficient at arriving at cooperative and hence jointly profitable solutions, but, in comparison, subjects in the PD seem almost deliberately pig-headed. If one counts the number of C (cooperative) moves that either player makes over a series of trials of the game, without even requiring such cooperation to be mutual, one typically finds that the C option will be chosen on only about one occasion in three. Occasionally the proportion of C moves may rise to 40 per cent but rarely beyond this without some rather special change in the typical experimental situation. The main focus of experimentation has therefore been with identifying the factors that inhibit the development of cooperation.

Pruitt and Kimmel (1977) have argued that what is crucial is whether subjects view their outcomes in terms of a 'short-range' or 'long-range' perspective—whether they are concerned more with immediate profit or loss, or consider how the interaction may develop over a series of trials.

The goal of achieving mutual cooperation, which involves 'long-range' thinking is seen to depend on perceived interdependence, pessimism about the chances of exploiting the other, and insight into the need to cooperate with the other so that he will also cooperate. However: 'While usually necessary, the goal of achieving mutual cooperation is insufficient to elicit cooperative behaviour. It must be accompanied by an *expectation that the other will cooperate* either immediately or in response to the actor's cooperation' (page 375.)

The perception of mutual interest is thus important for the emergence of cooperation, but subjects also need to think how the other person's behaviour may change, or be changed by them, over a series of trials. Even in the barren atmosphere of the minimal social situation, 'cooperative' responding should emerge rapidly if subjects adopted a simple 'win-stay, lose-change' principle. However, they clearly do not (Sidowski, 1957; Kelley, Thibaut, Radloff, and Mundy, 1962), and the reason may be that subjects treat each new trial as an independent event, and do not choose to learn from their outcome on the immediately preceding trial. Even such simple learning, however, may involve a departure from 'short-range thinking' which may not seem appropriate if one is ignorant even of the existence of another player about whom one could form social expectations. In the PD, some of the features that have been criticized as artificial may contribute to short-range rather than long-range thinking, and a number of factors most frequently manipulated in PD experiments may also be interpreted in the light of this distinction. Let us therefore briefly consider three of these factors: the other player's strategy, the nature of the rewards, and the opportunity to communicate with the other player.

THE OTHER PLAYER'S STRATEGY

Although subjects in the PD are made aware of the relationship between their own outcomes and the choices of the other player, the 'other player' is often simulated, or is a confederate of the experimenter playing according to a predetermined strategy. A large number of studies have manipulated this strategy as an independent variable (Oskamp, 1971). Two extreme strategies are when the other player unconditionally cooperates, or alternatively unconditionally competes, on every trial irrespective of the subject's own choice (100 per cent C vs. 100 per cent D). In the PD, a 100 per cent C strategy produces higher average levels of cooperation than does the 100 per cent D strategy, which forces subjects to respond D in self-defence. The higher average level produced by the 100 per cent C strategy, however, disguises a bimodal distribution in the pattern of subjects' responses: whereas some subjects reciprocate by consistently cooperating in return, other subjects take advantage of the situation to gain the maximum individual pay-off by choosing D. This tendency to exploit an unconditionally cooperative partner is particularly marked when the standard PD matrix is changed to one in which the subject sees the other player as more powerful than himself (Swingle, 1970).

When the other player's response pattern is less consistent, the important question is whether it is at all determined by the subject's own responses. One of the most commonly used pre-programmed strategies is the 'tit-for-tat' (TFT) strategy, in which the confederate chooses, on each trial, the response chosen by the subject on the previous trial. This has the result of rewarding the subject for cooperation and punishing him for defection, and is one of the more effective strategies for increasing cooperation—more effective, at any rate, than a strategy containing the same proportion of C responses but in a random order unrelated to the subject's actual behaviour. Bixenstein and Gaebelein (1971) compared a TFT strategy with conditions involving 'slow reciprocation' of C and/or D responses. Cooperation was highest when reciprocation of both C and D responses was 'slow', i.e., when the subject had to make the same move on three consecutive trials before the other player was certain to reciprocate.

THE NATURE OF REWARDS

One of the commonest general criticisms against gaming research is that subjects might not take their task seriously but see it as 'just a game', and thus be less concerned with the actual rewards or punishments they receive. This is plausible, since the stakes in such games have generally been very low by absolute standards. The actual pay-offs are often in the form of points which have no value outside the experiment, or are the equivalent of only minimal real money amounts (e.g., 1 point = 1¢). Since mutual cooperation is the way to achieve highest joint profit, by giving subjects only negligible rewards one may effectively be removing any incentive for cooperation.

This suggestion, that small rewards inhibit cooperation, has received only equivocal empirical support, however. One study which shows more cooperation as a function of increased reward level is that by Gallo (1966). Using a modified version of the Deutsch and Krauss trucking game, he found that subjects playing for real money won an average of nearly $5 each over 20 trials, whilst whose playing for imaginary rewards ended up with imaginary losses of nearly $20 each. McClintock and McNeel (1966) also found more cooperation in a high reward (2 points = 1 Belgian Franc), than in a low reward, condition (20 points = 1 Belgian Franc) over 100 trials of a 'Maximizing Differences' game. This game resembles the PD, in format, but not in the rules governing the relative sizes of the pay-offs. The pay-offs actually used were $x_1 = 6$, $x_2 = 0$, $x_3 = 5$, and $x_4 = 0$.

However, both these studies used games which present subjects with a qualitatively different kind of choice from that involved in the PD. In the trucking game, the maximum *joint* pay-off is achieved by subjects agreeing to each take the maximum *individual* pay-off on alternative trials, but a unilateral competitive move does not yield any individual profit: it simply produces losses for the other. In the Maximizing Differences game, the highest individual pay-off is obtained when both players choose C. In this game the *only* incentive for choosing D is to beat the other player. On the other hand, in the PD, the CC pay-off is obtained only if each player is prepared to forego the chance of the maximum individual pay-off (x_3) in order to produce a mutually rewarding outcome: he has, effectively, to curtail his aspirations for individual gain.

In the PD, increasing the real money equivalents of the pay-offs does not only increase the motivation to cooperate, it also increases the temptation to exploit the other player. For this reason, it is perhaps not too surprising that manipulations of absolute reward level in the PD have not produced very clear or consistent effects on level of cooperation (Oskamp and Kleinke, 1970). Where differences are found, they tend to be in the direction of more cooperation for real than for imaginary pay-offs (Radlow, Weidner, and Hurst, 1968). Gumpert, Deutsch, and Epstein (1969) found an opposite result, but Gallo and Sheposh (1971) replicated their study with a modified procedure and found that real money rewards again enhanced cooperation. None of these effects, however, are sufficiently strong to justify the assumption that the use of imaginary pay-offs seriously inhibits the emergence of cooperation in the PD.

A more powerful manipulation is to vary the *relative* sizes of the different pay-offs. Rapoport and Chammah (1965) proposed that the tendency to cooperate in a PD should be related to the ratio $(x_1 - x_4)/(x_3 - x_2)$, which they term the 'Cooperation Index'. As this ratio increases, there is less that may be gained, and more that may be lost, by trying to exploit the other player. Terhune (1968) found more mutual cooperation when the Cooperation Index was increased. The *structure* of the pay-offs in the PD and other games thus appears to be generally a more important factor than the absolute level of the rewards. It is this structure that gives most information to the subjects concerning the prior probability of the other player cooperating or failing to cooperate, and so will influence not only the goals which they themselves adopt, but also their expectations concerning whether such goals may be attained.

THE OPPORTUNITY TO COMMUNICATE

One obviously artificial feature of experimental games is the fact that the players typically cannot communicate with one another. Often this restriction is imposed with no more sinister motive in mind than to maintain the experimental deception that the subject's partner is only simulated. Nonetheless, this may be an important factor contributing to low levels of cooperation in some circumstances (Nemeth, 1972).

Since uncertainty concerning the other player's intentions, and the consequent risk associated with the cooperation, constitute the basic dilemma of the PD and similar games, it can reasonably be expected that the opportunity to communicate may clear up some of this uncertainty and hence lead to greater cooperation. A free discussion halfway through the game has been found to lead to greater subsequent cooperation in the PD (Scodel, Minas, Ratoosh, and Lipetz, 1959) and in a modification of the PD for six-person groups (Bixenstein, Levitt, and Wilson, 1966). Voissem and Sistrunk (1971) found that subjects who could pass each other notes expressing their intentions and/or expectations before each trial of a 100 trial PD became progressively more cooperative as compared with a no-communication group, who became more competitive as the game progressed; two other conditions with partial communication opportunities showed intermediate levels of cooperation. In coordination games, Mintz (1951) found that subjects removed their cones from the narrow-necked bottle more efficiently when discussion was permitted. On the other hand, Deutsch and Krauss (1962) observed that simply providing subjects with the opportunity to communicate is no guarantee that they will in fact make use of this opportunity. Subjects talked to each other most in the 'no-gate' condition and least in the 'two-gate' condition. Even in the 'no-gate' condition, most subjects did not communicate, possibly because communication took time, and time cost money.

To a great extent, whether communication opportunities increase cooperation depends on how much the players *want* to cooperate. As Deutsch (1958) points out:

> When subjects are competitively oriented, there is little commitment to what one communicates and hence little basis for trust as a result of the communication one receives. It would seem that the situation has to be ambiguous as to whether the individuals will interrelate themselves co-operatively or competitively, rather than clearly competitive, before an individual will assume that communications are informative rather than misleading. (Page 275.)

If a communicative act can be seen as a move in the game, by the same token a move in the game can be a means of communicating one's intentions to the other player. It is therefore important to specify what is being communicated, and how. A common criticism of the trucking game experiments is that the gates may have been used as a means of signalling whose turn it was to use the one-lane road, rather than as threats (see Kelley, 1965; Shomer,

Davis, and Kelley, 1966; and Deutsch, 1969, for a discussion of this point). Using a modified PD, Tedeschi, Bonoma, and Novinson (1970) found that bilateral threat capacity led to greater retaliation, but not to smaller earnings as in the Deutsch and Krauss (1960) study. The fact that threats took time to administer in the trucking game, and time cost money, may have contributed to this difference in outcomes.

According to Tedeschi (1970), the gates are an example of a *noncontingent threat*, which he defines as 'any stimulus which signals punishment, but which does not indicate any specific avoidance responses' (page 166). Although it is assumed that subjects will interpret the other player's use of his gate as a signal not to try and use the one-lane road, this is not made explicit. By comparison, a *contingent threat* is typically operationalized as 'a clear verbal if—then communication which promises administration of punishment for noncompliance' (page 167). Horai and Tedeschi (1969) demonstrated greater compliance on the part of a threatened player in a modified PD, the greater the credibility of the threat and the magnitude of the punishment. Promises similarly can be contingent or non-contingent. A *non-contingent promise* 'signals a reward in a situation in which the reward is not contingent upon any particular response' (page 176). A simple commitment to choose C in the PD is an example. As implied by Deutsch (1958), credibility is again a crucial variable. Gahagan and Tedeschi (1968) had a confederate communicate non-contingent promises after every 10 trials of a 110-trial modified PD; of the ten promises, either 3, 6, or 9 were in fact honoured. More credible promises produced more cooperation on the trial following the promise, but the effect did not spread to other trials (this finding is supported by one of the conditions of Voissem and Sistrunk, 1971). The effectiveness of *contingent promises* (defined as promises of administering a reward in return for compliance) does not seem similarly related to their credibility (Lindskold and Tedeschi, 1969).

Restricting the opportunity to communicate, however, may also have a more symbolic effect. The very fact of being isolated from one another may make the players see their interaction as a more impersonal affair, to which the norm of reciprocity (Nemeth, 1970) and other codes of conduct which operate in everyday encounters are somehow less applicable. Wichman (1970) reported median levels of cooperation, among female students playing a PD, of 41 per cent in an isolation condition in which they could neither see nor hear each other, of 48 per cent when they could see but not hear each other, of 72 per cent when they could hear but not see each other, and of 87 per cent when they could both see and hear each other. Wichman mentions that even here the opportunity to communicate was not always used: subjects who could see but not hear each other would often avoid looking at each other. But the overall conclusion is clear: the more freely and naturally subjects can communicate, the more likely they are to cooperate.

A somewhat bizarre but suggestive experiment by Durkin (1967) also testifies to the importance of visual contact. His main condition involved subjects making their choices while seated in total darkness, looking into opposite ends of a two-way tachistoscope. A mutually cooperative, or mutually competitive, combination of choices by the two players automatically illuminated the tachistoscope, so that they found themselves looking straight at each other for half a second. This led to an increase in the number of individual and especially joint cooperative choices as compared with a condition of constant illumination, which in turn produced more cooperation than a condition run in total darkness throughout. It is not clear whether subjects in the first condition may not have construed their task as one of illuminating the tachistoscope as often as they could rather than achieving a maximum number of points, but the possibility that manipulations of this kind can alter the phenomenological nature of the experimental situation should not be ignored.

In general, one would expect that any manipulation, such as increased opportunity to communicate, that encouraged subjects to think of the other player as a real person with whom they might have some relationship outside the laboratory, would tend to lead subjects to adopt what Pruitt and Kimmel (1977) call a long-range perspective. A long-range perspective, however, will not produce cooperation if the other player remains exploitative. In accordance with this argument, Marlowe, Gergen, and Doob (1966) and Gruder (1971) found that subjects reciprocated the other player's level of cooperation more when they anticipated informal contact with him after the experiment.

PERCEIVING THE OTHER'S INTENTIONS

The structure of the PD is such that unilateral cooperative intentions will not produce a stable pattern of cooperative responding unless the other player's intentions are also seen by the subject as cooperative. Of the three factors influencing the level of cooperation which we have just been considering, the two which directly affect the subject's outcomes are the strategy of the other player, and the level of reward. If the subject's own behaviour is simply a function of the outcomes he receives, then these should be the factors with the most influence on his level of cooperation. The most dramatic increases in cooperation, however, have generally been produced by giving subjects the opportunity to communicate with one another. These findings suggest that an understanding of strategic interaction in experimental games is likely to depend as much upon an understanding of how individuals attribute intentions to one another as upon a consideration of their overall gains and losses.

Kelley and Stahelski (1970b) have proposed that the extent to which a player in the PD or any similar game will see his partner as having cooperative or competitive intentions will be related to his *own* intentions in the interaction. In what they call the 'triangle hypothesis', they propose that, whereas cooperative individuals may see their partner as likely to be either cooperative or competitive, competitive individuals will predominantly interpret their partner's intentions as competitive. If one were to test a group of

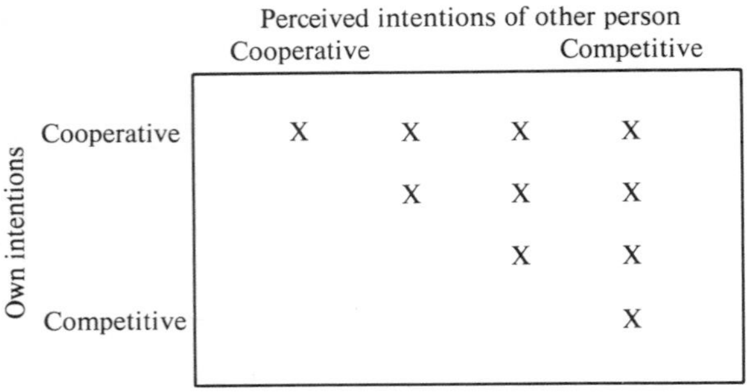

Perceived intentions of other person

	Cooperative			Competitive
Cooperative	X	X	X	X
		X	X	X
			X	X
Competitive				X

Own intentions

Figure 7.3 The 'triangle hypothesis' concerning relation between own intentions and perceived intentions of the other person. [*Adapted from Kelley and Stahelski (1970b).*]

subjects, and then plot their own intentions against their expectations of their partners' intentions, a triangular shape should result (see Figure 7.3).

Of most significance are the attributions made by subjects when the other player chooses D. Such a choice might represent either an attempt at exploitation (if the other player felt the subject would choose C) or an attempt at self-defence (if he felt the subject would choose D). Thus even if the other's original intentions were cooperative, he might be forced to choose D if the subject himself competed. Kelley and Stahelski argue that competitive individuals make an 'attributional error' in taking insufficient account of the causative influence of their *own* behaviour in forcing the other to act competitively. Thus, by attributing competitive intentions to their partner, they force him to act competitively, and so their attributions become self-fulfilling.

In support of this hypothesis, Kelley and Stahelski (1970a) show that, whilst the intentions of a competitive player in the PD tend to be accurately perceived, a player whose original intentions are cooperative tends to be seen as cooperative by a cooperative partner and competitive by a competitive partner. This is largely because he is forced to *behave* competitively, if faced with a competitive partner. Kelley and Stahelski see the differences in the attributions made by cooperators and competitors as evidence that they 'have different views of their worlds' (1970b, page 66), which reflect differences in personality, particularly in authoritarianism, generalizable to other interactions, and not specific to their behaviour in the PD or mixed-motive games generally.

Following the many other writers who have pointed out the very specific situational factors present in the PD as compared with other mixed-motive interactions (e.g., Sermat, 1970), Miller and Holmes (1975) have argued strongly against an interpretation of such findings in terms of players' general dispositions. They compared a standard PD with an 'expanded prisoner's dilemma' (EPD) as shown in Figure 7.4. The additional feature of the EPD was that both the subject and the other player had an extra response option, corresponding to the middle column and row of the matrix, which may be

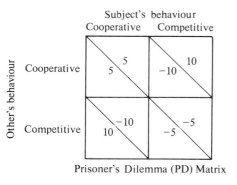

Prisoner's Dilemma (PD) Matrix

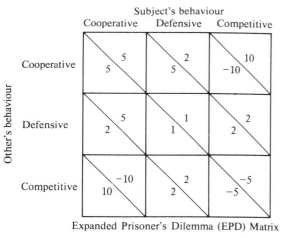

Expanded Prisoner's Dilemma (EPD) Matrix

Figure 7.4 The games used by Miller and Holmes (1975). [*Adapted from Miller and Holmes (1975)*.]

termed a 'defensive' move. If the other player acted competitively, a cooperative move by the subject would result in a high profit to the other and a serious loss to oneself. However, by acting 'defensively' the subject could prevent both these consequences if the other acted competitively, without penalizing the other if he acted cooperatively. The importance of this additional option is that a competitive move in the EPD cannot be construed as an attempt at self-defence, as it can be in the PD.

Miller and Holmes had subjects both declare their own intentions as cooperative or competitive, and also predict whether the 'typical person' would play cooperatively or competitively. As shown in Table 7.1, these data confirmed the Kelley and Stahelski prediction of a 'triangular' relationship in the case of the PD, but not the EPD. Subjects then played against a relatively

Table 7.1 Percentages of cooperative and competitive subjects predicting that the 'typical person' would respond cooperatively and competitively in the PD and EPD games used by Miller and Holmes (1975)

| | Predicted behaviour of 'typical person' | | | |
| | PD | | EPD | |
	Cooperative	Competitive	Cooperative	Competitive
Own intentions				
Cooperative	60	40	65	35
Competitive	10	90	32	68

cooperative or competitive programmed strategy. As predicted, cooperative subjects made fewer competitive choices in the EPD than the PD, when playing against a competitive strategy. Provision of a 'defensive' option removes the need for subjects to act competitively in self-defence. In general, EPD players were less influenced than were PD players by the kind of strategy which they had to play against.

Miller and Holmes do not dismiss the idea that attributions of intentions to the other person can operate as self-fulfilling prophecies, but stress the importance of specific situational variables in such attributions to a far greater extent than do Kelley and Stahelski. Subjects may choose to adopt a cooperative, or a competitive, goal in an interaction because of their prior expectations as to how the other will behave, just as plausibly as their expectations may be shaped by their own cooperative or competitive orientations. In addition, situational variables may be perceived differently by subjects with different orientations, so that it need not always be the other person's *behaviour* that is the basis for attributions of cooperativeness or competitiveness, but the *situation* that is seen as constraining anyone to act more or less competitively. These conclusions are reinforced by Kuhlman and Wimberley (1976), who also compared subjects' expectations of others' intentions in the PD and other experimental games. Whereas the data from the PD are consistent with the triangle hypothesis, the data from the other games (which allow 'individualistically' oriented subjects to be distinguished from those who are cooperative or competitive) show that subjects tend to assume that others will have broadly similar intentions to their own, whatever these happen to be.

A person's intentions can also affect the kind of information he will look for in a situation where his partner's intentions are unclear. Eiser and Tajfel (1972) had pairs of subjects exchange 'messages' in the form of coloured cards from a choice of five colours. Depending on its colour, each message sent cost the sender a certain number of points, and was worth a certain number of points to the other player who received it. Each subject was told the cost to himself of the messages he could send and the value to himself of those he could receive. No information was given about the value to his partner of the messages he sent, nor about his partner's costs, but this information could be 'bought' from the experimenter for a specified number of points. Subjects asked for much more information concerning the value to the other of their own messages than concerning the cost to the other of those they received. This difference, however, was significantly smaller among subjects whose declared intentions were less competitive. Knowing the costs incurred by the other person should provide a basis for attributions concerning his intentions. If the other person seemed merely to be acting so as to minimize his own costs, the outcomes received by the subject, whether high or low, would convey no information about the other's intentions (cf. Eiser, Aiyeola, Bailey, and Gaskell, 1973; Enzle, Hansen, and Lowe, 1975). It would appear, then, that the more cooperative subjects showed relatively more interest in information which would enable them to infer the reasons for their partner's apparent behaviour, and less interest in information that would enable them to control their partner's outcomes, than the less cooperative subjects.

These conclusions require qualification in the light of a modified replication conducted by Eiser and Eiser (1976a). Subjects in this study were young adolescents rather than university students, and one of the main findings was a significant tendency for older subjects in the sample (about 14 years old) to ask for more information concerning the other's costs than younger subjects (about 12 years old). Since information about another's costs provides insight into the reasons for his behaviour, this result is consistent with theories of socialization which suggest that children become increasingly capable, with age, of taking the viewpoint of another person in social interactions (e.g., Piaget, 1932; Kohlberg, 1969). As in the Eiser and Tajfel study, there were more requests for information concerning the other's value than concerning the other's costs, this tendency being most marked among those subjects who acted in such a way as to provide the other player with low value outcomes. In addition, measures were derived, on the basis of a pre-test, of the extent to which subjects' orientations were *individualistic* (concerned with one's own outcomes, but not with beating or helping the other) as distinct from cooperative or competitive. These measures suggested that it was the most individualistically oriented subjects who were least interested in providing themselves with an attributional basis for inferring the other's intentions by asking for cost information. Subjects who scored highly on the pre-test measure of competitiveness (trying to beat the other, rather than just maximizing one's own outcomes) showed at least as much interest in cost information as did less competitive subjects.

The age differences in relation to cost information are interesting when set against those of a study by McClintock and Moskowitz (1976), which looked at the individualistic, competitive and cooperative responses of children aged five to eight-and-a-half years playing differently structured experimental games. As expected, the frequency of cooperative choices increased with age. However, even the youngest subjects adopted primarily competitive, rather than individualistic, strategies. This led McClintock and Moskowitz to conclude that 'children as young as 5 years of age *systematically* take into consideration outcomes to self and other in making choices' (page 553). It would seem, therefore, that children are able to consider the effects of their own cooperative or competitive behaviour on another person before they can use information concerning another's costs as a basis for inferring his intentions.

SELF-PRESENTATION AND THE SUBJECTS' DEFINITION OF THE SITUATION

As important as the attributions subjects make about each other's intentions are their expectations of how their own behaviour will be seen by others. Such 'others' may include not only the partner with whom they are interacting, but also the experimenter and anyone else who may witness their behaviour. In many situations, the *symbolic* value of a person's behaviour is likely to be as important to that person as the pay-offs which his behaviour produces. This even applies to a variable which directly affects the subject's monetary outcomes, namely the size of the real money equivalent of the points in the pay-off matrix. Messé, Dawson, and Lane (1973) have shown that subjects' motivation to earn substantial rewards by mutual cooperation depends on what they consider an equitable rate of pay for their participation in the experiment. When playing a PD for high monetary rewards, subjects who had previously spent a long period completing questionnaires for the experimenter were more cooperative than subjects who did not have to complete the questionnaires first; this difference disappeared when subjects played for minimal rewards. Similarly, Gallo (1968) reports anecdotal evidence that, when subjects are questioned during debriefing as to why they had not cooperated more consistently and so earned more money, they often get indignant and reply that they are not greedy. Thus the same subjects, whom the experimenter regards as competitive, may, from their own point of view, be acting cooperatively *towards the experimenter* by not exploiting their opportunity to obtain inequitably large remunerations for their services.

Considerations of equity may also be involved in the findings that cooperation is less likely in situations where it will benefit one player more than the other (Tedeschi, Lindskold, Horai, and Gahagan, 1969; Marwell and Schmitt, 1975), or when the two players start the game with unequal assets (Aranoff and Tedeschi, 1968). This is why the concept of CL (Thibaut and Kelley, 1959) is so important. The same outcomes may be seen as satisfactory or unsatisfactory, depending on the CL or standard against which they are judged. This standard will reflect what the subject feels he deserves from the interaction, which is likely to be influenced by what he sees the other player getting.

Clear differences in level of cooperation can also be produced if the format of the pay-off matrix is altered so as to emphasize different implications of cooperative and competitive play. Evans and Crumbaugh (1966) found that subjects cooperated at a rate of 48 per cent against a TFT strategy when presented with a standard PD matrix, the matrix being $x_1 = 3$, $x_2 = 0$, $x_3 = 4$, and $x_4 = 1$. However, when subjects had to choose between the responses 'Give him 3' and 'Give me 1', cooperation increased to 63 per cent. The point is that both these procedures are logically equivalent (if both players chose 'Give him 3' this would be the same as if both chose C) but they do not appear to be equivalent *psychologically*. The latter procedure is closely related to what Pruitt (1967) calls a 'decomposed' PD. The essential feature of a decomposed PD is that the pay-offs are presented to each player in the form shown in Figure 7.5.

This would be equivalent to 'give him 3' and 'give me 1' if $a = 0$, $b = 3$, $c = 1$, and $d = 0$. The values a, b, c, and d can take any values provided the following rules are observed governing the relationship between the decomposed PD and the standard PD from which it is derived: $x_1 = a + b$; $x_2 = a + d$; $x_3 = b + c$; $x_4 = c + d$. (These rules also imply the additional restriction on the standard PD that $[x_1 - x_3] = [x_2 - x_4]$.) Pruitt compared the level of cooperation obtained with a PD presented in standard format with three decomposed PDs, as shown in Figure 7.6, all of which are mathematically equivalent to each other and to the standard PD. Cooperation on the standard PD was around 50 per cent. Over the last 5 of a series of 20 trials, the level was around 15 per cent on game II, but as high as 82 per cent and 78 per cent on games III and IV respectively. There is also evidence that decomposed PDs that produce greater cooperation lead subjects to reciprocate cooperation quickly, but retaliate more slowly if the other fails to cooperate (Pruitt, 1970; Tognoli, 1975). Pruitt and Kimmel (1977) suggest that displays such as Games III and IV may emphasize one's dependence on the other's willingness to cooperate, and thus foster the goal of mutual cooperation.

Just as the presentation of the matrix can alter the meaning of cooperation and competition for the subject, while leaving the actual pay-offs unchanged, so can the wider context in terms of which he feels his behaviour will be evaluated. Eiser and Bhavnani (1974) found subjects cooperated more when led to interpret a PD as a simulation of international negotiations or of

	Your gains	Other's gains
Your behaviour C	a	b
D	c	d

Figure 7.5 Basic Form of a Decomposed Prisoner's Dilemma

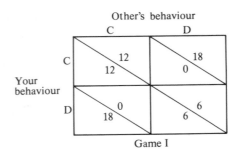

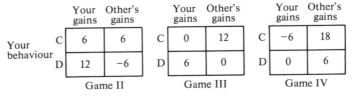

Figure 7.6 The PD game (Game I) and the derivative decompositions (Games II, III, and IV) used by Pruitt (1967). [*Adapted from Pruitt (1967)*.]

'real-life encounters between different individuals', than when given control instructions, or led to regard it as a simulation of economic bargaining. Alexander and Weil (1968) had subjects rate the players in a (supposedly genuine) previous game, in which one of the players had consistently cooperated and the other had been consistently exploitative. When subjects rated the two players in terms of traits chosen to emphasize 'good person' qualities, i.e., attached positive labels to cooperation and negative labels to competition (e.g., friendly, generous *vs.* treacherous, vicious), their own subsequent level of cooperation was higher than when the traits they had to use reflected 'good player' qualities, i.e., labelled cooperation negatively and competition positively (e.g., clever, enterprising *vs.* gullible, spineless)—a result which closely parallels the attitude change effects of evaluative labels (see Chapter 5).

Similar results have been found when the subject's own behaviour is evaluated. Using a modified trucking game, Brown (1968) found that subjects who had been exploited during the first ten trials of the experiment would be more likely to engage in retaliatory behaviour, even at high cost to themselves, if they received feedback from a simulated audience that they had looked foolish and weak than if they were told that they looked good because they had played fair. This tendency to restore face through retaliation is suppressed if the audience was supposedly aware of the subjects' costs for retaliation.

Brown (1970) has since generalized these findings beyond the context of experimental games. When male college students were required to give a full account of their sensations while sucking on a baby's rubber dummy (intended as an embarrassing activity), they were willing to forego monetary rewards of up to $1.50 in order to minimize personal embarrassment by choosing, for example, merely to produce a written description, as opposed to making a live presentation in front of a panel of peers, which would be recorded on videotape. Again, subjects were prepared to choose more embarrassing alternatives if they were told that the audience was aware of the costs they would incur by avoiding exposure.

Face-saving, then, is something people are prepared to pay for, provided that they do not lose face in the process by being seen to pay too much. A loss of face, of course, is itself a negative outcome and so conceivably could be included in a pay-off matrix. However, this would be a kind of 'second-order' pay-off, dependent on the meaning with which the subject invests the experimental situation, rather than on the monetary rewards and costs made available by the experimenter.

OUTDOOR GAMES

By 'outdoor' here, I mean outside the doors of the social psychology laboratory. Many of the less well considered criticisms of experimental gaming have appeared to treat it as self-evident that any experiment that is 'just a game' can provide no insight into 'real-life' encounters, not dictated by arbitrary constraints imposed by the experimenter: only *subjects* play games, *real* people don't. It is important to consider this general criticism apart from specific criticisms against the use of particular kinds of games, such as the PD. As I have argued, there are specific aspects of the PD, most importantly the fact that one needs to defend oneself against an exploitative other by making a move that itself could be construed as exploitative, that are a direct function of the pay-off structure and hence may be removed by alterations in that structure. Perhaps some people might wish to argue that the PD does not simulate real-life encounters, such as commercial or international rivalry, as well as might games that had a different kind of pay-off structure. To this, gaming researchers, or many of them at least, would probably answer that the PD is not intended to be a business game or war game or any other kind of simulation. But this debate would have little impression on those who felt that game-playing *as such* was, by definition, an inappropriate and irrelevant model for the study of 'real' social behaviour.

In one sense, this general criticism is unanswerable by either empirical research or logical argument. It is fairly easy to compare how people behave in particular experimental games with how they behave in 'real-life' situations which, *in the experimenter's judgement*, also should reflect the same behavioural tendencies of cooperation or competition, if the gaming approach is valid (e.g., Sermat, 1970). If the comparison shows an apparent similarity between subjects' experimental and nonexperimental behaviour, this will not necessarily be replicable, if other nonexperimental situations are used. Conversely, if differences are found between subjects' behaviour in the different situations, this may just point to the importance of situational variables, rather than to the invalidity of experimental situations as a basis for generalization. If other nonexperimental situations had been used, that more closely resembled the experimental situations in terms of crucial variables such as pay-off structure, greater similarity in behaviour might have been found. Interpretation of any empirical test of the general criticism against gaming research is thus dependent on researchers' (and critics') judgements about whether similar behaviours or similar situations really are similar. Logically, also, similarity does not establish identity, and to ask the gaming researcher to prove that there are no important differences between experimental and nonexperimental situations and behaviour is to set him the impossible task of proving a negative.

Perhaps a more reasonable approach is to see whether concepts developed in the gaming literature appear useful in the explanation of wider social behaviour. I hasten to stress that this short section attempts no such 'explanation of wider social behaviour' whatsoever. Instead, I shall briefly mention one or two of the ways in which gaming concepts have been used outside not only the physical, but also the disciplinary, confines of the social psychology laboratory. The thesis is that 'real-life' social interaction itself has important game-like properties, and that insights may often be gained into why people behave the way they do through the metaphor that they are playing parts in a socially defined game, identifying to greater or lesser extents with the roles assigned them. Evaluation of this thesis is more properly within the competence of sociology than of social psychology. For present purposes, it is enough to note that those who object to gaming experiments in social psychology on *a priori* grounds must similarly object to the use of gaming metaphors in sociological theory and related disciplines.

TRANSACTIONAL ANALYSIS

A popular application of gaming concepts to interpersonal relationships has been presented by Berne (1961, 1968). Transactional analysis, as Berne calls his approach, offers accounts of particular incidents in an interpersonal relationship ('transactions') by categorizing communicative acts as reflecting an adoption of a particular role by the communicator ('agent'), and the implicit expectation by the agent of the particular role he expects the audience or addressee ('respondent') to adopt in return. Within a theoretical framework which has a clear psychoanalytic heritage, Berne distinguishes three basic roles: Parent, Adult, and Child. Fulfilling the role of Parent in a transaction does not require that one actually is a parent, still less the parent of the other person in the transaction. All that is implied is that one adopts a relatively dominant (critical or nurturant) role. Berne distinguishes between 'complementary' and 'crossed' transactions. Examples of complementary transactions are those where both agent and respondent adopt the same role and expectations of the other's role (a departure here from the definition of complementarity in terms of Leary's 1957 scheme), be the transaction Parent-Parent, Adult-Adult or Child-Child. Another kind of complementary relationship is where the agent transmits a Parent-Child communication, and the respondent replies with a Child-Parent communication (or vice versa).

Crossed transactions occur when the respondent does not share the agent's role expectations. For example, the agent may try to communicate with the respondent on an Adult-to-Adult basis, but the respondent will reply on a Child-to-Parent basis, i.e., may unilaterally adopt a dependent position designed to elicit guidance, nurturance or dominance from the agent. Berne (1968, page 29) rather sweepingly claims that this particular example of a crossed transaction is 'the one which causes and has always caused most of the social difficulties in the world, whether in marriage, love, friendship, or work' and also 'is the principal concern of psychotherapists and is typified by the classical transference reaction of psychoanalysis'.

Again with shades of Freud showing through, Berne distinguishes between the analysis of a transaction at the ostensible or 'social' level, and its analysis at the ulterior or 'psychological' level. The actual words used in a communication might appear to convey one kind of relationship (e.g., Adult-Adult), where the ulterior 'psychological' relationship is of a different kind (e.g., Child-Child). A statement like: 'I've still got some of my original Beatles records. Would you like to come and listen to them?' thus might 'really' mean, 'Would you like to play with me?'

It is easy to understand how transactional analysis provides an appealingly homely conceptual framework for those who feel that they are engaged in some kind of 'crossed transaction' with a significant other and want to try to sort things out. For many people, the analysis that one is playing the wrong kind of role is also likely to be a lot more comforting, in the sense of implying greater possibility for change, than the diagnosis that one is suffering, or one's partner is suffering, from some kind of 'mental illness'. This appeal is considerably strengthened by Berne's graphic description of a number of supposedly typical games. One example, described as 'the most common game played between spouses' is called, 'If It Weren't For You' (IWFY), which is analysed as follows:

Mr White: 'You stay home and take care of the house.'
Mrs White: 'If it weren't for you, I could be out having fun.'

At a 'psychological' level, the game is analysed as a Child-Child game, as follows:

Mr White: 'You must always be here when I get home. I'm terrified of desertion.'
Mrs White: 'I will be if you help me avoid phobic situations.'

Among other games given similar treatment are, 'Now I've got you, you son of a bitch' (NIGYSOB) and 'Why don't you—yes but' (YDYB). Each of these games follows a 'social' and a 'psychological' paradigm. With NIGYSOB, the social paradigm is:

Adult: 'See, you have done wrong.'
Adult: 'Now that you draw it to my attention, I guess I have.'
The psychological paradigm, however, goes as follows:
Parent: 'I've been watching you, hoping you'd make a slip.'
Child: 'You caught me this time.'
Parent: 'Yes, and I'm going to let you feel the full force of my fury.'
With YDYB, the social paradigm is again ostensibly Adult-Adult:
Adult: 'What do you do if ....'
Adult: 'Why don't you ....'
Adult: 'Yes, but ....'
On a psychological level, though, YDYB is Parent-Child:
Parent: 'I can make you grateful for my help.'
Child: 'Go ahead and try.'

These examples should suffice to give a general impression of what Berne is trying to do. The implication is that it may sometimes be useful for psychiatric patients and others to dwell less on the particularities of their own problems, and pay more attention to the manner in which their behaviour reflects the adoption of a role in a game which others also have played. This approach depends upon the metaphor of the game as the best means both of summarizing clinical experience and of communicating this experience to the patients or clients.

But are such interpretations of personal relationships correct? This is strictly speaking a question for psychiatry rather than social psychology. One source of validation would be the client's own preparedness to admit that he is playing a particular kind of game, but then it can be all too easy for psychiatrists and therapists to make their own interpretations of a client's problem seem authoritative and persuasive to the client. Another approach would be to examine the frequency and reliability with which such games can be recognized in everyday encounters, among people who do not constitute as self-selected a sample as clients of a particular therapist or agency. Inspite of Berne's comments that a particular form of a game may be particularly 'common', nothing approaching hard data on this point is produced. Perhaps it is no more fruitful to bother whether one game, such as IWFY, is or is not a 'typical' game for married couples, than to speculate whether the PD is 'typical' of real life conflicts. The question of frequency may be less important than the understanding of the *processes* that operate within the constraints of a specific game or role, but are nonetheless more general than that game or role.

GAMES AND ROLES

Within sociology, a much more substantial application of gaming and role concepts has been developed by Goffman. An important concept in Goffman's writings is that of face-work (Goffman, 1955), in broad terms, the devices a person will adopt in order to present himself to others in a socially acceptable manner. In, *The Presentation of Self in Everyday Life*, (1959) numerous examples are given of more or less successful social 'performances', while in, *Asylums*, (1961) and, *Stigma*, (1963) Goffman deals, among related issues, with the problems of self-presentation posed for specific groups, such as psychiatric patients and persons with physical deformities. In, *Strategic Interaction*, (1970) he goes into detail regarding the performances required of spies and diplomats. Role-playing, then, is seen as relevant to a wide range of social encounters, although, unlike Berne, Goffman does not attempt to identify any archetypal roles (such as Parent, Adult, and Child) to encompass the whole range within a common dynamic framework. In Goffman's more authentically empirical analysis of specific games and role relationships, there is a firmer basis for extrapolating to game-like behaviour in general. By examining the structure of particular relationships, one can draw inferences about the processes involved in role-playing generally, and how such processes interact with structure. Such inferences, moreover, do not require statistical assumptions about what are 'typical' roles.

Of particular relevance to the present discussion, however, are the two papers published together in his volume *Encounters* (1972). In *Fun in Games* Goffman presents a powerful argument against dismissing game-playing as something which is trivial and unilluminating about social encounters in general. This argument is not based on a contention that the superficial structure of games is like that of more 'serious' interactions, but rather that the question of why any game is fun is a question which deserves to be taken seriously. Games are defined in the first instance by 'rules of relevance and irrelevance'. These define what should, or should not be, attended to in the game. In a football match, the colour of each team's strip is relevant, in that it is something that players and spectators can attend to so as to determine which side a player is on. The colour of their skin is not. Similarly, although the official rules of football lay down details of how many players constitute a team, the size and separation of goal-posts, etc., these rules may often be amended by local contract, as one can see on any park or common. When a pair of coats are put down on the ground to serve as goalposts, their attributes as coats cease to be relevant to the game. The fact that they are coats rather than 'real' goalposts can easily be seen, but this fact is ignored through 'selective inattention.'

Goffman argues that a game will be fun for the players to the extent that it defines a reality for them in which they can become engrossed. Violation of rules of irrelevance can threaten this engrossment, by diverting players' attention away from the game itself to aspects of external reality. The boy who starts complaining that his coat, which is being used as a goalpost, has been trampled on and is getting muddy will not be thanked for reminding his friends that they are not playing *proper* football. It doesn't matter if *proper* goalposts get muddy. Goffman talks of games being separated from external reality by a 'membrane' which can easily be punctured, and much of his discussion concerns the means adopted by players to preserve this membrane, or to repair it if it is punctured. Typically this requires a tacit recognition of aspects of external reality that are officially ruled to be irrelevant to the game itself. The question of who gets on well with whom may need to be taken into account in choosing partners for a game, if the game is to be fun. Similarly, for experienced bridge players, it will make an important difference to the kind of game being played whether or not husbands and wives are supposed to partner one another.

It is also important that games should be played with a certain degree of seriousness if they are to be fun. Blatantly to show that one doesn't care about the result will undermine one's opponent's fun, whatever the result may be. On the other hand, to appear over-exultant at winning or depressed at losing may similarly destroy the 'membrane' that keeps the game in its place. Stakes at poker are thus set at a level where players will try to win, but will (hopefully) not lose more than they can reasonably afford. On this point, what Goffman has to say is of direct relevance to the criticism that experimental games are not taken seriously by subjects. He argues that whether an activity is taken seriously depends primarily not on whether it is categorized as work or recreation, but on 'whether external pulls upon one's interest can be selectively held in check so that one can become absorbed in the encounter as a world in itself. The problem of too-serious or not-serious-enough arises in gaming encounters not because a game is involved but because an encounter is involved' (1972, page 63).

The second paper in the same volume is entitled 'Role Distance', and to a large extent follows on from the preceding discussion by showing how people who may be performing a particular role give notice to others that they do not fully identify with the role to the point that they could be accused of taking it too seriously. Here again recreational and work roles are treated alike with both seriousness and humour. Graphic descriptions are given of how people of different ages from toddlers to young adults will set about the business of riding a merry-go-round horse. As just remaining in the saddle becomes less of an achievement, it also becomes increasingly necessary for the individual to make it clear to his spectators that he does not expect to be judged simply on the basis of that achievement. Another example is of a group of high-school girls 'not of the horsey set' on a pony-trek, who manifest 'role distance' by generally larking around so that nobody could think they were really trying: 'Whatever their showing, they avoid having to be humbled before those who are socially placed to make a much better showing' (1972, page 99).

The manifestations of role distance, however, may do much more than allow the performer of a role to protect himself against personal criticism for failure. Surgery teams are used as an example of how distancing oneself from a role may serve as a kind of safety valve which allows for better performance both by oneself and the people around one. Just as games are less fun and more tension-provoking as rules of irrelevance come under pressure, so even something as serious as a surgical operation can run less efficiently if it is taken *too* seriously. The problem again is one of selective inattention. To try and deny that there is a world outside the theatre, faces behind the masks or bodies beneath the gowns is to put a strain on the 'situated activity system' of the operation which not all of the individuals involved may be able to sustain. For this reason, although the surgeon is entitled by virtue of his authority to expect the junior members of his team to carry out his orders as orders and not as requests, and to do so in a manner of high seriousness, medical etiquette requires that he phrases his instructions as requests and thanks his juniors for their help. It is also clear from Goffman's observations that a certain measure of good-humoured irreverence and teasing, if the surgeon gives the lead, can be a fairly typical part of how the different roles on the surgical team are *performed* although not a part of the roles themselves. Such irreverence essentially takes the form of limited violation of rules of irrelevance, and itself follows predictable patterns depending on the status of the performer.

The phenomenon of role distance thus shows, not just that people engaged in social interaction can be described as performing roles, but that, even as they identify with the activities they are performing, they are aware of their roles *as* roles—as only a specific part of their identity set apart from wider considerations by accepted rules which define which of their attributes are or are not relevant to their place in the interaction. However, the fact that no game or role can usually claim to represent the total reality of a social relationship or of an individual's identity, does not mean that it can be lightly dismissed. It is in fact the selective aspect of games and roles that enables us to take them seriously.

CONCLUSIONS

In this chapter I have described how a particular experimental game has been used by social psychologists in order to study cooperation and competition, and have also attempted to give a glimpse of the way the gaming metaphor has been applied to social interactions outside the laboratory. What assessment can be made of this large, but often by-passed, area of experimental social psychology?

There are many comments that can be made about the very special situation involved in the PD and some of its close variants, and typically these comments are presented as criticisms. It is undeniable that the PD is an 'artificial' situation in many respects. The removal of opportunities for communication and the impoverished response repertoire are the two most salient features. Other arbitrary rules of the game, such as the need to make a move before one knows what the other's move will be, and the particular relationships between the different outcomes in the matrix, also have a direct impact on behaviour in a way that implies that different behaviour would be observed if the rules were different. Such considerations mount up to a general criticism that the PD cannot be assumed to be paradigmatic of real-life encounters—and also, though this extension is not logically entailed, that behaviour in the PD is unrepresentative of behaviour outside the laboratory.

Implicit in this is the notion that, for the PD to be a useful topic for social research, its *structure* must be seen to be representative of the structure of real-life relationships. This representativeness is sometimes assumed, sometimes denied, but never put to any really thorough-going empirical test. My own view is that the question is irrelevant. There will be some real-life relationships that conform to the particular structure of the PD, and many others that do not, but their proportionate frequency of occurrence is not important theoretically. What is important for an understanding of human social behaviour is the interaction between any given social structure or relationship and the cognitive processes of the individuals involved. This can conceivably be studied as appropriately within one situational context as another, but it is still to be regretted that the experimental gaming literature is so one-sided in its reliance on the PD over and above all other games.

When one considers both how the PD is played in the laboratory, and how 'real' games and roles are played outside, it is apparent that an interaction can be recognized as a game—a world in itself set apart from external reality—and still be taken seriously. The artificiality of the PD is certainly something that players will recognize, but what is important is how they define the game for themselves within that artificial context. In all gaming encounters there is a potentially troublesome borderline to be drawn between the official definition of the game in terms of the rules, and the wider social context which can have impact on its meaning for the participants. The information given to subjects in the PD is slender and ambiguous. To a large extent it remains up to the subjects to define their 'rules of irrelevance.' Depending on how they define these rules, different kinds of behaviour and different relative outcomes will be seen as fair or appropriate. The theoretical preconception of gaming research is that only absolute outcomes should matter, but these do not seem to be the preconceptions of many subjects who play experimental games.

It is difficult to judge the place that will be accorded to experimental gaming in the long-term history of social psychology. As a simulation of war and peace, the PD, the trucking game, and similar little puzzles seem dangerously naive. But as specific situations posing an interesting dilemma for the participants, such games have had much to recommend them as a means of studying the impact of cognitive processes on social interaction. To take this point of view is not to deny their artificiality, which is evident even to the subjects. The subjects, however, attempt to cope with this artificiality by investing their encounters with some kind of social definition, and it is this process of social definition, not the artificiality, that is important.

SUMMARY

* Research on experimental games has used paradigms which many have seen as too artificial to allow for extrapolations to real-life conflict. The evaluation of such artificiality, and of any extrapolations, however, depends on the analysis of the processes underlying behaviour in such games.
* Such behaviour is not predictable from a simple reinforcement learning principle of 'win-stay, lose-change'.
* The most frequently used game is the Prisoner's Dilemma (PD). Its special feature is that, for subjects to achieve maximum joint outcomes through mutual cooperation, they must both forego the chance of exploiting their partner and leave themselves open to exploitation.
* Levels of cooperative responding in the PD are typically low (30–40 per cent). They may be increased if cooperation by the partner is contingent on cooperation by the subject.
* Levels of cooperation may be influenced by the relative sizes of the incentives to cooperate or compete, but only minimally by the absolute real money equivalents of these incentives.
* In general, cooperation is increased when subjects are more able to communicate with each other.
* In the PD, a competitive move by the other player could be seen as an attempt at exploitation, or as an act of self-defence. Subjects whose own intentions are competitive tend to attribute uniformly competitive intentions to their partner, whereas cooperative subjects are more heterogeneous in their attributions. This finding does not generalize to other games where players can defend themselves without acting in a way that could be misconstrued as exploitative.
* Levels of cooperation can be markedly influenced by manipulations which seem to change the perceived social desirability of cooperative or competitive behaviour, while leaving the actual pay-offs unaffected.
* Concepts based on gaming metaphors have been used by people other than experimental social psychologists in attempts to understand aspects of social interaction. Examples are transactional analysis, and Goffman's analysis of the concept of role.

EIGHT

JUSTICE, ALTRUISM, AND VICTIMIZATION

THE NOTION OF EQUITY

An emerging theme throughout the last few chapters has been the extent to which individuals judge their outcomes from an interaction in comparison with what they feel they deserve. This is implicit in Nuttin's (1975) challenge to cognitive dissonance theory, with regard to the finding that inequitably high *or* low rewards for a task can lead to 'dissonance' effects. It is implicit in the definition of CL proposed by Thibaut and Kelley (1959), and is also essential for an understanding of the results of research on experimental games. The importance of the concept of deservedness for social psychological theory may be difficult to overestimate. It allows us to deal with the fact that individuals decide on a course of action at least partly because of what they expect to get out of it, but does not require us to assume that the law of effect applies to social interaction deterministically and without regard to personal norms and values. It allows for a motivational analysis, but also enables the relevant motives to be treated as potentially under cognitive control.

Stimulated by such considerations, researchers have recently paid increasing attention to the issue of how people judge what is just, fair, deserved, or equitable, and how such judgements influence behaviour. Corporately this research has adopted the name of 'equity theory'. At present, however, the 'theory' consists for the most part of rather loosely formulated predictions and generalizations, and is in need of more precise definition and empirical validation (Berkowitz and Walster, 1976).

The fundamental question of equity research is that of how a desired resource should be distributed. This resource will often be limited, as in the case of money, employment, admission to a university, membership of a sports team, helpings of food or drink, the company of a mutual friend, and so on. In such cases, there is a potential conflict of interest between the participants in a relationship, and the function of an equity norm is to provide a guideline for its resolution. By extension, the same norm is treated as applicable to cases where one or more of the participants is deprived of certain resources, or receives undesirable outcomes, through accident, malice, neglect, or punishment.

A simple solution to the issue of resource allocation is that all participants should receive the same. So, in a situation involving two people A and B, an equitable relationship might be assumed to exist if:

$$O_A = O_B \qquad (8.1)$$

where O_A represents A's outcomes and O_B represents B's outcomes. This simple formula may be termed a 'parity' principle. As can be seen, it deals only with outcomes, and takes no account of the respective *inputs* of the participants, i.e., what they each contribute to the relationship or achieve through effort or quality of performance. Developmental evidence suggests that a feature of socialization may be a shift from a reliance on parity towards a greater consideration of relative inputs (Eiser and Eiser, 1976b; Lerner, 1974). Brickman and Bryan (1976) have also suggested that principles of parity and equity may 'operate independently and simultaneously' in determining children's moral judgements of various acts and exchanges.

A possible solution which also takes account of the relative inputs (I_A and I_B) of the two participants was proposed by Adams (1963, 1965). This basic formulation of an 'equity' principle assumes that a relationship will be seen as equitable if the ratio of all participants' outcomes to their inputs are equal. Thus:

$$\frac{O_A}{I_A} = \frac{O_B}{I_B} \qquad (8.2)$$

For example, in an industrial setting, an employee's outcomes (pay, prestige, etc.) would be seen as more or less equitable depending on their relation to his inputs (skill, training, experience, productivity, responsibility, danger and discomfort endured, etc.) when set against the outcomes and inputs of other employees. Disputes over 'differentials' involve just this sort of comparison. The fact that there are such disputes implies that the relative importance of different kinds of inputs and outcomes may not be viewed in the same way by all participants. In any context, there are likely to be powerful cultural and personal norms operating to define how any individual's outcomes and especially inputs should be evaluated.

Notwithstanding such considerations, attempts have been made to improve upon Adam's formula. Walster, Berscheid, and Walster (1976) point out that the formula cannot handle situations involving negative inputs, i.e., relationships where one or more of the participants' contributions may be directly damaging. According to Formula (8.2), a relationship could still be defined as equitable if person A contributed positive inputs but had negative outcomes, while person B gained positive outcomes inspite of negative inputs. For example, if $O_A = -10$, $I_A = 5$, $O_B = 10$, and $I_B = -5$, both sides of the equation would equal -2, which would imply that the relationship was equitable, which it clearly is not. To deal with such anomalies, Walster et al. therefore proposed the following revision of the formula, whereby, if

$$k_A = \text{sign} (I_A) \times \text{sign} (O_A - I_A)$$

and

$$k_B = \text{sign} (I_B) \times \text{sign} (O_B - I_B)$$

then a relationship is said to be equitable if

$$\frac{O_A - I_A}{(|I_A|)^{k_A}} = \frac{O_B - I_B}{(|I_B|)^{k_B}} \tag{8.3}$$

A simpler, and interestingly different, definition of equity has been proposed by Anderson (1976). He leaves aside the problem of negative inputs, and instead turns Adams' formula around to read as follows:

$$\frac{O_B}{O_A + O_B} = \frac{I_B}{I_A + I_B} \tag{8.4}$$

This means that a relationship is said to be equitable if each participant's proportionate share of the outcomes equals his proportionate share of the inputs. Discussing the difference between Formulas (8.2) and (8.4), Anderson (1976, page 293) writes:

> The contrast between them highlights a basic structural assumption. In general, equity judgments require two comparison processes, one between input and outcome, the other between persons. [Formula (8.2)] implies that an initial comparison is made between outcome and input within each person separately, and a second comparison is then made between persons on these two outcome/input ratios. [Formula (8.4)] implies a reverse order of comparisons, first between persons for input and outcome separately and then between these interpersonal ratios.

Anderson reports data which show that his model is reasonably successful at predicting how subjects allocate hypothetical monetary rewards to two imaginary people on the basis of information given about their performance on a task, the best fit being obtained when subjects were constrained to divide a fixed sum between the two people. He then attempts to deal with two conceptual problems. The first, which has already been mentioned, is that of negative inputs. Anderson makes no attempt to revise the basic equity equation to take account of negative inputs, but proposes a separate 'justice' equation:

$$O = kI \tag{8.5}$$

in which the punishment O fits the crime I. He does not regard this as an equity equation since 'it exhibits no interpersonal comparison structure' (page 296), and suggests that 'it might not overstate the case too far to say that equity theory does not apply to negative input' (page 296).

The second conceptual problem considered by Anderson concerns the distinction between equity and inequity. His recommendation is that the emphasis should shift from attempts to model equity, which he sees as an ideal rarely attained in everyday interaction, to attempts to model inequity. In other words, what is important is to be able to specify the extent to which any given situation will be judged as inequitable.

'Each person's accomplishments, efforts, needs, and aspirations are more salient to himself than to another, and so he will rate his own input higher than will the other. Any objectively fair division will, therefore, tend to leave all parties dissatisfied' (page 297).

In fact, it is only really when it comes to defining the degree of inequity that the distinction between Formulas (8.2) and (8.4) becomes important. For the ideal state of equity, the two formulas are mathematically equivalent. In situations of relative inequity, derivations from Formula (8.4) are found to be predictively superior (Anderson and Farkas, 1975). Most social psychological research on 'equity theory' has not, as yet, been designed so as to discriminate between different formulations. Nonetheless, Anderson's reformulation makes good intuitive sense regarding the order in which the different comparison processes are assumed to operate. It seems implausible that one typically compares one's absolute outcomes with one's absolute inputs, as Adams' formula implies, except in situations where one has already compared one's outcomes and inputs with those of others.

INTERVENTION IN EMERGENCIES

A central assumption of the various applications of equity theory is that a person who perceives himself, or another person, to be receiving inequitable outcomes will attempt to resolve this apparent inequity, either by acting directly to bring the level of outcomes back to what would be equitable, or by finding justifications for the outcomes experienced or observed. An important instance where this should apply is when one observes another person who has suffered from some kind of accidental misfortune, for example, physical injury or assault. There appears to be a generally accepted moral obligation to help others in emergencies, if one is in a position to do so. This obligation is consistent with the precepts of equity theory, though obviously no mere derivation from them.

Possibly an important impetus for the criticisms made of experimental gaming research has been the assumption that players' responses are artificially biased towards competitiveness, and that, in 'real-life', people are much more helpful towards one another. Any social psychologists who were attracted to the study of helping behaviour and altruism in the hope of discovering the silver lining of human interaction must have been quickly disillusioned. As in gaming research, the main question soon emerged as being one of why people tend *not* to help one another as often as they 'should'. The seriousness of this question was strongly emphasized by reports of non-altruistic behaviour in real life, notably the assault and murder of Kitty Genovese in New York City, passively witnessed by 38 onlookers (Rosenthal, 1964).

As with many problems that are 'important' in a broad sense, it took social psychologists some time to identify questions that could be meaningfully submitted to empirical investigation. An approach which showed considerable early promise was the 'diffusion of responsibility' notion proposed by Darley and Latané (1968). They suggest that, when there is a large number of people who are all in a position to offer help, the responsibility for any individual actually doing so appears to be reduced. Any single individual can say to himself: 'I don't have to do anything. Someone else can.' This suggests that any single individual within a group will be less likely to offer help than if he were alone.

Darley and Latané (1968) found support for this prediction in an experiment which involved subjects supposedly having a discussion about personal problems with other students over an intercom system. During the course of the discussion, subjects heard the other person, who was speaking at the time, begin to stammer, become incoherent, choke, and then fall silent, in an imitation of a fit. Depending on the condition, subjects had been led to believe that there were no other, one other, or four other participants in the discussion, apart from themselves and the 'victim'. All subjects who believed that they were alone with the victim reported the incident to the experimenter within an average of 52 seconds from the beginning of the fit. Of those who believed that there was a third participant in the discussion, only 85 per cent reacted in this way, and took on average 93 seconds to do so. Finally, only 62 per cent reacted, taking on average 166 seconds to do so, when they believed that they were in a six-person discussion group.

Also important is whether any bystander appears *able* to give effective assistance. Bickman (1971) had female students communicate over an intercom supposedly either with one other subject, who was the 'victim' of an accident, or with two others, one of whom was the 'victim' and the other a 'bystander'. By virtue of supposed distance from the 'victim', this 'bystander' was presented as either able or unable to give help. After hearing what sounded like a bookcase falling on the 'victim', 80 per cent of subjects left their cubicles within a minute to report the accident when there was no 'bystander'. When there was a 'bystander' who was too far away to help, 74 per cent of subjects reacted within the same period of time, but only 40 per cent did so when the 'bystander' was equally near to the 'victim' and so equally able to help.

In a subsequent study, Bickman (1972) modified the procedure so that the 'bystander' offered the subject one of three interpretations of the accident, varying in seriousness of concern. The greater the 'bystander's' apparent concern (irrespective of her ability to help), the faster subjects responded. In a similar vein, Clark and Word (1972) found that subjects were quick to go to the help of a workman whom they heard fall off a ladder and call out in agony, but were quite slow when they heard only the crash of the falling ladder but no cries.

The ambiguity of an emergency thus seems to be an important factor inhibiting bystanders from intervening, and it seems plausible that individuals will rely upon the reactions of others as a means of resolving such ambiguity. This was demonstrated clearly by Ross and Braband (1973). The subjects in their study were required to work on a card-sorting task alone, or in the presence of a confederate, who was either obviously normally-sighted, or disguised as a blind person. After the experimenter had left the room where the subjects were performing their task, one of two emergencies occurred. A 'scream' emergency consisted of the sound of a workman hurting himself and screaming, and the alternative 'smoke' emergency consisted of the sound of glass breaking followed by smoke pouring into the experimental room from part of the laboratory that had supposedly been taken over by the chemistry department, who had advertised their presence with a notice on their door saying, 'Dangerous work in progress'.

In both emergency conditions, the confederate showed no reaction. In the 'scream' condition, 64 per cent of the subjects tested alone broke off from their task within five minutes of the emergency to go and investigate. This compared with a response rate of 28 per cent among those paired with a blind confederate, and 35 per cent among those paired with a sighted confederate. In the 'smoke' condition, the response rates were 50 per cent for those working alone, 64 per cent (a non-significant improvement) for those paired with a blind confederate, and 14 per cent for those paired with a sighted confederate. These results argue strongly for an approach that emphasizes the information that others' reactions provide. If all that was happening was diffusion of responsibility, then only the presence of the sighted confederate would be expected to inhibit helping, regardless of the type of emergency. An apparently blind confederate could not reasonably be expected to offer help, and might well be in need of protection himself. On the other hand, the failure of the blind confederate to react could well provide subjects with the cue that 'nothing serious' had happened, but only, of course, in the 'scream' condition. The blind confederate would have heard the scream, but could not have noticed the smoke.

It is important to remember that there are potentially two kinds of ambiguity that subjects, or witnesses of real-life emergencies, may need to resolve. The first is ambiguity over what is happening. Until this is resolved, the would-be helper cannot plan effective action. Removing this ambiguity, however, does not immediately open the way for intervention if the would-be helper is still uncertain over what should be done. The failure of another

failure v
other person to react in any way to an emergency, when he is capable both of
noticing the emergency and of offering assistance, may provide cues which
imply both that nothing serious has happened, and that the most appropriate
reaction is to do nothing. Even where it is quite obvious that something
untoward has happened, however, the inactivity of others may still be enough
to inhibit subjects from taking the initiative by going to help or investigate.

As will be clear, experiments of the kind just described require the
efficient stage-management of elaborate deceptions. As elsewhere in social
psychology, there are no doubt experimenters who can make the most bizarre
procedures convincing for their subjects, and others who manage to arouse
their subjects' suspicions even before a single half-truth has been spoken.
There are also likely to be differences in gullibility between individual subjects. Although experimenters attempt to elicit from their subjects (during
ethically obligatory debriefings) the extent to which they may have seen
through any experimental deception, there may yet be a number of subjects
who may have felt that there was something strange going on, but not have
tumbled to the fact that the emergency was actually contrived by the experimenter. Combined with the possibility that some subjects may see through
the deception, but not want to hurt the experimenter's feelings (or data) by
saying so, and that others may on principle distrust indiscriminately any
instructions given to them during a social psychology experiment, we end up
with a situation in which an artefactual bias may be operating to reduce the
possibility of experimental subjects reacting as quickly as they might in a
genuine emergency. This would not matter too much if it operated evenly in
all conditions, but it might well interact with experimental manipulations,
becoming more acute as more elaborate stage-management is called for. The
acting skills of experimental confederates are not easy to assess from typical
experimental reports, which is why face-to-face interactions may require more
subtle handling than simulated interactions over intercoms.

THE COSTS OF HELPING

Some of the theoretically most provocative studies in the area have in fact
used field situations, rather than laboratory deceptions. Among these are a
number relevant to another of the predictions made by Darley and Latané
(1970), namely that a person's preparedness to help another will be a function
of the costs or risks incurred in doing so. Such costs might include consequences such as physical injury, monetary loss or sacrifice, loss of time,
embarrassment, and so on.

Piliavin, Rodin, and Piliavin (1969) observed the responses of travellers
on the New York subway to a 'victim' who collapsed onto the floor of the
train, where he remained staring at the ceiling. In some cases, the 'victim'
smelt of alcohol and was carrying a bottle of liquor; in other cases, he carried

a cane so as to give the appearance of being an invalid. Four different male stooges (three white and one black) took the part of the victim. The performance was convincing enough to elicit help about 60 per cent of the time from the other passengers, with little effect due to the number of bystanders. Males tended to offer help more frequently than females, and when the victim appeared drunk, he was more likely to be helped by members of his own race. Overall when the victim appeared to be an invalid, he received more help than when he appeared drunk. In sequels to this study, a victim who 'bled' from the mouth after falling was less likely to be helped, or was helped more slowly, than one who did not bleed (Piliavin and Piliavin, 1972), as was a victim with a disfiguring birthmark (Piliavin, Piliavin, and Rodin, 1975).

Darley and Latané (1970) cite a similar study by Allen, again conducted on the New York subway. The reactions of passengers were observed when they heard one fellow-passenger ask in which direction the train was going, and another reply with what was obviously the wrong answer. The issue was whether the genuine traveller would interrupt to correct the stooge who had given the false information. It was found that travellers would be more likely to correct the stooge if the request for directions had been addressed to them specifically (so that it was the stooge who had interrupted), rather than to the occupants of the carriage generally. They were also less likely to intervene if the stooge who had given the wrong information was made to look like a dangerous character. This was achieved by him having previously looked up from a magazine on muscle-building and shouted threats of physical assault at a fourth traveller (another stooge) who tripped over his feet!

Darley and Latané also report data from observations of the responses of passers-by to requests from a stranger for very minimal amounts of help. Requests which cost the giver nothing, such as to tell the time, or to give simple street directions, were granted more readily than requests for even minimal amounts of money (10¢). It should be noted, though, that even when no reason was given for the request, 34 per cent of the passers-by who were approached handed over the 10¢. This percentage rose to 64 per cent when the person making the request explained that he needed to make a telephone call, and to 72 per cent when he explained that his wallet had been stolen.

An implication which Darley and Latané draw from such findings is that it is more reasonable to look for the mediating influence of self-interest on helping than to seek to explain helping by postulating the presence of norms to act altruistically. Discussing how variations in costs to the helper influence whether or not help will be given, they argue that 'any serious attempt to deal with the various response rates in normative terms must involve the postulation of a proliferation of norms' (1970, page 99).

Clearly it is not much good, whenever any new instance of behaviour comes up for explanation, simply to say that 'this behaviour is determined by a norm' and to assume that one has thereby explained it. Equally, though, it is not much good *simply* to say that 'this behaviour is determined by self-interest'. What is important is how self-interest may operate within normative constraints, and how self-interest may set limits to the viability of norms. Furthermore, one does not need a 'proliferation of norms' to allow for situational variation within an approach that includes consideration of normative factors. All one needs to assume is that the perceived applicability or salience of any norm or moral principle will depend on the specific situation in question. To assume instead that all requests for help or all apparent emergencies are equally obligating from an ethical point of view—or alternatively that no principles can be found on the basis of which to predict any variations in the perceived level of obligation—is greatly to oversimplify the ways in which norms can operate.

There is no reason to view normative explanations as necessarily incompatible with the operation of a principle of self-interest. While the studies described by Darley and Latané (1970) show how response rates may vary as a function of the helper's costs, they do not provide a clear answer to the question of why anyone should give any help *at all* if it is not in his interest to do so. One possible explanation is that giving help is self-gratifying, in other words, that it makes one 'feel good'. There is evidence, for instance, that generosity may be determined by the mood of the helper. Cialdini and Kenrick (1976) had subjects of various ages from 6 up to 18 years old think of either neutral or depressing events, before being given the opportunity to be privately generous, by giving up prize coupons in favour of their fellow students. Whereas the youngest subjects tended to be less generous when they had been thinking about depressing events, this difference was reversed in the case of the older subjects, consistent with the notion that children are socialized into finding altruistic behaviour self-gratifying. This finding, however, does not 'reduce' altruism to a mere instance of self-gratificatory behaviour. It can be interpreted just as easily as showing that individuals acquire a norm for altruism during the course of socialization, and that any self-gratification comes from knowing that one has 'been good' within the context of that norm.

Pomazal and Jaccard (1976) applied Fishbein's (1967) model of attitude and behavioural intention to the problem of predicting who would donate blood during a 'blood drive' on a university campus. According to the model, one's attitude towards performing an altruistic act, in this case giving blood, would depend on one's 'evaluative beliefs' about the consequences of doing so. In comparison with those who said that they intended to give blood, those who said that they did not intend to do so were significantly more likely to say that they thought that giving blood would make them feel anxious, tired or faint, or would take up too much of their time. In addition, however, they found that predictions of intention were significantly improved when account was taken of subjects' levels of agreement with the statement, 'I personally feel I have a moral obligation to donate blood at the upcoming drive', indicating the importance of a 'moral norm' over and above a consideration of the pleasantness of the personal consequences.

THE NEED FOR HELP AND THE LEGITIMACY OF DEMANDS

It is, of course, one thing to posit a general norm or moral obligation to help others, and quite another to define the principles in terms of which an individual will decide whether this norm is applicable to a given situation. It is here that equity theory has an important part to play. The finding that people are less likely to help when helping can be costly is quite compatible with equity theory. If one believes that one's own outcomes, possessions, status, freedom from hazard or injury, etc., are no more than what one is equitably entitled to, then depriving oneself of any of these benefits by giving help to another person may be seen to produce a new inequity. *Indiscriminate* altruism is thus not predicted by equity theory.

Even in the data which Darley and Latané (1970) cite in support of a reward-cost analysis of helping behaviour, however, there is evidence of the importance of an additional factor—how much the victim, or the person making the request, needs or deserves to be helped. The finding by Piliavin *et al.* (1969) that a 'drunk' victim was helped less readily than an 'ill' victim could be explained in these terms, though the inhibitory effects of blood (Piliavin and Piliavin, 1972) seem to go against this. A drunk might appear less deserving of help, and less likely to come to serious harm if left to 'sleep it off', as compared with someone who passed out when apparently ill. The moral obligation to help an ill person in distress, related as it may be to apparent urgency, would seem to be at least as important a factor as the possibility of being hurt by a barely conscious inebriate. Similarly, the finding by Darley and Latané that passers-by would be much more likely to give 10¢ to a stranger who gave reasons for his request, suggests that even minimal help of this kind may be given in proportion to its perceived need. The experimental studies that have manipulated the ambiguity of an emergency (e.g., Bickman, 1972; Clark and Word, 1972) may also be interpreted as showing that help is less likely to be given if the victim's need for help is uncertain.

In an application of Abelson's (1976) script theory (see Chapter 2), Langer and Abelson (1972) have shown that the wording of a request for help can strongly influence a person's willingness to give assistance if approached. They distinguish in the first place between appeals which are 'victim-oriented', which evoke sympathy by stressing the victim's urgent personal need, and those which are 'target-oriented', where emphasis is placed on the responsibility of the person approached to help the victim. This distinction may be conveyed by opening phrases such as 'I've hurt myself' as opposed to 'Would you do something for me?' and Langer and Abelson manipulated this variable by simply changing the order of phrases in the appeal. The second distinction is that between 'legitimate' and 'illegitimate' requests, which essentially relates to the difference between cases of genuine need and others where the request is an imposition.

Langer and Abelson report the results of two field experiments in which passers-by were confronted with appeals for help worded so as to be victim- or target-oriented, and legitimate or illegitimate. The two factors were found to interact, with legitimate requests eliciting more help than illegitimate requests only when they were victim-oriented. Langer and Abelson conclude that victim-oriented appeals focus attention on the victim's state of need, and will tend to elicit more help if the need seems genuine. 'But there is also a strong cultural imperative ("rugged individualism") that people should not let others take illegitimate advantage of them' (page 31). This 'cultural imperative' could just as easily be called a norm. These results therefore imply that an approach which takes account of normative factors is quite capable of dealing with situational variations in levels of helping without, as Darley and Latané (1970) argue, needing to postulate a new norm for each situation.

A field study by Dorris (1972) provides evidence of the operation of a norm to act equitably towards others in a vulnerable position, and shows that this norm can be made more or less salient depending on how an appeal is phrased. Dorris approached a number of coin dealers with a set of rare coins which he said he had just inherited from his grandfather. He explained that he wanted to sell the coins, but that he knew nothing about how much they were worth. Through this admission of ignorance, therefore, he left himself open to exploitation, if the dealer wished to offer an unfairly low price.

In the 'neutral appeal' condition, the experimenter then simply continued by saying that he had no wish to become a collector, and that he did not want to take a lot of time over getting different estimates, so he was ready to sell the coins for whatever he was offered. Contrasted with this was a 'moral appeal' condition, in which the experimenter explained that he was afraid that he might get exploited selling them, and so had asked a stamp collector friend, who had recommended the dealer as someone he could trust to give a fair price. He then explained: 'Normally I wouldn't sell the coins, but I'm in a kind of jam. I need to buy some textbooks for my summer school class to get ready for exams, and for some reason my check got held up at work.' (Page 389.)

The average initial offer from dealers who received the moral appeal was 56 per cent higher than from those who received the neutral appeal. Also, when making their offer, those in the moral appeal condition maintained more eye-contact, and stood closer to the experimenter.

Although this study is concerned with exploitation or nonexploitation, rather than clear-cut altruism, the results reinforce those of Langer and Abelson (1972). The 'moral appeal' emphasized the personal circumstances of the experimenter, the fact that he needed the money urgently for the 'worthy cause' of buying textbooks for his studies, and the fact that his present temporary insolvency was no fault of his own. The effects of this appeal are notable in that the role of the dealer was already defined, his relationship with the experimenter involved no more than an ordinary business transaction, and that there were other dealers also in the position to buy the coins if they wished. It may be that the appeal functioned partly so as to invite the dealer to distance himself from the role of the profiteer. What is clear, however, is that dealers in the moral appeal condition to some extent resisted the opportunity to increase their own outcomes at the experimenter's expense, owing to features of the appeal that implied that it would be inequitable for them to do so.

Although these findings can be interpreted without the help of any of the mathematical formulations of equity theory discussed at the beginning of this chapter, they clearly demonstrate the importance of some kind of equity principle in moderating the demands of immediate self-interest. This principle or norm is not invoked indiscriminately. What counts as fair or equitable in a given situation may depend upon quite subtle features of the interaction that takes place, just as, in studies of the decomposed prisoner's dilemma game (Pruitt, 1967; see also Chapter 7), subtle differences in presentation of a task can make it appear one in which self-interested behaviour is more or less appropriate.

At the same time, however, an equity principle can act as a protection against demands for help that are themselves exploitative. The issue of whether a request for help is, or is not, an imposition, seems to depend primarily upon a consideration of the needs of the victim and the costs of the helper. If nothing particularly terrible is likely to happen to the victim if he or she does not receive help, then it is unreasonable to expect the helper to go to any great pains on the victim's behalf. To do so would be to create a new imbalance in outcomes in favour of the victim and to the detriment of the helper. The fact that such comparisons between *outcomes* can be made quite readily is consistent with Anderson's (1976) suggestion that the primary comparisons in equity judgements are interpersonal rather than intrapersonal, although it is far short of being a proof of his formulation.

Although the terms are sometimes used interchangeably, the *deservedness* of the victim should be distinguished from the victim's *need* for help. Deservedness seems to be more appropriately construed in terms of inputs rather than outcomes, in that it depends on the victim's attributes and previous behaviour, i.e., on why he comes to be in need of help. A 'good' person, who has not acted selfishly or carelessly, may be seen to be entitled to better outcomes, and hence more help if in distress, than a 'bad' person who appears to be responsible for his own misfortunes. This again may imply an interpersonal comparison, in that the would-be helper may consider his own attributes and entitlement to his relatively happy position. The less deserving he considers the victim to be in comparison to himself, the less obliged will he feel to help the victim out of considerations of equity. Granted a tendency for individuals to over-evaluate their own relative inputs, therefore, the principle of equity may frequently serve as a justification for self-interested, as well as altruistic, behaviour.

LIMITS TO SOCIAL OBLIGATIONS—THE 'JUST WORLD' HYPOTHESIS

Emphasis on the individual's perception of his own inputs and entitlements is central to a version of equity theory proposed by Lerner (1970; Lerner, Miller, and Holmes, 1976), referred to as the 'just world' hypothesis. In contrast to the attempts by writers such as Anderson (1976) and Walster *et al.* (1976) to formulate the notions of equity and inequity in more precise mathematical terms, Lerner's approach is more 'broad brush', highlighting paradoxes in how the equity principle appears to operate rather than offering a purer definition of the principle itself.

An individual is assumed to develop a sense of deserving and justice during socialization, at which time he makes a 'personal contract' with himself

> ... to orient himself to the world on the basis of what he earns or deserves via his prior investments rather than on the basis of what he can get at any given moment. He learns and trusts that his world is a place where additional investments often entitle him to better outcomes, and that 'earning' or 'deserving' is an effective way of obtaining what he desires. (Lerner *et al.*, 1976, page 135.)

This notion, highly reminiscent of the 'Protestant Ethic' (Weber, 1958) has implications for how a person will evaluate others also, since 'We want to believe we live in a world where people get what they deserve or, rather, deserve what they get' (Lerner, 1970, page 207).

This belief in a 'just world' is threatened, however, whenever an individual comes across others in greater need than himself, who clearly do not deserve their misfortunes, One possibility, directly predicted by other equity theorists (e.g., Walster *et al.*, 1976), is that he will attempt to remove the inequity by compensating those in need. He thus may give donations to charity, pay taxes to support welfare services, do voluntary work in his spare time, and so on. However, as Lerner rightly emphasizes, while such altruistic acts might discharge one's social obligation, they rarely go very far towards removing the inequality of outcomes. Even if the would-be champion of social justice obeyed the commandment to 'sell all that he had and give to the poor', he could still find others less fortunate than himself, not simply destitute but impossibly in debt or otherwise deprived. If others' relative deprivation was the sole measure of social obligation, such obligation could never be met.

To preserve his positive view of himself derived from his observation of his 'personal contract', therefore, the individual must find a way of reconciling his belief that he deserves what he has with the fact that others, no less deserving, have less. The answer suggested by Lerner is that a social comparison process is involved, so that the individual says to himself 'I deserve what others who are like me have' (Lerner *et al.*, 1976). Basically, this is analogous to the problem of relevance of judgemental standards, which were considered in Chapter 3 (see page 59). Judgements of stimuli may be influenced by the presence of qualitatively similar, but not dissimilar, standards (Brown, 1953). Knowledge of the plight of starving millions in a far-off country may thus have less impact on the level of outcomes to which one feels personally entitled than extremely minor discrepancies in salary or possessions that may differentiate one from one's neighbours or colleagues. *Unilateral* altruism is thus likely to reduce one's outcomes to below those of others whom one has chosen as relevant standards for social comparison, so that a demand for such altruism, even if justified by the needs of the victim, would appear 'unfair'— unless, that is, it was also addressed to others like oneself. If others like oneself also answered the appeal, even quite large sacrifices might be tolerable if the individuals who made them did not feel they were thereby depriving themselves or their dependents below the level enjoyed by comparable others, that is to say, below their comparison level.

The aspect of appeals for help that can be most threatening to the person's concept of a 'just world' is their potential open-endedness. Once a person has admitted the entitlement of one victim to receive help, how can he then deny help to another, no less deserving? One way in which it may be possible to elicit higher levels of altruism, therefore, is if the individual can define the situation as one in which his altruism would not imply any such open-ended commitment. This may be achieved if the appeal for help is presented under the guise of a trade or exchange, or more generally in situations where the individual can feel that he is gaining some positive outcomes, which may partially compensate for the help he has given. Answering such appeals does not imply a commitment to answer other appeals where one gets nothing in return.

These notions were explored in an experiment by Holmes, Miller, and Lerner (cited by Lerner *et al.*, 1976, pages 151–152). The experimenters approached students on a university campus, offering candles for sale as part of a supposed fund-raising activity on behalf of either a deserving, or less deserving, cause (respectively, handicapped children or a children's sports team). The candles were offered for $3 each, and subjects were told that $1 of this would go to the cause in question. They were also told that the candles sold for $2, $3, or $4 in most stores.

Subjects showed little interest in buying the candles to help the less deserving cause. (Incidentally, it was not the Christmas season.) On the other hand, more than half those approached were prepared to buy the candles to help the handicapped children, *provided* they were told that they would be getting the candles at a fair or bargain price. In these conditions, they were able to respond to the perceived need of the handicapped children without taking action which implied that the children had an unqualified claim upon their resources. They could act as though they were simply making a fair economic transaction. Far fewer subjects were prepared to buy the candles if they were given to believe that they would be paying more than the candles were worth.

A person's willingness to improve another's outcomes at his own expense may also be inhibited by normative factors relating to what Lerner and Lichtman (1968) refer to as *justified self-interest*. These 'imply equal opportunity and risk among the participants as well as the pursuit of self-interest within the rules of what is fair and equal' (page 226). Running counter to these are other norms which may be elicited by a plea for special help or consideration ['the participant confesses he is not able to compete on an equal basis' (page 226)], or by an intentionally gracious act ['It is possible for a participant clearly and openly to refuse to profit from a fortuitous opportunity and at the same time to establish the expectation that ... the other competitors should not take advantage of any fortuitous opportunities which may become available to them' (pages 226–227)].

The reference to 'competitors' is significant, particularly as such considerations might relate to the experimental gaming research reviewed in the last chapter. Games, *par excellence*, are interactions in which self-interest is justified. At the same time, games are played according to rules, and it is not 'playing fair' to try to circumvent them. Many of the manipulations used by gaming researchers may be interpreted as affecting levels of cooperation through influencing subjects' perceptions of a 'fair' degree of self-interested behaviour (e.g., the decomposed PDs used by Pruitt, 1967, Chapter 7). Many games and sports also have special rules or handicaps designed to make competitions (and hence competitiveness) between participants of unequal skill or strength fairer and more enjoyable.

Lerner and Lichtman conducted their study on pairs of female students who had volunteered for a learning experiment. On arrival, subjects were told that one of them, depending on a draw, would be in a condition in which she would receive electric shocks which would be 'painful', but causing no 'permanent damage', whereas the other would receive no shocks. Subjects then drew numbers to determine who would have the choice of condition, and were taken to separate cubicles before being told the outcome of the draw. The experimenter then informed each subject individually about the supposed outcome of the draw.

In a 'justified self-interest' condition, each subject was told that she had won the draw and could choose the condition she preferred. Naturally, if she chose the control condition, the other subject would supposedly be put in the shock condition. Only 9 per cent of these subjects chose the shock condition for themselves. This was compared with four other conditions. A 'gracious act' condition involved the subject being told that her partner had won the draw, but asked for the choice to be given to the subject instead. Here 88 per cent of the subjects chose the shock condition for themselves. A 'plea for help' condition, in which the subject was told that her partner was really scared about the shocks, led to 72 per cent of the subjects choosing the shocks for themselves. An 'illicit gracious act' condition was designed so that the partner's 'gracious act' appeared to be a piece of manipulative calculation, and here only 22 per cent chose the shock condition. Finally, an 'illicit plea for help' condition involved the experimenter arbitrarily over-ruling the draw, and putting the partner, who seemed 'really scared' into the control condition. Subjects were offered the right to object to being put in the shock condition, but 86 per cent acquiesced. However, when asked to rate their partner, subjects gave far more negative evaluations in this condition than in any of the other four.

In a replication of this study using male students, Lerner (1971) found that subjects were almost as likely to choose the shock as the control condi-tion for themselves under 'justified self-interest' instructions. Presumably, Lerner argues, it was not appropriate for *men* to use the wish to avoid pain as a justification for causing another person to suffer. However, when the control condition was rendered even more attractive by turning it into a *positive* reinforcement condition, involving the chance of considerable monetary reward, the principle of justified self-interest reasserted itself.

The quite remarkable variations in choice rates in the Lerner and Licht-man study testify to the influence that norms of fairness and justice have on both 'altruistic' and 'selfish' behaviour. In some situations, it is culturally defined as fair and equitable for one person to preserve or improve his own outcomes at another's expense. In other situations it is not. The results just described provide some indications of how such situations might be discri-minated. The important contribution of equity theory in this context is thus the demonstration that classes of behaviour which might be viewed as com-plete opposites of each other may be accounted for within a common framework. These results also give further support to the generalization that some of the most powerful manipulations employed in experimental social psychology are those that influence the subject's interpretation of the exper-imental situation through increasing the salience of specific extra-experimental norms and values.

JUSTIFICATION AND DEROGATION

So far I have concentrated on responses to perceived inequity that take the form of a redistribution of outcomes. In other words, subjects have been placed in situations where they have been given the opportunity to intervene on behalf of the victim, or to compensate the victim through donations or other favours, or through turning down the chance to increase their own outcomes at the victim's expense. The importance of the perceived need or deservedness of the victim, however, stresses the fact that equity theory is concerned not only with interpersonal comparisons of *outcomes,* but also with how a person will evaluate another's *inputs* in comparison to his own. An unequal distribution of outcomes may thus be seen as equitable if the person with lower outcomes contributed lower inputs—if, in other words, the victim deserved his misfortunes, either through defects of character, errors of judge-ment, or reproachable behaviour. As Walster *et al.* (1976) have hypothesized:

'Harmdoers tend either to *compensate* their victims (and so restore actual equity) or to *justify* the victim's deprivation (and restore psychological equity). Harmdoers rarely use both techniques in concert; compensation and justification seem to be alternative, rather than supplementary, techniques for restoring equity' (page 12).

It should be stressed that this prediction concerns the reactions of people who have actually harmed another individual. From this point of view, there is no particular need for the 'just world' hypothesis, over and above notions such as dissonance reduction and defensive attribution (Shaver, 1970a). Presumably the cognition that one has inequitably harmed another person is dissonance-arousing. If this is so, then dissonance may be reduced by either making amends through compensation, or denying one's own responsibility for the harm done, and instead attributing responsibility to the victim through either blame or derogation. Walster and Prestholdt (1966), for instance, led trainee social workers to harm their clients inadvertently, and then gave them the chance to volunteer to help their clients in their free time. The more positively subjects evaluated their clients, the more time they were prepared to volunteer. Derogation could thus be a technique for justifying the original harmful act and the failure to offer compensation.

Whereas such results are unsurprising in view of the weight of experimental evidence and everyday knowledge which points to the importance of processes of self-justification, the predictions derived from the 'just world' hypothesis are less obvious. What matters, in terms of Lerner's approach, is not that one has *oneself* harmed another person, but that an unjust incident has occurred. If a victim has been harmed inequitably, this is offensive to one's belief in a just world, regardless of the identity of the perpetrator. Observers should be as likely to derogate victims whom they cannot compensate as are the inadvertent perpetrators of the harm which the victims suffer. Lerner (1970) also proposes that there is a kind of 'trade-off' function between attributing responsibility to a victim ('It was his own fault') and derogation ('He's such a nasty person that he deserved to have it happen to him'). Derogation should thus be *negatively* related to blame, as well as to compensation. Similarly, positive outcomes may be justified by reference to a person's efforts, or attractiveness, but not both.

In support of the 'just world' position, there is evidence that observers will rate the recipients of fortuitous *rewards* as deserving their good fortune by virtue of their task performance, or as being generally more attractive. Even here, though, rated attractiveness and entitlement to rewards tend, if anything, to be positively related (Lerner, 1965; Apsler and Friedman, 1975). The reactions of observers to victims of *misfortune*, however, present a varied picture. Jones and Aronson (1973) presented male and female students with written accounts of a rape case, and then asked them to recommend a sentence for the convicted rapist, and to say how much they considered the crime to be the victim's fault. Varied details in the case accounts informed subjects that the victim was either a divorcee, a married woman, or a virgin. More fault was attributed to the victim when she was a divorcee than when she was married, or a virgin.

This result was interpreted as consistent with the 'just world' hypothesis, on the assumption that divorcees are less respectable than married women or virgins (which is itself a revealing assumption from a 'just world' perspective). It seems that subjects were less willing to accept that *chance* catastrophes happen to good or respectable people, since this would imply that they themselves (as good and respectable people, of course) might also be vulnerable to disasters beyond their control. To be able to see the rape as at least partly the victim's fault allows one to retain the belief that bad things don't 'just happen' to good people, if they behave correctly. Such an attribution thus restores one's feeling of personal control over one's environment, and with it one's sense of relative security. No such attribution is needed, on the other hand, when the victim is less respectable, in that it is seen as less offensive to notions of justice for bad things to happen to bad people, even if they are in no way responsible. However, Jones and Aronson still found that lighter sentences were recommended when the victim was a divorcee. If punishment of the rapist can be interpreted as a kind of compensation for the victim, these results do not support the Walster *et al.* (1976) prediction that compensation and justification (in this case, through attribution of responsibility) should be inversely related.

Probably the most influential study in this field is that by Lerner and Simmons (1966). The basic procedure of this study involved groups of female students taking part in an experiment supposedly to do with the perception of emotional cues. On arrival at the laboratory they were introduced to another 'subject' who was supposedly taking part in a learning experiment. It was explained that it had been arranged that subjects in the learning experiment should also serve as target persons for the emotional cues experiment: their performance on the learning task would be observed, as it occurred, over a closed circuit television system by the remaining subjects. Actually, what subjects saw was a standard videotape which showed the target person apparently receiving several painful electric shocks for wrong responses.

After subjects had viewed the tape, they were given differing sets of instructions. In the 'midpoint' condition, they were told that they were now halfway through the experiment, and that, after they had made some ratings, there would be another negative reinforcement session for the same 'victim'. In the 'reward' condition, subjects were also told that there would be a second session, but they were then asked to vote on whether the victim should continue in the negative reinforcement condition, or be transferred to a control or a reward condition for the second session. The experimenter then announced that the group had chosen the reward condition for the victim, and then asked them to give their ratings. In the 'reward decision' condition, the procedure was identical, except that subjects gave their ratings before the experimenter told them of the outcome of the vote. (Almost all subjects did in fact vote for the second session to be a reward treatment.)

In the 'end point' condition, subjects were told that the learning experiment was now over, and no mention was made of a second session. In the 'past event' condition, subjects were told that what they would see would in fact be a videotape of someone who had been shocked in the past. They were given an opportunity to meet the victim to determine that she was now fine and had been paid for her participation. Finally, in the 'martyr' condition, the procedure was similar to that for the 'end point' condition, except that, before the 'learning experiment' started, an argument took place between the victim and her 'experimenter' in front of the subjects, in which the victim first protested against being put in the negative reinforcement condition, but when withdrew her refusal so that the subjects could receive their experimental course credits for taking part in the emotional cues experiment. After subjects had given their ratings, following what they believed to be the first or only session, the experiment was terminated.

The task required of the subjects in each condition was to rate the victim on a number of scales. The main dependent variable was a composite measure of the perceived attractiveness of the victim, minus subjects' self-ratings, and negative scores were taken as a sign of derogation. The means for each condition were: 'midpoint' -26, 'reward' -5, 'reward decision' -25, 'end point' -13, 'past event' -11, and 'martyr' -34, compared with a maximum possible derogation score of -120.

With the exception of the 'martyr' condition, these results show that the victim was derogated less in conditions where her suffering was at an end than when subjects believed it would ('midpoint') or could ('reward decision') continue. Most derogation, however, occurred in the 'martyr' condition, and Lerner and Simmons regard this as particularly strong vindication of the 'just world' hypothesis: '... the suffering of someone who has acted out of altruistic motives should be most threatening to the belief in a just world. If this is true, then the observer should reject the willing martyr even more than the innocent victim' (page 205).

As has been pointed out, the 'just world' hypothesis predicts derogation of victims by observers, and not just by perpetrators, of injustice. Subsequent research, as well as critiques of the Lerner and Simmons (1966) study, have questioned whether derogation in fact occurs, other than in conditions where the subjects (observers) feel that they are in some way responsible for the victim's suffering. Subjects in the 'martyr' condition might have felt particularly responsible, since the victim explicitly chose to go on with the experiment so that they could obtain their experimental credits, and as was seen, this was the condition in which most derogation occurred. Some feelings of responsibility might still have been present among subjects in the other conditions, however, since the 'emotional cues' experiment still required the victim to serve as a target person.

Lerner and Matthews (1967) in fact manipulated personal responsibility using a modification of the Lerner and Lichtman (1968) procedure, involving a rigged draw to determine whether the subject or her partner was put in a shock condition of a learning experiment. The crucial comparison was between a condition where the subject drew before her partner, with the result that she was in a control or reward condition while her partner was in the shock condition, and a condition where her partner drew first, drawing the shock condition for herself and leaving the control or reward condition for the subject. Apparently, the order of the draw was sufficient to produce an illusion of differential responsibility. The results showed derogation of the partner (compared with ratings of the 'average college student') in the former but not the latter condition.

Lerner and Matthews interpret these results as consistent with the 'just world' hypothesis, on the grounds that blame and derogation should be inversely related to each other. If one can point to something the victim did which led to her suffering, one does not need to derogate her as a person. Apparently, when the victim had supposedly drawn first and put herself in the shock condition, she 'was perceived as responsible for her own suffering, and the subject's need to believe in a just world was not threatened' (page 324). On the other hand, an equally plausible interpretation of these data is that one only derogates victims if one feels oneself to be in some way responsible for their suffering.

A number of studies have attempted to define the limiting conditions of victim derogation through modified replications of the Lerner and Simmons experiment. Aderman, Brehm, and Katz (1974) showed female students a 10-minute videotape of a victim receiving shocks as part of a negative reinforcement learning experiment. Derogation occurred when subjects were instructed to 'watch' or 'observe' the victim (as in the Lerner and Simmons experiment), but not when they were told to imagine how they would feel if they were the victim.

Sorrentino and Boutelier (1974) had subjects observe a victim suffering under a negative reinforcement schedule in either a 'similar fate' condition, in which they believed they might have to undergo the same experience, or a 'dissimilar fate' condition, when they knew they would not. The victim was rated as *more* attractive than 'the average university student' in the 'similar fate' condition, but was derogated in the 'dissimilar fate' condition. This difference was only significant, however, among subjects who regarded the experiment as unfair. This last finding is somewhat troublesome for the 'just world' hypothesis. The *unfair* suffering of another person should offend one's notions of a 'just world' more than suffering which is perceived as fair, and so should lead to more derogation. Once derogation has occurred, however, presumably there is less need to see the situation as unfair. Also, such unfair suffering should be particularly threatening to one's belief in a 'just world' if one anticipated the possibility of a similar fate oneself. Yet subjects in the 'similar fate' condition did *not* derogate the victim—presumably because this would imply the potential derogation of themselves.

Very similar conclusions were reached by Chaikin and Darley (1973), who had pairs of male students view a videotape of what was supposedly a previous trial of an experiment in which they would be participating later. The tape showed two students acting as a 'worker-supervisor team' on a communication task which required the worker to build several stacks of blocks according to the supervisor's instructions. The worker's output was measured by the number of blocks stacked. At the end of the session, the supervisor accidentally knocked over the worker's blocks as he stood up. This had either mild consequences for the worker (he could be compensated), or severe consequences (he could not). Half the subjects were told that they would later be taking the part of the supervisor, and half that they would be taking that of the worker.

Derogation of the worker was shown only by future supervisors when the consequences were severe. Future workers saw the supervisor as clearly responsible for the accident, particularly when the consequences were severe. Chaikin and Darley interpret their data as evidence of defensive attribution, rather than as support for the 'just world' hypothesis, arguing that individuals are more concerned with making attributions for harmful accidents so as to avoid seeing themselves as potentially responsible for any similar mishap, than they are with defending any belief that the world is 'just'.

Such results lead one to ask what kind of attributions might have been made by subjects in the different conditions of the Lerner and Simmons (1966) study. Was the learner in fact seen as an 'innocent victim', or as someone who was responsible for her own suffering because of her poor performance on the learning task? Did subjects see themselves as mere 'observers', or did they feel responsible for the learner's suffering, in that she had to go through this procedure so that they would complete their own experiment? Piliavin, Hardyck, and Vadum (1967) failed to find derogation of the victim in a replication of the Lerner and Simmons 'midpoint' condition, as compared with the 'end-point' condition, when subjects were informed that the machine controlling the shocks had been wrongly programmed, so that the victim was completely helpless, and unable to avoid the shocks even by giving correct responses. This situation should of course be even more threatening to one's belief in a 'just world'. On the other hand, it poses no problems from a defensive attribution point of view, since the experimental equipment was clearly to blame, and so no responsibility need be attached to either observers or victim.

Similarly, comparing the effects of the Lerner and Simmons 'midpoint' and 'past event' conditions under different experimental instructions, Simons and Piliavin (1972) found evidence of relative derogation in the 'midpoint' condition only, as in the original study, when subjects were kept in ignorance of the true purpose of the experiment, and of the fact that the victim was only pretending to be shocked. When told that the purpose of the experiment was to study reactions to victims of misfortune, subjects did not derogate the victim, regardless of whether or not they were told that the shocks were only simulated. Apparently, seeing the learner as a 'victim of misfortune' was enough to inhibit derogation. The concept of 'misfortune' seems to invoke a different kind of attributional set from that which is required for victim derogation.

Even more directly, Cialdini, Kenrick, and Hoerig (1976) have argued that victim derogation by observers in the Lerner and Simmons paradigm is not due to a wish to restore their belief in a 'just world', but is instead a means of justifying their complicity in the victim's suffering. 'After all, they discover themselves to be willing and nonprotesting participants in a procedure that seems to involve the instigation of another's suffering' (pages 719–720). Cialdini *et al.* therefore replicated the 'midpoint' condition with the Lerner and Simmons instructions, and also with these instructions modified to reduce subjects' perceived complicity. Subjects in this latter condition were told that the learning experiment they would be viewing was taking place in another department, that it had been going on for some time but had only recently come to the attention of the experimenters running the 'emotional cues' study, and that these experimenters, and the psychology department generally, were relatively unfamiliar with the procedures involved. Orthogonally with this manipulation, half the subjects observed the learner undergoing a shock schedule, and half saw her perform under a schedule involving no shocks. The prediction derived from the 'just world' hypothesis, for derogation of the learner in the 'shock' but not in the 'no shock' condition, was supported only under the original instructions, when subjects could have felt in some way responsible for the victim's fate.

The assumption of a trade-off function between derogation and compensation also requires some qualification in the light of a study by Kenrick, Reich, and Cialdini (1976). They used a modification of the Lerner and Simmons 'midpoint' condition, with half the subjects seeing the learner receive shocks for incorrect responses on a serial learning task, and half seeing her receive no shocks (errors instead being identified by a buzzer). Half the subjects then made evaluative ratings of the learner, and then were asked to vote on how much compensation (from 50¢ to $5) she should receive 'for her effort'. The remaining subjects were given the opportunity to compensate the learner *before* rating her. Derogation occurred in the 'shock' and not in the 'no shock' condition, but was far less marked when subjects made their ratings *after* voting for compensation. This suggests that compensation does, indeed, inhibit derogation. However, the reverse relationship did not hold. Subjects voted for about $4.50 compensation for the learner in the 'shock' condition (as compared with about $3 in the 'no shock' condition) regardless of whether they had already rated her. Within the 'shock' conditions, there was no correlation ($r = 0.02$) between compensation and evaluation for subjects who gave their ratings first, but there was a strong correlation ($r = 0.81$) when they gave their ratings after compensating the victim.

On balance, therefore, there seems little evidence for the more 'non-obvious' predictions from the 'just world' hypothesis. It does indeed seem to be the case that the perception of inequity has important implications for both social interaction and social cognition. If inequity cannot be removed by redistribution or compensation, some kind of 'cognitive work' will ensue to find a justification. When a person receives unjustified rewards, there is some limited evidence that observers will still try to see his good fortune as earned or deserved, although it seems unlikely that this would apply to *all* kinds of windfalls. On the other hand, there seems to be no real evidence that observers will derogate an innocent victim, except when they feel in some way responsible for his or her fate. According to any social psychological theory that deals with problems of attitude organization and person perception, individuals should resist the cognition that good people are responsible for bad effects, and since (non-depressed) individuals seem to cling on to a positive view of themselves whenever possible, it follows that they should resist the idea that they themselves are the perpetrators of inequity.

If one does indeed believe the world to be a just place then the suffering of others is undoubtedly distressing and threatening. Even without such a 'world view', however, one does not wish to see the suffering of others left unexplained, since what is unexplained is also less predictable. Observers, therefore, seem prepared to undertake an attributional inquiry until they can find a cause or culpable agent for the victim's suffering. In some cases, observers might blame the victim's own judgement—he should have been more careful, but it was a mistake anyone might make—but such an attribution places relatively little emphasis on the *personal distinctiveness* of the victim's behaviour and hence stops short of derogation of his character. But suppose one feels oneself to be responsible for the victim's suffering, even if only indirectly? In a sense, the attributional inquiry has been completed but its recommendations have been vetoed. As a just person, one cannot possibly see oneself as responsible for the unjust suffering of another individual. Either someone, or something, else must be responsible, or the suffering itself has to be seen as justified by the kind of person the victim really is. For a good person to do harm to a bad person, in terms of balance theory or any of its derivatives, is cognitively more acceptable than for a good person to do harm to a good person. It appears, therefore, that when derogation occurs, this is not necessarily due to a belief in a 'just world', but rather to a belief in a 'just self'.

OBEDIENCE

In the studies on victim derogation just described, subjects have typically been asked to make attributions *after* they have observed the victim's suffering, with the expectation that it has now finished, and nothing can be done about it, or alternatively that the suffering will continue in a later session. Depending upon the conditions, subjects appear to feel some measure of responsibility, even though they themselves do not administer the electric shocks which the victim receives. Even in the Lerner and Lichtman (1968) study, where subjects chose to assign their partner to the shock condition, they did not actually administer the shocks themselves. They merely put her into a condition where she would receive shocks from the experimenter, if she made errors. Once the 'learning experiment' was under way, the subject, however remorseful, was a helpless observer. The focus of Milgram's (1963, 1964, 1974) research, however, has been on identifying the conditions under which subjects will obey an instruction knowingly to inflict pain, and possibly physical damage, on another individual.

The political significance of this question is all too obvious. In war, ordinary soldiers will obey orders which will lead to the death or injury of enemy combatants and civilians. Under oppressive regimes, ordinary officials will condemn citizens of an 'undesirable' race or political persuasion to death, torture, or imprisonment. Such acts, when revealed, are often 'justified' in terms of some supposedly noble ideal, such as preservation of national security, racial identity, law and order, democracy, the revolution, civilization, and so on and so forth. The invocation of such value-laden concepts is the cornerstone of political propaganda, of whatever orientation, and it enables ordinary citizens of the states concerned to 'sleep soundly in their beds', reassured that Right, however defined, is on their side. But what of the individuals who actually carry out the acts of cruelty or carnage? One possibility is that they are sadists of dubious sanity who deliberately choose the role of executioner or torturer, or who are deliberately recruited by some government agency wishing to capitalize on their perversions. No doubt such individuals exist, and may occasionally be thrown into prominence. To attribute the *generality* of institutionalized cruelty to such individual perversions, however, is no more persuasive or illuminating than attempts to reduce the causes of group conflict to the irrational motives or drives of individuals (Billig, 1976).

The alternative viewpoint, favoured by Milgram, is that most acts of inhumanity are in fact carried out by quite ordinary people, who are simply doing their job. Their role, as defined within a political or organizational system, or a military command structure, is perceived to oblige them to carry out instructions received from higher up the hierarchy. It is not their place to question the decisions of their 'superiors'. Disobedience, within such organizations, carries its own penalties, which may well be severe, but such penalties may not be absolutely necessary for authority to be obeyed. Milgram's studies claim to demonstrate 'obedience that is willingly assumed in the absence of threat of any sort, obedience that is maintained through the simple assertion by authority that it has the right to exercise control over the person' (Milgram, 1974, page xiii).

Milgram's basic procedure is as follows: two people come to the laboratory to take part in a study which, the experimenter explains, is concerned with the effects of punishment on learning. One of them is assigned the role of the 'learner' and the other that of the 'teacher'. The learner is taken into a room and, watched by the teacher, is strapped into a chair and an electrode is attached to his wrist. He is told that his task is to learn a list of word pairs, and that any errors he makes will be punished by the teacher with electric shocks of increasing intensity.

The learner is then seated (usually in another room) in front of a simulated shock generator with a row of thirty switches, ranging from 15 volts to 450 volts in 15-volt increments. The switches also bear verbal labels from 'slight shock' to 'danger—severe shock'. When the learner responds correctly, the teacher goes on to the next item in the test, but when the learner makes a mistake, the teacher is supposed to give him an electric shock, starting with the lowest voltage, but increasing the voltage level by 15 volts with each further error. In fact, only the teacher is a genuine subject. The learner is a paid actor, who deliberately makes errors so that the teacher is put in the position of having either to administer the shocks or to disobey the experimenter.

Of crucial importance are the learner's reactions to the shocks, which are coordinated with the supposed voltage levels. Thus, in the condition described by Milgram (1974, page 23), the learner indicated no discomfort below 75 volts; shocks from 75 to 105 volts produced grunts, 120 volts produced a shout of complaint, 135 volts a painful groan, and 150 volts a demand to be released from the experiment. Such demands and painful groans persisted with rising intensity until 300 volts, when the learner shouted desperately that he refused to provide any more answers to the test. The teacher would then usually turn to the experimenter for guidance, and would be told to treat the absence of a response as a wrong answer, and continue to administer shocks with increasing intensity. The 315-volt shock produced a violent scream and a repeated refusal to give more responses, and after 330 volts, the learner remained silent and gave no responses to the test items.

While all this was going on, the subject would frequently turn to the experimenter to ask whether he should continue, or to say that he did not wish to. The experimenter responded to such queries or protests with a series of standard 'prods', as follows: 'Please continue' or 'Please go on'; 'The experiment requires that you continue'; 'It is absolutely essential that you continue'; 'You have no other choice, you *must* go on'. If the subject expressed concern about possible injury to the learner, this sequence started with, 'Although the shocks may be painful, there is no permanent tissue damage, so please go on'. If the subject pointed to the learner's unwillingness to continue, the experimenter responded, 'Whether the learner likes it or not, you must go on until he has learned all the word pairs correctly. So please go on'. If, in spite of these 'prods', the subject insisted that he was not going to administer any more shocks to the learner, his refusal was accepted, and he was then debriefed and allowed to meet the learner again, who, of course, was perfectly well and in good spirits.

Milgram (1974) starts by reporting, not subjects' actual behaviour, but the predictions made by three groups (psychiatrists, college students, and middle class males) as to how far they themselves would go if they had to serve as 'teachers'. All these subjects predicted that they would defy the experimenter and refuse to administer shocks beyond a given level. The modal break-off point was around 150 volts, and no subjects were prepared to say that they would go beyond 300 volts. These predictions were in marked contrast to the levels of obedience observed among real subjects, recruited from adult male members of the general public who responded to an advertisement in a local newspaper. In the standard condition already described, 62·5 per cent of subjects obeyed the experimenter all the way through to the maximum shock level of 450 volts, and none showed defiance before the 135-volt level. The results were even more chilling in a 'remote' condition, in which there was no vocal feedback from the learner, but in which he was heard to pound the laboratory walls in protest at 300 volts, falling silent after 315 volts. Here 65 per cent of subjects showed complete obedience, and no subject broke off before the 300-volt level. Complete obedience was reduced to 40 per cent in a 'proximity' condition in which the subject could not only hear the learner, but see him also, as he was seated in the same room. A 'touch-proximity' condition was also run, which involved the teacher having to hold the learner's hand down onto the electric shock plate. As might be imagined, this condition produced lower levels of compliance, but nonetheless 30 per cent of subjects still obeyed right through to the maximum shock level. Of those who disobeyed the experimenter in this condition, most did so at 150 volts, which was the point at which the learner demanded to be let free and refused to leave his hand on the shock plate, and at which the experimeter told the teacher to keep the learner's hand in position by force.

A series of modified replications were then conducted. A new base-line condition was run in which the learner asked the experimenter before the session started whether the shocks were dangerous, as he had 'a slight heart condition'. The experimenter then replied, 'in a confident, somewhat dismissive tone that although the shocks may be painful, they cause no permanent tissue damage' (page 56). The vocal feedback from the learner during the experiment was also modified to contain references to this heart condition ('My heart's bothering me'). A less elegant room was also used as the laboratory. Inspite of these modifications, 65 per cent of subjects were completely obedient.

Women were also used as subjects in the base-line condition, though with a male experimenter and learner. Again, 65 per cent showed complete obedience, although Milgram refers to certain stylistic differences in their behaviour during the session and postexperimental interview. Many more women than men 'related their experience to problems of rearing children' (page 63). Additional manipulations were introduced to remove some of the experimenter's authority. If the experimenter no longer remained in the same room as the teacher, but instead gave his instructions by telephone, the number of completely compliant subjects dropped sharply to 22·5 per cent. Rather more (40 per cent) remained obedient throughout in a variation of the base-line condition which involved the learner stating at the outset (when signing a release form absolving the university from legal liability) 'I'll agree to be in it, but only on condition that you let me out when I say so; that's the only condition'. A particularly important variation sought to divest the experimenter of the prestige and respectability of Yale University, by conducting the study in a nearby industrial city 'in a three-room office suite in a somewhat rundown commercial building located in the downtown shopping area' (page 68) in the name of a fictitious organization called Research Associates of Bridgeport. The reduction in compliance was very slight. Although 5 per cent refused to administer any shocks at all, 47.5 per cent remained completely obedient. These results contrast sharply with those in a condition in which subjects were free to choose the level of shock they wanted to administer to the learner on any trial. With the requirement of escalation removed, only 1 subject out of 40 went as high as the 450-volt maximum, another went to 375 volts, but the remaining 38 gave shocks of 150 volts or below.

Further conditions were introduced to try to reduce compliance by putting the subject in situations where his obligation to complete the experiment conflicted with his acceptance of the experimenter's authority. In one condition, the learner insisted, at 150 volts, that he wanted to go on, even though the shocks were painful. However, the experimenter instructed the teacher to break off the experiment regardless, and all subjects indeed did so at this point. Another variation involved the experimenter taking on the role of the learner, while a third person, supposedly another subject, took on the experimenter's role, instructing the teacher to continue. All subjects in this condition broke off at 150 volts, when the experimenter, in the role of learner, demanded to be let out, even though the 'ordinary man' who had been told to give them orders instructed them to continue. When two confederates were used, so that the teacher received his orders from an 'ordinary man' with the experimenter out of the room, but with the learner also being an 'ordinary man' recruited like himself, only 20 per cent continued to the maximum shock level. However, of those who disobeyed their instructor at some point, fewer than one in three interfered with his taking over their role as teacher and administering the shocks himself up to the maximum level. When two experimenters instructed the teacher, with the learner supposedly being another subject, but gave contradictory instructions when the learner protested, all subjects refused to proceed beyond 165 volts. When two experimenters were used, and one took the role of the learner, 65 per cent of subjects remained completely obedient to the experimenter who instructed them to continue. When subjects did not have to administer the shocks themselves, but instead fulfilled a subsidiary role while another 'subject' did so, only 7·5 per cent interfered to stop the experiment continuing. However, if the teacher was required to administer the shocks with the assistance of two other 'subjects' who rebelled against the experimenter and refused to carry on, obedience to the experimenter was considerably reduced: 62·5 per cent broke off at, or before, the 210-volt level, but 10 per cent remained obedient to the experimenter throughout.

ROLES AND RESPONSIBILITY

Milgram's results are certainly some of the most challenging and provocative in experimental social psychology. At their face value, they imply that individuals will perform actions that appear to be severely hurting an innocent person, recruited in the same way as themselves, even to the point of possibly precipitating a heart attack, for no better reason than because the experimenter told them to do so. Somehow, the experimenter is accepted as a legitimate authority who can command behaviour which, in almost any context, would be regarded as offensive and immoral. In addition to giving commands, the experimenter defines the situation for the subject. '*There is a propensity for people to accept definitions of action provided by legitimate authority.* That is, although the subject performs the action, he allows authority to define its meaning' (Milgram, 1974, page 145). Milgram interprets his results as showing that the subject takes on the role of an 'agent' so that he 'feels responsible *to* the authority directing him but feels no responsibility *for* the content of the actions that the authority prescribes' (pages 145–146). The notion of perceived responsibility is thus central to Milgram's analysis. Subjects may be deeply concerned and distressed about the possible consequences of their actions for the victim, but they do not tend to see these actions as *their* actions, in the sense of being their responsibility.

Evidence of the harmful consequences for the victim of their performance of their role as 'agents' is said to produce 'strain', which may lead some of the subjects to disobey, i.e., to refuse to be 'agents' any more. Such an act of refusal, however, is not undertaken lightly. It involves the subject breaking his initial promise to help the experimenter, and offering a personal affront to the experimenter by negating his definition of the situation. 'The experimental situation is so constructed that there is no way the subject can stop shocking the learner without violating the experimenter's self-definition' (page 150). As Milgram points out, in terms of Goffman's (1959) approach, there is a 'moral demand', or social obligation, on individuals to respect each other's self-definitions.

It is nonetheless fair to say that the weight of Milgram's contribution has been empirical, rather than more broadly theoretical. The notion of perceived responsibility is emphasized, but is not related to the wider literature on attribution processes. Explanations based upon assumptions of aggressive instincts are mentioned but quickly dismissed. Milgram presents his findings as evidence that ordinary people will tend to carry out 'immoral' orders if they perceive their roles as requiring them to do so, and apart from identifying certain limiting conditions and drawing comparisons with real-life atrocities, he seems content to let his experiments speak for themselves. This interpretation, however, has not gone unchallenged.

An extensive critique of Milgram's research has been published by Mixon (1972). Mixon's thesis seems to contain three distinct, but purportedly related themes: a general metatheoretical argument concerning the nature of explanation and investigation in social psychology; a more methodological part involving the advocacy of a particular role-playing technique as an alternative to experimental deception; and a more speculative, but nonetheless more directly relevant, reinterpretation of Milgram's results.

The general metatheoretical position adopted by Mixon is shared by Harré and Secord (1972). Central to this position is a distinction between 'role/rule governed behaviour' and 'performance' within a given role/rule context. It is argued that an understanding of social interaction requires consideration not only of differences in performance, but also of the roles and rules which apply to the interaction and provide the context within which individuals may differ stylistically in performing the roles which they adopt. It is alleged that psychology has traditionally been concerned only with performance, and has ignored the roles and rules which define the social context of such performance.

> Psychologists have traditionally confined their interest to questions of performance—or, more specifically to the effects of particular treatments on performance. Implicit knowledge of the roles, rules, and aims of social situations and the limits of their chosen experimental method has made it difficult for psychologists even to formulate questions about role/rule governed behaviour.
>
> In effect psychologists have examined the effects of treatments on performance within a single role/rule context—that of the psychological experiment. Performance that is context-specific simply cannot be studied in the conventional experiment unless the context it is specific to is the social psychological experiment. Role and rules cannot be directly studied at all. It is, I believe, an intuitive notion of the limitations of conventional method and the desire to change its role/rule context that leads experimenters to deceive their subjects. For example, ordinarily it is a non-problematic fact that subjects obey the experimenter, for such obedience is clearly part of the role/rule context. Yet, as Milgram so clearly saw, a problem like that of destructive obedience is most important and should be somehow amenable to laboratory study. But for obedience to be studied in the laboratory people must be made to disobey—an act uncharacteristic of laboratory behaviour. Thus deception is used with the hope of somehow shattering the role/rule context of the experiment. I think that I have been able to show that deception of necessity only partially succeeds in moving the experiment from under the role/rule conventions of the psychological experiment. Though at times roles and rules are made more enigmatic by deception, the naturalistic experiment is essentially confined to examining performance within a single role/rule context. (Mixon, 1972, pages 168–169.)

This proposition certainly has its seductive features, but its acceptance depends, of course, on what is meant by 'single'. To imply that the role of the experimental subject is the same in all psychological experiments is a gross over-simplification. Mostly the experimenter gives instructions to the subject and the subject attempts to carry them out, but this does not necessarily entail that the subject sees himself in a subservient or inferior role. In experiments on recognition and recall, or on visual and auditory descrimination, the ground rules of the encounter imply that the experimenter is deliberately trying to stretch the subject's cognitive and perceptual abilities to their limit

Essentially what is involved is a contest of wits. Another kind of contest of wits is typically involved when subjects play the Prisoner's Dilemma Game, although here the challenge is to work out what the *other* subject will do. The experimenter stays discretely in the background after giving the initial instructions. Similarly in studies of communication accuracy (e.g., Mehrabian and Reed, 1968), the experimenter exerts little direct control after explaining the purpose of the task and providing the stimulus materials. Such 'brain-teaser' experiments form a major part of psychological research, including social psychological research, and even when a paradigm appears overworked, unoriginal, and tedious to the specialist who has read scores of papers on 'the same old stuff', it is remarkable how involving such experimental procedures can be for the naive subject.

Again, there are many procedures in which the subject's role comes close to that of an 'expert witness'. Here the ground rules assume that the subject has some kind of special knowledge or experience which makes the experimenter in some way *dependent on him* for information. Many social judgement studies involve the implicit theme that 'We want to know what people like you think about these statements'. The subject's *extra*-experimental status, be it is as a pupil, student, male or female, member of a particular age, occupational, political, religious, or ethnic group, makes him or her in an important way *special* and respected. Studies of interpersonal attraction, aesthetic appreciation, etc., similarly imply a genuine interest by the experimenter in the subject's likes and dislikes. Studies of counter-attitudinal advocacy also use this kind of approach, though of course more manipulatively.

Then there is the important and increasing body of research that exploits 'field situations' in which subjects typically do not know that they are being observed or experimented upon, and where there is no experimenter to give them instructions. These are still 'psychological experiments', nonetheless, since they use experimental designs to investigate psychological questions. Yet the role relationships involved are very different from the kind of situation which Mixon would presumably regard as archetypical, in which the subject is brought into an experimental room, and told by the experimenter to perform some task that is neither physically nor intellectually demanding, nor relevant to any special interests, skills, or experience of the subject. In such situations, the subject is the experimenter's operative, doing what the experimenter tells him because of some extrinsic purpose, be it to earn money, fulfil a course requirement, or get vicarious satisfaction from helping the experimenter to 'push back the frontiers of science'. For subjects in these kinds of experiments, admittedly, 'Theirs is not to reason why', but it is debatable how many studies in social psychology, apart from Milgram's, really fall into this category.

It is even debatable whether, in many paradigms, a 'single role/rule context' operates across different conditions of the same experiment. The statement that subjects' behaviour depends upon their interpretation or definition of the experimental situation, would be denied, if at all, only by the most hardline of behaviourists. Cognitively oriented social psychologists are well aware that the effects of different experimental treatments cannot be properly understood without attention being paid to how subjects interpret the information available to them—how they work out what is happening and decide upon a course of action which they consider situationally appropriate. What is intriguing about experimental social psychological research is the way in which individual subjects define their own roles and rules of conduct, do so differently under different treatments, but yet often do so in a manner predictable from theory. A few studies have attempted explicitly to introduce extra-experimental norms into the experimental situation, simply by varying the information given to subjects concerning the supposed purpose of the experiment (e.g., Eiser and Bhavnani, 1974; Simons and Piliavin, 1972). More generally, the implicit norms involved in most social psychological experiments, that one should behave in a way that appears to others, if not to oneself, to be reasonable, ethical, and justifiable, do not appear to be the manufactured product of social psychologists, nor their sole discovery.

Furthermore, Mixon's argument that psychologists have traditionally been interested in *performance* ignores, or at best disguises, the fact that their main concern has been with the cognitive *processes* which underly such performance. The experimental paradigms involved in studies of attention, memory, and perceptual discrimination are extremely restrictive and tightly controlled, yet the conclusions of such research can be directly applicable to applied contexts. It simply does not make sense to assume that human beings have evolved separate mechanisms of information processing which serve no function outside the experimental laboratory. The information which subjects in social psychological experiments are required to process may be more complex, evaluative, and symbolic than the stimuli used in many studies in cognitive psychology, but the main question is still that of how they will come to judgemental and/or behavioural decisions. Again, it is implausible that such processes of social decision-making, *considered as processes*, should be relevant only to laboratory behaviour.

Milgram's general criticisms of the social psychology experiment, though, are particularly inappropriate in the case of Milgram's research. It is precisely because disobedience is 'an act uncharacteristic of laboratory behaviour' that the experimenter-subject relationship can be used as a plausible analogue of superordinate-subordinate relationships outside the laboratory. In hierarchical social systems, disobedience may not only be uncharacteristic, it may carry severe punishments or reprimands. The presumed *absence* of such sanctions in the laboratory experiment makes Milgram's results all the more compelling.

The methodological part of Mixon's paper presents a distinction between 'active' and 'non-active' role-playing. Mixon argues that what typically passes for role-playing—when subjects are given an outline description of a procedure and asked to *predict* how they would respond—is 'non-active' and insufficiently involving. In 'active' role-playing situations, however, the subject goes through a simulation of the same procedure as a 'real' subject, and is asked to *pretend* that the situation is real. In other words, he has to act out the role assigned to him. Using the technique, Mixon reports a number of modified replications of Milgram's basic paradigm.

The levels of pretended obedience found by Mixon were, in general, comparable to the levels of actual obedience found by Milgram, but varied as a function of the script read out by the experimenter. Four conditions were run which 'differed only in the amount of concrete detail included' (page 162). Unfortunately, we are given almost no concrete detail about such variations in concrete detail. The script containing 'the least' information produced 40 per cent complete 'obedience', whereas the level was 80 per cent in a condition where the script 'included details noting the *duration* of each shock, that is details, that emphasized the fact that the length of each shock was at the teacher's discretion' (page 162). Remaining conditions varied cues pertaining to the shock's severity. When the verbal labels (e.g., 'Danger—Severe Shock') were removed from the imitation shock generator, 9 out of 10 subjects showed complete 'obedience'. Only 1 out of 10 did so, however, when the script contained feedback from the 'experimenter' that 'The learner's health is irrelevant. Experimental procedure requires that you treat the absence of a response as a wrong answer and continue as directed. Please go on!' (page 164.) The one 'obedient' subject in this condition remarked that the script had contained a reassurance from the 'experimenter' to the 'learner' that the shocks were not dangerous. When even this reassurance was removed, no subjects 'obeyed'.

The implications of these results depend on whether one believes, as Mixon argues, that the behaviour of 'active' role-playing subjects will generally be the same as that of deceived subjects in actual experiments with the same 'script'. If Mixon is right, then the utility of deceiving subjects is seriously questioned. His data, however, are nowhere near strong enough to justify recommending 'active' role-playing as a valid general alternative to conventional methodology. It is extremely difficult to determine exactly what went on in his different conditions. The descriptions of procedure are probably the vaguest and flimsiest of those in any of the studies I have read while writing this book, yet Mixon's is a major article of more than thirty printed pages, and no mere research note. One simply cannot tell whether Mixon's various scripts were adequate simulations of any of Milgram's conditions, and Mixon does not put their adequacy directly to the test himself by running them under Milgram-type deception procedures to compare the results. Nor are we given any basis for judging if other differences in method and procedure between specific role-playing and deception treatments are crucial or irrelevant. In this context, it is worth noting that Mixon was quite happy to use introductory psychology students as subjects, which surely must have had implications for how the 'role/rule context' of his experiment was interpreted. Milgram (1974), in comparison, not only draws subjects from other backgrounds, but also provides information about the individual characteristics of particular subjects in a way that suggests the presence of important differences in styles of coping with authority. Such individual differences presumably could be incorporated into a role-playing approach, but Mixon does not do so.

I have discussed Mixon's general theoretical and methodological viewpoints at some length, since his specific interpretation of Milgram's results is not strictly dependent on them, and acceptance of this interpretation need not necessarily imply a rejection of more conventional theories and methods. The way Mixon suggests that Milgram's results should be interpreted is in fact quite simple. Subjects tend to do what experimenters tell them, however bizarre or dangerous it might appear, so long as they believe that 'safeguards are in place', that is, so long as they can maintain their initial expectation that people do not get hurt in psychological experiments. In Milgram's experiments, subjects did in fact have considerable evidence of the victim's suffering—the feedback from the victim, the voltages indicated on the shock generator, and the verbal labels (e.g., 'Danger—Severe Shock') which explained the different voltage levels. On the other hand, this evidence was contradicted by continued reassurance from the experimenter, implying that everything was under control. Subjects were thus faced with contradictory interpretations of the situation, and their compliance or disobedience might therefore be explained on the assumption that they give greater or less weight to the cues provided by the experimenter rather than the victim. Mixon argues that his own results support this view, since manipulations designed to vary the salience of the conflicting types of information resulted in the changes in 'obedience' that would be expected.

Attractively simple though this might be, a number of problems still remain. First, if obedient subjects attach more weight to the cues provided by the experimenter, why should this be so? Mixon assumes that subjects will have clear 'background expectations' about what happens in experiments, but it will be remembered that Milgram deliberately recruited members of the general public for his studies, and also controlled for the perceived expertise and respectability of the experimenter. Second, Milgram's subjects continued to obey even after they had begun to doubt the credibility of the experimenter's assurances—at least, this seems to be the clear implication of the individual protocols presented by Milgram (1974), and of the available film records. Third, in his emphasis on subjects' expectations about the effects on the victim, Mixon pays little attention to the issue of perceived *responsibility* for such effects. Central to Milgram's analysis is the assumption that subordinates do not tend to see themselves as responsible for the effects of their actions when they are acting under instructions. Perhaps, in real life just as in experiments, people do not expect that anything they are instructed to do will involve seriously harming another person, but this does not mean that they will necessarily disobey their instructions as soon as such expectations are disconfirmed. Instead, they might assume that there must be some good reason for the instructions they have been given, and thus might see their actions as *justifiable* in terms of a wider context of which they cannot be blamed for being unaware.

Milgram, no less than Mixon, realizes that it is part of the role of the experimental subject, *within certain paradigms*, to obey the experimenter without being entitled to an explanation of the instructions until after the experiment is completed. The extraordinary thing about Milgram's results is the extent to which subjects find it difficult to break out from their roles, even when obviously distressed by the functions they are instructed to perform. In the next chapter (pages 285–287) I shall describe an even more striking example of this phenomenon, the simulated prison experiment at Stanford, in which young male volunteers took on the roles of prisoners and guards (Haney, Banks, and Zimbardo, 1973). As will be seen, the participants in this study, even including the senior investigators, became so engrossed in their roles that it ceased to be just a simulation, but instead an experience with brutalizing effects which were all too real. Ambiguity of cues may be an important feature of Milgram's procedures, but this by itself would not seem to be a sufficient, and perhaps not even a necessary, condition of people's preparedness to carry out instructions, even when to do so may cause distress or pain to another person. If there is some room for doubt concerning the negative effects of the actions a person is instructed to perform, it appears that this will inhibit defiance and disobedience. Even where there is no reasonable doubt, however, experimental subjects, and others in defined roles, may cling on to the excuse that they are 'only doing their job' and hence are not personally responsible.

CONCLUSIONS

In this chapter I have described research which may seem altogether more serious in its implications than the experimental gaming studies reviewed in Chapter 7. It might be supposed that the norms which seem to govern behaviour in gaming encounters, and which allow for degrees of competitiveness within conventionally accepted rules, have little relevance to interactions in which the participants are not 'just playing'. In fact, the issues involved are quite similar. The basic questions are those of how the individual perceives the situation with which he is confronted, which frequently means that he has to interpret ambiguous or contradictory information, and how he defines his own role in the situation, that is, what he sees as expected or required of him, and what he sees as his entitlement, relative to other participants. As in gaming research, the notion that individuals will simply act so as to maximize their own self-interest cannot account for the considerable situational variance in levels of selfish and unselfish behaviour. In some circumstances, a person may help another at considerable cost to himself. In other circumstances, he may directly or indirectly allow the other to suffer without receiving any special benefits for doing so.

An important factor throughout is the ambiguity of the situation. To help a victim, either through intervention or defiance of experimental instructions, is rarely devoid of risk. To overreact to a false alarm may make one feel foolish, and in laboratory studies may mean that one incurs the displeasure of the experimenter. A variety of situational cues will therefore influence the would-be helpers judgement of whether the victim is in need of help: the more evident the victim's need, the more likely will he be to receive help. Ambiguity, however, is not the only factor, since it would seem that individuals may allow a victim to continue suffering beyond the point at which the balance of evidence points to his need being genuine. Another factor, emphasized by Darley and Latané (1970), is the cost to the helper. The greater the cost to the helper, relative to the victim's perceived need, the less likelihood will there be of help being given.

To interpret this last factor merely as a special case of the law of effect, however, is to miss the central theoretical point. The studies reviewed in this chapter put subjects in a dilemma, which requires them to compare their perceived obligations and entitlements. Such obligations and entitlements relate to the inputs and outcomes dealt with by equity theory. Equity, however, does not depend simply on a comparison of one's *own* outcomes with one's *own* inputs, but rather on an interpersonal comparison of one's outcomes and inputs with those of other participants in the relationship. But what defines the relationship? What, in other words, defines the individual's frame of reference for social comparisons of inputs and outcomes? In many of the more mathematically oriented attempts to discriminate between different equity formulations (e.g., Anderson, 1976), the context is defined by experimental instructions. For instance, subjects may be told to imagine a situation in which two workers were cooperating on a particular task, and each received particular levels of remuneration. In studies of bystander intervention, however, the subject has to decide for himself whether or not to take account of a stranger's predicament—that is, whether or not to treat the stranger as a relevant comparison stimulus within his frame of reference.

If a person does take account of a victim's predicament, he then puts himself in a position where he has obligations to offer help or compensation. In return, he is entitled to gratitude from the victim and enhanced self-respect, instead of having to feel guilty at his own better fortune. Such obligations and entitlements define the role of the helper, but the salience of this role depends upon the frame of reference of interpersonal comparison. If this frame of reference consists simply of the bystander and the victim, and the victim's need is legitimate, the bystander is under an obligation to help if able to do so. Rarely, though, will things be so simple. If other bystanders are present, these also may serve as relevant standards for comparison. Depending on the situation, there may be a number of reasons why this may inhibit helping.

The first possible reason is that the individual relies upon the reactions of other bystanders to resolve the ambiguity over the victim's state of need, and hence his entitlement to receive help. A second possible reason—the so-called 'diffusion of responsibility' notion—is that the bystander, while recognizing the victim's need for help, does not regard himself as the person most obliged to take the initiative and give such help. A third possible reason, which comes closest to some of Lerner's arguments, is that, by giving help, the bystander may risk reducing his own outcomes to below those of other people (such as other bystanders) with whom he chooses to compare himself.

The presence of other bystanders is only one aspect of a more general problem. With the exception of institutionalized 'helping professions'— though even here the situation may appear more complex on closer examination—the obligation to help frequently conflicts with alternative role demands and perceived entitlements. The delay that might be involved in giving help could mean that one is late for an appointment at work, and hence that one would fail to fulfil one's obligations to one's colleagues, or alternatively that one kept friends or family waiting beyond the time at which one was expected, which again would constitute a violation of established role obligations. Such obligations might appear minor, but they depend upon established role relationships. Similarly, even when the delay would not in- convenience any third party, the inconvenience or danger that helping would cause oneself, might appear inconsistent with one's entitlement 'not to be bothered', which has been earned by fulfilment of other obligations. What this means is that the frame of reference for interpersonal comparisons may imply a *multiplicity of roles* between which the bystander has to choose.

In a number of studies of bystander intervention, as well as in Milgram's studies of obedience, the obligation to help is potentially incompatible with subjects' *previously contracted* obligations to the experimenter to complete the task assigned to them. Similarly, in naturalistic studies of helping in emergen- cies, bystanders would typically have to break off from what they were previously doing in order to help the victim. Helping a total stranger thus may require a *change of roles* which may not be easily accomplished without violation of established obligations. Such obligations might appear trivial when set against the urgency of the victim's need, but their primacy may give them greater subjective salience.

Such prior obligations, though, are more than mere distractions. If a subject accepts a functionary role in which he agrees to carry out the instruc- tions of the experimenter, and is given little or no room for personal choice and initiative in how he does so, he earns a number of entitlements in return for discharging his obligations to the experimenter. The most obvious of these, his entitlement to financial remuneration, is barely relevant to the theoretical debate. More relevant is his *entitlement not to be held responsible* for the consequences of the actions he has performed. As a mere functionary, he was not required to make personal decisions in order to perform his task in accordance with the instructions, so he should not, as he sees it, be held personally responsible as though the decisions were his own. This is why it is so important to distinguish the particular kind of role assigned to subjects in the Milgram studies from those fulfilled by subjects in most other psychological experiments. What distinguishes Milgram's 'teacher' subjects is that they are *not* treated as decision-makers. Milgram's paradigm thus offers subjects the chance to deny responsibility for their actions, just as do many hierarchical organizations which require subordinates to carry out instructions without requiring *or expecting* them to evaluate the wisdom of these instructions within a wider context.

Derogation of victims appears to operate primarily as a means of restoring one's perception of oneself as a 'just person' in situations where one's responsibility for the victim's suffering is not easily denied. What this amounts to is a refusal to admit that the victim's outcomes ought to be more comparable to one's own—a refusal, in other words, to treat the victim as a relevant standard for comparison—which is 'justified' by a devaluation of the victim's intrinsic deservedness. To deny the victim's deservedness is thus to deny one's own obligations towards him, and to down-grade the salience of any relationship with him.

The studies reviewed in this chapter have often involved subjects being placed in ambiguous, confusing, or distressing situations. As in other fields of research, the main theme that emerges is one of individuals trying to make sense of complex information through processes of selection, simplification, and evaluative comparison, in order to be able to decide on appropriate action. The actions taken as a result may range from the heroic to the horrifying, yet all tend to be seen as justifiable by the subjects involved. The perceived justice of one's actions towards another individual depends upon the kind of person one perceives him to be, the nature of one's obligations towards him, and the outcomes to which one feels one is legitimately entitled. As will be seen in the next chapter, such factors affect not only relationships between individuals, but also relationships between groups.

SUMMARY

* Equity theory assumes that people will evaluate each other's outcomes in relation to the perceived extent of their respective inputs, contributions or deservedness.
* It is further assumed that, when faced with a situation where their own, or another's, outcomes appear inequitable, people will either intervene to remove or lessen the inequity, or reappraise the situation so that the outcomes appear equitable.
* This implies that individuals should help others whom they perceive to be the victims of (inequitable) accidents. However, intervention by bystanders in emergencies can be very slow, especially when there is ambiguity regarding the seriousness of the emergency and when others are also seen as able to intervene.
* When helping involves risks or costs to the helper, its likelihood tends to be reduced but not eliminated.

* Help is more likely to be given to a victim who appears to be in genuine need, and/or whose reasons for requesting help appear legitimate.
* According to the 'just world' hypothesis, people are committed to a view of the world in which injustices do not happen to people who themselves act justly.
* One implication of this is the concept of 'justified self-interest', according to which a person may see himself as justified in increasing his own outcomes, or in refusing to help others beyond a certain point, when to do otherwise would reduce his own outcomes to below the level to which he feels entitled, and which he feels would be obtained by others comparable to himself.
* Another implication is that observers of a victim's suffering, who are unable to offer compensation, will try to see the suffering as justified, either by seeing the victim as responsible, or by derogating the victim as the kind of person who deserves to suffer.
* Victim derogation seems to occur mainly in conditions where subjects could feel themselves to be directly or indirectly responsible for the victim's suffering. This lends support to a defensive attribution interpretation rather than the 'just world' hypothesis.
* Subjects may obey experimental instructions apparently to inflict suffering on another person.
* Such obedience persists over a variety of conditions, tending to be reduced when the victim is in close physical proximity to the subject, when the experimenter gives instructions from a distance, when another subject takes over the role of the experimenter, or when there are two experimenters who give contradictory instructions.
* Although uncertainty over the extent of the victim's suffering may increase obedience, subjects will often still obey when there is no real doubt that the victim is suffering.
* The single most important requirement for the occurrence of destructive obedience seems to be that the subject should construe his role as one where he is absolved from personal responsibility for the consequences of his actions in carrying out the instructions.

NINE

GROUP PROCESSES

GROUPS AND INDIVIDUALS

The trouble with chapter headings is that they suggest a separation of subject matter that can often be quite misleading. How come, you might ask, that the topic of groups has been postponed to this late stage in the book, when surely all social psychology should be about groups and the behaviour of individuals within them? The answer is that all social psychology *is* about groups, but often does not admit it, and sometimes, perhaps, does not know it. The various topics covered in previous chapters are essential features of the inter-action between individuals in groups, and the functioning of groups cannot be understood if they are ignored.

In many respects, the problem is one of terminology. The language of social psychology is largely the language of individual cognition. We talk about likes and dislikes, judgements, evaluations, interpretations of feelings and events, attributions, intentions, and so on. These all pertain to indivi-duals. We cannot talk about groups having likes or dislikes, except as a shorthand way of saying that the individuals in the groups always or mostly have such feelings. Even when we talk about groups making decisions, what we are talking about is individuals in a group coming to decisions together. To suggest otherwise might seem to be incompatible with any claims to empiricism. Yet in dissociating themselves from the mysticism that still sur-rounds much of the talk about groups and group experiences, many social psychologists have failed to acknowledge, or adequately convey, the fact that the individual cognitive processes in which they are interested operate the way they do because the individual is embedded in a social context.

Studies of group processes, then, are not concerned with different cognitive processes from those involved in other areas of social psychology. Rather, they are concerned with how such processes, for instance the need to ascribe meaning to the events around one and the need to maintain a positive self-evaluation, translate themselves into particular contexts where the group membership of the subjects is made more explicit than in most of the paradigms described in previous chapters. Such studies, however, by no means constitute a homogeneous set. On the contrary, there is a deep division between approaches that deal primarily with normative influences of various kinds on individuals within a single group, and those which focus on the psychological consequences of relationships between groups. Cultural and even ideological aspects of this division have been detected by some writers (e.g., Billig, 1976), but the findings of studies on either side need not be irreconcilable empirically. This chapter will, therefore, provide a selective review of both approaches in turn.

INTRAGROUP RELATIONS: SOCIAL INFLUENCE IN AMBIGUOUS SITUATIONS

In one of the classic studies of social psychology, Sherif (1935) demonstrated that individuals would rely upon the responses of other people, albeit no more expert than themselves, when making judgements about an ambiguous perceptual stimulus, so that judgements made in a group setting would show a convergence towards a collective norm. His study made use of the optical illusion known as the autokinetic phenomenon, first noted by astronomers. If a stationary point of light is shown against a completely dark background, so that there is no visible frame of reference, it will appear to wander or waver. Subjects will then be found to give varying estimates of the amount the point of light has moved. Sherif compared two conditions, one where subjects first made judgements individually, and then were brought together into a group, and another where the order of sessions was reversed. In the first condition, subjects modified their initial individual judgements so as to lessen the discrepancy between themselves and the other group members. In the second condition, the collective norm established in the group session still affected subjects' judgements when made individually. There was even evidence of some influence due to the collective norm when subjects were re-tested one year later.

One recent legacy of this study has been the work described in Chapter 8 on the role of situational ambiguity on bystander intervention in emergencies. Other research, based more directly on Sherif's paradigm, has examined whether the emergence of a collective norm is inevitable in such situations, or whether it depends upon subjects' expectations about the stimulus, and their relationships with one another. Sperling (1946) compared Sherif's original situation, in which subjects were led to believe that the point of light really would move, with a situation in which they were told that 'This is just an optical illusion and the only truth is what each of you sees'. While replicating Sherif's results in the first condition, Sperling found that 60 per cent of the subjects in the second condition showed no convergence either towards the judgement of the other group members, or to those made by an experimental confederate.

In a similar vein, Alexander, Zucker, and Brody (1970) informed subjects that the phenomenon was in fact an illusion, before asking them to make judgements of the apparent movement of the point of light over a series of trials, first individually and then in pairs. Neither sets of responses showed any convergence, remaining as variable at the end as at the beginning of the session. In a second experiment, subjects were not informed about the nature of the illusion, but were instead paired with a confederate of the experimenter who made increasingly convergent and stable responses over time, or alternatively made judgements that became increasingly divergent and variable. In the former condition, subjects' responses became increasingly close to those of the stooge, whereas in the second, they appeared to give up the attempt to make their responses either internally consistent, or consistent with those of the stooge.

Other studies have explored the effects of subjects' attraction towards others in a group (or dyadic) judgement situation, and have suggested a greater tendency for judgements to converge when the interpersonal relationships are positive. Sampson and Insko (1964) paired subjects with a stooge (a drama student) who acted during the preliminary session of the experiment (supposedly concerned with 'empathy') so as to make himself be seen by the subjects as either very likeable or very objectionable. Then, over an initial series of trials, the stooge made either similar or dissimilar judgements of the autokinetic phenomenon to those that had been made by the naive subject. Subjects were more likely to change their judgements from before to after hearing the judgements given by the stooge, if the stooge was liked but gave dissimilar judgements to their own, or if he was disliked but gave similar judgements. In addition, subjects reported feeling more 'nervous' rather than 'calm' when making their judgements in those conditions where most shift was observed. These results are interpreted by Sampson and Insko as consistent with Heider's (1946) balance theory (see Chapter 2).

Pollis (1967), using a situation in which subjects listened to a series of sound beats and had to estimate their number, found that pairs of subjects who were friends made closer judgements to each other, and stood by their initial responses more when afterwards paired with a stranger, than did pairs of subjects who initially did not know each other. Similarly, Pollis and Montgomery (1968), using the autokinetic phenomenon, had subjects make judgements either individually, partnered by a friend, or partnered by a stranger, before making judgements individually in a second phase of the experiment. The subjects who were initially partnered by a friend showed less change between the two phases, and less variability of judgement within the second phase.

Status as well as friendship can also affect such judgements. Sampson (cited by Sherif and Sherif, 1969, page 169) used members of a monastery as subjects. Each subject was paired with another whose initial judgements of the autokinetic phenomenon showed an average discrepancy of about twelve centimeters from their own. Within this restriction, three kinds of couples were formed: (1) couples of young novices after only one week of noviciate who barely knew each other; (2) couples of novices who had been together for a year and therefore knew each other well; (account was also taken of their sociometric choices, so that one member of each pair was the first choice of his partner, but had not placed his partner among his top three choices); (3) unequal couples consisting of novices and non-novices. In the first condition, subjects were influenced by each other and tended to converge over time. In the second condition, they also converged, but the less preferred member of each pair shifted his judgements most. In the final condition, the higher status non-novices showed the greater stability in their judgements, while the novices initially shifted their judgements towards those of their partner, before going back to their original position.

There seems reasonable evidence, therefore, that individuals will tend to be influenced by one another when making judgements of ambiguous perceptual stimuli in a dyad or group setting. Nonetheless, the emergence of a 'collective norm' is by no means as automatic as Sherif may have originally supposed. Convergence of judgement is generally more marked when the others are more liked, or perceived as more similar to oneself. Also of critical importance is the extent to which subjects are, or are not, led to believe that the phenomenon they have to judge is objective or illusory. Whereas disagreement over the size of an illusion is quite tolerable, disagreement over objective reality is far less so. In terms of Kelley's (1967) formulation of attribution theory, there should be consensus among the judgements of different (but comparable) perceivers if their judgements are to be attributable to objective properties of the stimulus rather than to the idiosyncrasies of the perceivers. Some initial disagreement is nonetheless to be expected, even when judging objective reality, where the judgement task is difficult. In such situations, the adoption of a 'collective norm' is by no means an irrational solution, but on the contrary may be seen as a quite efficient way of estimating the correct answer.

SOCIAL INFLUENCE IN UNAMBIGUOUS SITUATIONS

Some of the most challenging studies are those which produce results which surprise even the investigators who conduct them. Such were the experiments by Asch (1951, 1956), which established the term 'conformity' as a major part of the social psychologist's explanatory repertoire, but which still have subleties which resist easy explanation. His basic paradigm was as follows:

Groups of subjects, usually numbering between four and ten, are seated together in front of a screen, and are asked to judge the lengths of sets of lines.

The judgements require a comparison of a standard line with a simultaneously presented set of three comparison lines, of which one is equal in length to the standard. Each subject in turn has to say out loud which of the three comparison lines is equal to the standard. The discrimination is so easy that mistakes are quite implausible. On two-thirds of the trials, however, one of the subjects hears all the others unanimously give a response which is blatantly wrong. Usually, this is the subject whose turn it is to respond last. In fact, the other subjects are all confederates of the experimenter responding in accordance with instructions. As the experiment progresses, the one naive subject exhibits growing nervousness, sometimes getting off his seat to go and look at the lines from the same angle as the other subjects, and hesitating before responding, sometimes by making the correct response, sometimes by 'conforming' to the incorrect response given by the rest of the group, and sometimes even giving a response which is incorrect but different from the group response.

Over a variety of conditions, the proportion of incorrect conformist responses made by naive subjects averages out at about one in three. This proportion is lower if there are fewer than four people in the group, but remains essentially unchanged for groups containing from three up to sixteen confederates in addition to the single naive subject. Beyond a certain point, therefore, the absolute size of the majority does not seem to matter. What does seem to matter very considerably, however, is if the naive subject has an 'ally' among the confederates. If this ally responds correctly throughout, the subject's level of conformity to the majority response is very drastically reduced. If the ally starts by giving correct judgements, but then adopts the majority norm, the subject tends to conform at the typical level (one trial in three) on later trials. On the other hand, if the ally starts giving correct responses only on the later trials, the subject shows greater independence as the experiment goes on.

The importance of unanimity is underlined by Mouton, Blake, and Olmstead (1956), who seated subjects in separate cubicles where they were asked to estimate the number of metronome clicks in sequences of 14, 32, or 49 clicks played back to them through earphones at the rate of 180 per minute. This was, therefore, a rather more ambiguous situation than that used by Asch, but less so than that used by Sherif. Before making their responses, each subject also heard what were supposedly the responses of four other subjects. These responses were in fact pre-recorded, and either under- or over-estimated the correct number of clicks on each trial by one, two or three. In one condition, when the responses of the pre-recorded majority were unanimous, more than half the total number of subjects' responses conformed to the majority norm. However, when the majority was not unanimous, the subjects accepted the normative response on only one occasion out of eight.

How is this importance of unanimity to be interpreted? Is what is crucial the lack of a consensus within the majority, or the fact that the subject has direct support for his own judgement for another person? An experiment which allows us to distinguish these two possibilities was performed by Allen and Levine (1968). In one of their conditions, the majority responded incorrectly, apart from one confederate who gave the correct responses. In another condition, this confederate disagreed with the majority, but in fact gave a response which was even more incorrect than the majority norm. In both of these conditions, the number of trials on which the naive subject conformed to the majority norm was greatly reduced, suggesting that the lack of consensus within the majority, rather than the presence of social support for the naive subject, is the crucial factor. Such an interpretation fits in well with attribution theory, since the absence of consensus allows the individual to say, 'This is the kind of situation in which people can disagree', and hence to feel the fact of his isolation less threatening to his concept of himself as a sane and reasonably accurate perceiver of objective reality.

Such an interpretation makes a number of assumptions. It assumes that the naive subject regards the other subjects as making their responses in good faith, which implies that he does not see through the experimental deception. Conformity experiments are now so much a part of the folklore of social psychology that this might appear a risky assumption. However, it has to be remembered that, at the time, these were novel procedures, and subjects were less hypersensitive to deceptive manipulations generally. Another assumption is that the naive subject also makes his response in reasonably good faith. He may not know what's up with his eyesight, but if *everyone* else agrees on a different answer, perhaps they are right and he is wrong. In other words, this interpretation assumes that the main influence of the group is at a cognitive level—the unanimous opposition of the other members of the group makes the subject less certain of his own judgement.

Such feelings of uncertainty might be quite confusing and distressing for the subject. Indeed, he is posed with a problem to which there is no easy solution. Sometimes his perceptions do coincide with the judgements of the other group members, but there seems no way in which he can predict when this will happen. If anything, things get worse rather than better as the experiment progresses. (The confederates in fact gave correct responses on trials 1, 2, 5, 10, 11, and 14 of the 18 trials in the Asch, 1956, experiment.) Such confusion and distress, however, is, as described, still a personal affair. The subject asks himself, 'What's happening to me?' and cannot find an answer.

This is very different from an alternative interpretation, which assumes that the subject fears ridicule or rejection by the group if he makes a deviant response. In other words, the question he asks himself is not, 'What's happening to me?' but instead, 'What will happen to me?' In support of this possibility, it should be remembered that the naive subject is typically readily identifiable by the other members of the group. In the Asch studies, he is sitting together with them in the same room. In the Mouton *et al.* study, he has to speak his name before giving his response. If he makes a deviant response, everyone will know.

There is also evidence, in a different situation, that deviants are rejected by other group members. Schachter (1951) had groups of students discuss a short case history concerning a juvenile delinquent, and recommend alternative courses of action, varying in harshness or leniency. A confederate who stubbornly defended a punitive recommendation, to which the majority was opposed, was clearly rejected by the other subjects, and was rated as an undesirable group-member. The largest proportion of remarks made during the discussion were also addressed to this confederate. In comparison, a confederate who adopted the modal position of the group was not rejected, and was addressed less frequently in the discussion, whereas another who moved from a deviant to a modal position in the course of the discussion received fewer communications after changing his position.

Possibly Asch's subjects feared a similar kind of rejection if they disagreed with the majority. This seems less likely in view of the fact that no group discussion took place, and is not easily reconciled with the findings that the unanimity of the majority was far more important than its sheer numerical preponderance. Nonetheless, one needs to know what would happen if subjects were able to make their responses in private, unobserved by other members of the group. Deutsch and Gerard (1955) found that subjects made, on average, just over 7 out of 13 conforming responses in an Asch line-judgement situation when responding publicly. Significantly fewer conforming responses were made when the naive subject responded in private, but the level (just under 6 out of 13) is still very high for any attempt to 'explain away' Asch's results as purely the result of a fear of rejection. Similar conclusions come from a study by Raven (1959), who presented subjects with the same case description used by Schachter (1951). Having made initial recommendations individually, subjects were presented with false information that the other members of the group, unlike them, were mostly in favour of an extremely punitive solution. Each subject was then asked to write an account of the case, either anonymously, or so that it could be passed round for the other group members to see. Having done so, the subjects again made individual recommendations. Of those who expected their accounts to be passed round, 39 per cent yielded to the bogus majority, as compared with 26 per cent of those had no such expectation. Once again, fear of being an *identified* deviate appears to have some effect, but not to be the whole story.

On balance, the evidence from studies of group influence on individual judgements, both in cases where the stimulus is ambiguous, and more dramatically even when it is not, suggest that a conforming response is best seen as an attempted solution to a dilemma that is essentially cognitive in nature. How can the subject deal with the fact that his perceptions appear to be different from those of other people who appear similar to himself? There is no real problem if the others' responses are in any way an unstable variable. The stimulus is simply not the kind of stimulus where one gets inter-observer consensus. But if everyone else *is* in consensus, some cognitive work has to be done: cognitive, that is, but not necessarily perceptual. As in more general kinds of psychophysical judgements (see Chapter 3), the question of whether changes on a response scale do, or do not, reflect changes in how a stimulus is 'really' perceived, remains complex, and not at all easy, and perhaps even impossible in principle, to settle empirically. There is an important middle ground between viewing a conforming response as a deliberate lie, and supposing that naive subjects begin to actually 'see' the stimuli in accordance with the majority norm. This is perhaps a reasonable possibility in the case of the autokinetic phenomenon, but rather less so in the Asch experiments. But we do not need to go nearly this far. It is enough to say that the violation of the subject's expectations is enough to make him uncertain as to which *response* is correct. Such uncertainty is likely to be even greater if his perceptions remain veridical, since then his expectations will remain violated. The problem is not whether his perceptions are in fact accurate, but whether he has confidence that they are. If such confidence is undermined, he may respond, even in private, in accordance with what he thinks he *ought* to see. That is, he may give the response which he regards as the best estimate of the correct answer, even if it does not correspond to what he *actually* sees.

DEVIANCE AND DIFFERENTIATION

In the experiments just described, the focus has been primarily on how the individual will adjust to the pressures exerted on him by other members of the group. In other words, the question of the relationship between groups and individuals, or between majorities and minorities, has been posed traditionally in terms of the influence of the group on the individual, or of the majority on the minority. Such an approach may provide insights into how individuals become socialized into a given system, but is arguably less relevant to the question of how that system may come to change. Moscovici has described this tradition: 'The phenomenon of deviance has been barely skimmed, and viewed only in relation to conformity. Very few studies have looked at the conditions in which a minority may take innovative initiatives and change group norms. Nor has the function of independence within the group been the object of any research.' (1976, page 43.)

Our attitudes towards nonconformists often can be quite ambivalent. In Schachter's (1951) study, there was clear evidence of rejection of the stubborn deviate by the majority, but on the other side Gerard and Greenbaum (1962) interviewed subjects who had taken part in conformity studies, and found that they gave stereotypically negative judgements of other members of the group who appeared to yield to a majority norm. As Moscovici points out, such results are difficult to reconcile with a view that individuals conform in order to gain esteem, since 'the only advantage of conformity that might be gained was to change in the eyes of the others from the status of deviant to the status of sheep' (1974, page 203). Innovation and originality receive acclaim just as surely as deviance and defiance cause offence. Historical examples abound where one person's hero has been another's heretic. Contemporarily, opposition to political systems from within may be seen as dissident or treacherous, radical or subversive. From a cynical point of view, it might be argued that nonconformists are admired only if they challenge *other people's* norms, or after history has 'proved them right'. But there is also a more positive possibility: that groups may themselves seek change, perhaps especially as desired goals appear more difficult to obtain, and therefore welcome or give prominence to those who will show them a new direction.

To deviate, in terms of its Latin derivation, means to 'leave the main road', and the metaphor can be quite revealing. If one can be sure that the main road is leading to where one wants to go, and that what is important is arriving at one's destination, then a suggestion that a better way of getting there would be to take another ('devious') route might seem stupid, inefficient, or dangerous. By the same token, forced diversions (or, as the French say, *déviations*) can cause frustration and delay. The Roman *via* was not 'just a road', but a major highway, essential to commerce and political control, and often passing through potentially hostile country. It would also represent the shortest and straightest route to one's destination. A reasonable analogy might be the railroads of America a century ago. To the ordinary traveller, as opposed to the explorer or adventurer, territories away from the main route would be inhospitable—unknown, uncivilized, undefended. Yet at the same time, the destination of the *via*, like that of the railroad, was fixed. If new territories were to be acquired, at some point an expedition would need to leave the familiar route, and strike out in a new direction, and this would be when the services of guides or pathfinders, either from among the native population, or from the less conforming colonists would be indispensable.

Lemaine (1974) has argued forcibly that an individual's need to differentiate himself from others is as essential to his feeling of identity as is his need to feel similar to others. He relates the notion of psychological differentiation to aspects of both Durkheim's and Darwin's theories, and, in the latter case particularly, the territorial metaphor is still appropriate: 'Darwinian competition is above all competition between close relations, and natural selection comes into play when, in a given region, there exist what might be called *vacant places* which can be better occupied when some of the existing inhabitants have undergone certain modifications' (page 18).

The traditional conformity model, in terms of which the group is seen as the source of rewards (acceptance) and punishments (rejection), thus appears far too simplistic. The individual can be in competition with the other members of his group for rewards such as those of status, recognition, or affection, and to achieve such rewards, he must take the essentially risky option of differentiating himself from the other members—in other words, he must find a 'vacant place' within the group where his presence will be valued, and of course he may fail in his search. Lemaine points to the diversification of research activity within the scientific community as being one of a number of real-life examples of this search for 'vacant places'. Scientific 'distinction' requires finding questions which others have not answered, and then answering them, and the rewards for doing so can far outweigh, at least symbolically, those for more conventional activity.

This need for an individual to differentiate himself from others implies that he might *not* wish to see himself, in all circumstances, as completely similar to the other members of his group. This may be so in spite of a general tendency for individuals to expect members of their own reference group to behave in similar ways to themselves, even to the extent of overestimating such similarity. (Hansen and Donoghue, 1977; Ross, Greene, and House, 1977; see Chapter 4, page 123 of the present book.)

Codol (1975) presents an abundance of evidence that individuals tend to see their own behaviour as more 'normative' than that of other members of their group. Codol's use of the term 'normative' deliberately implies the operation of two kinds of norms: 'factual' norms, which refer to conventional practices or customs, and 'desirable' norms, which refer to conventional values or ideals. Unfortunately, Codol does not commit himself with regard to the factors which may make either one of these two kinds of norms the more salient in any situation. Nonetheless, according to Codol, whether the individual is asked to compare himself with other members of an experimentally created group, or of a real-life social category to which he belongs, he will tend to describe himself as closer to the standard or ideal of the group than he describes the other group members. This tendency, which Codol calls 'superior conformity of the self', seems to imply that the individual sets a positive value on his group membership. The interesting thing is that he can do so at the same time as he attempts to distinguish himself from the rest of his group.

The contest for 'vacant places', however, does not simply occur within a group. It may also occur between groups. The more general significance of this for intergroup relations will be dealt with shortly, but one immediate implication which seems to follow is that there will be many circumstances in which *groups need their deviants*, or active minorities. If a group is unsure of its own direction, it will be more likely to listen to someone who claims to know the way, even if that way is different.

In an experimental context, what may be involved may be no more than the need to achieve a reasonable consensus on a group discussion topic, or a successful solution to a problem. Sometimes an element of intergroup competition is introduced explicitly, but even without this, a confident minority can have a marked influence on the behaviour of the majority. A question that arises, therefore, is how a minority presents itself as being confident of its position without permanently antagonizing the other group members.

Recognizing the dangers to group members who take an innovative stance, Hollander (1964) suggested that an individual would be more likely to be accepted as a leader if he accumulates 'credits' by first showing competence and conforming to expectations. Moscovici (1976, page 48) cites this as an example of research which is 'solely concerned with innovating behaviour and non-conformity at the top end of the social scale'. The very mention of the term 'leader' invokes memories of an earlier era of 'small group' research, concerned with issues such as the qualities of a 'good leader', and the efficiency of different kinds of hierarchical structures and communication systems. Accounts of this systematic body of research are easily available in the textbooks of the 'sixties, such as Hollander's own (1964), and those by Jones and Gerard (1967), and Secord and Backman (1964). It is not therefore my purpose to redescribe it here. On the other hand, Moscovici's (1976, page 67) assertion that 'Every group member, irrespective of his rank, is a potential source and receiver of influence' suggests that questions may be asked in this field which do not presuppose a rigid structure or network of relationships. Indeed, the function of innovation may be precisely to change the nature of any such prevailing structure or social system.

Contrary to Hollander's hypothesis, Wahrman and Pugh (1972) demonstrated that an *early* innovative stand can have greater influence. They had groups of four subjects perform a task which required them to decide on a common strategy before each trial. One member of each group was a confederate, who showed varying degrees of disruptive or deviant behaviour, claiming that he was better at the task than the other subjects. The timing of this deviant behaviour constituted the main manipulation, and it was found that the earlier the confederate started asserting himself in this way, the more likely it was that the other subjects would accept his suggestions.

There is also evidence that a consistent minority can influence a majority to change its position. In an experiment by Moscovici, Lage, and Naffrechoux (1969), female subjects were tested in groups of six and were required to judge whether a series of colour slides were blue or green. In fact, all the slides were blue, but they varied in light intensity. In a control condition, only 0.25 per cent of subjects' responses were 'Green'. However, in an experimental condition, where two of the subjects, acting as confederates, consistently said, 'Green' on every trial, the total number of 'Green' responses made by the naive subjects increased to 8·42 per cent. Nearly one in three of these subjects made at least one 'Green' response. These judgements were made publicly in a group setting, but in a second part of the same experiment, each subject was presented privately with sixteen more slides to categorize as 'Blue' or 'Green'. Of these, three were unambiguously blue and three were unambiguously green, while the remainder were blue-green. Subjects who had been in the experimental condition were more likely than the controls to judge these blue-green stimuli as 'Green' rather than 'Blue'. Interestingly, this tendency was even stronger among those subjects who had *not* given any judgements of 'Green' in the group setting. On the basis of these data, public compliance would not seem to be a necessary condition of private change in judgement in response to social influence.

Nemeth, Swedlund, and Kanki (1974) followed up this study with an investigation of the effects of the consistency of the minority's position. As in the Moscovici *et al.* (1969) study, the stimuli were blue slides varying in light intensity, and subjects were tested in groups of six which included two confederates. In the main phase of the experiment, the two confederates responded 'Green' to half the stimuli and 'Green and Blue' to the other half. In one condition, these responses were given in a random order, unrelated to the light intensity of the stimuli. In a second condition, the confederates responded 'Green' to the dimmest half of the stimulus series and 'Green and Blue' to the brightest half. In a third condition, the pattern of the confederates' responses were reversed. The naive subjects were influenced by the two confederates in the latter two conditions, to the extent that they gave 'Green' responses on nearly a quarter of the trials. In the first condition, however, almost no 'Green' responses were given, suggesting that majorities are unlikely to be influenced by minorities whose judgements appear inconsistent. These results confirm those of an additional experiment reported by Moscovici *et al.* (1969) in which naive subjects were not influenced by confederates who similarly responded 'Green' to half the stimuli, and 'Blue' to the other half, but in a random order.

The assumption that there should be reasonable interpersonal consensus in judgements of physical reality does not seem to oblige individuals to accommodate, in such a consensus, the judgement of deviants who fail to show even *intra*personal consistency. On the other hand, the judgements of a *consistent* and apparently confident minority cannot be dismissed so easily, and indeed such minorities appear to have far greater influence than might have been inferred from the early demonstrations of individuals yielding to groups, or of groups rejecting their deviants. Consistency appears to be a more important ingredient of social influence than numerical superiority, suggesting that the phenomena described in this chapter cannot be understood if groups are seen as purely coercive, rather than as sources of information and comparison.

GROUP DECISIONS AND THE 'RISKY SHIFT'

In most of the studies described so far in this chapter, the emphasis has been on the confrontation of majorities and minorities over simple perceptual judgements, where the stimuli have no special significance in themselves. The question therefore arises of how groups resolve divergences of opinion over issues where disagreement may be less atypical, but possibly more threatening to the group's goals.

Much of the early interest in group decision-making stemmed from the work of Lewin (1943, 1958) on the commitment of individuals to behavioural changes agreed upon in groups. Lewin showed that students were more prepared to change their diets, and housewives were more prepared to cook less popular meats (e.g., offals) or to feed their babies cod liver oil, orange juice, etc., after agreeing on group goals than after simply listening to lectures. Since then, there has been a considerable volume of research, which I shall not attempt to review here, concerning decision-making in particular kinds of real-life groups (or their experimental analogues) such as management-union negotiating teams, and juries. However, one finding from this mainly applied literature somehow caught the imagination of more laboratory-based social psychologists and led to a quite remarkable spate of research during the late 'sixties and early 'seventies. This was, that groups who had to make decisions involving risk appeared to make 'riskier' decisions together than they did individually—the so-called 'risky shift'.

This effect was first noted by Ziller (1957) in a military context, but it was a study by Stoner (1961) which set the tone for most of the experiments in this area. Stoner's interest was in the riskiness of management decisions, and for this reason he administered to his subjects a questionnaire developed by Wallach and Kogan (1959, 1961) as a supposed measure of generalized individual differences in the tendency to take risks. This questionnaire (see Kogan and Wallach, 1964) consists of 12 'choice-dilemmas', each of which presents subjects with an hypothetical situation requiring a choice between a cautious option, which if chosen would lead to moderate but certain outcomes for the central hypothetical character, and a risky option, which might lead to much better outcomes, if successful, or to much worse outcomes, if it failed. Subjects are required to state the *lowest* probability of the risky option succeeding (in terms of so many chances in 10 of success) which they feel would be sufficient to justify recommending the risky course of action. A selection of a higher probability is thus taken to imply greater caution. The dilemmas themselves involve such situations as an engineer choosing whether to leave a steady job for a more speculative one, a graduating chemist deciding whether to apply for an easy or difficult graduate school, a captain of a football team deciding whether or not to play for a draw, and so on. Stoner's innovation was to present subjects with these choice-dilemmas as topics for group discussion, after they had completed the questionnaire individually. When subjects were required to reach a consensus, they tended to make riskier recommendations in the group than they had done individually.

The earlier researchers in this field seemed in little doubt that it was indeed risk-taking which they were measuring, and the theories they proposed to account for this effect treated risk as a central concept. One such theory proposed that groups were riskier than individuals because of 'diffusion of responsibility' within the group (Wallach, Kogan, and Bem, 1964). A major empirical problem with this explanation is that it attributes the shift to shared responsibility for the *decision*, rather than to anything that might have happened in the preceding discussion. Lamm (1967) found risky shifts of normal size when subjects watched a live discussion group, but did not participate in the group's decision. Pruitt and Teger (1969) failed to find a risky shift in a gambling situation where groups decided on a level of risk without discussion. Wallach and Kogan (1965) observed risky shifts when subjects had to reach a consensus after discussion, or had to reformulate their individual opinions after discussion without needing to reach a consensus, but not when they had to reach a consensus without discussion. Intuitively also, the notion of diffusion of responsibility for such purely hypothetical decisions seems pretty far-fetched.

Another set of explanations involve variations on an idea proposed by Brown (1965), that there is a generalized 'value for risk' in Western culture. One possible implication of this idea is that people who are *generally* more predisposed to take risks are more likely to be seen as influential by their fellow group-members, that is, to assume a leadership position in the group. The evidence does not support this prediction (Wallach, Kogan, and Burt, 1968), although, *on individual items*, those subjects whose positions are adopted by other group-members are seen, not surprisingly, as being the most influential.

Some supportive evidence comes from studies which have attempted to find the levels of risk which subjects evaluate most positively. Levinger and Schneider (1969) asked subjects to state not only the level of risk which they would find acceptable, but also the level which they felt that most of their 'fellow students here' would choose, and in addition the choice which they 'would admire most'. For most of the items on the choice-dilemma questionnaire, subjects perceived themselves as more likely to endorse a risky choice than their fellow group members, but still perceived the ideal ('most admired') choice as riskier than their own. This result is clearly in line with Codol's (1975) notion of the 'superior conformity of the self', discussed earlier in this chapter. On the other hand, Pruitt (1969) had subjects first rate the different levels of risk as 'risky' or 'cautious', and then make their own decisions in a separate booklet. Contrary to what would be predicted from Brown's (1965, page 701) suggestion that 'people mean to be risky', subjects decided in favour of levels of risk which they had previously rated as 'cautious'.

The observation that most influenced the development of 'value' explanations, however, was the finding of relatively stable differences between the different items in the choice-dilemma questionnaire regarding the size of the risky shift. On one of the 12 items, in fact, the shift was usually in a *cautious* direction, and on another, it was often so. Because of this, Brown (1965, page 705) qualifies his position to say that 'we value both risk and caution, according to the circumstances'. In other words, both a cultural value for risk and one for caution are postulated, and the appearance of risky or cautious shifts depends on which of these general values is the more predominant. It is important to note that the suggestion is that value is attached to risk or caution *as such*, rather than to specific risky or cautious options on the individual dilemmas. Compatible with this approach is the finding that the riskiness or cautiousness of initial choices on an item is a good predictor of whether the group shifts in a risky or cautious direction (e.g., Teger and Pruitt, 1967).

To a large extent, the 'value for risk' notion appears to be an historical accident of the composition of the Wallach and Kogan questionnaire and the scaling assumptions on which it was based. As has already been mentioned, it was originally intended as a personality test of stable individual differences in the tendency to take risks. It was assumed, therefore, that someone who said he would accept odds of only 3 in 10 on a given dilemma was 'riskier' than someone who said he would accept odds of no less than 7 in 10. Moreover, the common practice of summing ratings over different items to derive an overall score of 'riskiness' assumes that (1) subjects' selections of acceptable odds can be treated as scores on an absolute scale of riskiness, i.e., the level of riskiness represented by any given response (e.g., 3 in 10) is the same across the different dilemmas; and (2) the choice-dilemmas are somehow representative of a known universe of such situations. Both of these assumptions distract attention from an analysis of the individual items. Thus, in spite of the finding of some cautious shifts, the hypothesis of a predominant value for risk survived for apparently no better reason than the fact that 'risk-oriented' items predominate over 'caution-oriented' items in the Wallach and Kogan questionnaire.

With respect to the first assumption, it seems unreasonable to regard a given chance-level as risky or cautious, without considering the importance of the possible consequences. There is nothing 'cautious', for instance, about playing Russian roulette, even if the chances of killing oneself are only 1 in 6. An approach based on subjective expected utility theory (Vinokur, 1971; Vinokur and Burnstein, 1974; Vinokur, Trope, and Burnstein, 1975) analyses preferences and shifts towards risk or caution in terms of subjects' perceptions of the utility (desirability) of the different possible outcomes on each dilemma *taken individually*. Although some of the assumptions of this approach are challenged by Coombs and Huang (1970, 1977), the emphasis on *specific* expected values is more amenable to empirical investigation than the notion of *general* values for risk or caution as such.

With respect to the second assumption, it is not in fact difficult to construct dilemmas which are biased towards caution rather than risk. The item in the original questionnaire which produced the most reliable cautious shifts has as its central character a man who is contemplating marriage, but is so worried by recent disagreements with his fiancée that they have consulted a marriage counsellor. The cautious option here is *not* to get married, which is what most subjects recommend. Fraser, Gouge, and Billig (1971) succeeded in constructing a number of such dilemmas, where both initial preferences and group shifts went in a cautious direction, and also showed that these effects were not restricted to the original 'minimal odds' response scale, but could be reproduced on a Likert-type scale of degree of preference for the risky or cautious option. Even so, these authors were still prepared to entertain the idea that a general value for risk, applicable to all situations, might operate over and above other specific factors to produce the finding that risky shifts are typically more frequent than cautious shifts.

Similar conclusions were reached by Madaras and Bem (1968), who had subjects rate risk-takers and risk-rejectors in the context of each dilemma on a number of semantic differential scales. On dilemmas where initial preferences and group shifts tend to be 'risky', Madaras and Bem claimed to show that risk-takers were rated more positively than risk-rejectors, although the scales which showed the largest differences were not, in fact, purely evaluative, but were loaded on the potency and activity factors (cf. Osgood, Suci, and Tannenbaum, 1957). On caution-oriented items, this preference for risk-takers over risk-rejectors was reduced or reversed, but the general overall preference for risk-takers is taken as support for Brown. In fact, these data are weakened by a simple confounding of evaluative and descriptive meaning in the labelling of the scales. The scale showing the largest differences in evaluation was 'passive-active'. Madaras and Bem regard 'active' as the more positive term, and derive support for their conclusions from the finding that risk-takers are rated as definitely active on risk-oriented items and still moderately active on caution-oriented items. An alternative interpretation is that risk-takers are rated as more active than risk-rejectors on descriptive grounds, but the size of this difference depends on the subjects' evaluations of risk or caution on each dilemma.

To test this interpretation, I presented subjects with a series of 10 novel choice-dilemmas, so constructed that on 5 most people would favour the risky alternative and on the others most people would favour the cautious alternative (Eiser, 1976). Subjects individually rated both the risky and cautious options described in each dilemma on four scales, two of which were chosen so that the term denoting risk would be the more positive in value connotation (cowardly-courageous, unenterprising-enterprising) and two where the direction of value connotation was reversed (careful-foolhardy, prudent-imprudent). As was predicted on the basis of the attitudinal judgement effects found by Eiser and Mower White (1974a, 1975; see Chapter 3), the difference in rating between the risky and cautious options was larger on the former pair of scales for those dilemmas where the risky alternative was preferred, but larger on the latter pair of scales for dilemmas where the cautious alternative was preferred. On the basis of these data, one cannot infer that any general value for risk predominates over a value for caution.

Madaras and Bem also report an experiment in which groups discussed only five of the ten risk-oriented dilemmas in the Wallach and Kogan questionnaire, but gave recommendations on all ten. Their reasoning was that, if the crucial factor was the *general* level of risk preferred by others in the groups, this should be communicated adequately by just the five dilemmas discussed, and so any risky shift on these items should generalize to the other items also. The data failed to support this prediction, implying instead that 'the crucial information transmitted in group discussion is not the risk level of others, but information relevant to the specific items discussed' (1968, page 360).

GROUP POLARIZATION

More recent research suggests that so-called risky and cautious shifts may have little to do with risk at all, but are simply examples of a more general phenomenon termed 'group polarization'. Moscovici and Zavalloni (1969) had French high school students give individual ratings of their opinions towards de Gaulle and towards Americans, discuss these opinions until they reached a consensus, and then give their individual ratings again. In a further condition, subjects had to discuss the favourability or unfavourability of the items used in the attitude scale about de Gaulle—that is, they had to give typical social judgements before and after group discussion, without rating their own agreement with the statements. In all conditions, the extremity of subjects' responses was greater after than before the group discussion. Other studies have also shown that groups, on average, become more extreme in their responses following group discussion, using material unrelated to risk. Myers and Bishop (1970) used the issue of racial attitudes, and found that group discussion led groups consisting of prejudiced subjects to become more racist in their expressed attitudes, and groups consisting of less prejudiced subjects to become even less racist. Doise (1969) also found shifts towards extremity following group discussion using the issue of French students' attitudes towards their academic institution. These shifts were more marked when the students also had to indicate how they felt their school was perceived by students of a rival institution.

McCauley (1972), however, has pointed out that such increases in group extremity do not necessarily imply that all, or even most, of the individuals in the group become more extreme after group discussion. The paradox arises because the initial judgements of the group members can lie on either side of the neutral point. In such cases, individuals can converge on a consensus which is *more* extreme than the average of their initial positions, but still *less* extreme (in absolute terms) than their initial positions considered individually. McCauley found increases in group extremity without increases in individual extremity with both attitudinal and risk material, pointing out that the previously cited studies of group polarization report changes in group averages, but not individual extremity. Group polarization is therefore not necessarily an exception to the tendency which one would predict from the conformity literature for a convergence of individual judgements as a result of group interaction.

But what is it about the group discussion that produces these shifts anyway? It is only recently that researchers have started to give this question the attention it deserves. As Cartwright (1971, page 376) commented on the earlier work: 'Despite the demonstrated importance of group discussion for the occurrence of shifts, almost nothing is known about its nature. It is clear that discussion serves in some way to reconcile differences in initial choices and brings about a reduction in their variance, but it is not clear how this is accomplished.'

A few indicators do now seem to be emerging as to the important ingredients of group discussion. The size of a group shift appears generally to be a direct function of the divergence of the initial opinions of the individual group members (Hermann and Kogan, 1968; Hoyt and Stoner, 1968). Brown (1965, page 702) assumed that it was awareness of others' choices that produced shifts: 'The content of the discussion, the arguments pro and con, are of no importance by this theory. It is the information about other people's answers that makes individuals move toward greater risk after group discussion.'

However, this proposition is clearly incompatible with the regular finding that mere exchange of information about others' opinions without group discussion fails to produce shifts (Teger and Pruitt, 1967; Wallach and Kogan, 1965). Moscovici, Doise, and Dulong (1972, page 390) therefore argue instead that: 'Divergence or the presence of an extreme individual in a group has no influence as such. What is decisive is the interaction triggered by this divergence and this presence.'

Moscovici et al. report two experiments in which the size of group shifts was reduced by devices designed to make subjects try to reach a compromise, instead of fully discussing the reasons for their differences of position. These devices consisted of instructions which encouraged subjects, in one experiment, to follow strict rules of procedure during the group decision process and the preceding discussion, and, in the other experiment, to pay attention to the time. The positive correlations between the size of group shifts and divergences of initial individual positions found under control conditions were also absent when these requirements were imposed. Moscovici et al. interpret these data as showing that interactions in which subjects communicate their 'preferences' but not their 'opinions' (i.e., the arguments in favour of their preferences) do not lead to polarization.

The importance of the arguments put forward during the course of group discussion has also been stressed by a number of researchers. In one condition of an experiment by St Jean (1970), subjects were instructed to 'discuss only the pros and cons attached to the risky action without revealing their own risk preferences'. This produced almost as large shifts as in normal discussion conditions. Vinokur and Burnstein (1974) and Vinokur, Trope, and Burnstein (1975) have analysed the persuasive arguments put forward in the course of group discussion in terms of how they relate to the utilities of the specific risky and cautious actions. In terms of simple frequency, more pro-risk arguments were generated on items shifting to risk, and more pro-caution arguments on items shifting to caution. Arguments were found to be most influential when they contained information which was only 'partially shared', i.e., not previously thought of by all group members. Furthermore, shifts were produced by having subjects simply read the arguments (Vinokur and Burnstein, 1974). Such arguments were directed towards changes in the assessment of utilities specific to each dilemma, rather than concerned with the values of risk or caution as such (Vinokur et al., 1975).

Vinokur and Burnstein (1978) have extended their 'persuasive arguments' theory to cover cases where the group-members' attitudes become *less* polarized as a result of discussion. These cases are predicted to arise when there is no initial majority in favour of one side of the issue, so that a fairly even distribution of arguments on either side is expected. Vinokur and Burnstein show clear evidence of depolarization effects, and although they do not report any content analysis of the arguments generated in the discussion, they found stronger effects on items dealing with less familiar issues. This is taken as support for their theory, since, if the issue is unfamiliar, there should be more novel or 'partially shared' information contained in the arguments.

With a few such exceptions, however, the last few years seem to have witnessed some decline in the popularity of this area. The reason may partly be that the questions now being asked are very different from those which led to the first 'gold rush' to find an explanation for the 'risky shift'. These newer questions demand attention to the ways in which the individuals within the discussion groups process the information communicated to them by the experimenter and the other members of their group, to how *specific* values and arguments are made salient during the course of discussion, and to how the need for individuals to justify their opinions in front of their peers can lead to changes in attitude and level of commitment. The early excitement in this field seemed to be based on the expectation that groups could be shown to make different kinds of decisions from individuals, and that therefore there was a special kind of discontinuity between small group phenomena and the rest of social psychology. Perhaps it came as some disappointment to find that those effects which could be replicated still required for their explanation a consideration of individual cognitions.

INFORMATION INTEGRATION AND DECISIONS IN GROUPS

Such a consideration of individual cognitions is basic to recent applications of integration theory to group decision processes. Anderson and Graesser (1976) have looked at the issue of the effects of persuasive argumentation from a different point of view from that proposed by Vinokur and Burnstein. Their principal objection to the Vinokur and Burnstein approach is that they regard the single argument as too small a unit of analysis, since a simple tally of pro and anti arguments takes no account of the manner in which such arguments are presented, and by whom. Instead, they propose that the contribution of each individual group-member should be considered as a 'molar unit' of information, and that the attitude change produced by group discussion can be predicted from a combination of these units according to the weighted average rule of integration theory.

Assuming an asymmetrical distribution of initial attitudes, group polarization should occur if the information (arguments) contributed by each member is more extreme than his own position. For this to be so, all that is required, according to integration theory, is that each individual should simply convey the information on which his own opinion is based, since his own opinion should be a weighted average of this information and a neutral initial impression, and hence less polarized than the information itself. If, on the other hand, the initial opinions of the group-members are symmetrically distributed, the weighted average rule predicts depolarization, as found by Vinokur and Burnstein (1978).

Integration theory has also been applied to the judgements of guilt or innocence made by jurors. Immediately, it should be stressed that one is hardly ever, in this field of research, talking about the actual judgements made in real-life juries, whose deliberations are protected from outside scrutiny for very good reasons. Instead, conclusions are based on either of two basic paradigms: (1) the presentation of case summaries to individual subjects, who then state their assessment of the hypothetical defendant's guilt or innocence; or (2) group decision situations varying considerably in their degree of correspondence to those encountered by real-life juries, in which the subjects have to reach a verdict on the basis of evidence presented in summary form, or in a form corresponding more or less closely to the content of actual case transcripts. Inspite of the rather chaotic procedural heterogeneity of this research field, though, two questions for integration theory stand out: first how individuals integrate different pieces of evidence so as to form a personal judgement of the defendant's guilt or innocence, and second how these personal judgements change as a function of the information and arguments presented by the other 'jurors' during the course of discussion.

The first of these questions is no different, in principle, from that of how individuals integrate information in any other person perception task. Nonetheless, some specific features of the integration process have relevance to the broader question of how far the way jurors react to evidence corresponds to the assumptions and prescriptions of the judicial system. Are jurors able to disregard information about personal characteristics of the defendant which would not be strictly admissible as evidence? An experiment by Kaplan and Kemmerick (1974) suggests that they do not, but instead average information about personal characteristics in with the information contained in the trial evidence.

Do jurors start from a presumption that the defendent is innocent, as the law prescribes, or do they take the very fact that the defendant has been sent for trial as a basis for assuming something nearer to, say, a fifty-fifty chance of guilt? Ostrom, Werner, and Saks (1978) estimated initial presumptions of guilt or innocence by presenting subjects with differing amounts of information in the form of written statements of evidence, and concluded that the presumption of innocence held both for student subjects, and for subjects who had served on a real jury during the preceding two-and-a-half years. However, they are careful to stress that their results, '... show only that jurors can presume innocence under the present idealized, abstract conditions. It does not show that jurors do, in fact, presume innocence in the much more complex setting of the courtroom.' (Page 446.)

Less comforting evidence comes from an experiment reported by Kaplan (1977). Subjects were presented with a one-page summary of a case, which was either very, or not very, incriminating, and were told either that the summary was an unreliable account of the evidence (written by an inept clerk, since dismissed) or a reliable account (written by a respected judge). As would be expected, the evidence had less influence when categorized as unreliable. Particularly interesting, though, is the finding that unreliable less-incriminating evidence led to *less* definite judgements of innocence than reliable less-incriminating evidence, at least for subjects who held relatively punitive attitudes in general. This suggests that these subjects started from a *neutral* initial position—from which they were moved more by the reliable than unreliable evidence—rather than from a presumption of innocence.

When it comes to considering how the opinions of different jurors are integrated in the course of discussion, the model suggested by Anderson and Graesser (1976) seems as plausible as in the case of group decisions concerning risk. As in other situations, polarization occurs in the direction of the predominant prediscussion impression of the weight of evidence; furthermore, polarization is stronger, the less redundancy in the information content of the discussion (Kaplan, 1977), as would be expected from both persuasive arguments theory and integration theory. Anderson and Graesser suggest that polarization results from individuals conveying the information on which their own opinions are based, but holding opinions which are initially less extreme than such information, i.e., opinions which are a weighted average of a *neutral* initial impression and that information. If they are right, the presence of polarization implies that jurors start from an initial position close to the neutral point on the innocent-guilty scale, rather than a presumption of innocence.

There is a vitally important difference, however, between predicting how individual group members will change their attitudes during the course of group discussion, and predicting how such change will be translated into a group decision. A theory of decision-making by *jurors*, therefore, is incomplete if it is to be used as a theory of decision-making by *juries*. Predicting group decisions requires not only a consideration of individual cognitive processes as a starting point, but also an understanding of the rules used by the group-members to translate a *distribution* of preferences into a *single* judgement. A variety of such rules, or 'social decision schemes' have been described by Davis (1973). In a 'risky shift' experiment, the use of a continuous response scale, for example, allows for a 'consensus' to be achieved through compromise or averaging of individual judgements. This is very different from the simple majority rule used by representative bodies such as parliament, and different rules again are used to choose the members of such representative bodies under different electoral systems.

With juries, there may be both variations in the prescribed social decision scheme (e.g., the directions given by the judge) and also differences between the prescribed scheme and that actually used by the jurors. For example, a difference in the social decision scheme is implied if jurors are faced with a simple choice between 'Guilty' and 'Not guilty', or have the additional option, as under Scottish law, of returning a verdict of 'Not proven'. Yet another difference is implied if multiple charges are being considered, so that the defendant might, for example, be acquitted of murder but convicted of manslaughter. Also, the judge may require a unanimous verdict, or alternatively say he would accept a majority verdict. This is particularly important, in that jurors may adopt a majority-rule scheme even when instructed to achieve unanimity, as when a minority may be persuaded to 'go along with the majority' to produce a unanimous verdict, even if they still dissent in their private opinions. The points which Davis raises, therefore, are an important reminder of the need to understand the explicit and implicit ground-rules of concrete social situations if one is to make any useful or valid generalization from the laboratory to the outside world, or from abstract theory to application.

DEINDIVIDUATION

An approach which seems to start from the assumption that group behaviour is qualitatively different from other social psychological phenomena is that of Zimbardo (1969a,b). His basic distinction is between 'individuated' and 'deindividuated' behaviour. The individuated person is viewed as acting rationally and consistently, in control of his own behaviour and, as far as possible, of his environment: 'consistency becomes a self-imposed principle in order for the individual to maintain a conception of himself as a normal member of society who, in behaving as others expect him to, gains their social recognition (the most potent of all reinforcers) as a rational decision-maker, whose decisions help him to control his environment.' (1969a, page 280).

This familiar picture is contrasted with that of the deindividuated person, acting on unrestrained primitive impulse, engaging in orgies of rape, murder, torture, theft, and vandalism, or indeed any evil or delinquent act that is not easily explained in other ways (Zimbardo, 1969b). Although not proposed as an absolutely necessary, let alone sufficient, condition for these effects, anonymous membership of a group is assumed to be an important antecedent of the 'deindividuation process'. This process is supposed to involve a minimization of self-observation and concern for social evaluation, followed by a weakening of controls based upon guilt, shame, fear, and commitment, and a lowered threshold for expressing inhibited behaviours. The person may then get 'carried away' by the contagious arousal of group activity, and enter a chain reaction of destruction and brutality.

Although the debt to Freud is not acknowledged in Zimbardo's (1969b) paper, the notion of primitive impulses (the id?) held in check by rational control (the ego?) and socialized ideals and moral norms (the superego?) is by no means innovatory. Perhaps, though, these older ideas are the right ones after all: so what is Zimbardo's evidence?

The evidence which Zimbardo presents can be crudely summarized as follows: that (1) acts of brutality by individuals acting in groups are a feature of modern life, and (2) acts of brutality can also be performed by experimental subjects, granted suitably 'deindividuating' conditions. The first of these points is never in dispute, although it is for historians to judge whether things are better or worse than they used to be: what is problematic is how such events are to be explained. The second point is more provocative, although by now you will be familiar with the experiments on obedience and victim derogation described in Chapter 8. The data which Zimbardo (1969b) presents are in fact obtained from a very similar paradigm, with naive subjects being put in the situation where they have the opportunity to deliver electric shocks to a victim. Zimbardo's innovation was to run subjects in groups, and, in the critical experimental condition, have them wear over-sized lab coats and a hood over their heads, making them look strikingly similar to members of the Ku Klux Klan, and, of course, unidentifiable by each other. Female college students administered longer durations of electric shock to a simulated victim when thus 'deindividuated' than when identifiable by each other. Contrary to expectations, however, opposite results were obtained using Belgian soldiers as subjects. Zimbardo explains this contradiction by suggesting that the soldiers in the 'deindividuation' condition in fact felt *more* alone than those who were not required to wear a hood, but instead were tested together with their friends (who were all uniformed anyway).

This leaves the rather unsatisfactory state of affairs that the principal experimental manipulation can have opposite effects, depending on its significance for the particular group of subjects used, and this significance is inferred *post hoc*. Decreased self-consciousness should lead to greater aggression, but the bizarre business of donning a hood could make subjects feel more, not less, self-conscious. To attempt to clarify this problem, therefore, Zimbardo repeated his first experiment, with one change: subjects were tested alone. What happened as a result was that the hooded subjects were *less* aggressive than those not made to wear a hood. The inference is that a manipulation that makes subjects feel anonymous within a group can set the 'deindividuation process' in motion and lead to less inhibition of aggressive acts, but if the same manipulation makes subjects feel alone, it can have the reverse effect. There are nonetheless some untidy loose ends to this argument. Why should the soldiers have acted more aggressively when identifiable by their peers, whereas the reverse was true of the college students? Because they were already uniformed? Because they were a more cohesive group in terms of previous acquaintanceship? Because of their military training? The list is almost endless. There is also the obvious confounding of sex, which, though not necessarily important, would have been easy to control. Clearly, these experiments, whilst showing that strange manipulations can have strange effects, leave many questions unanswered with regard to the inter-relationships between identification with a group, anonymity, feelings of being alone, and what Duval and Wicklund (1972) term 'objective self-awareness' (see Chapter 6).

The aggression shown by these subjects was, nonetheless, only simulated, and was administered at a distance. Not so in Zimbardo's most controversial study, commonly known as the Stanford prison experiment. The most complete account of the data obtained in this study is to be found in Haney, Banks, and Zimbardo (1973), but a more vivid impression of what went on is conveyed by the photographs and accompanying recordings which have been edited and marketed as a teaching package. The study was an attempt to look at 'interpersonal dynamics in a prison environment', using what the authors term a 'functional' simulation of a prison, in which male students played the roles of prisoners and guards for an extended period of time. Activities and experiences were created, which, while not 'literal' simulations of actual prison life, 'were expected to produce qualitatively similar psychological reactions in our subjects—feelings of power and powerlessness, of control and oppression, of satisfaction and frustration, of arbitrary rule and resistance to authority, of status and anonymity, of machismo and emasculation' (page 72).

Subjects were male students who answered a newspaper advertisement for volunteers for a psychological study of prison life, in return for payment of $15 per day. The final sample consisted of 10 'prisoners' and 11 'guards', whose roles were assigned on a random basis. The mock prison was built in a basement corridor of the Stanford University psychology building, and included three small cells (6 ft × 9 ft) in which the prisoners slept in threes, as well as a solitary confinement room (2 ft × 2 ft × 7 ft). The prisoners remained in the prison 24 hours a day, wore nylon stocking caps on their head (to simulate having their hair cut short), a loosely fitting muslin smock with an identification number in front, no underclothes, rubber sandals on their feet and a chain and lock around one ankle. The guards wore plain khaki shirts and trousers, reflecting sun glasses (to prevent eye contact), and carried whistles and wooden batons, and attended in shifts. Various other details of the initial set-up also served to stress the inferiority of the prisoners such as a 'delousing' procedure, and the rule that they could refer to each other only by number. They also had all been unexpectedly 'arrested' with the cooperation of the local police and charged with suspicion of burglary or armed robbery 'often as curious neighbours looked on' (page 76).

Apart from some minor restrictions, the guards were given extremely wide discretion in the methods they could devise to keep order in the prison. Very quickly, however, the guards' use of their arbitrary authority escalated as they were faced first with taunts, and then more hostile resistance from the prisoners, until the prisoners' will was broken.

A very clear picture emerges of almost everyone involved losing touch with the reality that it was only a simulation, and being completely consumed by their roles. Essentially, the experiment got completely out of hand, to the point where five of the prisoners had to be released 'because of extreme emotional depression, crying, rage, and acute anxiety' (page 81). Finally: 'When the experiment was terminated prematurely after only six days [it had originally been scheduled for two weeks], all the remaining prisoners were delighted by their unexpected good fortune. In contrast, most of the guards seemed to be distressed by the decision' (page 81).

Was it all worth it? This question has to be considered in two parts. The first is whether it served a useful social purpose. Certainly the experiment attracted sufficient publicity to allow it to provide a springboard for a more general criticism of penal institutions. Yet this criticism is weakened considerably by the fact that so many departures from actual prison procedure were employed that those people whom Zimbardo might have wished to persuade could well say to themselves 'That wouldn't happen in a real prison'. Indeed, the fact that things go so out of hand might even be used as a justification for existing practices. The authors talk of ethical and legal considerations which led them to devise a 'functional' rather than a 'literal' simulation. The end product does not strike me personally as noticeably more ethical than the real thing. Moreover, there seems to have been no ethical, legal, or practical imperative (at least, none that is explained) that required a simulation study rather than a naturalistic observation study, or even a participant observation study of the kind courageously performed by Rosenhan (1973) in psychiatric hospitals. The main justification seems to lie in the need felt by the authors to disprove the 'dispositional hypothesis' that 'the state of the social institution of prison is due to the "nature" of the people who administer it, or the "nature" of the people who populate it, or both' (page 70). Indeed, the battery of personality measures administered to subjects before the start of the simulation predicted little of their behaviour.

The second aspect to the question 'Was it worth it?' concerns the value of any findings from a scientific point of view. Apart from the 'dispositional hypothesis' just mentioned, the analysis does not set out to test specific hypotheses. About all that can be said is that a very strong and unpleasant experimental procedure had some very strong and unpleasant effects, but no real attempt can be made to try to separate out which aspects of the situation had the greatest influence. In this respect, this study compares unfavourably with the much more systematic approach of Milgram (1974).

Was deindividuation the crucial factor? We simply can't say. Certainly the guards thought of themselves as guards, and seemed to lose any initial self-consciousness about playing their roles, to the point where the roles became reality. On the other hand, the anonymity imposed on the prisoners does not seem to have facilitated the expression of similar aggressive 'impulses', except perhaps towards themselves. In neither case, however, does there seem to be particularly strong evidence of the kind of irrational frenzy postulated by Zimbardo (1969b). The prisoners' depression may be seen as a quite 'rational' response to their loss of control over their environment. The escalation of punitiveness on the part of the guards until resistance to their authority was crushed may also be seen as a quite 'rational' response to a situation in which they may have believed that if they were soft they would have a riot on their hands. Both groups seem to have been searching for some meaning and consistency in the situation, and found it in the administration and observation of the prison rules.

Even, therefore, where one has people of normal healthy backgrounds acting in a destructive or self-destructive way, it cannot be definitely said that this is the result of deindividuation. If the individuated person is someone who attempts to gain the social recognition of others by behaving as they expect him to, then the same could be said of the guards and prisoners in this study, as well as people indulging in the kinds of 'deindividuated' behaviour which Zimbardo describes. The difference between individuated and deindividuated behaviour, as postulated by Zimbardo, seems to depend on the *particular* social expectations involved and the *particular* kind of social recognition that is being sought, rather than on the presence or absence of a group, or on the rationality or irrationality of the thought processes of the individuals involved. Even frenzied behaviour may be susceptible to cognitive analysis, and by no means all, or most, acts of intergroup hostility are frenzied. Simply invoking the concept of primitive, destructive impulses, therefore, makes little contribution to the understanding of intergroup behaviour.

THE MINIMAL CONDITIONS FOR INTERGROUP DISCRIMINATION

It does not require social psychological experiments to show that groups, classes, races, and nations discriminate against one another, both at the level of hostile actions and at the level of negative stereotypes. Often there is a history of conflict of interest between opposing groups to which such behaviour and attitudes can be attributed. But can discrimination still occur in the absence of any such 'realistic' conflict? Is conflict perhaps sometimes the effect rather than the cause of a perception of difference between one's own and another group? Might even the mere presence of another group, different from one's own in some way, be sufficient to trigger discrimination? To answer such questions, a number of researchers have attempted to create group divisions experimentally from individuals with no previous history of conflict, in order to observe the effects of such group divisions on judgements and behaviour.

Early studies of this kind were conducted by Sherif (1951; Sherif and Sherif, 1953), on boys attending American summer camps, who were quite unaware that an experiment was going on. For the first period after they arrived at the camp, the boys mixed freely with each other, establishing friendships, etc. After about a week, however, the camp organizers divided the boys into two groups (taking care to split up previously established friendship pairs), which from then on slept and ate apart and performed separate activities. As a result, each group developed its own separate hierarchy and miniature culture. After this, the two groups were put in competition with each other in sports activities, which had the effect of producing strong overt hostility between them. In a later study, Sherif (1966) added a fourth stage, in which the groups were brought together to perform cooperative tasks (e.g., combining to pull a broken down food truck), and the introduction of such 'superordinate goals' helped to relieve the intergroup tension that had been created.

Since Sherif's original study, a number of studies have been designed to identify the minimal conditions under which intergroup discrimination can occur. Subjects' assignment to groups in these studies has typically been extremely short-term, relating merely to performance of experimental tasks, and not extending through whole days and nights as in the Sherif studies, or the Stanford prison experiment. Nonetheless, clear evidence of intergroup rivalry is often observed. Ferguson and Kelley (1964), for instance, had pairs of groups perform tasks within sight of one another, but without any formal competition between them having been introduced. Subjects still consistently overvalued the products of their own group and undervalued those of the other group.

Rabbie and Horwitz (1969) tested an hypothesis derived from Lewin (1948), that the main criterion for feeling that one belongs to a group is interdependence of fate with the other group members. To this end, equal numbers of boys and girls of about 15 years old were tested in groups of eight, and were randomly subdivided into groups of four. After some preliminary tasks, the experimenter announced that he would like to give them a reward for participating, a transistor radio, but unfortunately he only had four radios to give away instead of eight. He then arbitrarily gave the radios to one of the two subgroups, or alternatively did so on the toss of a coin, or else arbitrarily let one of the two subgroups decide, and led subjects to believe that the subgroup had decided in its own favour. Half the subjects thus experienced reward and half relative deprivation by virtue of their membership of one of the experimentally created groups. They then each had to rate their impressions of the other subjects in their session, who came from different schools and were, therefore, not previously acquainted with one another. Disregarding some minor variations between conditions and different dependent variables, the overall picture that emerges is one of subjects rating members of their own subgroup more favourably than members of the other subgroup, whether they were themselves rewarded or not, and whether the cause of their deprivation was chance, the experimenter, or the decision of their own or the other group. No such ingroup bias was observed in a control condition without any reward manipulation. Rabbie and Wilkens (1971) similarly found greater evidence of ingroup bias among subjects who anticipated working together as a group, particularly when this would be in competition with another group, than when they were given no such expectation.

The absence of a bias by subjects in favour of their own group in the control conditions of these two experiments might imply that the mere presence of an outgroup is not enough to elicit discrimination, or ingroup favouritism. Some details of these conditions, however, should be borne in mind. Subjects were divided at random into the two groups, and the two groups were sat on opposite sides of a screen so that they could not see each other. Subjects were told that the division was 'for administrative reasons only' and that they would not work together in any way. The two groups were labelled as 'Greens' and 'Blues', but were not addressed as the green or blue *group*. It is, therefore, possible that the cues of group membership were so weak that subjects did not see the situation as involving any kind of intergroup comparison. Rabbie and Horwitz (1969, page 272) concluded that: 'Group classification *per se* appears to be insufficient to produce discriminatory evaluations'. One might ask, though, whether any group classification *was* perceived by the control subjects.

Very different conclusions were reached by Tajfel, Flament, Billig, and Bundy (1971). Their concern was with whether 'the very act of social categorization' could lead to discriminatory behaviour against an outgroup and in favour of one's ingroup. The emphasis is very much on the cognitive functions that intergroup categorization could serve, in terms of simplifying the individual's perception of his social world and providing guidelines for social action. Their experiments were, therefore, designed to satisfy six criteria, so as to be able to say whether the mere perception of a difference between one's own group and another was sufficient to lead to discriminatory behaviour in favour of the ingroup. These criteria were, that there should be: (1) no face-to-face interaction between subjects, either within or between groups, (2) complete anonymity of group membership, and (3) no connection between the basis on which subjects are categorized into groups and the kind of ingroup and outgroup responses they are asked to make. Also, these responses should: (4) have no utilitarian value to the individual making them, (5) pose a direct conflict between a strategy of differentiation in favour of the ingroup and against the outgroup, and other more 'rational' strategies, such as the production of maximum benefit for all, and finally (6) be made as important as possible to the subjects.

The two experiments reported by Tajfel *et al.* shared the following basic paradigm. Subjects (all of them boys of 14–15 years old) are brought from school together in small parties to the university's psychology department. Since all of those in a party come from the same class at school, they are well acquainted with each other before the experiment starts. The first phase of the experiment then consists of them being shown a number of visual stimuli projected onto a screen. Supposedly on the basis of their individual responses to these stimuli (but in fact randomly), the subjects are then divided into two groups, but in such a way that they do not know the composition of the two groups. Each subject is taken individually into a separate room and seated in a cubicle, and is told which of the two groups he belongs to. This division into groups and the task which follows it are introduced in a way that seems intended to lead subjects to believe that they are taking part in a second study which is separate from the first phase. It is not too clear, though, how convincing the instructions would have been on this point. They then perform a task which they are told consists of giving real money rewards and penalties to others. In no case do they assign money to themselves. In fact they have to make quite a number of reward assignments, which in all cases involve a comparative choice between two other boys from their party. Sometimes the two recipients of the rewards are both members of the same group to which the subject himself was assigned, sometimes they are both members of the other group, and sometimes one of them is a member of the subject's group and the other a member of the other group. It is this last category—that of ingroup-outgroup choices—that is the main focus of interest. Subjects are told that after completing this task, they will be taken back into the first room and given the money that the others have assigned to them.

The form in which these reward assignments are made is fairly complex, and requires subjects, on each trial, to choose one column or 'box' in a two-row matrix. The numbers in the top row refer to the rewards to be assigned to one person, and those in the bottom row refer to the other person's rewards. Examples of two such matrices are shown in Table 9.1. The numbers represent units of 0·1d (one-tenth of an old penny). The matrices are designed to assess, in the case of ingroup-outgroup choices, the relative 'pull' of different strategies which subjects might adopt. Specifically, those compared are:

MJP—'maximum joint profit'—responding so as to maximize the total amount given to the two others combined.

MIP—'maximum ingroup profit'—responding so as to maximize the individual outcomes of the member of the subject's ingroup.

MD—'maximum difference'—responding so as to maximize the relative difference between the outcomes of the two others, to the advantage of the ingroup member and to the disadvantage of the outgroup member.

On the type (A) matrix, the MIP and MD strategies both exert a pull towards the left-hand extreme, while the MJP strategy exerts a pull to the right, if the top row represents the outcomes of the ingroup member and the bottom row the outcome of the outgroup member. However, if the outgroup member's outcomes are on top, and those of the ingroup member on the bottom, all three strategies pull to the right. On the type (B) matrix, MJP and MIP pull to the right, and MD pulls to the left when the ingroup member's outcomes are on top, while all three strategies pull to the right if the ingroup member's outcomes are on the bottom. By comparing each subject's responses over a series of different matrices, scores can be derived which represent the relative strengths of these different strategies.

In the first of the Tajfel *et al.* experiments, subjects were required to estimate the number of dots in a series of slides, and were divided into those

Table 9.1 Examples of response matrices used by Tajfel *et al.* (1971)

A	19	18	17	16	15	14	13	12	11	10	9	8	7
	1	3	5	7	9	11	13	15	17	19	21	23	25

B	7	8	9	10	11	12	13	14	15	16	17	18	19
	1	3	5	7	9	11	13	15	17	19	21	23	25

who were supposedly more and less accurate, or who tended to over- and underestimate. In the second experiment, subjects were shown slides of paintings by Klee and Kandinsky, and were split into groups, supposedly on the basis of their preferences for either one of the painters. In both experiments, the division was actually made on a random basis, and in both, subjects assigned 'rewards' which favoured the members of their own group over the members of the outgroup, typically choosing responses which represented a compromise between complete fairness (the middle box in the matrix) and complete bias in favour of the ingroup.

Particularly challenging are the results of the second experiment. On matrices of type A, subjects consistently responded to increase the absolute (MIP) and relative (MD) outcomes of the ingroup, and this tendency was not significantly affected by a consideration of joint outcomes (MJP). On matrices of type B, subjects' responses reflected an apparent wish to give more to the ingroup than the outgroup member (MD), even when this was incompatible with giving a larger absolute amount to the ingroup member (MIP) or to the ingroup and outgroup member combined (MJP).

A sequel to these experiments was conducted by Billig and Tajfel (1973) to provide an even more stringent test of the assumption that social categorization—explicit division of subjects into groups—is sufficient to lead to ingroup bias. Even though the basis for division into groups used by Tajfel *et al.* (1971) might appear to be essentially trivial, subjects were still given to believe that there was some real similarity between themselves and the other members of their own group which was not shared by members of the outgroup. The perceptual judgements which subjects had to make might not have seemed that important in themselves, but, from the subjects' point of view, they must have been of interest to the experimenters or why would they have been included in the experimental task at all? Effectively, the Tajfel *et al.* experiments confound social categorization with perceived similarity in terms of an attribute to which some implicit importance has been attached by the experimenters. In view of the literature on similarity and interpersonal attraction (see Chapter 6) the finding of ingroup bias may be less surprising than it at first appears.

Billig and Tajfel, therefore, manipulated the variables of social categorization and similarity in a simple 2 × 2 design. In the 'categorization-similarity' condition, subjects were divided into groups on the basis of their supposed preferences for Klee or Kandinsky pictures, as in the second experiment by Tajfel *et al.* The response matrices were labelled so that, e.g., the top row might refer to rewards for, 'Member No. 49 of the Kandinsky group', and the bottom row to rewards for, 'Member No. 79 of the Klee group'. The 'noncategorization-similarity' condition followed the same procedure, except that the word 'group' was carefully avoided. Subjects were told that they would know only the code numbers of the other subjects to whom they were awarding money. They were told in an off-hand way that some of the code numbers were in the forties and some were in the seventies, and that those with numbers in the forties had tended to prefer the Kandinsky pictures, and those with numbers in the seventies had preferred the Klee pictures. In the 'categorization-nonsimilarity' condition, subjects were told that the two parts of the experiment had nothing to do with each other, and that for the second part they would be divided into 'group X' and 'group W' on the toss of a coin. The response matrices were labelled with these group designations (e.g., 'Member No. 49 of the W group'). Finally, in the 'noncategorization-nonsimilarity' condition, the word 'group' was avoided, subjects being told that their code numbers, some of which would be in the forties and some in the seventies, had been allotted to them on the toss of a coin. The results showed that ingroup favouritism increased as a function of both categorization and similarity, being strongest in the 'categorization-similarity' condition and weakest in the 'noncategorization-nonsimilarity' condition. In other words, categorization *per se* seems to have an effect, over and above any due to similarity.

More recently, Deschamps, and Doise (1978) have explored the effects of categorization on ingroup favouritism from a slightly different perspective. Their concern is with the fact that, in real life, there are many alternative criteria for dividing people up into categories, which are to a large extent independent of one another. Their first experiment, using girls aged between 13 and 15 years as subjects, required judgements in terms of 32 traits of the four concepts 'people of the female sex', 'people of the male sex', 'young people', and 'adults' in the 'simple categorization' condition, and of the four concepts 'young people of the female sex', 'young people of the male sex', 'female adults', and 'male adults' in the 'crossed categorization' condition. In the simple categorization condition, the girls rated males as more different from females, and young people more different from adults, than when they had to deal with both age and sex categories independently. In a second experiment, they used a similar design with subjects of both sexes, and with the categories being sex and an experimentally imposed group division (into a 'group of reds' seated one side of a table, and a 'group of blues' on the other side). Interpersonal evaluations generally showed greater bias in favour of subjects' own sex, or own group, when subjects had to consider only one criterion of classification than when they had to consider the two independent criteria simultaneously.

DISCRIMINATION BETWEEN MINIMAL GROUPS: WHAT FUNCTION DOES IT SERVE?

In many ways, the longer one thinks about the Tajfel *et al.* (1971) and Billig and Tajfel (1973) findings, the stranger they seem. We all know that discrimination takes place in the outside world, so at one level it might not seem too surprising that it can be reproduced in the laboratory. Also, we know that categorization is an extremely important process in both social and perceptual judgements, so perhaps the special place accorded to this process by these studies is not all that extraordinary. But however irrational and arbitrary the criteria for discrimination in the outside world may be, the discrimination itself usually seems interpretable as an attempt by the discriminating group to protect or enhance its own interests or integrity. In the minimal group, it is difficult to see what subjects possibly hope to get out of discriminating, particularly when it does not serve their own individual interests to do so.

One possibility, albeit rather an anticlimactic one, is that subjects discriminate because they feel that that is what the experimenter wants them to do. Criticizing the Tajfel *et al.* experiments, Gerard and Hoyt (1974, page 837) argue: 'Faced with the forced-choice situation of favoring one or the other of two groups, ... it is not surprising that the subject distributed outcomes with regard to the ingroup-outgroup distinction ... indeed, Tajfel *et al.* recognized that the subject saw the situation as one "in which social categorization *ought* to lead to discriminatory behaviour ...."'

Gerard and Hoyt overstate their case by talking of a 'forced-choice situation'. It is worth noting that they do not complete the sentence which they quote from Tajfel *et al.* The fuller context is as follows:

> It will be clear that we interpret our results in terms of a 'generic' social norm of ingroup-outgroup behaviour which guided the Ss' choices. This was so because they classified the social situation in which they found themselves as one to which this norm was pertinent, in which social categorization *ought* to lead to discriminatory intergroup behaviour *rather than to behaviour in terms of alternatives that were offered to them.* (1971, page 174, italics added to last phrase.)

The Tajfel *et al.* position is that, because of the way in which the response matrices were constructed, subjects were *not* forced to choose which of the two groups to favour at the expense of the other. In other words, they were not forced to base their responses on a strategy of MD or even MIP rather than MJP. Gerard and Hoyt do not comment on this feature of the experiments. Nor is the concept of an experimenter effect (e.g., Orne, 1962), which is implicit in the Gerard and Hoyt criticism, ignored by Tajfel *et al.* In the paragraph which follows the passage just quoted, Tajfel *et al,* write:

> The experimenter effect can be defined for present purposes as the use of experimental procedures which may have caused the Ss to entertain certain hypotheses as to how the experimenters expected them to behave, and then to conform to these expectations. There is no doubt that this was an important aspect of the situation. The term 'group' was used extensively in the instructions to the Ss preceding their choices and on the pages of the booklets of matrices which they found in their cubicles. The experimenter effect is not, however, a concept which presents a theoretical alternative to the interpretation of the findings presented here. The point of the experiments was to activate for the Ss the norm of 'groupness' under certain specified conditions .... What does seem theoretically important is the fact that a few references to 'groupness' in the instructions were sufficient to release the kind of behaviour that was observed despite its 'non-rational', 'non-instrumental' and 'non-utilitarian' character, despite the flimsy criteria for social categorization that were employed, and despite the possibility of using alternative and in some ways 'better' strategies. (1971, page 174.)

If there is any basis to the Gerard and Hoyt argument, it lies in the fact that responding in accordance with the MD strategy rather than any other was the only means whereby subjects could express an intergroup *comparison*. The MIP and MJP strategies are non-comparative. If subjects saw the situation as one involving intergroup comparison, then indeed there is some sense in the argument that MD was the only appropriate strategy available to them. By implication, then, part of any norm of 'groupness' activated in the experimental situation should be the tendency to engage in intergroup comparison. This point is quite crucial, but it is by no means one with which Tajfel would disagree. On the contrary, the central assumption of Tajfel's approach is that individuals are attracted to a group to the extent that it provides them with a positive 'social identity' through comparisons with other groups (Tajfel, 1978).

But again, we return to the basic question of why this should happen in *minimal* groups. This question has been considered at some length by Turner (1975). Turner proposes a basic distinction between 'conflict of interests' and what he terms 'social competition', which depends primarily on the individual's desire to be able to evaluate himself positively in comparison with others. If he is a member of a group which can prove itself 'better' than another group on some dimension of comparison, then that group and that dimension will be salient to his self-concept and 'social identity'. The minimal group situation thus provides subjects with the opportunity of being the 'winners', if they respond discriminatively in favour of their ingroup and against the outgroup, and with the threat of coming out the 'losers' if they do not. The monetary rewards, according to this analysis, are not an end in themselves, but merely a symbolic means to enhance one's self-image.

To test these assumptions, Turner conducted an experiment which closely followed the Tajfel *et al.* paradigm, with two innovatory manipulations. The first of these was that half the subjects allocated real money rewards in terms of the matrices, whereas for the other half of the subjects, the points had only symbolic value. Discrimination in favour of the ingroup was even stronger when symbolic rewards were used, suggesting that in this condition the motivation to do 'better' than the outgroup was even less encumbered by a consideration of the absolute level of outcomes (cf. Oskamp and Kleinke, 1970).

The second manipulation involved half the subjects first allotting rewards, as in the Tajfel *et al.* experiments, to two subjects other than themselves ('other-other' choices), but then also allotting rewards between themselves and another subject, who could be either a member of the ingroup or a member of the outgroup ('self-other' choices). In this condition, subjects still showed evidence of intergroup discrimination even in their self-other choices. In other words, their responses were more discriminatory in their own favour when they allotted rewards between themselves and an outgrouper than when they did so between themselves and another member of their own group. For the other subjects, the order of tasks was reversed, so that they made their self-other choices first. In this condition, subjects showed about the same levels of discrimination in their own favour whether the other was an in-grouper or outgrouper. In other words, the distinction between the two groups was only used by subjects as a basis for discrimination in their self-other choices if they had *already* used it in their other-other choices. The task order manipulation had no significant effect on the extent of intergroup discrimination in subjects' other-other choices. Turner concludes that:

> subjects will identify with a social category to the extent that such identification enables them to achieve value significance, to the extent that it is the category most relevant to the desire for positive self-evaluation in the experimental situation. Thus it can be said that in the experiment by Tajfel *et al.* it was not the *division into groups which caused discrimination* but rather that the group dichotomy was the only existing categorization through which a more basic motivation might be expressed—the subjects therefore *had* to use the categories provided. (Pages 19–20.)

Mention of this 'more basic motivation'—the desire for positive self-evaluation validated through social comparison—returns us, as you will recognize, to more familiar theoretical ground.

COMPARISONS BETWEEN UNEQUAL GROUPS

If what attracts individuals to groups is the hope of achieving a 'positive social identity', then it would seem, at first sight, that some real-life groups should be much more attractive to their members than others. I say 'at first sight' because, as we shall see towards the end of this chapter, things are not quite so simple. Nonetheless, it is undeniable that differences do exist between groups on conventionally accepted dimensions of status, power, achievement, numerical strength, etc., and perhaps the most significant question that can be asked of research on intergroup behaviour concerns how groups which are unequal in terms of such criteria relate to one another.

Shortly, I shall be describing a recent attempt at a theoretical synthesis of this area, but first let us consider some of the relevant experimental data. Two of the experiments already described contained manipulations which *might* be construed as relevant to the question of whether high and low status groups show different levels of intergroup discrimination. In the Rabbie and Horwitz (1969) study, half the experimental subjects were rewarded, and half relatively deprived by virtue of their membership of an arbitrary group. One might have expected different levels of discriminatory behaviour between the rewarded and deprived groups, but no clear effects were found. Similarly, in the first of the Tajfel *et al.* experiments, some subjects were told that they were more accurate, and others that they were less accurate, in their estimates of numbers of dots, but both groups showed comparable levels of ingroup favouritism.

Differences are found, however, when one looks at real-life social groups.

Doise and Sinclair (1973) conducted a study within the context of the Swiss secondary education system, in which a higher status is conventionally attributed to the more academically oriented *collégiens* than to the more technically oriented *apprentis*. Subjects drawn from both these groups were asked to rate both their own and the other group on a series of attributes. In a 'no encounter' condition, subjects first rated the characteristics of their own group, and then those of the other group, but were not told until after they had made their ingroup ratings that they would also have to describe the other group. In a 'symbolic encounter' condition, subjects were told from the outset that they would have to rate both *collégiens* and *apprentis*. In an 'individual encounter' condition, subjects were tested in pairs consisting of one *collégien* and one *apprenti*, and in a 'collective encounter' condition, subjects were tested in fours, with two from each group. In these last two conditions, rating were obtained before and after discussion.

In the 'no encounter' condition the ingroup evaluations which subjects made (when they did not know they would also have to rate the other group) were evaluatively neutral rather than favourable. In the 'symbolic encounter' condition, however, subjects gave much more favourable ratings of their ingroup (so that their ingroup came out 'better' than the outgroup) than did subjects in the 'no encounter' condition. The difference between the two conditions is stronger for *collégiens* than for *apprentis*, among whom some gave very favourable, and others less favourable, ingroup ratings. The last two conditions confirmed a stronger tendency for the *collégiens* to evaluate their ingroup more favourably, and the outgroup less favourably, than was the case in the ratings given by the *apprentis*. Overall, bias in favour of the ingroup was stronger in the 'collective' than in the 'individual encounter' condition. In general, the *collégiens* rated the ingroup more favourably than the outgroup, whereas the reverse was true in the case of the *apprentis* (to which one should add the important qualification: *on the specific attributes presented*).

These findings do not allow us to conclude that in general, higher status groups show more ingroup bias, since the results of a study by Branthwaite and Jones (1975) appear to point in exactly the opposite direction. They used the issue of national attitudes between the Welsh and English. In the context of their historical position of political and economic pre-eminence, and their majority status within the United Kingdom, the English were regarded as having the higher status of the two national groups. Subjects in this study were undergraduate students at University College, Cardiff, who unambiguously categorized themselves as English or Welsh. The experimental procedure was modelled after that of Tajfel *et al.* (1971) and involved the allocation of rewards to others in terms of the same response matrices. The crucial feature of this experiment was that subjects were explicitly divided on the basis of nationality, so that the response booklet contained references to, e.g., 'Member No. 32 of Welsh group', and 'Member No. 22 of English group'. Although, overall, about one-third of the subjects responded so as to give equal outcomes to the two groups, the Welsh tended to show more discrimination against the English than the English did against the Welsh. Conversely, discrimination in favour of the *outgroup* was more common on the part of the English. (As a warning against too broad a generalization from these data, however, it should be pointed out that *if* any English students were negatively disposed towards the Welsh, they would be unlikely to choose to go to university of Cardiff.)

Even without using broader social categories of this kind, differences in the level of *ingroup* bias can be produced experimentally by varying the numerical size of the ingroup compared with the outgroup. Gerard and Hoyt (1974) divided subjects into those who were supposedly 'overestimators' and those who were supposedly 'underestimators' on a visual estimation of number task. Subjects were told that 'estimation tendencies are an interesting and important personality attribute, although it's not 'better' to be one way or the other' (page 839). Groups of ten subjects were led to believe that they had been split either into two subgroups of five, or into one subgroup of eight and one of two. Subjects then had to evaluate two essays, one supposedly written by another member of their ingroup and one by a member of their outgroup. Both male and female subjects were used, and when the results for both sexes are combined, they show a tendency for ingroup bias to decrease with the size of the ingroup. Subjects who believed they were in a minority of two evaluated the ingroup essay more favourably than the outgroup essay— very slightly so in the case of females but strongly so in the case of males. When the groups were supposedly of equal size, both male and female subjects were somewhat more favourable in their ratings of the outgroup than the ingroup essay. When subjects believed that they were in the majority, males indicated a slight preference, and females a strong preference, for the outgroup essay. Females were thus, overall, more favourable in their ratings of the outgroup essay relative to the ingroup essay than were males, although this effect was only marginally significant (p < 0.1).

Once again, though, results can be found that support the opposite conclusion: that majorities discriminate more than minorities. Moscovici and Paichelier (1978), using first-year university students as subjects, replicated the main condition of the Tajfel *et al.* (1971) study, with subjects being split into equal groups on the basis of their supposed preference for pictures by Klee or Kandinsky, and compared this 'control' condition with a 'majority' condition, in which they were told that their preferences were shared by just over 80 per cent of the total subject population, and a 'minority' condition in which they were told that their preferences put them in a minority of under 20 per cent. Subjects then filled out the standard response matrices, allotting rewards to members of the Klee and Kandinsky groups. The data are presented in the form of the percentages of responses demonstrating ingroup favouritism, fairness, or outgroup favouritism. For the control group, these percentages were respectively 32, 47, and 21. For subjects who thought they were in the majority, they were 70, 14, and 16; and for those who thought they were in the minority, 44, 29, and 27. In other words, the 'majority' subjects were the most discriminatory in their own favour. The 'control' subjects seem to have been less discriminatory than would have been expected on the basis of the Tajfel *et al.* data, although the different ages of the subjects might have played some part.

These last two experiments, however, do not deal directly with the issue of whether belonging to a majority or minority has positive or negative value for the individual, so it is possible that some such variable might account for the discrepancy between the results. It might also help explain the low levels of ingroup favouritism shown by the *apprentis* in the Doise and Sinclair (1973) study, but the relatively higher levels shown by the Welsh students in the Branthwaite and Jones (1975) study. To test this possibility, Moscovici and Paichelier conducted a second experiment in which subjects were again led to believe that they were in a majority or minority group, but this time the division was supposedly made on the basis of their scores on a test of creativity, and subjects were also given feedback which implied that they were personally high or low in creativity. As can be seen in Table 9.2, most ingroup favouritism was shown by subjects who believed they were high in creativity and in a minority, or low in creativity and in a majority. The value attached to group membership and the minority-majority status of the group thus appear to have interactive effects on the level of discrimination. Although such an interpretation would be entirely *post hoc*, it is possible that the criteria for group division led to the Gerard and Hoyt subjects having a more positive image of their ingroup than was the case in the first of the Moscovici and Paichelier experiments. Similarly, one might suppose, on a more substantial basis, that the Welsh students in the Branthwaite and Jones study valued their own group more positively than did the *apprentis* in the Doise and Sinclair study.

Moscovici and Paichelier discuss these results in the context of Moscovici's (1976) distinction between 'nomic' and 'anomic' groups. Broadly speaking, 'nomic' groups are sure of their position and opinions and have experience of success. 'Nomic' majorities can afford to tolerate minorities and

Table 9.2 Percentages of ingroup favouritism, fairness, and outgroup favouritism responses as a function of self-image and minority-majority status, found by Moscovici and Paichelier (1978)

	Positive self-image (High creativity)		Negative self-image (Low creativity)	
	Minority	Majority	Minority	Majority
Ingroup favouritism	61	29	46	62
Fairness	24	56	38	24
Outgroup favouritism	15	15	17	14

act equitably towards them, while 'nomic' minorities will tend to assert their differences from the majority and hence show strong ingroup bias. By contrast, 'anomic' groups are unsure of their position and have experience of failure. 'Anomic' majorities will avoid comparisons with the minority and will show strong ingroup favouritism, whereas 'anomic' minorities will tend to identify more with the majority outgroup, which is seen as conforming to accepted norms.

This highlights an important distinction between the position of a group on some valued dimension, such as status, and the stability of that position. An attempt to manipulate these as independent factors has been made by Turner (1978). Groups of students were presented with the task of improving a passage of prose. There were two groups of subjects in each session, and they each read out their revised versions and rated each other's performance. The instructions introduced the task as a measure of verbal intelligence, related to linguistic and literary skills, as distinct from spatial-motor intelligence, related to scientific and technical skills. Subjects were drawn from either the Arts or the Science faculty of the university. In the 'unstable' condition, they were told that verbal intelligence was more important for Arts students, and spatial-motor intelligence for Science students. In the 'stable' condition, they were told explicitly that Arts students were definitely superior to Science students in verbal intelligence, but inferior to them in spatial-motor intelligence. The intended implication of this rather subtle distinction seems to be that, in the 'unstable' condition, Science students were likely to do worse than Arts students, in that the task required skills which were 'less important' to them, but this result was not inevitable. Ratings were obtained of the respective merits of the two groups' performances, subjects' preferences for belonging to either group, and perceived task importance.

When both groups were drawn from the same faculty, Arts students were more likely to evaluate their own group's performance more highly than that of the outgroup, whereas Science students were more likely to rate the task as unimportant, particularly under 'stable' instructions. When the two groups were drawn from different faculties, the only subjects who consistently rated their own group's performance more highly than that of the other group were the Arts students under 'unstable' instructions. The Arts students who received the 'stable' instructions, and therefore knew that they were anyway 'definitely' superior, acted more as though they felt that they could afford to 'give credit where credit was due'. Arts students, under either set of instructions, were not at all keen to change groups for another similar task, whereas Science students were not too bothered if they changed groups or not. The task was rated as less important by Science students under 'stable' instructions.

These results suggest that comparisons between unequal groups differ from those between equal groups in a way that depends upon the stability of that inequality. In particular, groups in a position of unstable superiority seem to discriminate more than those in a position of stable superiority. One has to be careful, though, to remember what was meant by 'superior' and 'inferior' in this context. Science students do not necessarily perceive themselves as 'inferior' to Arts students. Superiority and inferiority were manipulated purely by instructions which gave information about the nature of the task. This information related, on the one hand, to expected levels of performance, and on the other hand, to the relevance of the task to the subject's self-evaluation. It is by no means clear that the stability manipulation in fact succeeded in manipulating perceived *stability* of status inequality (i.e., inequality of the relevant skills) independently of the perceived *size* of that inequality. In addition, it seems quite plausible that the 'stable' instructions may have further increased the perceived relevance of the task as a dimension of self-evaluation in the case of the Arts students, and decreased it further in the case of the Science students. It is an experiment where the conceptual distinctions are clearer at a theoretical than at an operational level.

A similar procedure was employed by Turner and Brown (1978) in an experiment designed to distinguish the stability of a perceived difference in status (i.e., task ability) from its perceived *legitimacy*. The meaning of legitimacy in this context will be best understood if the experimental design is first described. Subjects were 48 male students, half from the Arts, and half from the Science faculty. Sixteen experimental sessions were run, each with a single group of three subjects, all from the same faculty. Subjects were told that the experiment was an investigation of reasoning skills, and they would be required to work on a group task which consisted of discussing for 20 minutes the statement: 'No individual is justified in committing suicide.' They were told that research had shown either that Arts students, or that Science students, tended to do better. This information was manipulated orthogonally with subjects' faculty membership, so that half the students from each faculty were led to expect that they would do relatively well ('high status'), and half that they would do relatively badly ('low status'). This was achieved by giving different instructions in the 'legitimate' and 'illegitimate' conditions. In the 'legitimate' conditions, subjects who were told that Arts students did better were told that this was 'not surprising', as the task was probably influenced by 'verbal intellectual skills', and this was 'widely recognized by psychologists. So it does not amount to any kind of a handicap for Science students'. When it was the Science students who were supposed to do better, the instructions were changed appropriately, with the phrase 'mathematico-deductive skills' replacing 'verbal intellectual skills'. In the 'illegitimate' conditions, the difference was instead described as 'worrying' and 'not sufficiently well recognized by psychologists', and that the bias . . . undoubtedly amounts to quite a handicap for people like Science (Arts) students'. In the 'stable' conditions, subjects were told that the differences were 'a highly consistent finding', whereas those in the 'unstable' conditions were told the opposite. Collapsing over subjects' faculty membership, the three independent variables of status, legitimacy, and stability constituted a $2 \times 2 \times 2$ factorial design.

After subjects had held their group discussion, which was recorded, the experimenter told them that he wanted to know how well they thought they had done, and so would play them a recording of an earlier group, 'so that they had a standard against which to compare their work'. This tape was in fact constant for all conditions, but was introduced to subjects as being that of a group from the *other* faculty from their own. They then had to evaluate the 'relative merits' of the two groups' performances on response matrices adapted from Tajfel *et al.* (1971), and also had to assess their own and the other group on a number of rating scales. 'Creativity' measures were also included, in which subjects were invited to list other methods they could think of for measuring 'reasoning skills', and other factors which they thought were important and ought to be 'taken into account in assessing overall intellectual ability'.

The impact of this ingeniously designed experiment is weakened by a barely defensible statistical treatment of the data. In fact, Turner and Brown performed a factor analysis on 44 dependent variables, and extracted 10 orthogonal factors, which together accounted for less than 60 per cent of the total variance. Analyses of variance were then performed on the factor scores. With a sample of only 48 subjects, this procedure comes nowhere near to recommended practice (Gorsuch, 1974), and the factors extracted simply cannot be regarded as at all reliable. More informative are the analyses conducted on a few of the dependent variables treated separately. The familiar measure of ingroup favouritism derived from the Tajfel *et al.* matrices showed significant main effects with high status subjects showing more ingroup bias than low status subjects, and more ingroup bias being shown by subjects in the illegitimate than legitimate conditions. Contrary to prediction, there was no overall tendency for 'unstable' instructions to produce more ingroup bias than 'stable' instructions, but instead a three-way interaction occurred as can be seen in Table 9.3. As shown by the group means, the low status subjects tended to be more favourable to the outgroup than towards their own group when allocating points for performance, except in the illegitimate unstable

Table 9.3 Ingroup bias as a function of status, legitimacy, and stability, found by Turner and Brown, 1978.

	Legitimate		Illegitimate	
	Stable	Unstable	Stable	Unstable
High status	0·1	2·3	3·6	0·9
Low status	−1·2	−2·1	−0·9	1·1

Note: Figures are mean scores with a range from +12 (maximum discrimination in favour of the ingroup) to −12 (maximum discrimination in favour of the outgroup).

condition. The high status subjects who perceived their superiority to be both legitimate and stable showed no bias (as predicted), but those who perceived their superiority to be neither legitimate nor stable, and who thus should be the most 'anomic' in Moscovici's (1976) terms, showed far less bias than Turner and Brown predicted. Perhaps there comes a point when groups in a superior position perceive their superiority to be so unreliable and indefensible that they no longer seek to differentiate themselves from others in an 'inferior' position on the relevant dimension.

Among the remaining data of this experiment, perhaps the most interesting finding is that low status subjects tended to be more 'creative', in the sense of suggesting more methods for measuring reasoning ability and more factors of relevance to general intelligence, when they perceived their inferiority to be illegitimate. High status subjects tended to be somewhat more 'creative' under 'unstable' instructions.

TAJFEL'S THEORY OF INTERGROUP BEHAVIOUR

One of the most ambitious undertakings in research on group processes during recent years has been Tajfel's attempt to develop a theory of intergroup behaviour from a cognitive social psychological perspective. The theory and related research is presented in detail in Tajfel's (1978) volume, so what follows is intended merely as the barest outline. At the outset it should be stressed that the theory is not just an attempt to synthesize established experimental findings, but is intended to be applicable to the analysis of more large-scale phenomena of societal change and social movements, beyond the scope of the relatively narrowly based experimental approaches described elsewhere in this chapter. To a large extent, it constitutes a framework for the possible *future* development of research in this area, rather than a derivation from what has already been found. The questions to which such future research will need to address itself, therefore, are not just theoretical, but also methodological, since a major problem remains—that of validly and unambiguously operationalizing the conceptual distinctions to which Tajfel draws attention.

Tajfel sees the various issues of intergroup relations as turning on the individual's sense of belonging to, or identification with, his group. Definitions of what is or is not a group thus depend on this process of identification, rather than on any other single factor. As an illustration of this point, Tajfel cites the definition of a 'nation' offered by the historian Emerson (1960, page 102): 'The simplest statement that can be made about a nation is that it is a body of people who feel that they are a nation; and it may be that when all the fine-spun analysis is concluded this will be the ultimate statement as well.'

The salience of an individual's identification with his group (and indeed the particular group with which he identifies) will not be constant across all situations. On the contrary, social situations can be characterized as lying on a continuum from the extremely interpersonal to the extremely intergroup. Towards the interpersonal extreme (which may be rarely if every reached) individuals relate to each other purely as individuals, without regard to their membership of any social categories. Towards the intergroup extreme, individual attributes of the participants lose relevance, interactions being based purely on people's membership of social categories. The major common features of behaviour in intergroup rather than interpersonal situations are a shared ingroup affiliation of the individuals concerned, and a shared interpretation of the relations between the ingroup and outgroup as applied to the particular situation. The corollary of this interpersonal-intergroup continuum is a continuum of variability-uniformity of behaviour in the ingroup and of its treatment of members of the outgroup; in other words, as one approaches the intergroup extreme, different members of the ingroup will adopt similar behaviour towards the outgroup, and no differentiations will be made by them between individual outgroup members. The interesting and important departure in this argument from similar interpretations of earlier research on prejudice and stereotypes (see Chapter 3) is that these phenomena are treated as a function of the specific social *situation*, rather than of individuals' deep-seated drives and dispositions. In that much attitude research has been concerned with intergroup attitudes, Tajfel's emphasis here is entirely in accordance with the main theme of Chapter 2 in this book, where I argued that attitudes are to be understood in terms of the meaning of specific acts of expressive behaviour, rather than as situationally invariant entities.

Of crucial relevance to the extent of differentiation between and within groups is assumed to be the perceived permeability of the boundaries between the groups. The basic condition for extreme forms of intergroup behaviour is said to be the belief that the boundaries are sharply drawn and immutable, so that it is impossible or extremely difficult for individuals to pass from one group to the other. Similarly, the basic condition for predominantly interpersonal behaviour is the belief that the boundaries are flexible and that individuals can pass through them with no special difficulty. This becomes particularly important, in terms of generalizations to society at large, if one is considering the relations between groups which occupy different positions in some status hierarchy. To preserve or improve his status, can the individual just look after himself, or must he act as a member of his group? Tajfel discusses some of the ways in which social stratifications may present themselves in psychological terms:

We can distinguish *a priori* between several major sets of social psychological attributes of these stratifications which are likely to determine different forms of social behaviour relating to them. The first consists of the consensus in *all* the groups involved that the criteria for the stratification are both legitimate and stable (i.e. incapable of being changed). The second consists of the consensus existing (or developing) in one or more groups that the criteria are neither legitimate nor incapable of change. The third arises when one or more groups believe that the criteria are illegitimate but unchangeable (because of e.g., drastic differences in power between the groups). And the fourth—conversely—when they are believed to be legitimate but unstable (i.e., capable of change). The third and fourth sets of attributes most probably interact in many cases—in the sense that perceived illegitimacy is likely to determine, sooner or later, attempts to change the situation; and the perceived instability (which can be translated as the development in a group of the awareness of cognitive alternatives to the existing situation) is likely to be associated, sooner or later, with the decrease in that group of the perceived legitimacy of the situation. It will be obvious that a combination of illegitimacy and instability would become a powerful incitement for attempts to change the intergroup status quo or to resist such changes on the part of the groups which see themselves as threatened by them. (Tajfel, 1978, pages 51–52.)

Tajfel summarizes this position by assuming another corollary to the interpersonal-intergroup continuum. This is the 'social mobility–social change' continuum which refers to differences in individuals' beliefs concerning the nature of intergroup relations (or more specifically, intergroup stratifications). At the 'social mobility' end, the basic assumption is that the social system is flexible and permeable, and allows improvement of individual status on the basis of luck, effort, ability, etc. At the 'social change' end, the basic assumption is that the only way the individual can change or preserve his status and conditions is 'together with his group as a whole'. Implicit or explicit in much of Tajfel's argument is the thought that the bulk of social psychological research on groups has been premised on a 'social mobility' rather than a 'social change' conception of intergroup relations, and the correspondence between this conception and the traditional American ethos of 'rugged individualism' is seen as no coincidence. Tajfel's position is that intergroup discrimination and hostility cannot be adequately understood unless the structure of beliefs at the 'social change' end is more directly examined.

The three main 'independent variables' of the theory thus emerge as being those of *status*, *legitimacy*, and *stability*. All three relate to the structure of the relationship between any pair of groups *as perceived by the group members*. At a conceptual level, it is freely admitted that these three classes of perception can influence each other, so that, for instance a superior group might be more likely to perceive its status as legitimate, and unstable relations might also tend to be seen as illegitimate. A very real methodological problem to which this gives rise, though, is the difficulty of manipulating these perceptions as truly *independent* factors within an experimental design (as in the studies by Turner, 1978, and Turner and Brown, 1978), which can lead to ambiguities in the interpretation of results.

The concept of stability also needs additional clarification. Tajfel seems to use the term 'stability' to refer both to the stability of the status differences between groups, and to the rigidity, as opposed to the permeability, of the intergroup boundaries. A clearer differentiation between the effects of stability and permeability appears to be called for. One can easily think of situations in which the boundaries between groups (e.g., nations) are clearly defined and impermeable, but where the status differences are quite unstable. In other words, it is possible to envisage changes in the status positions of groups as a whole without any implication that the boundaries between the groups are permeable. Indeed, this is precisely what Tajfel means by a 'social change' system of beliefs. Increasing the permeability of intergroup boundaries, on the other hand, would seem to encourage individuals to adopt a 'social mobility' system of beliefs. Arguments against calls for radical social change (at least in Western democracies) are rarely, if ever, premised on the untenable assumption that class differences are non-existent. Instead, some argue that the class boundaries are permeable, (i.e., there is equality of opportunity) so that the class differences that do (or will) exist are not really *class* differences at all, but differences between achieving and non-achieving *individuals*. Permeability, actual or perceived, may thus legitimate a social system containing inequalities of status, and hence contribute to its stability.

Having dealt with the relations between groups in terms of status, legitimacy and stability, Tajfel then discusses the probable effects of these variables on the individual's commitment to his group. The basic assumptions are as follows:

(a) It can be assumed that an individual will tend to remain a member of a group and seek membership of new groups if these groups have some contribution to make to the positive aspects of his social identity; i.e., to those aspects of it from which he derives some satisfaction.

(b) If a group does not satisfy this requirement, the individual will tend to leave it *unless*
   (i) leaving the group is impossible for some "objective" reasons, or,
   (ii) it conflicts with important values which are themselves a part of his acceptable self image.

(c) If leaving the group presents the difficulties just mentioned, then at least two solutions are possible:
   (i) to change one's interpretations of the attributes of the group so that its unwelcome features (e.g., low status) are either justified or made acceptable through a reinterpretation; or,
   (ii) to accept the situation for what it is and engage in social action which would lead to desirable changes in the situation.

(d) No group lives alone—all groups in society live in the midst of other groups. In other words, the 'positive aspects of social identity' and the reinterpretation of attributes and engagement in social action only acquire meaning in relation to, or in comparisons with, other groups. (Page 64.)

The similarity of this part of the theory to the ideas proposed by Thibaut and Kelley (1959, see Chapter 6) is quite striking. According to Thibaut and Kelley, a person should remain in a group so long as his outcomes derived from membership do not fall below his comparison level (CL). The concept of CL has at least two distinct advantages in this context. First, since CL is defined as the level of outcomes to which a person feels he is *entitled*, it directly incorporates the notion of perceived legitimacy. Second, since CL is a judgemental standard, and standards shift with experience (see Chapter 3), it is an easy prediction that individuals will tend to adjust their CLs, and hence their levels of aspiration, to the levels of outcomes which they habitually experience, thus tending to adopt a relatively 'conservative' ideology. A possible criticism of the balance of Tajfel's theory is that, with its emphasis on the preconditions for social *change*, proportionately less attention tends to be given to psychological basis of the inertia which any forces for change need to overcome, and to the processes underlying the continued perception of a system as legitimate and stable, inspite of inequalities.

The concept of CL_{alt} is also relevant to the question of when a person will leave or stay in his group. A person may remain in his group, even if it produces outcomes for him below his CL, if these outcomes are still above his CL_{alt}, i.e., what he could expect to get from leaving his group. This would be equivalent to a system which was perceived as illegitimate but stable. On the other hand, in a system which allowed for upward individual social mobility, a person's outcomes within a group could be below his CL_{alt}, and under such circumstances he would be motivated to leave his group. Whereas Tajfel's theory is phrased in terms of 'positive social identity', that of Thibaut and Kelley is phrased in terms of 'outcomes', but that is no problem—a contribution to a person's positive social identity can be easily regarded as an outcome.

One of the most important aspects of Tajfel's theory, however, is the assumed dependence of a person's social identity, or self-evaluation, on processes of social comparison (cf. Festinger, 1954). Whereas Thibaut and Kelley were more concerned with comparisons within a group, Tajfel stresses the role that intergroup comparisons play in a person's self-evaluation. It is through such comparisons that a person acquires a better or worse image of himself by virtue of his group membership:

> The characteristics of one's group as a whole (such as its status, its richness or poverty, its skin colour or its ability to reach its aims) achieve most of their significance in relation to perceived differences from other groups and the value connotation of these differences. For example, economic deprivation acquires its importance in social attitudes, intentions and actions mainly when it becomes 'relative deprivation' ... the definition of a group (national, racial or any other) makes no sense unless there are other groups around. (Page 66).

From this follows the crux of Tajfel's argument: that *individuals will tend to engage in intergroup comparisons which are seen as likely to make a positive contribution to their social identity* (self-evaluation as group members), *and will tend to avoid intergroup comparisons which are seen as likely to make a negative contribution.* For intergroup comparisons to make any (positive) contribution of this kind, however, the other group must be seen as potentially similar or comparable to one's own. Yet in society comparisons will tend to be made between groups that are often quite dissimilar in terms of status. This is why it is necessary to take the variable of legitimacy into account:

> Social comparisons between groups which may be highly dissimilar are based on the perceived legitimacy of the perceived relationships between them. The concept of social identity ... is linked to the need for a positive and distinctive image of the ingroup; this is why the perceived illegitimacy of an intergroup relationship transcends the limits of intergroup similarity in the relevant social comparisons and reaches out wherever the causes of illegitimacy are thought to reside .... The perceived legitimacy of an intergroup relationship presents no problem for a social comparison theory, based on the assumption of similarity,

when the groups are (at least potentially) of similar status .... Again, the assumption of similarity seems valid in the case of stable and clear-cut status differences which are perceived as legitimate, in the sense that dissimilarity implies here the *absence* of comparisons The difficulties arise when this kind of a stable and legitimate intergroup system begins to break down .... The important issue ... is that the perceived illegitimacy of an existing relationship in status, power, domination or any other differential implies the development of *some* dimensions of comparability (i.e., underlying *similarity*) where none existed before .... Paradoxically, this means that the perceived illegitimacy of the relationship between groups which are highly dissimilar leads to the acknowledgement or discovery of *new* similarities, actual or potential .... The perceived illegitimacy of an intergroup relationship is thus socially and psychologically the accepted and acceptable lever for social action and social change in intergroup behaviour. (Pages 74–76.)

What is the link, finally, between individuals' choice to engage (or not engage) in intergroup comparisons and behaviour in minimal groups and similar experimental situations? Ingroup bias, as shown by the 'pulls' of the MIP and (more directly) MD strategies on the response matrices, and also as shown by differential evaluations of group performance or attributes of ingroup and outgroup members, is taken as evidence that subjects are engaging in intergroup comparisons—that is, in behaviour towards the intergroup end of the interpersonal–intergroup continuum. Such bias is seen primarily as action designed to enhance subjects' social identity or self-image, in the sense of allowing them to feel, 'Our side won'. As distinct from how such bias might be viewed by writers such as Berkowitz (1962), who treats outgroup aggression as a response to individual frustration, or Zimbardo (1969b), who treats it as a result of deindividuation, it is not seen by Tajfel as an end in itself, but rather as a means through which the individual can enhance his self-evaluation as a member of his group, through seeing his own group as both *distinctive* and also as *better* than the outgroup on the (only) available dimensions of comparison.

This assumption is consistent with the findings of ingroup bias in those minimal group studies (e.g., Billig and Tajfel, 1973; Tajfel *et al.*, 1971) where the status variable has not been incorporated. Since the groups are comparable, subjects tend to make intergroup comparisons. Where status has been incorporated, as in the Turner (1978) and Turner and Brown (1978) studies, unequal status should reduce comparability, and hence the degree of intergroup comparison (and hence bias) except where the status difference is presented as illegitimate and/or unstable. The results of these studies to date are partially, but not completely, consistent with this assumption (see Table 9.3, page 301). The results of minority-majority intergroup comparisons (Gerard and Hoyt, 1974; Moscovici and Paichelier, 1978) are also compatible with Tajfel's approach if one assumes that, in general, minorities will be more likely to compare themselves with majorities than vice versa. In conditions when the minority can evaluate themselves positively along a relevant dimension, the minority is likely to show bias against the outgroup, but in conditions where they are told that the majority is 'better' than them on the relevant dimension, it is less in their interest to compare themselves directly with them. By the same token, a majority that is sure of its own merits stands to gain nothing by comparing itself with an inferior minority (it is 'on a hiding to nothing'), but is likely to show more bias if its 'normative' status is threatened by the possibility of being 'bettered' by the minority.

One issue which future research in this area will undoubtedly have to consider is the relationship of such effects to processes more traditionally studied within the framework of attribution theory and equity theory. This is not to imply that Tajfel's theory is likely to prove reducible to either of these, but it is certainly the case that the experiments in this area have frequently involved procedures with a family likeness to those used in studies of attributions for success and failure (see Chapter 4), or of equity principles (see Chapter 8) in the distribution of rewards on the basis of task performance. The term 'reward' appears throughout the Tajfel *et al.* (1971) matrices, and it is not necessarily an idle speculation to wonder whether the same results would have been obtained if the word 'gift' had been used instead.

As things stand, it seems quite reasonable to suppose that subjects saw their task, at least partly, as that of distributing money or points in accordance with what they felt was *deserved* by the different ingroup and outgroup members—indeed, where subjects have to evaluate ingroup and outgroup performance in terms of rating scales, this seems to be precisely what subjects would have thought was required of them. The importance of the comparative MD strategy is quite compatible with this argument, provided one goes along with Anderson's (1976) formulation of the equity principle, that each participant's proportionate share of the outcomes should equal his proportionate share of the inputs. Equity, according to this view, is a matter primarily of interpersonal rather than intrapersonal comparisons. Furthermore, when one considers the factors which might affect such perceptions of deservedness, it seems more than a coincidence that 'ingroup bias' should be least marked where subjects are encouraged to attribute any differences in performance to stable and legitimate differences in the difficulty of the task for the different groups, rather than being led to expect that relative success or failure will be primarily determined by effort, or differences in ability not previously recognized. Nonetheless, the specifically intergroup applications of equity and attribution principles have hitherto been at best sporadic and incidental.

Potentially one of the most exciting aspects of intergroup behaviour dealt with by Tajfel is the phenomenon that groups who find themselves in a disadvantaged position in terms of one dimension will tend to look for new dimensions of comparison along which they can achieve a distinctive and positive social identity. Many striking examples are provided by Giles (1978) of how national or ethnic minorities will use and perceive their own language (as in the case of the Welsh or the French Canadians), or dialect and accent (as in the case of American blacks), to differentiate themselves from a majority outgroup, the use of such differentiating language or speech markers being predictable from the intergroup dynamics implicit in any given social situation. Turner and Brown (1978) included their measures of 'creativity' (sugg-estions of new assessment methods) to see if illegitimately disadvantaged groups would be the more likely to challenge the existing dimensions of comparison, and the direction of differences accorded with this prediction.

Particularly relevant here is the work of Lemaine (1974; Lemaine, Kast-ersztein, and Personnaz, 1978), who carried out a series of studies in children's summer camps. These involved two groups of children competing against each other for a single prize on tasks such as the construction of a hut in the woods. In each case, one of the groups was deprived of a resource vital to the completion of the task. This was done on a chance basis, after both groups had agreed to follow the 'rules of the game'. The main focus of interest was on how the disadvantaged group would react. In fact, a recognizable sequence was observed, with the disadvantaged group showing less efficient organiza-tion and division of labour, and with them, first of all, spending a lot of time watching the advantaged group. After a while, though, they set to work, but in doing so 'closed their frontiers' so as to keep away the children of the other group. Most interestingly, they then set about their task in a way which was deliberately different from the approach adopted by the advantaged group. For instance, when it was quite obvious that they could not built as good a hut as the other group, they diverted considerable energy towards making a garden around their hut—something not specifically prohibited under the rules.

Lemaine also observed comparable behaviour among older subjects in situations of interpersonal rather than intergroup competition. In one experi-ment, psychology students wrote a fictitious letter of application for a job in a marketing agency. At first they only believed that they would have to write one letter, but then were instructed to write a second letter, believing them-selves to be competing with another candidate who was either (1) similar to themselves, (2) had previous experience of the job in question, or (3) had a superior academic background to their own. Subjects changed the content of their letters more in conditions (2) and (3) than in condition (1), and whereas the changes made in condition (1) tended to be simple additions, those in the latter two conditions suggested that subjects sought to differentiate them-selves from their hypothetical rival by stressing new dimensions of compari-son. In another experiment, subjects performed a task involving painting in the presence of a confederate of the experimenters, who either claimed to have, or not to have, a talent for painting. The experiment was supposedly about people's subjective sense of colour, so the instructions were simply that subjects paint *colours*. Those paired with another person supposedly no better at painting than themselves obeyed these instructions, whereas those who felt the other person to be more expert paid attention to features of design and composition not mentioned in the instructions. Lemaine interprets such findings as part of a general tendency for individuals to attempt to differen-tiate themselves from others along dimensions which allow them to maintain a positive self-evaluation, and hence a sense of identity.

CONCLUSIONS

Recent years have witnessed an important change in the emphasis and direction of research on group processes. Before, attention was focused mainly on the normalizing and stabilizing effects of group interaction, and, with the important exception of Sherif (1951), most researchers neglected the question of intergroup processes. Wider issues of intergroup relations tended to be discussed in the context either of individual attitudes, or of cooperation and competition between individuals. These more traditional approaches have since been balanced by a concern with processes of differentiation and innovation, and with intergroup as well as intragroup behaviour.

It is undoubtedly the case that groups may impose conditions and restrictions on their individual members, and that individuals will frequently defer to the norms of their group, and will validate their own judgements by reference to others. Yet any role has its rights as well as its responsibilities, and mere performance of a role is not by itself an adequate basis for a sense of identity. As Goffman (1972, see Chapter 7) argued in his discussion of 'role distance', it is important to an individual's sense of identity and personal worth to be able to feel and show that he is more than the role he performs. It is good to be a good team-member, but not good to be *just* a good team-member. It is good to belong, but not good to be type-cast, to have nothing special to offer. An individual will compare himself with others, not simply to see how he can be the same, but also to see how he can be different.

Essentially, the same considerations apply to the study of intergroup behaviour. Earlier work tended to stress the competitive and essentially destructive aspects of relationships between groups, which were seen to arise from conflict of interest between groups and community of interest within groups. The competitive aspects continue to be stressed, but the goal of such competition is not simply or necessarily material profit, but rather the attainment of a 'positive social identity'—the ability to evaluate oneself positively as a member of a distinct and positively valued group. Such an identity is assumed to depend upon comparison with other groups. As with all other comparisons, the crucial factors will be the standards available for comparison and the dimensions perceived as relevant. The capacity of individuals and groups to create and discover standards and dimensions of comparison appropriate to their identity remains one of the most fundamental aspects of human social behaviour.

SUMMARY

* Individuals' judgements of ambiguous perceptual stimuli will tend to converge towards a group norm, or towards the judgements given by liked or respected others. However, it is important whether the phenomenon being judged is explained as being real or illusory.

* Individuals may also shift their judgements towards a group norm when the stimuli being judged are unambiguous, but when confederates give deliberately false responses.
* Whether such shifts represent changes in perception is doubtful, but may be less important than the fact that individuals seem to use others' judgements as the basis for inferring the correct *response*.
* Such effects depend more on the unanimity than the absolute size of the majority.
* Despite tendencies to conform to group norms, individuals may also seek to differentiate themselves from other group members. In certain contexts distinctiveness may be positively evaluated.
* Confident and consistent minorities may succeed in changing majority group norms.
* A number of studies have examined the hypothesis that decisions made by groups are 'riskier' than those made by individuals. Support for this hypothesis is contingent on a number of factors, particularly the content of the decision problems. The concept of riskiness is also poorly defined.
* Group decisions following discussion tend to be more polarized than the average pre-discussion individual judgements. Such effects seem to depend on the balance of arguments put forward during the course of the discussion. If group members simply communicate their judgements, but do not present supporting arguments, comparable shifts do not tend to occur.
* An integration theory approach explains group polarization effects by assuming that, in a discussion, individuals present simply the information on which their own pre-discussion opinions were based; this information will tend to be more extreme than their own opinions, however, which are assumed to be a weighted average of such information and a neutral initial impression held before any information is presented.
* Applied to the context of juries, this might imply that juries do not start from a presumption that the defendant is innocent, but from a position of uncertainty over whether he is guilty or innocent. However, much research on juror judgements has concentrated on individual judgements of guilt or innocence from case summaries, without specifying how such individual judgements are translated into a group verdict.
* Zimbardo has proposed that anonymous membership of a group may decrease people's inhibitions against acting in irrational or destructive ways. However, studies based on this proposal are criticized, and it is argued that manipulations designed to make individuals feel 'deindividuated' may have complex and potentially contradictory effects.
* Experiments have suggested that the mere act of categorizing individuals into groups can lead individuals to behave discriminatively in favour of their ingroup and against the outgroup.
* A suggested explanation for this is that individuals will seek opportunities to compare themselves with others in ways which contribute to a more positive self-image. An experiment where the subject could find himself in a 'winning' group provides such an opportunity.

* When groups of unequal status interact, they may each show different degrees of intergroup discrimination as a function of their perceptions of the legitimacy and stability of the difference in status.
* Tajfel has proposed that individuals will feel themselves to be committed members of a particular social group, so long as membership of that group contributes to their sense of 'positive social identity'.
* If membership of the group fails to make such a contribution (as when it occupies a low position in a status hierarchy), the individual may, depending on the circumstances, either attempt individually to leave the group ('social mobility'), or engage in direct action designed to improve the position of his group as a whole ('social change'), or seek new dimensions of comparison between his own and other groups, which may allow a more positive evaluation of his own group.

FOUR

CONCLUSIONS AND
PROSPECTS

TEN
CONCLUSIONS AND PROSPECTS

HOW FAR HAVE WE COME?

Social psychology is established. That, in a sentence, has been the main achievement of work over the last thirty years. After a long period of adolescent self-consciousness, and some phases of acute self-criticism, our discipline has fully come of age. It is still a young science, comparatively speaking, but it is by no means in its infancy. It is not rigidly set in its ways, but it can assert its right to ask questions, and have others listen to its answers. It cannot rest on its laurels, but enough has been accomplished to show that it has something to offer. These accomplishments have been at three levels, that of methodology, that of specific findings and the formulation of predictive models, and that of a more general theoretical approach to the understanding of human social behaviour.

At a methodological level, the major achievements have been in the field of scaling and measurement, and in the application of experimental methods to the study of social behaviour. In both these respects the heritage of general psychology is clearly evident. The development of techniques of attitude measurement dates back to the earliest days of social psychology, but recent years have seen research which strengthens the claims to validity of these techniques, while at the same time clarifying their limiting assumptions. Difficulties with the prediction of overt behaviour from verbal attitude measures now seem attributable to differences in degrees of generality or specificity. Difficulties arising from the fact that attitude statements are judged differently by individuals with different attitudes are now interpretable in accordance with more general principles of judgement, so long as it is realized that individuals may differ in the aspects of an attitudinal issue which they see as salient, and in the ways they choose to label such aspects linguistically. Attitudes are not entities, but meanings of forms of expression. For this reason, problems of prediction and of interpretation will arise when researchers attribute a different meaning to expressive acts from that attributed by the actors themselves.

The use of the experimental method has been one of the most distinctive features of social psychology, and the criticisms of it are well known. Most social psychological experiments have involved a fairly small number of basic laboratory paradigms, frequently using a captive population of psychology students as subjects. The kinds of social interaction which can take place in such laboratory settings are often very restricted and artificial. Sometimes it seems little more than an historical accident that a particular paradigm 'catches on', while others are ignored. Yet the experiment, for all its short-comings, is more than a device to enable social psychologists to align themselves with other branches of psychology. What is often overlooked is that experiments *work*, and social psychologists have continued to use them because they work, rather than because of some deliberately endorsed philosophical or ideological stance. What I mean by this is not that experiments always confirm the experimenter's hypotheses, nor that experimental effects may not be subject to important limiting conditions, be these procedural, individual, cultural, or historical. Nor, do I deny that experimentation may demand a measure of skill and sensitivity which may be unequally shared or acquired. An experiment is like a radio; if we twiddle the knobs at random, there's no telling what we will find, or any guarantee that it will be in a language we understand, even though the radio itself may be in perfect working order. On the other hand, if the radio is accurately tuned, we can expect to hear something, and also, which is especially important, we can expect others whose radios are similarly tuned to hear the same thing.

A basic assumption of the experimental method is that results are in principle reproducible, and that one should try to resolve apparent discrepancies. If two experiments produce results which seem to conflict, it matters. Sometimes such discrepancies may lead to important theoretical advances, sometimes they may arise because one of the experiments was confounded, or was measuring something different from the other, but they are not to be simply shrugged off with an, 'Oh well, different people find different things'. The experiment provides both a testing ground for ideas and a language for debate. Without it, it is difficult to see how social psychology could have avoided veering off course towards either of the twin dangers of speculative subjectivism or aimless head-counting that have characterized an unfortunately large proportion of what has passed for 'social research' over the years.

But of course, there are experiments and experiments. In their search for reproducible results, many experimenters have not worried too much about the correspondence between such results and behaviour outside the laboratory. Many have played safe, adding only minor variations to well-tried paradigms. Yet there has also been a trend, over recent years, away from rigidly controlled 'minimal' situations towards the study of behaviour both inside and especially outside the laboratory that has much more of a 'real-life' flavour. In a number of ways studies of this sort are not 'true' experiments, in that subjects may be allocated to conditions on the basis of prior attitudes or other characteristics, rather than by random selection from a homogeneous population, and procedures may be used which contain many aspects that cannot all, from a practical point of view, be controlled and manipulated independently. These studies, however, do not negate the value of the experimental method, but rather affirm the confidence that social psychologists now have in that method—a confidence which allows them to take a few risks and relax a few controls in the search for richer and more realistic social situations. Like radio broadcasts, laboratory experiments can only offer a selective account of social phenomena. One may need to check for oneself whether such selectivity is balanced, biased, or misleading.

At first sight, the specific 'discoveries' of social psychological research seem to be rather small scale. I have mentioned the problems of the overlap between social psychological knowledge and common sense, which make it difficult to show that research has anything 'new' to contribute. The important distinction, though, is between process and product. Someone who reads the literature in search of examples of 'new' kinds of social behaviour of which he was previously unaware may come across the occasional surprise, but in general will probably be disappointed. Compared, for example, with social anthropology, the subject matter of social psychology is not especially exotic. The central task of social psychology, however, is to identify the processes which underly common everyday social behaviour. What social psychologists have been able to say about such processes often *has* been new, even if the products of these processes are already quite familiar.

Specific 'effects' and predictive models have been described in the previous chapters, and I shall not reiterate them in detail here. Nonetheless, there are some themes that crop up with particular regularity, which together point the way towards a more general theoretical approach. The most important of these themes is the view of the individual as an active processor of information. Social stimuli influence behaviour by virtue of the information which they provide, and this influence is dependent on individuals' expectations and interpretations. Different aspects of such information-processing are emphasized by different theories. Cognitive consistency theories emphasize the need for evaluative simplicity, while complexity theories also stress that individuals will seek out new information. Integration theory attempts to describe mathematically how individuals will combine different items of information to form a composite impression. Social judgement research stresses the differential salience of different aspects of an issue for different individuals, and the self-justificatory functions of attitude organization and evaluative language. These self-justificatory functions remain an important theme of both attribution and cognitive dissonance research. Both these traditions, which seem far less at odds with each other than a few years ago, stress the importance of individuals' explanations of behaviour (including their own), and of perceptions of freedom and responsibility.

Such themes are not confined within the boundaries of the 'social perception' half of social psychology. Attraction research is in many respects the interpersonal counterpart to work on attitude organization, while the concept of attribution of intention is arguably the single most important key to an understanding of interpersonal competition and cooperation. Social judgement principles are centrally involved in people's evaluations of the desirability and equity of their outcomes from a relationship, be it dyadic, contractual, corporate, or intergroup. People's perceptions of the rights and responsibilities attached to specific roles are a crucial determinant of their willingness to act altruistically, or to obey instructions, and these areas also show evidence of people's remarkably adaptable capacity for self-justification. Finally research on group processes stresses the individual's reliance upon other people, who may be members of either his own or another group, as sources of information and as standards of evaluative comparison along personally salient dimensions.

It is sometimes argued that there are no general theories any more in social psychology, only specific hypotheses about specific effects. For instance, Eagly and Himmelfarb (1974) have discussed the development of 'limited range' theories of attitude change, in preference to more general integrative frameworks. Certainly theories which are only defined at a high level of abstraction do not easily generate empirical research, but such arguments tend to overlook the strong family resemblances between the underlying assumptions of such 'limited-range' theories and specific models. It is this family group of assumptions which adds up to what I have called a 'cognitive' approach to social psychology. Such a cognitive approach assumes that people make behavioural decisions on the basis of their expectations and their interpretation of information. It is not in itself, perhaps, a remarkable assumption, but its broader implications may be quite far-reaching.

To view human social behaviour as the product of decisions allows a strategy of inquiry which is neither crudely positivist nor romantically phenomenalist. Behavioural instances are of interest because of what they tell us about human decision processes, but at the same time people's thoughts and perceptions are of interest because they help us understand behaviour. It is also a view which may help to liberate the study of social behaviour from some of the more deterministic dogmas that still attract their disciples. Such dogmas come from many quarters, but they all seem to owe their appeal to the fact that they offer excuses for ignoring individual cognitive processes. In contrast, a cognitive social psychology at least attempts to credit its human subjects with some intelligence and capacity for choice. According to this view, therefore, constructs which pertain to this intelligence and this capacity are likely to be those which have most to offer for an understanding of human social behaviour.

WHERE DO WE GO FROM HERE?

While cognitive theories in social psychology are in the ascendant, it is vitally important to realize that the intelligence and capacity for choice possessed by the human subject, though impressive, are not unlimited, and future theoretical advances are unlikely to be made by ignoring these limitations. Cognitive social psychology is often accused of presenting too rationalist a picture of the individual. I have continually pointed out how people's interpretative and decision-making processes can show marked deviations from an ideal of perfect rationality. Cognitive bias and selectivity are in fact some of the most important topics for study in social psychology, so in that sense the accusation is unfair. Nonetheless, it is a fair criticism that the 'emotional side of life' has not been subjected to particularly sensitive or sympathetic scrutiny in much of the research I have described. As Manis (1977, page 562) has warned us:

> ... motivational variables are given scant consideration by many cognitive theorists. This is doubtless a healthy corrective from an earlier tradition in which unconscious motives, fantasies, and unbridled emotional reactions were too-freely invoked to account for social phenomena. On the other hand, the recent popularity of 'cool' cognitive formulations like attribution theory should not blind us to the important role of motivation and emotion in social phenomena.

A possible answer is that cognitive theories do not need to be so 'cool'. It remains an extremely important question how arousal, either pleasant or unpleasant, influences behaviour under specified circumstances. It could be argued that arousing stimuli are themselves a kind of 'information' and so can easily be incorporated within a cognitive approach. Strictly speaking, this is quite correct, but it detracts attention from the validity of Manis's criticism. A more reasonable response would be to acknowledge that arousal of various kinds undoubtedly influences the kinds of cognitive processes in which social psychologists have been interested, but that our knowledge of how it does so remains superficial and unsystematic. If such influence could be better understood, then we should be nearer not only to understanding the effects of arousal on behaviour, but also the nature of arousal itself.

The other accusation frequently made against cognitive social psychology is that it is too individualistic, and as such is inappropriate for an analysis of behaviour in larger social groups. If this is true, again, there is no reason why it should remain so. It could be pointed out, for example, that a number of theories of group behaviour (e.g., Tajfel's) are explicitly cognitive in orientation.

A stronger version of this criticism, however, challenges the assumption that ordinary people have any realistic 'capacity to choose', at least in those areas of their social lives which are most affected by their political, economic, or ethnic status. Implied in this criticism is the rider that studying the social cognitive processes of *individuals* is to indulge in a starry-eyed liberalism which ignores the basic structural inequalities that persist in society. To this I should answer that of course there are inequalities, and of course these influence the individual's capacity to choose, but that this influence is something which can and should be also investigated from a social psychological point of view. Such an investigation cannot, by its very nature, ignore the group membership and perceived social identity of the people concerned within a wider network of relationships. It is not, for instance, simply a matter of asking, 'Why are people prejudiced?' while ignoring the effects of institutionalized injustice on the aspirations and achievements of groups who are the targets of discrimination. Nor is it part of a cognitive social psychology necessarily to dismiss political alienation and dissent as an 'irrational' response to frustration. Neither is it for social psychology to prescribe a utopia, still less the political actions to bring it about.

The demand that social psychology should take account of societal structure is not a particularly new one, and possibly this demand has been resisted on account of the connotations of rigid determinism that seem implicit in the way that the concept of structure is sometimes used. No such connotations apply, however, to the question of societal change. Rather than trying to manufacture change within the laboratory, social psychology would, in my view, benefit considerably from directing more of its attention towards changes that are happening in society all the time. Access to social benefits such as housing, health, and education, fundamentally affects the way people live, and also varies both between regions and across time. Prospects for employment (and currently, the lack of them) show similar variations and are at least as significant for society and the individual. These changes may themselves be consequences of a host of other changes, such as in the availability of different sources of energy supply, policies of national governments and agreements between them, investments by multinational corporations, 'business confidence', and so on. Yet these important changes have been barely considered by social psychology.

To call for the social psychological study of these and other features of societal change is to call for a more 'applied' social psychology—but this would be a different kind of 'applied' psychology from much of what has gone on before. A large part of the traditional role of the applied psychologist has been to offer advice on how manipulations of the person's environment can lead to changes in his behaviour, and how people can be efficiently matched to the tasks they are required to perform. Doubtless, there will continue to be a considerable call for such advice. But there is also the question of how individuals themselves control their environment, and select their own goals, which is not only a return to the original Lewinian tradition, but also an issue which a cognitive social psychology is equipped to handle, both theoretically and methodologically.

Within such a context, it should also be possible for social psychology to start paying more attention to two familiar but by-passed concepts. The first of these is the concept of role. Apart from a few, typically polemical, treatises on 'the role of the experimental subject', the study of roles has remained mostly well within the province of sociology. Yet the concepts of role choice, role distance, and role conflict have profound social psychological implications, extending well beyond the laboratory experiment. The ways in which individuals perceive and perform their roles in (to name but a few examples) medical, legal, and familial contexts comprise large areas which social psychologists have only recently started systematically to explore.

The other concept that is frequently ignored is that of time. Social psychology has been shaped to a quite excessive extent by relatively trivial considerations of procedural convenience, such as how many hours one can demand of one's experimental subjects as part of a course requirement, how one can avoid off-putting intrusions into privacy or requests for longer-term cooperation, how one can control for previous patterns of friendship between members of groups, and so on. Thus, attitude change may be produced and measured within the hour, but for all we know may often vanish just as quickly. Interpersonal attraction tends to be studied mainly in terms of first impressions and invitations, and group membership is studied in contexts where subjects are kept in ignorance of the composition of their group. I do not wish to imply that these procedures cannot be justified, but their cumulative effect has been to make social psychology primarily the study of short-term behaviour. What seems needed is a concentration on forms of social interaction, on goals and choices which have longer-term implications. For a number of reasons, both practical and ethical, it may not be possible to submit subjects to experimental treatments over extended periods of time. There is then all the more reason for exploiting the 'natural experiments' that occur everyday in the outside world.

The roots of social psychology lie in the study of the everyday. If we disown these roots in searching only for ever more sophisticated theories and methods, we may yet end up with less than when we started. If we forget where we started from, we may loose our way.

SUMMARY

* Social psychology has made substantial contributions to the scientific study of human social behaviour at the levels of methodology, empirical prediction, and general theory.
* Although some would stress the separateness of various smaller-scale social psychological theories, strong family resemblances are discernible among many of these, and may be comprised within a common cognitive approach.

* Future research should pay increased attention to problems and concepts (e.g., emotion) which have hitherto been relatively neglected by cognitive social psychologists.
* Naturally occurring events and social change provide opportunities for a theoretically based social psychology both to lessen its reliance on artificial experimental situations and to apply itself more directly to the study of everyday social behaviour.

BIBLIOGRAPHY

Abelson, R. P., 'Models of resolution of belief dilemmas', *Journal of Conflict Resolution*, **3**, 343–352, 1959.

Abelson, R. P., 'The structure of belief systems', in *Computer Simulation of Thought and Language*, Colby, K., and R. Schank (eds.), Freeman, San Francisco, 1973.

Abelson, R. P., 'Script processing in attitude formation and decision making', in Carroll, J. S., and J. W. Payne (eds.), *Cognition and Social Behavior*, Erlbaum, Hillsdale, N.J., 1976.

Adams, J. S., 'Toward an understanding of inequity', *Journal of Abnormal and Social Psychology*, **67**, 422–436, 1963.

Adams, J. S., 'Inequity in social exchange', in Berkowitz, L., (ed.), *Advances in Experimental Social Psychology*, vol. 2, Academic Press, New York, 1965.

Aderman, D., 'Effects of anticipating future interaction on the preference for balanced states', *Journal of Personality and Social Psychology*, **11**, 214–219, 1969.

Aderman, D., D. Brehm, and L. B. Katz, 'Empathetic observation of an innocent victim: The just world revisited', *Journal of Personality and Social Psychology*, **29**, 324–347, 1974.

Ager, J. W., and R. M. Dawes, 'The effect of judges' attitudes on judgment', *Journal of Personality and Social Psychology*, **1**, 533–538, 1965.

Ajzen, I., 'Intuitive theories of events and the effects of base-rate information on prediction', *Journal of Personality and Social Psychology*, **35**, 303–314, 1977.

Ajzen, I., and M. Fishbein, 'Attitude-behavior relations: A theoretical analysis and a review of empirical research', *Psychological Bulletin*, **84**, 888–918, 1977.

Alexander, C. N., Jr., and H. C. Weil, 'Players, persons, and purposes: Situational meaning and the Prisoner's Dilemma game', *Sociometry*, **32**, 121–144, 1969.

Alexander, C. N., Jr., L. G. Zucker, and C. L. Brody, 'Experimental expectations and autokinetic experiences: Consistency theories and judgmental convergence', *Sociometry*, **33**, 108–122, 1970.

Allen, V. L., and J. M. Levine, 'Social support, dissent and conformity', *Sociometry*, **31**, 138–149, 1968.

Allport, G. W., *Personality: A Psychological Interpretation*, Holt, New York, 1937.

Allport, G. W., and H. S. Odbert, 'Trait-names: A psycho-lexical study', *Psychological Monographs*, **47**, (Whole no. 211), 1936.

Anderson, N. H., 'Application of an additive model to impression formation', *Science*, **138**, 817–818, 1962.

Anderson, N. H., 'Averaging versus adding as a stimulus-combination rule in impression formation', *Journal of Experimental Psychology*, **70**, 394–400, 1965.

Anderson, N. H., 'Application of a linear-serial model to a personality-impression task using serial presentation', *Journal of Personality and Social Psychology*, **10**, 354–362, 1968a.

Anderson, N. H., 'Likeableness ratings of 555 personality-trait words', *Journal of Personality and Social Psychology*, **9**, 272–279, 1968b.

Anderson, N. H., 'Functional measurement and psychophysical judgment', *Psychological Review*, **77**, 152–170, 1970.

Anderson, N. H., 'On the role of context effects in psychophysical judgment', *Psychological Review*, **82**, 462–482, 1975.

Anderson, N. H., 'Equity judgments as information integration', *Journal of Personality and Social Psychology*, **33**, 291–299, 1976.

Anderson, N. H., 'Some problems in using analysis of variance in balance theory', *Journal of Personality and Social Psychology*, **35**, 140–158, 1977.

Anderson, N. H., and A. J. Farkas, 'Integration theory applied to models of inequity', *Personality and Social Psychology Bulletin*, **1**, 588–591, 1975.

Anderson, N. H., and C. C. Graesser, 'An information integration analysis of attitude change in group discussion', *Journal of Personality and Social Psychology*, **34**, 210–222, 1976.

Anderson, N. H., and S. Hubert, 'Effects of concomitant verbal recall on order effects in personality impression formation', *Journal of Verbal Learning and Verbal Behavior*, **2**, 379–391, 1963.

Anderson, N. H., and A. Jacobson, 'Effect of stimulus inconsistency and discounting instructions in personality impression formation', *Journal of Personality and Social Psychology*, **2**, 531–539, 1965.

Anscombe, G. E. M., *Intention*, 2nd edn., Blackwell, Oxford, 1963.

Apsler, R., and H. Friedman, 'Chance outcomes and the just world: A comparison of observers and recipients', *Journal of Personality and Social Psychology*, **31**, 887–894, 1975.

Aranoff, D., and J. T. Tedeschi, 'Original stakes and behavior in the prisoner's dilemma game', *Psychonomic Science*, **12**, 79–80, 1968.

Argyle, M., F. Alkema, and R. Gilmour, 'The communication of friendly and hostile attitudes by verbal and non-verbal signals', *European Journal of Social Psychology*, **1**, 385–402, 1971.

Aronson, E., 'The theory of cognitive dissonance: A current perspective', in L. Berkowitz (ed.), *Advances in Experimental Social Psychology*, vol. 4, Academic Press, New York, 1969.

Aronson, E., *The Social Animal*, Freeman, San Francisco, 1972.

Aronson, E., and J. Mills, 'The effects of severity of initiation on liking for a group', *Journal of Abnormal and Social Psychology*, **59**, 177–181, 1959.

Asch, S. E., 'Forming impressions of personality', *Journal of Abnormal and Social Psychology*, **41**, 258–290, 1946.

Asch, S. E., 'Effects of group pressure upon the modification and distortion of judgment', in H. Guetzkow (ed.), *Groups, Leadership and Men*, Carnegie Press, Pittsburgh, 1951.

Asch, S. E., 'Studies of independence and conformity: A minority of one against a unanimous majority', *Psychological Monographs*, **70**, no. 9, Whole no. 416, 1956.

Ashley, W. R., R. S. Harper, and D. L. Runyon, 'The perceived size of coins in hypnotically induced economic states', *American Journal of Psychology*, **64**, 564–572, 1951.

Atkinson, J. W., 'Motivational determinants of risk-taking behavior', *Psychological Review*, **64**, 359–372, 1957.

Atkinson, J. W., *An Introduction to Motivation*, Van Nostrand, New York, 1964.

Becker, W. C., and R. S. Krug, 'A circumplex model for social behavior in children', *Child Development*, **35**, 371–396, 1964.

Beebe-Center, J. G., *The Psychology of Pleasantness and Unpleasantness*, Van Nostrand, New York, 1932.

Bem, D. J., 'An experimental analysis of self-persuasion', *Journal of Experimental Social Psychology*, **1**, 199–218, 1965.

Bem, D. J., 'Self-perception: An alternative interpretation of cognitive dissonance phenomena', *Psychological Review*, **74**, 183–200, 1967.

Bem, D. J., and H. K. McConnell, 'Testing the self-perception explanation of dissonance phenomena', *Journal of Personality and Social Psychology*, **14**, 23–31, 1970.

Benson, J. S., and K. J. Kennelly, 'Learned helplessness: The result of uncontrollable reinforcements on uncontrollable aversive stimuli?', *Journal of Personality and Social Psychology*, **34**, 138–145, 1976.

Berkowitz, L., *Aggression: A Social Psychological Analysis*, McGraw-Hill, New York, 1962.

Berkowitz, L., and E. Walster, *Advances in Experimental Social Psychology (Vol. 9). Equity Theory: Toward a General Theory of Social Interaction*, Academic Press, New York, 1976.

Berlyne, D. E., *Conflict, Arousal and Curiosity*, McGraw-Hill, New York, 1960.

Berne, E., *Transactional Analysis in Psychotherapy*, Grove Press, New York, 1961.

Berne, E., *Games People Play: The Psychology of Human Relationships*, Penguin, Harmondsworth, 1968.

Berscheid, E., K. K. Dion, E. Walster, and G. W. Walster, 'Physical attractiveness and dating choice: A test of the matching hypothesis', *Journal of Experimental Social Psychology*, **7**, 173–189, 1971.

Berscheid, E., and E. Walster, 'A little bit about love', in T. L. Huston (ed.), *Foundations of Interpersonal Attraction*, Academic Press, New York, 1974.

Bevan, W., and F. J. Pritchard, 'The anchor effect and the problem of relevance in the judgment of shape', *Journal of General Psychology*, **69**, 147–161, 1963.

Beyle, H. C., 'A scale of measurement of attitude toward candidates for elective governmental office', *American Political Science Review*, **26**, 527–544, 1932.

Bickman, L., 'The effect of another bystander's ability to help on bystander intervention in an emergency', *Journal of Experimental Social Psychology*, **7**, 367–379, 1971.

Bickman, L., 'Social influence and diffusion of responsibility in an emergency', *Journal of Experimental Social Psychology*, **8**, 438–445, 1972.

Billig, M., *Social Psychology and Intergroup Relations*, Academic Press, London, 1976.

Billig, M., and H. Tajfel, 'Social categorization and similarity in intergroup behaviour', *European Journal of Social Psychology*, **3**, 27–52, 1973.

Birnbaum, M. H., 'Using contextual effects to derive psychophysical scales', *Perception and Psychophysics*, **15**, 89–96, 1974.

Bixenstein, V. E., and J. W. Gaebelein, 'Strategies of "real" opponents in eliciting cooperative choice in a Prisoner's Dilemma game', *Journal of Conflict Resolution*, **15**, 157–166, 1971.

Bixenstein, V. E., C. A. Levitt, and K. V. Wilson, 'Collaboration among six persons in a Prisoner's Dilemma game', *Journal of Conflict Resolution*, **10**, 488–496, 1966.

Bogardus, E. S., 'Measuring social distance', *Journal of Applied Sociology*, **9**, 299–308, 1925.

Bonarius, J. C. J., 'Research in the personal construct theory of George A. Kelly: Role construct repertory test and basic theory', in B. Maher (ed.), *Progress in experimental personality research*, vol. 2, Academic Press, New York, 1965.

Borgatta, E. F., 'Rankings and self-assessments: Some behavioral characteristics replication studies', *Journal of Social Psychology*, **52**, 279–307, 1960.

Borgatta, E. F., 'The structure of personality characteristics', *Behavioral Science*, **9**, 8–17, 1964.

Borgatta, E. F., L. S. Cottrell, and J. H. Mann, 'The spectrum of individual interaction characteristics: An interdimensional analysis', *Psychological Reports*, **4**, 279–306, 1958.

Borgida, E., 'Scientific deduction—Evidence is not necessarily informative: A reply to Wells and Harvey', *Journal of Personality and Social Psychology*, **36**, 477–482, 1978.

Boucher, J., and C. E. Osgood, 'The Polyanna hypothesis', *Journal of Verbal Learning and Verbal Behavior*, **8**, 1–8, 1969.

Bradley, G. W., 'Self-serving biases in the attribution process: A re-examination of the fact or fiction question', *Journal of Personality and Social Psychology*, **36**, 56–71, 1978.

Branthwaite, A., and J. E. Jones, 'Fairness and discrimination: English versus Welsh', *European Journal of Social Psychology*, **5**, 323–338, 1975.

Brehm, J. W., 'An experiment on recall of discrepant information', in J. W. Brehm and A. R. Cohen (eds.), *Explorations in Cognitive Dissonance*, Wiley, New York, 1962.

Brehm, J. W., and A. R. Cohen, 'Revaluation of choice alternatives as a function of their number and qualitative similarity', *Journal of Abnormal and Social Psychology*, **58**, 373–378, 1959.

Brewer, M. B., 'An information-processing approach to attribution of responsibility', *Journal of Experimental Social Psychology*, **13**, 58–69, 1977.

Brickman, P., and J. H. Bryan, 'Equity versus equality as factors in children's moral judgments of thefts, charity, and third-party transfers', *Journal of Personality and Social Psychology*, **34**, 757–761, 1976.

Brigham, J. C., 'Ethnic stereotypes', *Psychological Bulletin*, **76**, 15–38, 1971.

Brown, B. R., 'The effects of need to maintain face on interpersonal bargaining', *Journal of Experimental Social Psychology*, **4**, 107–122, 1968.

Brown, B. R., 'Face-saving following experimentally induced embarrassment', *Journal of Experimental Social Psychology*, **6**, 255–271, 1970.

Brown, D. R., 'Stimulus-similarity and the anchoring of subjective scales', *American Journal of Psychology*, **66**, 199–214, 1953.

Brown, R., *Social psychology*, Free Press, New York, 1965.

Bruner, J. S., and C. C. Goodman, 'Value and need as organizing factors in perception', *Journal of Abnormal and Social Psychology*, **42**, 33–44, 1947.

Bruner, J. S., J. L. Goodnow, and G. A. Austin, *A study of thinking*, Wiley, New York, 1956.

Bruner, J. S., and L. Postman, 'Symbolic value as an organizing factor in perception', *Journal of Social Psychology*, **27**, 203–208, 1948.

Bruner, J. S., and J. S. Rodrigues, 'Some determinants of apparent size', *Journal of Abnormal and Social Psychology*, **48**, 17–24, 1953.

Bruner, J. S., D. Shapiro, and R. Tagiuri, 'The meaning of traits in isolation and in combination', in R. Tagiuri and L. Petrullo (eds.), *Person Perception and Interpersonal Behavior*, Stanford University Press, Stanford, California, 1958.

Burnstein, E., 'Sources of cognitive bias in the representation of simple social structures: Balance, minimal change, reciprocity and the respondent's own attitude', *Journal of Personality and Social Psychology*, **7**, 36–48, 1967.

Byrne, D., 'Interpersonal attraction and attitude similarity', *Journal of Abnormal and Social Psychology*, **62**, 713–715, 1961.

Byrne, D., 'Response to attitude similarity-dissimilarity as a function of affiliation need', *Journal of Personality*, **30**, 164–177, 1962.

Byrne, D., and G. L. Clore, Jr., 'Predicting interpersonal attraction toward strangers presented in three different stimulus modes', *Psychonomic Science*, **4**, 239–240, 1966.

Byrne, D., and G. L. Clore, Jr., 'Effectance arousal and attraction', *Journal of Personality and Social Psychology Monograph*, **6**, (**4**, whole no. 638), 1967.

Byrne, D., C. R. Ervin, and J. Lamberth, 'Continuity between the experimental study of attraction and real life computer dating', *Journal of Personality and Social Psychology*, **16**, 157–165, 1970.

Byrne, D., and W. Griffitt, 'A developmental investigation of the law of attraction', *Journal of Personality and Social Psychology*, **4**, 699–702, 1966.

Byrne, D., and D. Nelson, 'Attraction as a linear function of proportion of positive reinforcements', *Journal of Personality and Social Psychology*, **1**, 659–663, 1965.

Calder, B. J., and B. M. Staw, 'Self-perception of intrinsic and extrinsic motivation', *Journal of Personality and Social Psychology*, **31**, 599–605, 1975.

Campbell, D. T., 'Enhancement of contrast as composite habit', *Journal of Abnormal and Social Psychology*, **53**, 350–355, 1956.

Campbell, D. T., and D. W. Fiske, 'Convergent and discriminant validation by the multitrait-multimethod matrix', *Psychological Bulletin*, **56**, 81–105, 1959.

Campbell, D. T., W. H. Kruskal, and W. P. Wallace, 'Seating aggregation as an index of attitude', *Sociometry*, **29**, 1–15, 1966.

Campbell, D. T., N. A. Lewis, and W. A. Hunt, 'Context effects with judgmental language that is absolute, extensive, and extra-experimentally anchored', *Journal of Experimental Psychology*, **55**, 220–228, 1958.

Campbell, D. T., and J. C. Stanley, 'Experimental and quasi-experimental designs for research on teaching', in N. L. Gage (ed.), *Handbook of Research on Teaching*, Rand McNally, Chicago, 1963.

Cantor, J., D. Zillman, and J. Bryant, 'Enhancement of experienced sexual arousal in response to erotic stimuli through misattribution of unrelated residual excitation', *Journal of Personality and Social Psychology*, **32**, 69–75, 1975.

Cantril, H., 'The intensity of an attitude', *Journal of Abnormal and Social Psychology*, **41**, 129–136, 1946.

Carlsmith, J. M., B. E. Collins, and R. L. Helmreich, 'Studies in forced compliance: I. The effect of pressure for compliance on attitude change produced by face-to-face role playing and anonymous essay writing', *Journal of Personality and Social Psychology*, **4**, 1–13, 1966.

Carson, R. C., *Interaction Concepts of Personality*, George Allen and Unwin, London, 1969.

Carter, L. F., and K. Schooler, 'Value, need, and other factors in perception', *Psychological Review*, **56**, 200–207, 1949.

Cartwright, D., 'Risk taking by individuals and groups: An assessment of research employing choice dilemmas', *Journal of Personality and Social Psychology*, **20**, 361–378, 1971.

Cartwright, D., and F. Harary, 'Structural balance: A generalization of Heider's theory', *Psychological* Review, **63**, 277–293, 1956.

Cattell, R. B., *The Scientific Analysis of Personality*, Penguin, Harmondsworth, 1965.

Chaikin, A. L., and J. M. Darley, 'Victim or perpetrator? Defensive attribution of responsibility and the need for order and justice', *Journal of Personality and Social Psychology*, **25**, 268–275, 1973.

Chapanis, N. J., and A. C. Chapanis, 'Cognitive dissonance: Five years later', *Psychological Bulletin*, **61**, 1–22, 1964.

Chapman, L. J., 'Illusory correlation in observational report', *Journal of Verbal Learning and Verbal Behavior*, **6**, 151–155, 1967.

Cialdini, R. B., 'Attitudinal advocacy in the verbal conditioner', *Journal of Personality and Social Psychology*, **17**, 350–358, 1971.

Cialdini, R. B., S. L. Braver, and S. K. Lewis, 'Attributional bias and the easily persuaded other', *Journal of Personality and Social Psychology*, **30**, 631–637, 1974.

Cialdini, R. B., and D. T. Kenrick, 'Altruism as hedonism: A social development perspective on the relationship of negative mood state and helping', *Journal of Personality and Social Psychology*, **34**, 907–914, 1976.

Cialdini, R. B., D. T. Kenrick, and J. H. Hoerig, 'Victim derogation in the Lerner paradigm: Just world or just justification?', *Journal of Personality and Social Psychology*, **33**, 719–724, 1976.

Cialdini, R. B., and H. L. Mirels, 'Sense of personal control and attributions about yielding and resisting persuasion targets', *Journal of Personality and Social Psychology*, **33**, 395–402, 1976.

Clark, R. D., III, and L. E. Word, 'Why don't bystanders help? Because of ambiguity?', *Journal of Personality and Social Psychology*, **24**, 392–400, 1972.

Codol, J. P., 'On the so-called "superior conformity of the self" behavior: Twenty experimental investigations', *European Journal of Social Psychology*, **5**, 457–501, 1975.

Cohen, A. R., 'An experiment on small rewards for discrepant compliance and attitude change', in J. W. Brehm and A. R. Cohen, *Explorations in Cognitive Dissonance*, Wiley, New York, 1962.

Cohen, R., 'An investigation of the diagnostic processing of contradictory information', *European Journal of Social Psychology*, **1**, 475–492, 1971.

Collins, B. E., and M. F. Hoyt, 'Personal responsibility-for-consequences: An integration and extension of the "forced compliance" literature', *Journal of Experimental Social Psychology*, **8**, 558–593, 1972.

Cook, S. W., 'A comment on the ethical issues involved in West, Gunn, and Chernicky's "Ubiquitous Watergate: An attributional analysis"', *Journal of Personality and Social Psychology*, **32,** 66–68, 1975.

Cooley, C. H., 'The social self: On the meanings of "I"', in C. Gordon and K. J. Gergen (eds.), *The Self in Social Interaction, Vol. 1: Classic and Contemporary Perspectives*, Wiley, New York, 1968.

Coombs, C. H., 'Psychological scaling without a unit of measurement', *Psychological Review*, **57,** 145–158, 1950.

Coombs, C. H., *A Theory of Data*, Wiley, New York, 1964.

Coombs, C. H., and L. C. Huang, 'Tests of a portfolio theory of risk preference', *Journal of Experimental Psychology*, **85,** 23–29, 1970.

Cooper, J., and J. W. Brehm, 'Prechoice awareness of relative deprivation as a determinant of cognitive dissonance', *Journal of Experimental Social Psychology*, **7,** 571–581, 1971.

Cooper, J., and G. R. Goethals, 'Unforseen events and the elimination of cognitive dissonance', *Journal of Personality and Social Psychology*, **29,** 441–445, 1974.

Cooper, J., and S. Worchel, 'The role of undesired consequences in arousing cognitive dissonance', *Journal of Personality and Social Psychology*, **16,** 199–206, 1970.

Cooper, J., M. P. Zanna, and P. A. Taves, 'Arousal as a necessary condition for attitude change following compliance', *Journal of Personality and Social Psychology*, **36,** 1101–1106, 1978.

Cottrell, N. B., L. B. Ingraham, and F. W. Monfort, 'The retention of balanced and inbalanced cognitive structures', *Journal of Personality*, **39,** 112–131, 1971.

Crandall, V. C., W. Katkovsky, and U. J. Crandall, 'Children's beliefs in their own control of reinforcements in intellectual-academic achievement situations', *Child Development*, **36,** 91–109, 1965.

Crockett, W. H., 'Cognitive complexity and impression formation', in B. Maher (ed.), *Progress in Experimental Personality Research*, vol. 2, Academic Press, New York, 1965.

Crockett, W. H., 'Balance, agreement and subjective evaluations of the P-O-X triads', *Journal of Personality and Social Psychology*, **29,** 102–110, 1974.

Cromwell, R. L., and D. F. Caldwell, 'A comparison of ratings based on personal constructs of self and others', *Journal of Clinical Psychology*, **18,** 43–46, 1962.

Darley, J. M., and E. Berscheid, 'Increased liking as a result of the anticipation of personal contact', *Human Relations*, **20,** 29–39, 1967.

Darley, J. M., and B. Latané, 'Bystander intervention in emergencies: Diffusion of responsibility', *Journal of Personality and Social Psychology*, **8,** 377–383, 1968.

Darley, J. M., and B. Latané, 'Norms and normative behavior: Field studies of social interdependence', in J. Macaulay and L. Berkowitz (eds.), *Altruism and Helping Behavior*, Academic Press, New York, 1970.

Davis, D., and T. C. Brock, 'Heightened self awareness, self esteem, and egocentric thought', (Unpublished manuscript), Ohio State University, 1974.

Davis, J. H., 'Group decision and social interaction', *Psychological Review*, **80,** 98–125, 1973.

Dawes, R. M., D. Singer, and F. Lemons, 'An experimental analysis of the contrast effect and its implications for intergroup communication and the indirect assessment of attitude', *Journal of Personality and Social Psychology*, **21,** 281–295, 1972.

Deci, E. L., 'Effects of externally mediated rewards on intrinsic motivation', *Journal of Personality and Social Psychology*, **18,** 105–115, 1971.

DeFleur, M. L., and F. R. Westie, 'Verbal attitudes and overt acts: An experiment on the salience of attitudes', *American Sociological Review*, **23,** 667–673, 1958.

Delia, J. G., and W. H. Crockett, 'Social schemas, cognitive complexity and the learning of social structures', *Journal of Personality*, **41,** 413–429, 1973.

Deschamps, J. C., and W. Doise, 'Crossed category memberships in intergroup relations', in H. Tajfel (ed.), *Differentiation Between Social Groups: Studies in the Social Psychology of Intergroup Relations*, Academic Press, London, 1978.

Deutsch, M., 'A theory of cooperation and competition', *Human Relations*, **2,** 129–151, 1949.

Deutsch, M., 'Trust and suspicion', *Journal of Conflict Resolution*, **2,** 265–279, 1958.

Deutsch, M., 'Socially relevant science: Reflections on some studies of interpersonal conflict', *American Psychologist*, **24**, 1076–1092, 1969.

Deutsch, M., *The Resolution of Conflict: Constructive and Destructive Processes*, Yale University Press, New Haven, 1973.

Deutsch, M., D. Canavan, and J. Rubin, 'The effects of size of conflict and sex of experimenter upon interpersonal bargaining', *Journal of Experimental Social Psychology*, **7**, 258–267, 1971.

Deutsch, M., and H. B. Gerard, 'A study of normative and informational social influences upon individual judgment', *Journal of Abnormal and Social Psychology*, **51**, 629–636, 1955.

Deutsch, M., and R. M. Krauss, 'The effect of threat on interpersonal bargaining', *Journal of Abnormal and Social Psychology*, **61**, 181–189, 1960.

Deutsch, M., and R. M. Krauss, 'Studies of interpersonal bargaining', *Journal of Conflict Resolution*, **6**, 52–76, 1962.

Deutsch, M., and L. Solomon, 'Reactions to evaluations of others as influenced by self-evaluations', *Sociometry*, **22**, 93–112, 1959.

Dillehay, R. C., 'Judgmental processes in response to a persuasive communication', *Journal of Personality and Social Psychology*, **1**, 631–641, 1965.

Dillehay, R. C., and L. R. Jernigan, 'The biased questionnaire as an instrument of opinion change', *Journal of Personality and Social Psychology*, **15**, 144–150, 1970.

Doise, W., 'Intergroup relations and polarization of individual and collective judgments', *Journal of Personality and Social Psychology*, **12**, 136–143, 1969.

Doise, W., and A. Sinclair, 'The categorisation process in intergroup relations', *European Journal of Social Psychology*, **3**, 145–157, 1973.

Dorris, J. W., 'Reactions to unconditional cooperation: A field study emphasizing variables neglected in laboratory research', *Journal of Personality and Social Psychology*, **22**, 387–397, 1972.

Driscoll, R., K. Davis, and M. Lipetz, 'Parental interference and romantic love: The Romeo and Juliet effect', *Journal of Personality and Social Psychology*, **24**, 1–10, 1972.

Duck, S. W., *Personal Relationships and Personal Constructs: A Study of Friendship Formation*, Wiley, London, 1973.

Durkin, J. E., 'Moment-of-truth encounters in Prisoner's Dilemma', Paper presented at American Psychological Association convention, Washington, D.C., 1967. Also in L. S. Wrightsman, Jr., J. O'Connor, and N. J. Baker (eds.), *Cooperation and Competition: Readings on Mixed-Motive Games*, Wadsworth, Belmont, 1972.

Dutton, D. G., 'Effect of feedback parameters on congruency versus positivity effects in reactions to personal evaluations', *Journal of Personality and Social Psychology*, **24**, 366–371, 1972.

Dutton, D. G., and A. Aron, 'Some evidence for heightened sexual attraction under conditions of high anxiety', *Journal of Personality and Social Psychology*, **30**, 510–517, 1974.

Duval, S., and R. A. Wicklund, *A Theory of Objective Self-awareness*, Academic Press, New York, 1972.

Dweck, C. S., 'The role of expectations and attributions in the alleviation of learned helplessness', *Journal of Personality and Social Psychology*, **31**, 674–685, 1975.

Eagly, A. H., and S. Chaiken, 'An attribution analysis of the effect of communicator characteristics on opinion change: The case of communicator attractiveness', *Journal of Personality and Social Psychology*, **32**, 136–144, 1975.

Eagly, A. H., and S. Himmelfarb, 'Current trends in attitude theory and research', in S. Himmelfarb, and A. H. Eagly (eds.), *Readings in Attitude Change*, Wiley, New York, 1974.

Eagly, A. H., W. Wood, and S. Chaiken, 'Causal inferences about communicators and their effect on opinion change', *Journal of Personality and Social Psychology*, **36**, 424–435, 1978.

Edwards, A. L., *Manual for the Edwards Personal Preference Schedule*, Psychological Corporation, New York, 1953.

Edwards, A. L., and K. C. Kenney, 'A comparison of the Thurstone and Likert techniques of attitude scale construction', *Journal of Applied Psychology*, **30**, 72–83, 1946.

Eiser, C., and J. R. Eiser, 'Acquisition of information in children's bargaining', *Journal of Personality and Social Psychology*, **34**, 796–804, 1976a.

Eiser, C., and J. R. Eiser, 'Children's concepts of a fair exchange', *British Journal of Social and Clinical Psychology*, **15**, 357–364, 1976b.

Eiser, J. R., 'Categorization, cognitive consistency, and the concept of dimensional salience', *European Journal of Social Psychology*, **1**, 435–454, 1971a.

Eiser, J. R., 'Comment on Ward's "Attitude and involvement in the absolute judgment of attitude statements."', *Journal of Personality and Social Psychology*, **17**, 81–83, 1971b.

Eiser, J. R., 'Enhancement of contrast in the absolute judgment of attitude statements', *Journal of Personality and Social Psychology*, **17**, 1–10, 1971c.

Eiser, J. R., 'Judgement of attitude statements as a function of judges' attitudes and the judgemental dimension', *British Journal of Social and Clinical Psychology*, **12**, 231–240, 1973.

Eiser, J. R., 'Evaluation of choice-dilemma alternatives: Utility, morality and social judgement', *British Journal of Social and Clinical Psychology*, **15**, 51–60, 1976.

Eiser, J. R., 'Discrepancy, dissonance and the "dissonant" smoker', *International Journal of the Addictions*, **13**, 1295–1305, 1978.

Eiser, J. R., C. N. Aiyeola, S. M. Bailey, and E. J. Gaskell, 'Attributions of intention to a simulated partner in a mixed-motive game', *British Journal of Social and Clinical Psychology*, **12**, 241–247, 1973.

Eiser, J. R., and K.-K. Bhavnani, 'The effect of situational meaning on the behaviour of subjects in the Prisoner's Dilemma game', *European Journal of Social Psychology*, **4**, 93–97, 1974.

Eiser, J. R., and C. J. Mower White, 'Evaluative consistency and social judgment', *Journal of Personality and Social Psychology*, **30**, 349–359, 1974a.

Eiser, J. R., and C. J. Mower White, 'The persuasiveness of labels: Attitude change produced through definition of the attitude continuum', *European Journal of Social Psychology*, **4**, 89–92, 1974b.

Eiser, J. R., and C. J. Mower White, 'Categorization and congruity in attitudinal judgment', *Journal of Personality and Social Psychology*, **31**, 769–775, 1975.

Eiser, J. R., and B. E. Osmon, 'Judgmental perspective and the value connotations of response scale labels', *Journal of Personality and Social Psychology*, **36**, 491–497, 1978.

Eiser, J. R., and S. M. Pancer, 'Attitudinal effects of the use of evaluatively biased language', *European Journal of Social Psychology*, **9**, 39–47, 1979.

Eiser, J. R., and M. J. Roiser, 'The sampling of social attitudes: A comment on Eysenck's "Social attitudes and social class".', *British Journal of Social and Clinical Psychology*, **11**, 397–401, 1972.

Eiser, J. R., and M. Ross, 'Partisan language, immediacy, and attitude change', *European Journal of Social Psychology*, **7**, 477–489, 1977.

Eiser, J. R., and W. Stroebe, *Categorization and Social Judgement*, Academic Press, London, 1972.

Eiser, J. R., and H. Tajfel, 'Acquisition of information in dyadic interaction', *Journal of Personality and Social Psychology*, **23**, 340–345, 1972.

Ekman, P., 'Universals and cultural differences in facial expressions of emotion', *Nebraska Symposium on Motivation*, **19**, 207–284, 1971.

Ekman, P., and W. V. Friesen, 'Constants across cultures in the face and emotions', *Journal of Personality and Social Psychology*, **17**, 124–129, 1971.

Emerson, R., *From Empire to Nation*, Harvard University Press, Cambridge, Mass., 1960.

Enzle, M. E., R. D. Hansen, and C. A. Lowe, 'Causal attribution in the mixed-motive game: Effects of facilitatory and inhibitory environmental forces', *Journal of Personality and Social Psychology*, **31**, 50–54, 1975.

Evans, G., and C. Crumbaugh, 'Effects of Prisoner's Dilemma format on cooperative behavior', *Journal of Personality and Social Psychology*, **3**, 486–488, 1966.

Exline, R., 'Visual interaction: The glances of power and preference', *Nebraska Symposium on Motivation*, **19**, 163–206, 1971.

Exline, R. V., D. Gray, and D. Schuette, 'Visual behavior in a dyad as affected by interview content and sex of respondent', *Journal of Personality and Social Psychology*, **1**, 201–209, 1965.

Eysenck, H. J., 'Social attitudes and social class', *British Journal of Social and Clinical Psychology*, **10**, 201–212, 1971.

Eysenck, H. J., and S. Crown, 'An experimental study in opinion-attitude methodology', *International Journal of Opinion and Attitude Research*, **3**, 47–86, 1949.

Farr, R. M., 'Heider, Harré and Herzlich on health and illness: Some observations on the structure of "représentations collectives",' *European Journal of Social Psychology*, **7**, 491–504, 1977a.

Farr, R. M., 'On the nature of attributional artifacts in qualitative research: Herzberg's two-factor theory of work motivation', *Journal of Occupational Psychology*, **50**, 3–14, 1977b.

Fazio, R. H., M. P. Zanna, and J. Cooper, 'Dissonance and self-perception: An integrative view of each theory's proper domain of application', *Journal of Experimental Social Psychology*, **13**, 464–479, 1977.

Fechner, G. T., *Elemente der psychophysik*, Breitkopt and Hartel, Leipzig, 1860.

Federoff, N. A., and J. H. Harvey, 'Focus of attention, self-esteem and attribution of causality', *Journal of Research in Personality*, **10**, 336–345, 1976.

Fehrer, E., 'Shifts in scale values of attitude statements as a function of the composition of the scale', *Journal of Experimental Psychology*, **44**, 179–188, 1952.

Felipe, A. I., 'Evaluative and descriptive consistency in trait inferences', *Journal of Personality and Social Psychology*, **16**, 627–638, 1970.

Ferguson, C. K., and H. H. Kelley, 'Significant factors in over-evaluation of own group's product', *Journal of Abnormal and Social Psychology*, **69**, 223–228, 1964.

Ferguson, L. W., 'The influence of individual attitudes on construction of an attitude scale', *Journal of Social Psychology*, **16**, 115–117, 1935.

Festinger, L., 'The treatment of qualitative data by "scale analysis"', *Psychological Bulletin*, **44**, 149–161, 1947.

Festinger, L., 'A theory of social comparison processes', *Human Relations*, **7**, 117–140, 1954.

Festinger, L., *A Theory of Cognitive Dissonance*, Row, Peterson, Evanston, Ill., 1957.

Festinger, L., and D. Bramel, 'The reactions of humans to cognitive dissonance', in A. Bachrach (ed.), *The Experimental Foundation of Clinical Psychology*, Basic Books, New York, 1962.

Festinger, L., and J. M. Carlsmith, 'Cognitive consequences of forced compliance', *Journal of Abnormal and Social Psychology*, **58**, 203–210, 1959.

Festinger, L., S. Schachter, and K. Back, *Social Pressures in Informal Groups: A Study of Human Factors in Housing*, Harper and Row, New York, 1950.

Fischhoff, B., 'Attribution theory and judgment under uncertainty', in J. H. Harvey, W. J. Ickes, and R. F. Kidd (eds.), *New Directions in Attribution Research, Vol. 1*, Erlbaum, Hillsdale, N.J., 1976.

Fishbein, M., 'Attitude and the prediction of behavior', in M. Fishbein (ed.), *Readings in Attitude Theory and Measurement*, Wiley, New York, 1967.

Fishbein, M., and I. Ajzen, 'Attribution of responsibility: A theoretical note', *Journal of Experimental Social Psychology*, **9**, 148–153, 1973.

Fishbein, M., and I. Ajzen, 'Attitudes toward objects as predictors of single and multiple behavioral criteria', *Psychological Review*, **81**, 59–74, 1974.

Fishbein, M., and I. Ajzen, *Belief, Attitude, Intention and Behaviour: An Introduction to Theory and Research*, Addison-Wesley, Reading, Mass., 1975.

Fishbein, M., and R. Hunter, 'Summation versus balance in attitude organization and change', *Journal of Abnormal and Social Psychology*, **69**, 505–510, 1964.

Fontaine, G., 'Social comparison and some determinants of expected personal control and expected performance in a novel task situation', *Journal of Personality and Social Psychology*, **29**, 487–496, 1974.

Fraser, C., C. Gouge, and M. Billig, 'Risky shifts, cautious shifts, and group polarization', *European Journal of Social Psychology*, **1**, 7–29, 1971.

Freedman, J. L., 'Attitudinal effects of inadequate justification', *Journal of Personality*, **31**, 371–385, 1963.

Gahagan, J. P., and J. T. Tedeschi, 'Strategy and the credibility of promises in the Prisoner's Dilemma game', *Journal of Conflict Resolution*, **12**, 224–234, 1968.

Gallo, P. S., 'Effects of increased incentives upon the use of threat in bargaining', *Journal of Personality and Social Psychology*, **4**, 14–20, 1966.

Gallo, P. S., 'Prisoner's of our own dilemma?', Paper presented at the Western Psychological Association convention, San Diego, 1968. Also in L. S. Wrightsman, Jr., J. O'Connor and N. J. Baker (eds.), *Cooperation and Competition: Readings on Mixed-motive Games*, Wadsworth, Belmont, 1972.

Gallo, P. S., and J. Sheposh, 'Effects of incentive magnitude on cooperation in the Prisoner's Dilemma game: A reply to Gumpert, Deutsch and Epstein', *Journal of Personality and Social Psychology*, **19**, 42–46, 1971.

Gammage, P., 'Socialisation, schooling, and locus of control', Unpublished Ph.D. Thesis, University of Bristol, 1974.

Gerard, H. B., and L. Fleischer, 'Recall and pleasantness of balanced and imbalanced cognitive structures', *Journal of Personality and Social Psychology*, **7**, 332–337, 1967.

Gerard, H. B., and C. Greenbaum, 'Attitudes toward an agent of uncertainty reduction', *Journal of Personality*, **30**, 485–495, 1962.

Gerard, H. B., and M. F. Hoyt, 'Distinctiveness of social categorization and attitude toward ingroup members', *Journal of Personality and Social Psychology*, **29**, 836–842, 1974.

Giles, H., 'Linguistic differentiation in ethnic groups', in H. Tajfel (ed.), *Differentiation Between Social Groups: Studies in the Social Psychology of Intergroup Relations*, Academic Press, London, 1978.

Goffman, E., 'On face-work: An analysis of ritual elements in social interaction', *Psychiatry*, **18**, 213–231, 1955.

Goffman, E., *The Presentation of Self in Everyday Life*, Doubleday Anchor Books, New York, 1959.

Goffman, E., *Asylums: Essays on the Social Situation of Mental Patients and Other Inmates*, Doubleday Anchor Books, New York, 1961.

Goffman, E., *Stigma: Notes on the Management of Spoiled Identity*, Prentice-Hall, Englewood Cliffs, N.J., 1963.

Goffman, E., *Strategic interaction*, Blackwell, Oxford, 1970.

Goffman, E., *Encounters: Two Studies in the Sociology of Interaction*, Allan Lane, Harmondsworth, 1972.

Goldberg, G. N., C. A. Kiesler, and B. E. Collins, 'Visual behavior and face-to-face distance during interaction', *Sociometry*, **32**, 43–53, 1969.

Goldman, R., M. Jaffa, and S. Schachter, 'Yom Kippur, Air France, dormitory food, and the eating behavior of obese and normal persons', *Journal of Personality and Social Psychology*, **10**, 117–123, 1968.

Gollob, H. F., 'The subject-verb-object approach to social cognition. *Psychological Review*, **81**, 286–321, 1974.

Gorsuch, R. L., *Factor Analysis*, Saunders, Philadelphia, 1974.

Götz-Marchand, B., J. Götz, and M. Irle, 'Preference of dissonance reduction modes as a function of their order, familiarity and reversibility', *European Journal of Social Psychology*, **4**, 201–228, 1974.

Greene, D., B. Sternberg, and M. R. Lepper, 'Overjustification in a token economy', *Journal of Personality and Social Psychology*, **34**, 1219–1234, 1976.

Greenwald, A. G., 'On the inconclusiveness of "crucial" cognitive tests of dissonance versus self-perception theories', *Journal of Experimental Social Psychology*, **11**, 490–499, 1975.

Gregory, S. W., 'Ideology and affect regarding "law" and their relation to law-abidingness, Part I', *Character and Personality*, **7**, 265–284, 1939.

Gruder, C. L., 'Relationships with opponent and partner in mixed-motive bargaining', *Journal of Conflict Resolution*, **15**, 403–416, 1971.

Gullahorn, J. T., 'Distance and friendship as factors in the gross interaction matrix', *Sociometry*, **15**, 123–134, 1952.

Gumpert, P., M. Deutsch, and Y. Epstein, 'Effect of incentive magnitude on cooperation in the Prisoner's Dilemma game', *Journal of Personality and Social Psychology*, **11**, 66–69, 1969.

Gurwitz, S. B., and L. Panciera, 'Attributions of freedom by actors and observers', *Journal of Personality and Social Psychology*, **32**, 531–539, 1975.

Guttman, L., 'A basis for scaling qualitative data', *American Sociological Review*, **9**, 139–150, 1944.

Hadamovsky, E., *Propaganda und Nationale Macht*, Oldenburg, 1933. (Translated by A. Mavrogordato and I. De Witt as *Propaganda and National Power*, Reprint edition, Arno Press, New York, 1972).

Hamilton, D. L., 'Cognitive biases in the perception of social groups', in J. S. Carroll and J. W. Payne (eds.), *Cognition and Social Behavior*, Erlbaum, Hillsdale, N.J., 1976.

Hamilton, D. L., and R. K. Gifford, 'Illusory correlation in interpersonal perception. A cognitive basis of stereotypic judgments', *Journal of Experimental Social Psychology*, **12**, 392–407, 1976.

Hansen, R. D., and J. M. Donoghue, 'The power of consensus: Information derived from one's own and others' behavior', *Journal of Personality and Social Psychology*, **35**, 294–302, 1977.

Haney, C., C. Banks, and P. Zimbardo, 'Interpersonal dynamics in a simulated prison', *International Journal of Criminology and Penology*, **1**, 69–97, 1973.

Hardin, G., 'The tragedy of the commons', *Science*, **162**, 1243–1248, 1968.

Harré, R., and P. F. Secord, *The Explanation of Social Behaviour*, Blackwell, Oxford, 1972.

Harvey, J. H., B. Harris, and R. D. Barnes, 'Actor-observer differences in the perceptions of responsibility and freedom', *Journal of Personality and Social Psychology*, **32**, 22–28, 1975.

Harvey, O. J., D. E. Hunt, and H. M. Schroder, *Conceptual Systems and Personality Organization*, Wiley, New York, 1961.

Harvey, O. J., and R. Ware, 'Personality differences in dissonance resolution', *Journal of Personality and Social Psychology*, **7**, 227–230, 1967.

Heider, F., 'Social perception and phenomenal causality', *Psychological Review*, **51**, 358–374, 1944.

Heider, F., 'Attitudes and cognitive organization', *Journal of Psychology*, **21**, 107–112, 1946.

Heider, F., *The Psychology of Interpersonal Relations*, Wiley, New York, 1958.

Helson, H., 'Adaptation-level as frame of reference for prediction of psychophysical data', *American Journal of Psychology*, **60**, 1–29, 1947.

Helson, H., *Adaptation-level Theory*, Harper and Row, New York, 1964.

Hendrick, C., and A. F. Constantini, 'Effects of varying trait inconsistency and response requirements on the primacy effect in impression formation', *Journal of Personality and Social Psychology*, **15**, 158–164, 1970.

Hensley, V., and S. Duval, 'Some perceptual determinants of perceived similarity, liking, and correctness', *Journal of Personality and Social Psychology*, **34**, 159–168, 1976.

Hermann, M. G., and N. Kogan, 'Negotiation in leader and delegate groups', *Journal of Conflict Resolution*, **12**, 332–344, 1968.

Herzberg, F., B. Mausner, and B. B. Snyderman, *The Motivation to Work*, 2nd ed., Wiley, New York, 1959.

Herzlich, C., *Health and Illness: A Social Psychological Analysis*, Academic Press, London, 1974.

Hinckley, E. D., 'The influence of individual opinion on construction of an attitude scale', *Journal of Social Psychology*, **3**, 283–296, 1932.

Hiroto, D. S., and M. E. P. Seligman, 'Generality of learned helplessness in man', *Journal of Personality and Social Psychology*, **31**, 311–327, 1975.

Hollander, E. P., *Leaders, Groups and Influence*, Oxford University Press, Oxford, 1964.

Holmes, J. G., and L. H. Strickland, 'Choice freedom and confirmation of incentive expectancy as determinants of attitude change', *Journal of Personality and Social Psychology*, **14**, 39–45, 1970.

Holzkamp, K., 'Das Problem der "Akzentuierung" in der sozialen Wahrnehmung', *Zeitschrift für Experimentelle und Angewandte Psychologie*, **12**, 86–97, 1965.

Holzkamp, K., and E. Perlwitz, 'Absolute oder relative Grossenakzentuierung? Eine experimentelle Studie zur sozialen Wahrnehmung', *Zeitschrift für Experimentelle und Angewandte Psychologie*, **13**, 390–405, 1966.

Horai, J., and J. T. Tedeschi, 'The effects of credibility and magnitude of punishment upon compliance to threats', *Journal of Personality and Social Psychology*, **12**, 164–169, 1969.

Hovland, C. I., O. J. Harvey, and M. Sherif, 'Assimilation and contrast effects in reactions to communication and attitude change', *Journal of Abnormal and Social Psychology*, **55**, 244–252, 1957.

Hovland, C. I., and M. Sherif, 'Judgmental phenomena and scales of attitude measurement: Item displacement in Thurstone scales', *Journal of Abnormal and Social Psychology*, **47**, 822–832, 1952.

Hoyt, G. C., and J. A. F. Stoner, 'Leadership and group decisions involving risk', *Journal of Experimental Social Psychology*, **4**, 275–284, 1968.

Huston, T. L., 'Ambiguity of acceptance, social desirability, and dating choice', *Journal of Experimental Social Psychology*, **9**, 32–42, 1973.

Ickes, W. J., R. A. Wicklund, and C. B. Ferris, 'Objective self awareness and self esteem', *Journal of Experimental Social Psychology*, **9**, 202–219, 1973.

James, W., 'The self', in C. Gordon and K. J. Gergen (eds.), *The Self in Social Interaction, Vol. 1: Classic and Contemporary Perspectives*, Wiley, New York, 1968.

Jaspars, J. M. F., 'On social perception', Unpublished PhD Thesis, University of Leiden, 1965.

Johnson, T. J., R. Feigenbaum, and M. Weiby, 'Some determinants and consequences of the teacher's perception of causation', *Journal of Educational Psychology*, **55**, 237–246, 1964.

Jones, C., and E. Aronson, 'Attribution of fault to a rape victim as a function of respectability of the victim', *Journal of Personality and Social Psychology*, **26**, 415–419, 1973.

Jones, E. E., and K. E. Davis, 'From acts to dispositions: The attribution process in person perception', in L. Berkowitz (ed.), *Advances in Experimental Social Psychology*, vol. 2, Academic Press, New York, 1965.

Jones, E. E., K. E. Davis, and K. J. Gergen, 'Role playing variations and their informational value for person perception', *Journal of Abnormal and Social Psychology*, **63**, 302–310, 1961.

Jones, E. E., and H. B. Gerard, *Foundations of Social Psychology*, Wiley, New York, 1967.

Jones, E. E., and G. R. Goethals, 'Order effects in impression formation: Attribution context and the nature of the entity', in E. E. Jones, D. E. Kanouse, H. H. Kelley, R. E. Nisbett, S. Valins, and B. Weiner, *Attribution: Perceiving the Causes of Behavior*, General Learning Press, Morristown, N.J., 1971.

Jones, E. E., and V. A. Harris, 'The attribution of attitudes', *Journal of Experimental Social Psychology*, **3**, 1–24, 1967.

Jones, E. E., and R. E. Nisbett, 'The actor and observer: Divergent perceptions of the causes of behavior', in E. E. Jones, D. E. Kanouse, H. H. Kelley, R. E. Nisbett, S. Valins, and B. Weiner, *Attribution: Perceiving the Causes of Behavior*, General Learning Press, Morristown, N. J., 1971.

Jones, E. E., S. Worchel, G. R. Goethals, and J. F. Grumet, 'Prior expectancy and behavioral extremity as determinants of attitude attribution', *Journal of Experimental Social Psychology*, **7**, 59–80, 1971.

Jones, R. A., D. E. Linder, C. A. Kiesler, M. P. Zanna, and J. W. Brehm, 'Internal states or external stimuli: Observers' attitude judgments and the dissonance theory—self-persuasion controversy', *Journal of Experimental Social Psychology*, **4**, 247–269, 1968.

Jordan, N., 'Behavioral forces that are a function of attitudes and cognitive organization', *Human Relations*, **6**, 273–287, 1953.

Kahneman, D., and A. Tversky, 'On the psychology of prediction', *Psychological Review*, **80**, 237–251, 1973.

Kanouse, D. E., and L. R. Hanson, Jr., 'Negativity in evaluations', in E. E. Jones, D. E. Kanouse, H. H. Kelley, R. E. Nisbett, S. Valins, and B. Weiner, *Attribution: Perceiving the Causes of Behavior*, General Learning Press, Morristown, N.J., 1971.

Kaplan, M. F., 'Judgment by jurors', in M. F. Kaplan and S. Schwartz (eds.), *Human Judgment and Decision Processes in Applied Settings*, Academic Press, New York, 1977.

Kaplan, M. F., and G. D. Kemmerick, 'Juror judgment as information integration: combining evidential and nonevidential information', *Journal of Personality and Social Psychology*, **30**, 493–499, 1974.

Karniol, R., and M. Ross, 'The effect of performance contingent rewards on instrinsic motivation', Unpublished manuscript, University of Waterloo, 1975.

Kelley, H. H., 'Experimental studies of threats in interpersonal negotiations', *Journal of Conflict Resolution*, **9**, 79–105, 1965.

Kelley, H. H., 'Attribution theory in social psychology', in D. Levine (ed.), *Nebraska Symposium on Motivation*, **15**, 192–238, 1967.

Kelley, H. H., 'Causal schemata and the attribution process', in E. E. Jones, D. E. Kanouse, H. H. Kelley, R. E. Nisbett, S. Valins, and B. Weiner, *Attribution: Perceiving the Causes of Behavior*, General Learning Press, Morristown, N.J., 1971.

Kelley, H. H., and A. J. Stahelski, 'Errors in perception of intentions in a mixed-motive game', *Journal of Experimental Social Psychology*, **6**, 379–400, 1970a.

Kelley, H. H., and A. J. Stahelski, 'Social interaction basis of cooperators' and competitors' beliefs about others', *Journal of Personality and Social Psychology*, **16**, 66–91, 1970b.

Kelley, H. H., J. W. Thibaut, R. Radloff, and D. Mundy, 'The development of cooperation in the "minimal social situation"', *Psychological Monographs*, **76**, (19, Whole no. 538), 1962.

Kelly, G. A., *The Psychology of Personal Constructs*, Norton, New York, 1955.

Kenrick, D. T., and R. B. Cialdini, 'Romantic attraction: Misattribution versus reinforcement explanations', *Journal of Personality and Social Psychology*, **35**, 381–391, 1977.

Kenrick, D. T., J. W. Reich, and R. B. Cialdini, 'Justification and compensation: Rosier skies for the devalued victim', *Journal of Personality and Social Psychology*, **34**, 654–657, 1976.

Kiesler, C. A., B. E. Collins, and N. Miller, *Attitude Change*, Wiley, New York, 1969.

Kiesler, C. A., R. E. Nisbett, and M. P. Zanna, 'On inferring one's beliefs from one's behavior', *Journal of Personality and Social Psychology*, **11**, 321–327, 1969.

Kiesler, S. B., and R. L. Baral, 'The search for a romantic partner: The effects of self-esteem and physical attractiveness on romantic behavior', in K. J. Gergen and D. Marlowe (eds.), *Personality and Social Behavior*, Addison-Wesley, Reading, Mass., 1970.

Kinder, D. R., T. Smith, and H. B. Gerard, 'The attitude-labeling process outside of the laboratory', *Journal of Personality and Social Psychology*, **33**, 480–491, 1976.

Klein, D. C. E., E. Fencil-Morse, and M. E. P. Seligman, 'Learned helplessness, depression, and the attribution of failure', *Journal of Personality and Social Psychiatry*, **33**, 508–516, 1976.

Klein, G. S., H. J. Schlesinger, and D. E. Meister, 'The effect of values on perception: An experimental critique', *Psychological Review*, **58**, 96–112, 1951.

Kogan, N., and M. A. Wallach, *Risk-taking: A Study in Cognition and Personality*, Holt, New York, 1964.

Kohlberg, L., 'State and sequence: The cognitive-developmental approach to socialization', in D. Goslin (ed.), *Handbook of Socialization Theory and Research*, Rand McNally, Chicago, 1969.

Krantz, D. L., and D. T. Campbell, 'Separating perceptual and linguistic effects of context shifts upon absolute judgments', *Journal of Experimental Psychology*, **62**, 35–42, 1961.

Kruglanski, A. W., S. Alon, and T. Lewis, 'Retrospective misattribution and task enjoyment', *Journal of Experimental Social Psychology*, **8**, 493–501, 1972.

Kruglanski, A. W., and M. Cohen, 'Attributed freedom and personal causation', *Journal of Personality and Social Psychology*, **26**, 245–250, 1973.

Kruglanski, A. W., I. Friedman, and G. Zeevi, 'The effect of extrinsic incentives on some qualitative aspects of task performance', *Journal of Personality*, **39**, 606–617, 1971.

Kruskal, J. B., 'Multidimensional scaling by optimizing goodness of fit to a nonmetric hypothesis', *Psychometrika*, **29**, 1–27, 1964.

Kuhlman, D. M., and D. L. Wimberley, 'Expectations of choice behavior held by cooperators, competitors, and individualists across four classes of experimental game', *Journal of Personality and Social Psychology*, **34**, 69–81, 1976.

Kutner, B., C. Wilkins, and P. R. Yarrow, 'Verbal attitudes and overt behavior involving racial prejudice', *Journal of Abnormal and Social Psychology*, **47**, 649–652, 1952.

Laird, J. D., 'Self-attribution of emotion: The effects of expressive behavior on the quality of emotional experience', *Journal of Personality and Social Psychology*, **29**, 475–486, 1974.

Lamm, H., 'Will an observer advise high risk taking after hearing a discussion of the decision problem?', *Journal of Personality and Social Psychology*, **6**, 467–471, 1967.

Landfield, A. W., 'The extremity rating revisited within the context of personal construct theory', *British Journal of Social and Clinical Psychology*, **7**, 135–139, 1968.

Langer, E. J., and R. P. Abelson, 'The semantics of asking a favor: How to succeed in getting help without really dying', *Journal of Personality and Social Psychology*, **24**, 26–32, 1972.

LaPiere, R. T., 'Attitudes vs. actions', *Social Forces*, **13**, 230–237, 1934.

Lawrence, D. H., and L. Festinger, *Deterrents and Reinforcement*, Stanford University Press, Stanford, California, 1962.

Leary, T., *Interpersonal Diagnosis of Personality*, Ronald, New York, 1957.

Lefcourt, H. M., 'Recent developments in the study of locus of control', in B. Maher (ed.), *Progress in Experimental Personality Research*, vol. 6, Academic Press, New York, 1972.

Lemaine, G., 'Social differentiation and social originality', *European Journal of Social Psychology*, **4**, 17–52, 1974.

Lemaine, G., J. Kastersztein, and B. Personnaz, 'Social differentiation', in H. Tajfel (ed.), *Differentiation Between Social Groups: Studies in the Social Psychology of Intergroup Relations*, Academic Press, London, 1978.

Lepper, M. R., and D. Greene, 'Turning play into work: Effects of adult surveillance and extrinsic rewards on children's intrinsic motivation', *Journal of Personality and Social Psychology*, **31**, 479–486, 1975.

Lepper, M. R., and D. Greene, 'On understanding "overjustification": A reply to Reiss and Sushinsky', *Journal of Personality and Social Psychology*, **33**, 25–35, 1976.

Lepper, M. R., D. Greene, and R. E. Nisbett, 'Undermining children's instrinsic interest with extrinsic reward: A test of the "overjustification" hypothesis', *Journal of Personality and Social Psychology*, **28**, 129–137, 1973.

Lerner, M. J., 'Evaluation of performance as a function of performer's reward and attractiveness', *Journal of Personality and Social Psychology*, **1**, 355–360, 1965.

Lerner, M. J., 'The desire for justice and reactions to victims', in J. Macaulay and L. Berkowitz (eds.), *Altruism and Helping Behavior*, Academic Press, New York, 1970.

Lerner, M. J., 'Justified self-interest and the responsibility for suffering', *Journal of Human Relations*, **19**, 550–559, 1971.

Lerner, M. J., 'The justice motive: "Equity" and "parity" among children', *Journal of Personality and Social Psychology*, **29**, 539–550, 1974.

Lerner, M. J., and R. R. Lichtman, 'Effects of perceived norms on attitudes and altruistic behavior toward a dependent other', *Journal of Personality and Social Psychology*, **9**, 226–232, 1968.

Lerner, M. J., and G. Matthews, 'Reactions to suffering of others under conditions of indirect responsibility', *Journal of Personality and Social Psychology*, **5**, 319–325, 1967.

Lerner, M. J., D. T. Miller, and J. G. Holmes, 'Deserving and the emergence of forms of justice', in L. Berkowitz and E. Walster (eds.), *Advances in Experimental Social Psychology (Vol. 9)*. *Equity Theory: Toward a General Theory of Social Interaction*, Academic Press, New York, 1976.

Lerner, M. J., and C. H. Simmons, 'Observer's reaction to the "innocent victim" Comparison or rejection?', *Journal of Personality and Social Psychology*, **4**, 203–210, 1966.

Levinger, G., and D. J. Schneider, 'Test of the "risk as a value" hypothesis', *Journal of Personality and Social Psychology*, **11**, 165–169, 1969.

Lewin, K., *Principles of Topological Psychology*, McGraw-Hill, New York, 1936.

Lewin, K., 'Behind food habits and methods of change', *Bulletin of the Research Council*, no. 108, 1943.

Lewin, K., *Resolving Social Conflicts*, Harper, New York, 1948.

Lewin, K., 'Group decision and social change', in E. Maccoby, T. Newcomb and E. Hartley (eds.), *Readings in Social Psychology*, 3rd edn., Holt, Rinehart, New York, 1958.

Likert, R., 'A technique for the measurement of attitudes', *Archives of Psychology*, **22**, whole no. 140, 1932.

Lilli, W., 'Das Zustandekommen von Stereotypen über einfache und komplexe Sachverhalte: Experimente zum klassifizierenden Urteil', *Zeitschift für Sozialpsychologie*, **1**, 57–59, 1970.

Linder, D. E., J. Cooper, and E. E. Jones, 'Decision freedom as a determinant of the role of incentive magnitude in attitude change', *Journal of Personality and Social Psychology*, **6**, 245–254, 1967.

Lindskold, S., and J. T. Tedeschi, 'Effects of contingent promises on interpersonal conflict', Unpublished manuscript, University of Miami, 1969.

Lipetz, M. E., I. H. Cohen, J. Dworin, and L. S. Rogers, 'Need complementarity, marital stability and marital satisfaction', in K. J. Gergen and D. Marlowe (eds.), *Personality and Social Behavior*, Addison-Wesley, Reading, Mass., 1970.

Lombardo, J. L., R. F. Weiss, and W. Buchanan, 'Reinforcing and attracting functions of yielding', *Journal of Personality and Social Psychology*, **21**, 359–368, 1972.

Lorr, M., and D. M. McNair, 'Expansion of the interpersonal behavior circle', *Journal of Personality and Social Psychology*, **2**, 813–830, 1965.

Lott, A. J., and B. E. Lott, 'Group cohesiveness, communication level, and conformity', *Journal of Abnormal and Social Psychology*, **62**, 408–412, 1961.

Lysak, W., and J. C. Gilchrist, 'Value equivocality and goal availability', *Journal of Personality*, **23**, 500–501, 1955.

Madaras, G. R., and D. J. Bem, 'Risk and conservatism in group decision-making', *Journal of Experimental Social Psychology*, **4**, 350–365, 1968.

Maddi, S. R., 'The pursuit of consistency and variety', in R. P. Abelson, E. Aronson, W. J. McGuire, T. M. Newcomb, M. J. Rosenberg, and P. H. Tannenbaum (eds.), *Theories of Cognitive Consistency: A Sourcebook*, Rand McNally, Chicago, 1968.

Malpass, R., and L. Kravitz, 'Recognition for faces of own and other race', *Journal of Personality and Social Psychology*, **13**, 330–334, 1969.

Manis, M., 'The interpretation of opinion statements as a function of recipient attitude', *Journal of Abnormal and Social Psychology*, **60**, 340–344, 1960.

Manis, M., 'The interpretation of opinion statements as a function of message ambiguity and recipient attitude', *Journal of Abnormal and Social Psychology*, **63**, 78–81, 1961.

Manis, M., 'Comment on Upshaw's "Own attitude as an anchor in equal-appearing intervals"', *Journal of Abnormal and Social Psychology*, **68**, 689–691, 1964.

Manis, M., 'Cognitive social psychology', *Personality and Social Psychology Bulletin*, **3**, 550–566, 1977.

Marchand, B., 'Auswirkung einer emotional wertvollen und einer emotional neutralen Klassifikation auf die Schätzung einer Stimulusserie', *Zeitschrift für Sozialpsychologie*, **1**, 264–274, 1970.

Marlowe, D., K. J. Gergen, and A. N. Doob, 'Opponents' personality, expectation of social interaction, and interpersonal bargaining', *Journal of Personality and Social Psychology*, **3**, 206–213, 1966.

Marwell, G., and D. R. Schmitt, *Cooperation: An Experimental Analysis*, Academic Press, New York, 1975.

McArthur, L. A., 'Luck is alive and well in New Haven: A serendipitous finding on perceived control of reinforcement after the draft lottery', *Journal of Personality and Social Psychology*, **16**, 316–318, 1970.

McArthur, L. A., 'The how and what of why: Some determinants and consequences of causal attribution', *Journal of Personality and Social Psychology*, **22**, 171–193, 1972.

McArthur, L. Z., 'The lesser influence of consensus than distinctiveness information on causal attributions: A test of the person-thing hypothesis', *Journal of Personality and Social Psychology*, **33**, 733–742, 1976.

McCauley, C. R., 'Extremity shifts, risk shifts, and attitude shifts after group discussion', *European Journal of Social Psychology*, **2**, 417–436, 1972.

McClintock, C. G., and S. P. McNeel, 'Reward level and goal playing behavior', *Journal of Conflict Resolution*, **10**, 98–102, 1966.

McClintock, C. G., and J. M. Moskowitz, 'Children's preferences for individualistic cooperative, and competitive outcomes', *Journal of Personality and Social Psychology*, **34**, 543–555, 1976.

McGuire, W. J., 'A syllogistic analysis of cognitive relationships', in C. I. Hovland and M. J. Rosenberg (eds.), *Attitude Organization and Change*, Yale University Press, New Haven, Conn., 1960.

McGuire, W. J., 'Résumé and response from the consistency theory viewpoint', in R. P. Abelson, E. Aronson, W. J. McGuire, T. M. Newcomb, M. J. Rosenberg, and P. H. Tannenbaum (eds.), *Theories of Cognitive Consistency: A Sourcebook*, Rand McNally, Chicago, 1968.

McGuire, W. J., C. V. McGuire, P. Child, and T. Fujioka, 'Salience of ethnicity in the spontaneous self-concept as a function of one's ethnic distinctiveness in the social environment', *Journal of Personality and Social Psychology*, **36**, 511–520, 1978.

McGuire, W. J., and A. Padawer-Singer, 'Trait salience in the spontaneous self-concept', *Journal of Personality and Social Psychology*, **33**, 743–754, 1976.

McMahan, I. D., 'Relationships between causal attributions and expectancy of success', *Journal of Personality and Social Psychology*, **28**, 108–114, 1973.

Mead, G. H., 'The genesis of the self', in C. Gordon and K. J. Gergen (eds.), *The Self in Social Interaction, Vol. 1: Classic and Contemporary Perspectives*, Wiley, New York, 1968.

Mehrabian, A., 'Measures of the achieving tendency', *Educational and Psychological Measurement*, **29**, 445–451, 1969.

Mehrabian, A., and H. Reed, 'Some determinants of communication accuracy', *Psychological Bulletin*, **70**, 365–380, 1968.

Messé, L. A., J. E. Dawson, and I. M. Lane, 'Equity as a mediator of the effect of reward level on behavior in the Prisoner's Dilemma game', *Journal of Personality and Social Psychology*, **26**, 60–65, 1973.

Messick, D. M., and G. Reeder, 'Perceived motivation, role variations, and the attribution of personal characteristics', *Journal of Experimental Social Psychology*, **8**, 482–491, 1972.

Meyer, W. U., 'Selbstverantworklichkeit und Leistungsmotivation', Unpublished PhD Thesis, Ruhr-Universität Bochum, 1970.

Milgram, S., 'Behavioral study of obedience', *Journal of Abnormal and Social Psychology*, **67**, 371–378, 1963.

Milgram, S., 'Group pressure and action against a person', *Journal of Abnormal and Social Psychology*, **69**, 137–143, 1964.

Milgram, S., *Obedience to Authority*, Tavistock, London, 1974.

Miller, D. T., and J. G. Holmes, 'The role of situational restrictiveness on self-fulfilling prophecies. A theoretical and empirical extension of Kelley and Stahelski's Triangle Hypothesis', *Journal of Personality and Social Psychology*, **31**, 661–673, 1975.

Miller, D. T., and M. Ross, 'Self-serving biases in the attribution of causality: Fact or fiction?', *Psychological Bulletin*, **82**, 213–225, 1975.

Miller, N., 'Involvement and dogmatism as inhibitors of attitude change', *Journal of Experimental Social Psychology*, **1**, 121–132, 1965.

Miller, R. L., P. Brickman, and D. Bolen, 'Attribution versus persuasion as a means for modifying behavior', *Journal of Personality and Social Psychology*, **31**, 430–441, 1975.

Mills, J., and P. M. Mintz, 'Effect of unexplained arousal on affiliation', *Journal of Personality and Social Psychology*, **24**, 11–13, 1972.

Mintz, A., 'Nonadaptive group behavior', *Journal of Abnormal and Social Psychology*, **46**, 150–159, 1951.

Mirels, H. L., 'Dimensions of internal versus external control', *Journal of Consulting and Clinical Psychology*, **34**, 226–228, 1970.

Mischel, W., *Personality and Assessment*, Wiley, New York, 1968.

Mischel, W., 'Processes in delay of gratification', in L. Berkowitz (ed.), *Advances in Experimental Social Psychology*, vol. 7, Academic Press, New York, 1974.

Mixon, D., 'Instead of deception', *Journal for the Theory of Social Behaviour*, **2**, 145–178, 1972.

Moos, R. H., 'Situational analysis of a therapeutic community milieu', *Journal of Abnormal Psychology*, **73**, 49–61, 1968.

Moscovici, S., 'Social Influence, I: Conformity and social control', in C. Nemeth (ed.), *Social Psychology: Classic and Contemporary Integrations*, Rand McNally, Chicago, 1974.

Moscovici, S., *Social Influence and Social Change*, Academic Press, London, 1976.

Moscovici, S., W. Doise, and R. Dulong, 'Studies in group decision, II: Differences of positions, differences of opinion and group polarization', *European Journal of Social Psychology*, **2**, 385–399, 1972.

Moscovici, S., E. Lage, and M. Naffrechoux, 'Influence of a consistent minority on the responses of a majority in a color perception task', *Sociometry*, **32**, 365–380, 1969.

Moscovici, S., and G. Paichelier, 'Social comparison and social recognition: Two complementary processes of identification', in H. Tajfel (ed.), *Differentiation Between Social Groups: Studies in the Social Psychology of Intergroup Relations*, Academic Press, London, 1978.

Moscovici, S., and M. Zavalloni, 'The group as a polarizer of attitudes', *Journal of Personality and Social Psychology*, **12**, 125–135, 1969.

Mouton, J. S., R. R. Blake, and J. A. Olmstead, 'The relationship between frequency of yielding and the disclosure of personal identity', *Journal of Personality*, **24**, 339–347, 1956.

Mower White, C. J., 'Positivity and consistency in attitude organization and judgement', Unpublished PhD Thesis, University of Bristol, 1974.

Myers, D. G., and G. D. Bishop, 'Discussion effects on racial attitudes', *Science*, **169**, 778–779, 1970.

Nemeth, C., 'Bargaining and reciprocity', *Psychological Bulletin*, **74**, 297–308, 1970.

Nemeth, C., 'A critical analysis of research utilizing the Prisoner's Dilemma paradigm for the study of bargaining', in L. Berkowitz (ed.), *Advances in Experimental Social Psychology*, vol. 6, Academic Press, New York, 1972.

Nemeth, C., M. Swedlund, and B. Kanki, 'Patterning of the minority's responses and their influence on the majority', *European Journal of Social Psychology*, **4**, 53–64, 1974.

Newcomb, T. M., *Personality and Social Change: Attitude Formation in a Student Community*, Dryden Press, New York, 1943.

Newcomb, T. M., 'The prediction of interpersonal attraction', *American Psychologist*, **11**, 575–586, 1956.

Newcomb, T. M., *The Acquaintance Process*, Holt, Rinehart, and Winston, New York, 1961.

Newcomb, T. M., 'Interpersonal balance', in R. P. Abelson, E. Aronson, W. J. McGuire, T. M. Newcomb, M. J. Rosenberg, and P. H. Tannenbaum (eds.), *Theories of Cognitive Consistency: A Source Book*, Rand McNally, Chicago, 1968.

Nisbett, R. E., 'Taste, deprivation, and weight determinants of eating behavior', *Journal of Personality and Social Psychology*, **10**, 107–116, 1968.

Nisbett, R. E., and E. Borgida, 'Attribution and the psychology of prediction', *Journal of Personality and Social Psychology*, **32**, 932–943, 1975.

Nisbett, R. E., E. Borgida, R. Crandall, and H. Reed, 'Popular induction: Information is not always informative', in J. S. Carroll and J. W. Payne (eds.), *Cognitive and Social Behavior*, Erlbaum, Hillsdale, N.J., 1976.

Nisbett, R. E., C. Caputo, P. Legant, and J. Maracek, 'Behavior as seen by the actor and as seen by the observer', *Journal of Personality and Social Psychology*, **27**, 154–164, 1973.

Nisbett, R. E., and T. D. Wilson, 'Telling more than we can know: Verbal reports on mental processes', *Psychological Review*, **84**, 231–259, 1977.

Nuttin, J. M., Jr., *The Illusion of Attitude Change: Towards a Response Contagion Theory of Persuasion*, Academic Press, London, 1975.

Orne, M. T., 'On the social psychology of the psychological experiment: With particular reference to demand characteristics and their implications', *American Psychologist*, **17**, 776–783, 1962.

Osgood, C. E., and Z. Luria, 'A blind analysis of a case of multiple personality using the semantic differential', *Journal of Abnormal and Social Psychology*, **49**, 579–591, 1954.

Osgood, C. E., G. J. Suci, and P. H. Tannenbaum, *The Measurement of Meaning*, University of Illinois Press, Urbana, Illinois, 1957.

Osgood, C. E., and P. H. Tannenbaum, 'The principle of congruity in the prediction of attitude change', *Psychological Review*, **62**, 42–55, 1955.

Oskamp, S., 'Effects of programmed strategies on cooperation in the Prisoner's Dilemma and other mixed-motive games', *Journal of Conflict Resolution*, **15**, 225–259, 1971.

Oskamp, S., and C. Kleinke, 'Amount of reward as a variable in the Prisoner's Dilemma game', *Journal of Personality and Social Psychology*, **16**, 133–140, 1970.

Ostrom, T. M., 'The relationship between the affective, behavioral and cognitive components of attitude', *Journal of Experimental Social Psychology*, **5**, 12–30, 1969.

Ostrom, T. M., 'Perspective as a determinant of attitude change', *Journal of Experimental Social Psychology*, **6**, 280–292, 1970.

Ostrom, T. M., and H. S. Upshaw, 'Psychological perspective and attitude change', in A. G. Greenwald, T. C. Brock, and T. M. Ostrom (eds.), *Psychological Foundations of Attitudes*, Academic Press, New York, 1968.

Ostrom, T. M., C. Werner, and M. J. Saks, 'An integration theory analysis of jurors' presumptions of guilt or innocence', *Journal of Personality and Social Psychology*, **36**, 436–450, 1978.

Pancer, S. M., and J. R. Eiser, 'Expectations, aspirations and evaluations as influenced by another's attributions for success and failure', *Canadian Journal of Behavioral Science*, **9**, 252–264, 1977.

Parducci, A., 'Range-frequency compromise in judgment', *Psychological Monographs*, **77**, (2, Whole no. 565), 1963.

Parducci, A., 'Contextual effects: A range-frequency analysis', in E. C. Carterette and M. P. Friedman (eds.), *Handbook of Perception*, vol. 2, Academic Press, New York, 1974.

Parducci, A., and L. M. Marshall, 'Assimilation versus contrast in the anchoring of perceptual judgment of weight', *Journal of Experimental Psychology*, **63**, 426–437, 1962.

Parducci, A., and L. F. Perrett, 'Category rating scales', *Journal of Experimental Psychology*, **89**, 427–452, 1971.

Peabody, D., 'Trait inferences: Evaluative and descriptive aspects', *Journal of Personality and Social Psychology Monograph*, **7**, (2, Pt. 2, Whole no. 642), 1957.

Peabody, D., 'Group judgments in the Philippines: Evaluative and descriptive aspects', *Journal of Personality and Social Psychology*, **10**, 290–300, 1968.

Peabody, D., 'Evaluative and descriptive aspects in personality perception: A reappraisal', *Journal of Personality and Social Psychology*, **16**, 639–646, 1970.

Peevers, B. H., and P. F. Secord, 'Developmental changes in attribution of descriptive concepts to persons', *Journal of Personality and Social Psychology*, **27**, 120–128, 1973.

Piaget, J., *The Moral Judgement of the Child*, Harcourt, Brace, and World, New York, 1932.

Piliavin, I. M., J. Hardyck, and A. Vadum, 'Reactions to the victim in a just or non-just world', Paper presented at the meeting of the Society of Experimental Social Psychology, Bethesda, Maryland, August, 1967.

Piliavin, I. M., J. A. Piliavin, and J. Rodin, 'Costs, diffusion and the stigmatized victim', *Journal of Personality and Social Psychology*, **32**, 429–438, 1975.

Piliavin, I. M., J. Rodin, and J. A. Piliavin, 'Good Samaritanism: An underground phenomenon?', *Journal of Personality and Social Psychology*, **13**, 289–299, 1969.

Piliavin, J. A., and I. M. Piliavin, 'Effect of blood on reactions to a victim', *Journal of Personality and Social Psychology*, **23**, 353–361, 1972.

Piliavin, J. A., I. M. Piliavin, E. P. Loewenton, C. McCauley, and P. Hammond, 'On observers' reproductions of dissonance effects: The right answers for the wrong reasons?', *Journal of*

Personality and Social Psychology, **13**, 98–106, 1969.

Pintner, R., and G. Forlano, 'The influence of attitude upon scaling of attitude items', *Journal of Social Psychology*, **8**, 39–45, 1937.

Pollis, N. P., 'Relative stability of scales formed in individual togetherness and group situations', *British Journal of Social and Clinical Psychology*, **6**, 249–255, 1967.

Pollis, N. P., and R. L. Montgomery, 'Individual judgmental stability and the natural group', *Journal of Social Psychology*, **74**, 75–81, 1968.

Pomazal, R. P., and J. J. Jaccard, 'An informational approach to altruistic behavior', *Journal of Personality and Social Psychology*, **33**, 317–326, 1976.

Press, A. N., W. H. Crockett, and P. S. Rosenkrantz, 'Cognitive complexity and the learning of balanced and unbalanced social structures', *Journal of Personality*, **37**, 541–553, 1969.

Price, K. O., E. Harburg, and T. M. Newcomb, 'Psychological balance in situations of negative interpersonal attitudes', *Journal of Personality and Social Psychology*, **3**, 265–270, 1966.

Prociuk, T. J., and L. J. Breen, 'Defensive externality and its relation to academic performance', *Journal of Personality and Social Psychology*, **31**, 549–556, 1975.

Pruitt, D. G., 'Reward structure and cooperation: The decomposed Prisoner's Dilemma game', *Journal of Personality and Social Psychology*, **7**, 21–27, 1967.

Pruitt, D. G., 'The "Walter Mitty" effect in individual and group risk-taking', *Proceedings of the 77th Annual Convention of the American Psychological Association*, **4**, 425–426 (Summary), 1969.

Pruitt, D. G., 'Motivational processes in the decomposed Prisoner's Dilemma game', *Journal of Personality and Social Psychology*, **14**, 227–238, 1970.

Pruitt, D. G., and M. J. Kimmel, 'Twenty years of experimental gaming: Critique, synthesis, and suggestions for the future', *Annual Review of Psychology*, **28**, 363–392, 1977.

Pruitt, D. G., and A. I. Teger, 'The risky shift in group betting', *Journal of Experimental Social Psychology*, **5**, 115–126, 1969.

Rabbie, J. M., and M. Horwitz, 'Arousal of ingroup-outgroup bias by a chance win or loss', *Journal of Personality and Social Psychology*, **13**, 269–277, 1969.

Rabbie, J. M., and G. Wilkens, 'Intergroup competition and its effect on intragroup and intergroup relations', *European Journal of Social Psychology*, **1**, 215–234, 1971.

Radlow, R., M. F. Weidner, and P. M. Hurst, 'Effect of incentive magnitude and motivational orientation upon choice behavior in a two-person, non-zero-sum game', *Journal of Social Psychology*, **74**, 199–208, 1968.

Rapoport, A., 'Conflict resolution in the light of game theory and beyond', in P. G. Swingle (ed.), *The Structure of Conflict*, Academic Press, New York, 1970.

Rapoport, A., and A. Chammah, *Prisoner's Dilemma*, University of Michigan Press, Ann Arbor, 1965.

Raven, B. H., 'Social influence on opinions and the communication of related content', *Journal of Abnormal and Social Psychology*, **58**, 119–128, 1959.

Regan, D. T., and J. Totten, 'Empathy and attribution: Turning observers into actors', *Journal of Personality and Social Psychology*, **32**, 850–856, 1975.

Reiss, S., and L. W. Sushinsky, 'Overjustification, competing responses, and the acquisition of intrinsic interest', *Journal of Personality and Social Psychology*, **31**, 1116–1125, 1975.

Reiss, S., and L. W. Sushinsky, 'The competing response hypothesis of decreased play effects: A reply to Lepper and Greene', *Journal of Personality and Social Psychology*, **33**, 233–244, 1976.

Rodrigues, A., 'Effects of balance, positivity and agreement in triadic social relations', *Journal of Personality and Social Psychology*, **5**, 472–478, 1967.

Rodrigues, A., 'The biasing effect of agreement in balanced and unbalanced triads', *Journal of Personality*, **36**, 138–153, 1968.

Rosenberg, M. J., 'When dissonance fails: On eliminating evaluation apprehension from attitude measurement', *Journal of Personality and Social Psychology*, **1**, 28–42, 1965.

Rosenberg, M. J., 'Some limits of dissonance: Toward a differentiated view of counterattitudinal performance', in S. Feldman (ed.), *Cognitive Consistency: Motivational Antecedents and Behavioral Consequents*, Academic Press, New York, 1966.

Rosenberg, M. J., and R. P. Abelson, 'An analysis of cognitive balancing', in M. J. Rosenberg, C. I. Hovland, W. J. McGuire, R. P. Abelson, and J. W. Brehm (eds.), *Attitude Organization and Change: An Analysis of Consistency Among Attitude Components*, Yale University Press, New Haven, Conn., 1960.

Rosenberg, M. J., and C. I. Hovland, 'Cognitive, affective and behavioral Components of attitudes', in M. J. Rosenberg, C. I. Hovland, W. J. McGuire, R. P. Abelson, and J. W. Brehm (eds.), *Attitude Organization and Change: An Analysis of Consistency Among Attitude Components*, Yale University Press, New Haven, Conn., 1960.

Rosenberg, S., and K. Olshan, 'Evaluative and descriptive aspects in personality perception', *Journal of Personality and Social Psychology*, **16**, 619–626, 1970.

Rosenhan, D. L., 'On being sane in insane places', *Science*, **179**, 250–258, 1973.

Rosenthal, A. M., *Thirty-eight Witnesses*, McGraw-Hill, New York, 1964.

Ross, A. S., and J. Braband, 'Effect of increased responsibility on bystander intervention, II: The cue value of a blind person', *Journal of Personality and Social Psychology*, **25**, 254–258, 1973.

Ross, L., D. Greene, and P. House, 'The "false consensus effect": An egocentric bias in social perception and attribution processes', *Journal of Experimental Social Psychology*, **13**, 279–301, 1977.

Ross, M., 'Salience of reward and intrinsic motivation', *Journal of Personality and Social Psychology*, **32**, 245–254, 1975.

Ross, M., 'The self-perception of intrinsic motivation', in J. H. Harvey, W. J. Ickes, and R. F. Kidd (eds.), *New Directions in Attribution Research*, vol. 1, Erlbaum, Hillsdale, N.J., 1976.

Ross, M., C. A. Insko, and H. S. Ross, 'Self-attribution of attitude', *Journal of Personality and Social Psychology*, **17**, 292–297, 1971.

Ross, M., R. Karniol, and M. Rothstein, 'Reward contingency and intrinsic motivation in children: A test of the delay of gratification hypothesis', *Journal of Personality and Social Psychology*, **33**, 442–447, 1976.

Ross, M., and R. F. Shulman, 'Increasing the salience of initial attitudes: Dissonance versus self-perception theory', *Journal of Personality and Social Psychology*, **28**, 138–144, 1973.

Rossman, B. B., and H. F. Gollob, 'Social inference and pleasantness judgments involving people and issues', *Journal of Experimental Social Psychology*, **12**, 374–391, 1976.

Rotter, J. B., 'Generalized expectancies for internal versus external control of reinforcement', *Psychological Monographs*, **80**, (1, Whole no. 609), 1966.

Rotter, J. B., J. E. Chance, and E. J. Phares, *Applications of a Social Learning Theory of Personality*, Holt, Rinehart, and Winston, New York, 1972.

Rubin, Z., 'The measurement of romantic love', *Journal of Personality and Social Psychology*, **16**, 265–273, 1970.

Rubin, Z., *Liking and Loving: An Invitation to Social Psychology*, Holt, Rinehart, and Winston, New York, 1973.

Rubin, Z., and R. B. Zajonc, 'Structural bias and generalization in the learning of social structures', *Journal of Personality*, **37**, 310–324, 1969.

Rundquist, E. A., and R. F. Sletto, *Personality in the Depression*, University of Minnesota Press, Minneapolis, 1936.

Russell, M. A. H., 'Tobacco smoking and nicotine dependence', in R. J. Gibbins *et al.*, (eds.), *Research Advances in Alcohol and Drug Problems*, vol. 3, Wiley, New York, 1976.

Sampson, E. E., and C. A. Insko, 'Cognitive consistency and performance in the autokinetic situation', *Journal of Abnormal and Social Psychology*, **68**, 184–192, 1964.

Schachter, S., 'Deviation, rejection and communication', *Journal of Abnormal and Social Psychology*, **46**, 190–207, 1951.

Schachter, S., and L. Gross, 'Manipulated time and eating behavior', *Journal of Personality and Social Psychology*, **10**, 98–106, 1968.

Schachter, S., B. Silverstein, L. T. Kozlowski, D. Perlick, C. P. Herman, and B. Liebling, 'Studies of the interaction of psychological and pharmacological determinants of smoking', *Journal of Experimental Psychology: General*, **106**, 3–40, 1977.

Schachter, S., and J. E. Singer, 'Cognitive, social and physiological determinants of emotional state', *Psychological Review*, **69**, 379–399, 1962.

Schaefer, E., 'A circumplex model for maternal behavior', *Journal of Abnormal and Social Psychology*, **59**, 226–235, 1959.

Schaffer, D. R., 'Some effects of consonant and dissonant attitudinal advocacy on initial attitude salience and attitude change, *Journal of Personality and Social Psychology*, **32**, 160–168, 1975.

Schopler, J., and B. Layton, 'Determinants of the self-attribution of having influenced another person', *Journal of Personality and Social Psychology*, **22**, 326–332, 1972.

Scodel, A., J. S. Minas, P. Ratoosh, and M. Lipetz, 'Some descriptive aspects of two-person non-zero-sum games, I ', *Journal of Conflict Resolution*, **3**, 114–119, 1959.

Secord, P. F., 'Stereotyping and favorableness in the perception of Negro faces, *Journal of Abnormal and Social Psychology*, **59**, 309–315, 1959.

Secord, P. F., and C. W. Backman, *Social Psychology*, McGraw-Hill, New York, 1964.

Secord, P. F., and C. W. Backman, 'An interpersonal approach to personality', in B. Maher (ed.), *Progress in Experimental Research*, vol. 2, Academic Press, New York, 1965.

Secord, P. F., W. Bevan, and B. Katz, 'The Negro stereotype and perceptual accentuation', *Journal of Abnormal and Social Psychology*, **53**, 78–83, 1956.

Segall, M. H., 'The effect of attitude and experience on judgments of controversial statements', *Journal of Abnormal and Social Psychology*, **58**, 366–372, 1959.

Seiler, L. H., and R. L. Hough, 'Empirical comparisons of the Thurstone and Likert techniques', in G. F. Summers (ed.), *Attitude Measurement*, Rand McNally, Chicago, 1970.

Seligman, M. E. P., 'Learned helplessness', *Annual Review of Medicine*, **23**, 407–412, 1972.

Seligman, M. E. P., *Helplessness*, Freeman, San Francisco, 1975.

Seligman, M. E. P., and S. F. Maier, 'Failure to escape traumatic shock ', *Journal of Experimental Psychology*, **74**, 1–9, 1967.

Selltiz, C., H. Edrich, and S. W. Cook, 'Ratings of favorableness about a social group as an indication of attitude toward the group', *Journal of Personality and Social Psychology*, **2**, 408–415, 1965.

Sermat, V., 'Is game behavior related to behavior in other interpersonal situations?', *Journal of Personality and Social Psychology*, **16**, 92–109, 1970.

Shaffer, D. R., 'Some effects of consonant and dissonant attitudinal advocacy on initial attitude salience and attitude change', *Journal of Personality and Social Psychology*, **32**, 160–168, 1975.

Shapiro, M. B., 'The psychology of pleasantness and unpleasantness: A reminder of neglected work ', *Bulletin of the British Psychological Society*, **20**, no. 67, 1–10, 1967.

Shaver, K. G., 'Defensive attribution: Effects of severity and relevance on the responsibility assigned for an accident', *Journal of Personality and Social Psychology*, **14**, 101–113, 1970a.

Shaver, K. G., 'Redress and conscientiousness in the attribution of responsibility for accidents', *Journal of Experimental Social Psychology*, **6**, 100–110, 1970b.

Shaw, J. I., and P. Skolnick, 'Attribution of responsibility for a happy accident', *Journal of Personality and Social Psychology*, **18**, 380–383, 1971.

Shaw, M. E., and J. L. Sulzer, 'An empirical test of Heider's levels in attribution of responsibility', *Journal of Abnormal and Social Psychology*, **69**, 39–46, 1964.

Shaw, M. E., and J. M. Wright, *Scales for the Measurement of Attitudes*, McGraw-Hill, New York, 1967.

Shepard, R. N., 'The analysis of proximities: Multidimensional scaling with an unknown distance function, I ', *Psychometrika*, **27**, 125–140, 1962a.

Shepard, R. N., 'The analysis of proximities: Multidimensional scaling with an unknown distance function, II ', *Psychometrika*, **27**, 219–246, 1962b.

Sherif, C. W., M. Sherif, and R. E. Nebergall, *Attitude and Attitude Change: The Social Judgment-involvement Approach*, Saunders, Philadelphia, 1965.

Sherif, M., 'A study of some social factors in perception', *Archives of Psychology*, **22**, no. 187, 1935.

Sherif, M., 'A preliminary experimental study of intergroup relations', in J. H. Rohrer and M. Sherif (eds.), *Social Psychology at the Crossroads*, Harper, New York, 1951.

Sherif, M., *Group Conflict and Cooperation: Their Social Psychology*, Routledge and Kegan Paul, London, 1966.

Sherif, M., and C. I. Hovland, *Social Judgment: Assimilation and Contrast Effects in Communication and Attitude Change*, Yale University Press, New Haven, Conn., 1961.

Sherif, M., and C. W. Sherif, *Groups in Harmony and Tension*, Harper, New York, 1953.

Sherif, M., and C. W. Sherif, *Social Psychology*, Harper and Row, New York, 1969.

Sherif, M., D. Taub, and C. I. Hovland, 'Assimilation and contrast effects of anchoring stimuli on judgment', *Journal of Experimental Psychology*, **55**, 150–155, 1958.

Shomer, R. W., A. H. Davis, and H. H. Kelley, 'Threats and the development of coordination: Further studies of the Deutsch and Krauss trucking game', *Journal of Personality and Social Psychology*, **4**, 119–126, 1966.

Sidowski, J. B., 'Reward and punishment in a minimal social situation', *Journal of Experimental Psychology*, **54**, 119–126, 1957.

Simons, C. W., and J. A. Piliavin, 'The effect of deception on reactions to a victim', *Journal of Personality and Social Psychology*, **21**, 56–60, 1972.

Skolnick, P., 'Reactions to personal evaluation: A failure to replicate', *Journal of Personality and Social Psychology*, **18**, 62–67, 1971.

Slater, P. E., 'Parent behavior and the personality of the child', *Journal of Genetic Psychology*, **101**, 53–68, 1962.

Slovic, P., B. Fischoff, and S. Lichtenstein, 'Cognitive processes and societal risk taking', in J. S. Carroll and J. W. Payne (eds.), *Cognition and Social Behaviour*, Erlbaum, Hillsdale, N.J., 1976.

Smith, E. R., and F. D. Miller, 'Limits on perception of cognitive processes: A reply to Nisbett and Wilson', *Psychological Review*, **85**, 355–362, 1978.

Snyder, M., and E. Ebbesen, 'Dissonance awareness: A test of dissonance theory versus self-perception theory', *Journal of Experimental Social Psychology*, **8**, 502–517, 1972.

Snyder, M. L., W. G. Stephan, and D. Rosenfield, 'Egotism and attribution', *Journal of Personality and Social Psychology*, **33**, 435–441, 1976.

Solley, C. M., and R. Lee, 'Perceived size: Closure versus symbolic value', *American Journal of Psychology*, **68**, 142–144, 1955.

Sorrentino, R. M., and R. G. Boutelier, 'Evaluation of a victim as a function of fate similarity/dissimilarity', *Journal of Experimental Social Psychology*, **10**, 83–92, 1974.

Sperling, H. G., 'An experimental study of some psychological factors in judgment', N.S.S.R. Unpublished master's thesis, 1946.

St Jean, R., 'Reformulation of the value hypothesis in group risk taking', *Proceedings of the 78th Annual Convention of the American Psychological Association*, **5**, 339–340 (Summary), 1970.

Stephan, W., E. Berscheid, and E. Walster, 'Sexual arousal and heterosexual perception', *Journal of Personality and Social Psychology*, **20**, 93–101, 1971.

Stevens, L., and E. E. Jones, 'Defensive attribution and the Kelley cube', *Journal of Personality and Social Psychology*, **34**, 809–820, 1976.

Stevens, S. S., 'On the psychophysical law', *Psychological Review*, **64**, 153–181, 1957.

Stevens, S. S., 'Adaptation-level versus the relativity of judgment', *American Journal of Psychology*, **71**, 633–646, 1958.

Stevens, S. S., 'A metric for the social consensus', *Science*, **151**, 530–541, 1966.

Stevens, S. S., *Psychophysics: Introduction to Its Perceptual, Neural and Social Prospects*, Wiley New York, 1975.

Stewart, R. H., 'Effect of continuous responding on the order effect in personality impression formation', *Journal of Personality and Social Psychology*, **1**, 161–165, 1965.

Stoner, J. A. F., 'A comparison of individual and group decision involving risk', Unpublished doctoral dissertation, M.I.T., School of Industrial Management, 1961.

Storms, M. D., 'Videotape and the attribution process: Reversing actors' and observers' points of view', *Journal of Personality and Social Psychology*, **27**, 165–175, 1973.

Streufert, S., and S. C. Streufert, *Behavior in the Complex Environment*, Winston, Washington, D.D., 1978.

Stroebe, W., 'Self-esteem and interpersonal attraction', in S. Duck (ed.), *Theory and Practice in Interpersonal Attraction*, Academic Press, London, 1977.

Stroebe, W., A. H. Eagly, and M. S. Stroebe, 'Friendly or just polite? The effect of self-esteem on attributions', *European Journal of Social Psychology*, **7**, 265–274, 1977.

Stroebe, W., C. A. Insko, V. D. Thompson, and B. D. Layton, 'Effects of physical attractiveness, attitude similarity and sex on various aspects of interpersonal attraction', *Journal of Personality and Social Psychology*, **18**, 79–91, 1971.

Stroebe, W., V. D. Thompson, C. A. Insko, and S. R. Reisman, 'Balance and differentiation in the evaluation of linked attitude objects', *Journal of Personality and Social Psychology*, **16**, 38–47, 1970.

Sullivan, H. S., *The Interpersonal Theory of Psychiatry*, Tavistock, London, 1955.

Swingle, P. G., 'Exploitative behavior in non-zero-sum games', *Journal of Personality and Social Psychology*, **16**, 121–132, 1970.

Tajfel, H., 'Value and the perceptual judgment of magnitude', *Psychological Review*, **64**, 192–204, 1957.

Tajfel, H., 'Quantitative judgement in social perception', *British Journal of Psychology*, **50**, 16–29, 1959.

Tajfel, H., 'Cognitive aspects of prejudice', *Journal of Social Issues*, **25**, 79–97, 1969.

Tajfel, H., (ed.), *Differentiation Between Social Groups: Studies in the Social Psychology of Intergroup Relations*, Academic Press, London, 1978.

Tajfel, H., C. Flament, M. G. Billig, and R. P. Bundy, 'Social categorization and intergroup behaviour', *European Journal of Social Psychology*, **1**, 149–178, 1971.

Tajfel, H., A. A. Sheikh, and R. C. Gardner, 'Content of stereotypes and the inference of similarity between members of stereotyped groups', *Acta Psychologica*, **22**, 191–201, 1964.

Tajfel, H., and A. L. Wilkes, 'Classification and quantitative judgement', *British Journal of Psychology*, **54**, 101–114, 1963.

Tajfel, H., and A. L. Wilkes, 'Salience of attributes and commitment to extreme judgements in the perception of people', *British Journal of Social and Clinical Psychology*, **3**, 40–49, 1964.

Taylor, S. E., and S. T. Fiske, 'Point of view and perceptions of causality', *Journal of Personality and Social Psychology*, **32**, 439–445, 1975.

Taylor, S. E., and S. T. Fiske, 'Salience, attention and attribution: Top of the head phenomena', in L. Berkowitz (ed.), *Advances in Experimental Social Psychology*, vol. 11, Academic Press, New York, 1978.

Taylor, S. E., S. T. Fiske, N. L. Etcoff, and A. J. Ruderman, 'Categorical and contextual bases of person memory and stereotyping', *Journal of Personality and Social Psychology*, **36**, 778–793, 1978.

Tedeschi, J. T., 'Threats and promises', in P. G. Swindle (ed.), *The Structure of Conflict*, Academic Press, New York, 1970.

Tedeschi, J. T., T. V. Bonoma, and N. Novinson, 'Behavior of a threatener: Retaliation vs. fixed opportunity costs', *Journal of Conflict Resolution*, **14**, 70–76, 1970.

Tedeschi, J. T., S. Lindskold, J. Horai, and J. P. Gahagan, 'Social power and the credibility of promises', *Journal of Personality and Social Psychology*, **13**, 253–261, 1969.

Teger, A. I., and D. G. Pruitt, 'Components of group risk taking', *Journal of Experimental Social Psychology*, **3**, 189–205, 1967.

Terhune, K. W., 'Motives, situation and interpersonal conflict within the Prisoner's Dilemma', *Journal of Personality and Social Psychology Monograph Supplement*, **8**, 1–24, 1968.

Thibaut, J. W., and H. H. Kelley, *The Social Psychology of Groups*, Wiley, New York, 1959.

Thibaut, J. W., and M. Ross, 'Commitment and experience as determinants of assimilation and contrast', *Journal of Personality and Social Psychology*, **13**, 322–329, 1969.

Thomson, J. A. K., (Tr.), *The Ethics of Aristotle*, Penguin, Harmondsworth, 1955.

Thurstone, L. L., 'Attitudes can be measured', *American Journal of Sociology*, **33**, 529–554, 1928.

Thurstone, L. L., (ed.), *Scales for the Measurement of Social Attitudes*, University of Chicago Press, Chicago, 1931.

Thurstone, L. L., and E. J. Chave, *The Measurement of Attitude*, University of Chicago Press, Chicago, 1929.

Tognoli, J., 'Reciprocation of generosity and knowledge of game termination in the decomposed Prisoner's Dilemma game', *European Journal of Social Psychology*, **5**, 297–312, 1975.

Tom, G., and M. Rucker, 'Fat, full, and happy: Effects of food deprivation, external cues and obesity on preference ratings, consumption, and buying intentions', *Journal of Personality and Social Psychology*, **32**, 761–766, 1975.

Torgerson, W. S., *Theory and Methods of Scaling*, Wiley, New York, 1958.

Tresselt, M. E., 'The effect of experience of contrasted groups upon the formation of a new scale', *Journal of Social Psychology*, **27**, 209–216, 1948.

Triandis, H. C., 'Exploratory factor analyses of the behavioral component of social attitudes', *Journal of Abnormal and Social Psychology*, **68**, 420–430, 1964.

Triandis, H. C., 'Towards an analysis of the components of interpersonal attitudes', in C. W. Sherif and M. Sherif (eds.), *Attitudes, Ego Involvement, and Change*, Wiley, New York, 1967.

Triandis, H. C., and M. Fishbein, 'Cognitive interaction in person perception', *Journal of Abnormal and Social Psychology*, **67**, 446–453, 1963.

Tucker, L. R., and S. Messick, 'An individual differences model for multidimensional scaling', *Psychometrika*, **28**, 333–367, 1963.

Turner, J. C., 'Social comparison and social indentity: Some prospects for intergroup behaviour', *European Journal of Social Psychology*, **5**, 5–34, 1975.

Turner, J. C., 'Social comparison, similarity and ingroup favouritism', in H. Tajfel (ed.), *Differentiation Between Social Groups: Studies in the Social Psychology of Intergroup Relations*, Academic Press, London, 1978.

Turner, J. C., and R. Brown, 'Social status, cognitive alternatives and intergroup relations', in H. Tajfel (ed.), *Differentiation Between Social Groups: Studies in the Social Psychology of Intergroup Relations*, Academic Press, London, 1978.

Tversky, A., and D. Kahneman, 'Judgment under uncertainty; Heuristics and biases', *Science*, **185**, 1124–1131, 1974.

Upshaw, H. S., 'Own attitude as an anchor in equal-appearing intervals', *Journal of Abnormal and Social Psychology*, **64**, 85–96, 1962.

Upshaw, H. S., 'The effect of variable perspectives on judgments of opinion statement for Thurstone scales: Equal-appearing intervals', *Journal of Personality and Social Psychology*, **2**, 60–69, 1965.

Upshaw, H. S., 'The personal reference scale: An approach to social judgment', in L. Berkowitz (ed.), *Advances in Experimental Social Psychology*, vol. 4, Academic Press, New York, 1969.

Upshaw, H. S., 'Out of the laboratory and into wonderland: A critique of the Kinder, Smith and Gerard adventure with perspective theory', *Journal of Personality and Social Psychology*, **34**, 699–703, 1976.

Upshaw, H. S., T. M. Ostrom, and C. D. Ward, 'Content versus self-rating in attitude research', *Journal of Experimental Social Psychology*, **6**, 272–279, 1970.

Valins, S., 'Cognitive effects of false heart-rate feed-back', *Journal of Personality and Social Psychology*, **4**, 400–408, 1966.

Valins, S., 'Persistent effects of information about internal reactions: Ineffectiveness of debriefing', in H. London and R. E. Nisbett (eds.), *The Cognitive Alteration of Feeling States*, Aldine, Chicago, 1972.

van der Pligt, J., and J. A. van Dijk, 'Polarization of judgment and preference for judgmental labels', *European Journal of Social Psychology*, **9**, 233–242, 1979.

Vannoy, J. S., 'Generality of cognitive complexity-simplicity as a personality construct', *Journal of Personality and Social Psychology*, **2**, 385–396, 1965.

Verhaeghe, H., 'Mistreating other persons through simple discrepant role playing: Dissonance arousal or response contagion', *Journal of Personality and Social Psychology*, **34**, 125–137, 1976.

Vine, I., 'Communication by facial-visual signals', in J. H. Crook (ed.), *Social Behaviour in Birds and Mammals*, Academic Press, London, 1970.

Vinokur, A., 'Cognitive and affective processes influencing risk-taking in groups: An expected utility approach', *Journal of Personality and Social Psychology*, **20**, 472–486, 1971.

Vinokur, A., and E. Burnstein, 'Effects of partially shared persuasive arguments on group-induced shifts: A group-problem-solving approach', *Journal of Personality and Social Psychology*, **29**, 305–315, 1974.

Vinokur, A., and E. Burnstein, 'Depolarization of attitudes in groups', *Journal of Personality and Social Psychology*, **36**, 872–885, 1978.

Vinokur, A., Y. Trope, and E. Burnstein, 'A decision making analysis of persuasive argumentation and the choice-shift effect', *Journal of Experimental Social Psychology*, **11**, 127–148, 1975.

Voissem, N. H., and F. Sistrunk, 'Communication schedule and cooperative game behavior', *Journal of Personality and Social Psychology*, **19**, 160–167, 1971.

Volkmann, J., 'Scales of judgment and their implications for social psychology', in J. H. Rohrer and M. Sherif (eds.), *Social Psychology at the Crossroads*, Harper and Row, New York, 1951.

Wahrman, R., and M. D. Pugh, 'Competence and conformity: Another look at Hollander's study', *Sociometry*, **35**, 376–386, 1972.

Wallach, M. A., and N. Kogan, 'Sex differences and judgment processes', *Journal of Personality*, **27**, 555–564, 1959.

Wallach, M. A., and N. Kogan, 'Aspects of judgment and decision-making', *Behavioral Science*, **6**, 23–36, 1961.

Wallach, M. A., and N. Kogan, 'The role of information, discussion and consensus in group risk taking', *Journal of Experimental Social Psychology*, **1**, 1–19, 1965.

Wallach, M. A., N. Kogan, and D. J. Bem, 'Diffusion of responsibility and level of risk taking in groups', *Journal of Abnormal and Social Psychology*, **68**, 263–274, 1964.

Wallach, M. A., N. Kogan, and R. Burt, 'Are risk takers more persuasive than conservatives in group decisions?', *Journal of Experimental Social Psychology*, **4**, 76–89, 1968.

Walster, E., 'Assignment of responsibility for an accident', *Journal of Personality and Social Psychology*, **3**, 73–79, 1966.

Walster, E., '"Second guessing" important events', *Human Relations*, **20**, 239–250, 1967.

Walster, E., V. Aronson, D. Abrahams, and L. Rottman, 'Importance of physical attractiveness in dating behavior', *Journal of Personality and Social Psychology*, **4**, 508–516, 1966.

Walster, E., E. Berscheid, and G. W. Walster, 'New directions in equity research', in L. Berkowitz and E. Walster (eds.), *Advances in Experimental Social Psychology, Vol. 9. Equity Theory: Toward a General Theory of Social Interaction*, Academic Press, New York, 1976.

Walster, E., and P. Prestholdt, 'The effect of misjudging another: Over-compensation or dissonance reduction?', *Journal of Experimental Social Psychology*, **2**, 85–97, 1966.

Ward, C. D., 'Attitude and involvement in the absolute judgment of attitude statements', *Journal of Personality and Social Psychology*, **4**, 465–476, 1966.

Ware, R., and O. J. Harvey, 'A cognitive determinant of impression formation', *Journal of Personality and Social Psychology*, **5**, 38–44, 1967.

Warr, P. B., and P. Jackson, 'The importance of extremity', *Journal of Personality and Social Psychology*, **32**, 278–282, 1975.

Warr, P. B., and J. S. Smith, 'Combining information about people: Comparisons between six models', *Journal of Personality and Social Psychology*, **16**, 55–65, 1970.

Webb, E. J., D. T. Campbell, R. D. Schwartz, and L. Sechrest, *Unobtrusive Measures: Nonreactive Research in the Social Sciences*, Rand McNally, Chicago, 1966.

Weber, M., *The Protestant Ethic and the Spirit of Capitalism*, (translated by T. Parsons) Scribners, New York, 1958.

Weiner, B., 'New conceptions in the study of achievement motivation', in B. Maher (ed.), *Progress in Experimental Personality Research*, vol. 5, Academic Press, New York, 1970.

Weiner, B., I. Frieze, A. Kukla, L. Reed, S. Rest, and R. M. Rosenbaum, 'Perceiving the causes of success and failure', in E. E. Jones, D. E. Kanouse, H. H. Kelley, R. E. Nisbett, S. Valins, and B. Weiner (eds.), *Attribution: Perceiving the Causes of Behavior*, General Learning Press, Morristown, N.J., 1971.

Weiner, B., H. Heckhausen, W. Meyer, and R. E. Cook, 'Causal ascriptions and achievement behavior: The conceptual analysis of effort', *Journal of Personality and Social Psychology*, **21**, 239–248, 1972.

Weiner, B., and A. Kukla, 'An attributional analysis of achievement motivation', *Journal of Personality and Social Psychology*, **15**, 1–20, 1970.

Weiner, B., and J. Sierad, 'Misattribution for failure and enhancement of achievement strivings', *Journal of Personality and Social Psychology*, **31**, 415–421, 1975.

Wells, G. L., and J. H. Harvey, 'Do people use consensus information in making causal attributions?', *Journal of Personality and Social Psychology*, **35**, 279–293, 1977.

West, S. G., S. P. Gunn, and P. Chernicky, 'Ubiquitous Watergate: an attributional analysis', *Journal of Personality and Social Psychology*, **32**, 55–65, 1975.

Whitney, R. E., 'Agreement and positivity in pleasantness ratings of balanced and unbalanced social situations: A cross-cultural study', *Journal of Personality and Social Psychology*, **17**, 11–14, 1971.

Wichman, H., 'Effects of isolation and communication on cooperation in a two-person game', *Journal of Personality and Social Psychology*, **16**, 114–120, 1970.

Wicker, A. W., 'Attitudes versus actions: The relationship of overt and behavioral responses to attitude objects', *Journal of Social Issues*, **25**, 41–78, 1969.

Wicklund, R. A., 'Objective self-awareness', in L. Berkowitz (ed.), *Advances in Experimental Social Psychology*, vol. 8, Academic Press, New York, 1975.

Wicklund, R. A., and J. W. Brehm, *Perspectives On Cognitive Dissonance*, Erlbaum, Hillsdale, N.J., 1976.

Wishner, J., 'Reanalysis of "impressions of personality"', *Psychological Review*, **67**, 96–112, 1960.

Wortman, C. B., and D. E. Linder, 'Attribution of responsibility for an outcome as a function of its likelihood', *American Psychological Association 81st Annual Convention*, Montreal, 1973.

Wyer, R. S., Jr., *Cognitive Organization and Change: An Information Processing Approach*, Erlbaum, Potomac, Md., 1974.

Yuker, H. E., J. R. Block, and W. J. Campbell, 'A scale to measure attitudes toward disabled persons', Study No. 5, Human Resources Foundation, Albertson, N.Y., 1960.

Zajonc, R. B., 'Social facilitation', *Science*, **149**, 269–274, 1965.

Zajonc, R. B., 'Attitudinal effects of mere exposure', *Journal of Personality and Social Psychology Monograph Supplement*, **9**, (2, pt. 2), 1–27, 1968a.

Zajonc, R. B., 'Cognitive theories in social psychology', in G. Lindzey and E. Aronson (eds.), *Handbook of Social Psychology*, vol. 1, Addison-Wesley, Reading, Mass., 1968b.

Zajonc, R. B., and E. Burnstein, 'The learning of balanced and unbalanced social structures', *Journal of Personality*, **33**, 158–163, 1965.

Zajonc, R. B., and S. J. Sherman, 'Structural balance and the induction of relations', *Journal of Personality*, **35**, 635–650, 1967.

Zanna, M. P., and J. Cooper, 'Dissonance and the pill: An attribution approach to studying the arousal properties of dissonance', *Journal of Personality and Social Psychology*, **29**, 703–709, 1974.

Zavalloni, M., and S. W. Cook, 'Influence of judges' attitudes on ratings of favorableness of statements about a social group', *Journal of Personality and Social Psychology*, **1**, 43–54, 1965.

Ziller, R. C., 'Four techniques of group decision making under uncertainty', *Journal of Applied Psychology*, **41**, 384–388, 1957.

Zimbardo, P. G., *The Cognitive Control of Motivation*, Scott, Foresman, Glenview, Ill., 1969a.

Zimbardo, P. G., 'The human choice: Individuation, reason and order versus deindividuation, impulse and chaos', *Nebraska Symposium on Motivation*, **17**, 237–307, 1969b.
Zimbardo, P. G., M. Weisenberg, I. J. Firestone, and B. Levy, 'Communicator effectiveness in producing public conformity and private attitude change', *Journal of Personality*, **33**, 233–255, 1965.

AUTHOR INDEX

SUBJECT INDEX

PRINTED AND BOUND IN GREAT BRITAIN BY
WILLIAM CLOWES (BECCLES) LIMITED
BECCLES AND LONDON